legal shmegal!

URANUS LAD

PARADISE TOO: DRUNK DUCKS!
Copyright ©2002 Terry Moore
All Rights Reserved

First Edition: July 2002
ISBN 1-892597-18-7

Published by
Abstract Studio, Inc.
P. O. Box 271487
Houston, Texas 77277
www.Kixie.com
www.StrangersInParadise.com
email: SIPnet@StrangersInParadise.com

Printed In Canada by Quebecor Printing

DRUNK DUCKS!

by
Terry Moore

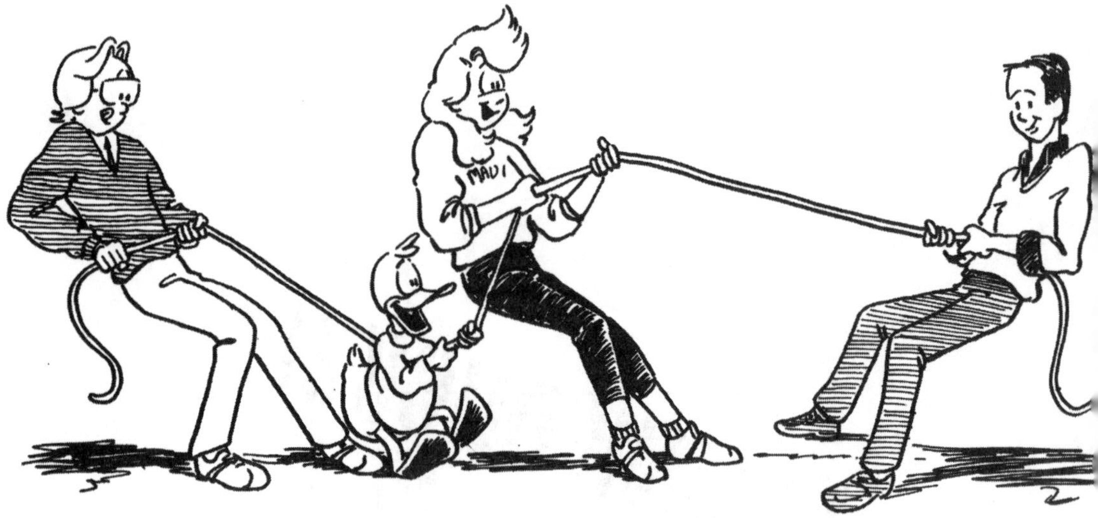
MAUI

Since 1993 I have been writing and drawing a comic book entitled Strangers In Paradise because I wasn't able to think of anything funnier.

See, in the comic book industry you can publish anything you like, but in the gazillion dollar world of newspaper syndication they have these stupid requirements like, be good. And be shorter than six inches. Well, who can work under such conditions? Granted, with years of practice, most cartoonists can figure out the six inch rule but, it's that good part that eludes the masses. For a select few who conquer both rules, it's nirvana six days a week with an extra helping on Sundays.

This book is a compilation of my various attempts to find syndicated nirvana over the past few years. I still pursue this, my Holy Grail of cartooning but, in the meantime, I have been writing and drawing a comic book filled with characters who were born in the strips you are about to read. And, although I have shown samples of my strips from time to time in the pages of SIP, this book contains no reprints. All of the strips contained in this collection are seeing print for the first time.

For the SIP reader, this book offers a lighthearted forensic look into the body of the Strangers In Paradise ensemble. However, if you just picked this book up and are discovering my work for the first time... it helps to have a glass of wine first.

Terry Moore

I suppose we should begin with a couple of examples from my earliest strip work. I have no idea what these creatures are exactly , but they seemed to be having a good time. The female of the two was named Kachoo but, I don't recall anybody else's name or a name for the strip. Mutants Of The Air seems a little harsh.

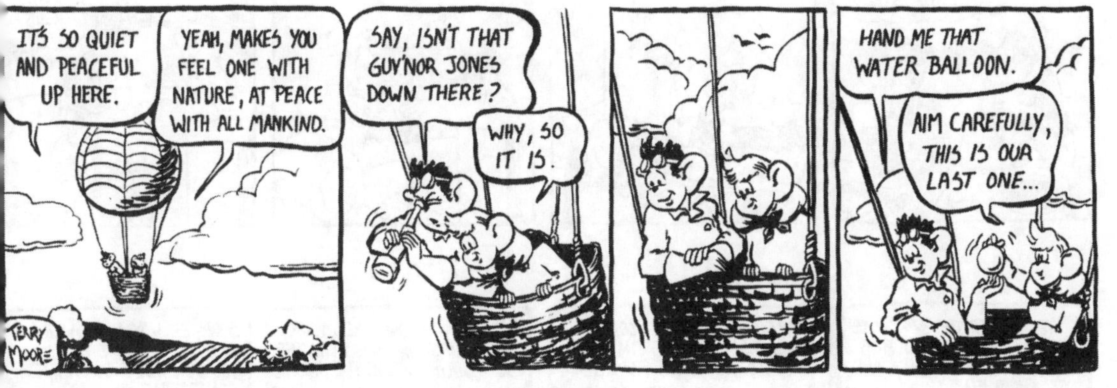
IT'S SO QUIET AND PEACEFUL UP HERE.
YEAH, MAKES YOU FEEL ONE WITH NATURE, AT PEACE WITH ALL MANKIND.
TERRY MOORE
SAY, ISN'T THAT GUV'NOR JONES DOWN THERE?
WHY, SO IT IS.
HAND ME THAT WATER BALLOON.
AIM CAREFULLY, THIS IS OUR LAST ONE...

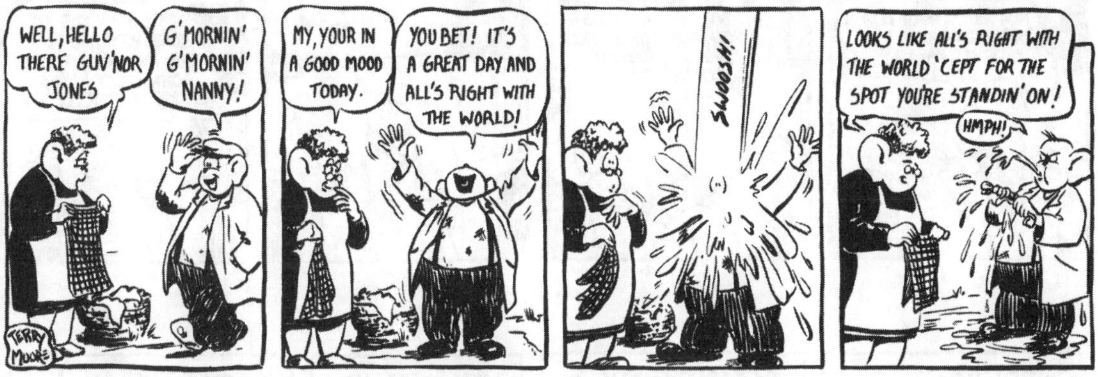
WELL, HELLO THERE GUV'NOR JONES
G'MORNIN' G'MORNIN' NANNY!
TERRY MOORE
MY, YOUR IN A GOOD MOOD TODAY.
YOU BET! IT'S A GREAT DAY AND ALL'S RIGHT WITH THE WORLD!
SWOOSH!
LOOKS LIKE ALL'S RIGHT WITH THE WORLD 'CEPT FOR THE SPOT YOU'RE STANDIN' ON!
HMPH!

I don't know what I was thinking. That lasted about a week before I abandoned the weird little animal look and came up with this guy named Oliver Wonderbee. Oliver had a thinking duck named Alex and a cute blonde girlfriend named Steffi Katchoo. I liked that name, it sort of fell out of your mouth like a bunch of SweetTarts... Steffi Katchoo. Try it.

Anyway, Oliver Wonderbee reeked of Bloom County influences because that was my favorite strip at the time (How many times has that poor guy been ripped off?). I have a bunch of these, but in the interest of public relations, I'll only drag out a few samples. Your welcome.

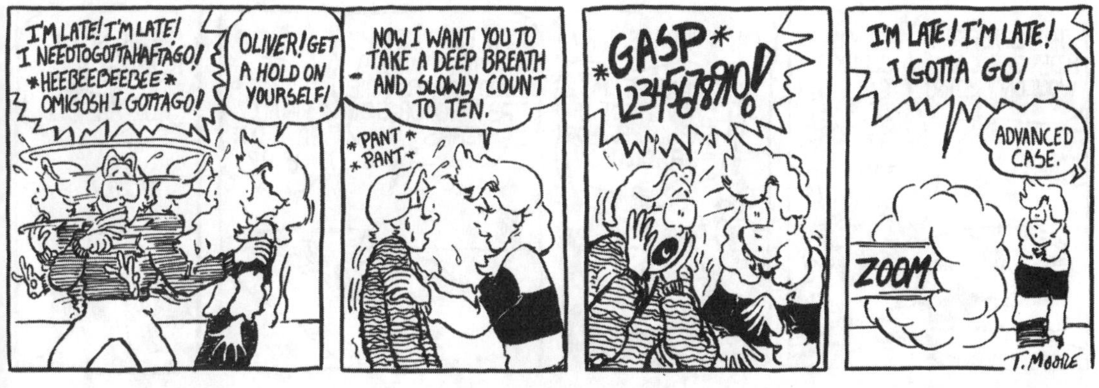
I'M LATE! I'M LATE! I NEEDTOGOTTAHAFTAGO! *HEEBEEBEEBEE* OMIGOSH I GOTTAGO!
OLIVER! GET A HOLD ON YOURSELF!
NOW I WANT YOU TO TAKE A DEEP BREATH AND SLOWLY COUNT TO TEN.
PANT *PANT*
GASP 12345678910!
I'M LATE! I'M LATE! I GOTTA GO!
ADVANCED CASE.
ZOOM
T. MOORE

OLIVER WONDERBEE

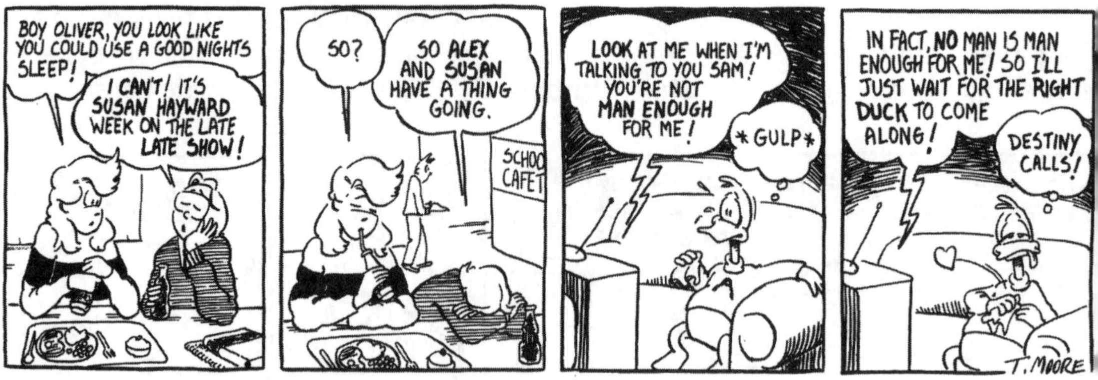
BOY OLIVER, YOU LOOK LIKE YOU COULD USE A GOOD NIGHTS SLEEP!
I CAN'T! IT'S SUSAN HAYWARD WEEK ON THE LATE LATE SHOW!
SO?
SO ALEX AND SUSAN HAVE A THING GOING.
SCHOO
CAFET
LOOK AT ME WHEN I'M TALKING TO YOU SAM! YOU'RE NOT MAN ENOUGH FOR ME!
GULP
IN FACT, NO MAN IS MAN ENOUGH FOR ME! SO I'LL JUST WAIT FOR THE RIGHT DUCK TO COME ALONG!
DESTINY CALLS!
T. MOORE

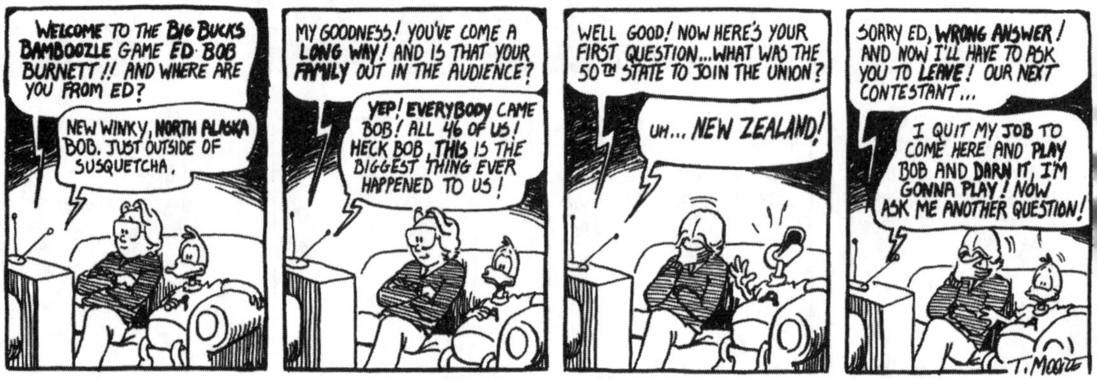
WELCOME TO THE BIG BUCKS BAMBOOZLE GAME ED·BOB BURNETT!! AND WHERE ARE YOU FROM ED?
NEW WINKY, NORTH ALASKA BOB. JUST OUTSIDE OF SUSQUETCHA.
MY GOODNESS! YOU'VE COME A LONG WAY! AND IS THAT YOUR FAMILY OUT IN THE AUDIENCE?
YEP! EVERYBODY CAME BOB! ALL 46 OF US! HECK BOB, THIS IS THE BIGGEST THING EVER HAPPENED TO US!
WELL GOOD! NOW HERE'S YOUR FIRST QUESTION...WHAT WAS THE 50TH STATE TO JOIN THE UNION?
UH... NEW ZEALAND!
SORRY ED, WRONG ANSWER! AND NOW I'LL HAVE TO ASK YOU TO LEAVE! OUR NEXT CONTESTANT...
I QUIT MY JOB TO COME HERE AND PLAY BOB AND DARN IT, I'M GONNA PLAY! NOW ASK ME ANOTHER QUESTION!
T. MOORE

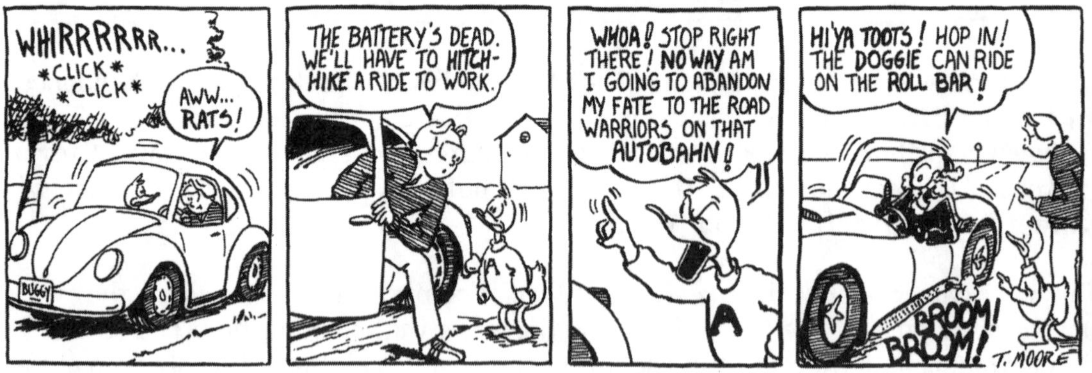
WHIRRRRRR...
CLICK
CLICK
AWW... RATS!
BUGGY
THE BATTERY'S DEAD. WE'LL HAVE TO HITCH-HIKE A RIDE TO WORK.
WHOA! STOP RIGHT THERE! NO WAY AM I GOING TO ABANDON MY FATE TO THE ROAD WARRIORS ON THAT AUTOBAHN!
HI'YA TOOTS! HOP IN! THE DOGGIE CAN RIDE ON THE ROLL BAR!
BROOM! BROOM!
T. MOORE

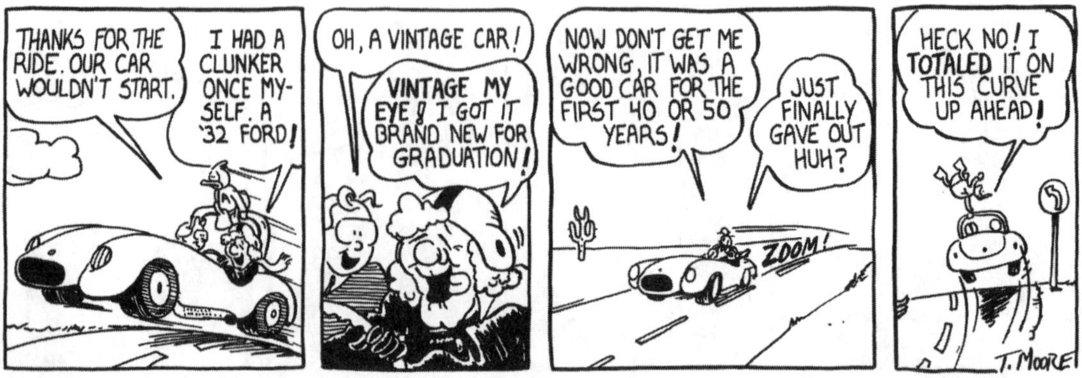
THANKS FOR THE RIDE. OUR CAR WOULDN'T START.
I HAD A CLUNKER ONCE MY-SELF. A '32 FORD!
OH, A VINTAGE CAR!
VINTAGE MY EYE! I GOT IT BRAND NEW FOR GRADUATION!
NOW DON'T GET ME WRONG, IT WAS A GOOD CAR FOR THE FIRST 40 OR 50 YEARS!
JUST FINALLY GAVE OUT HUH?
ZOOM!
HECK NO! I TOTALED IT ON THIS CURVE UP AHEAD!
T. MOORE

My favorite job before comics was working in a music store during my rock and roll days. I gave Oliver the same job. All this stuff really happened.

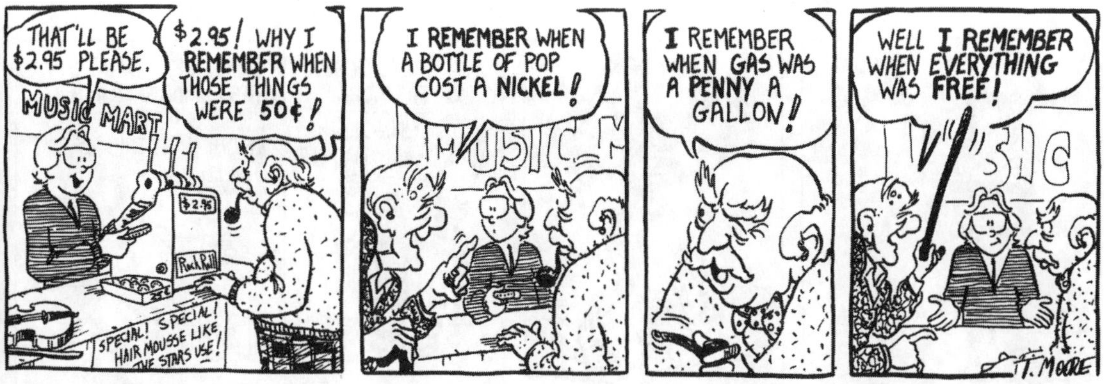
THAT'LL BE $2.95 PLEASE.
$2.95! WHY I REMEMBER WHEN THOSE THINGS WERE 50¢!
MUSIC MART
$2.95
SPECIAL! SPECIAL! HAIR MOUSSE LIKE THE STARS USE!
I REMEMBER WHEN A BOTTLE OF POP COST A NICKEL!
I REMEMBER WHEN GAS WAS A PENNY A GALLON!
WELL I REMEMBER WHEN EVERYTHING WAS FREE!
T. MOORE

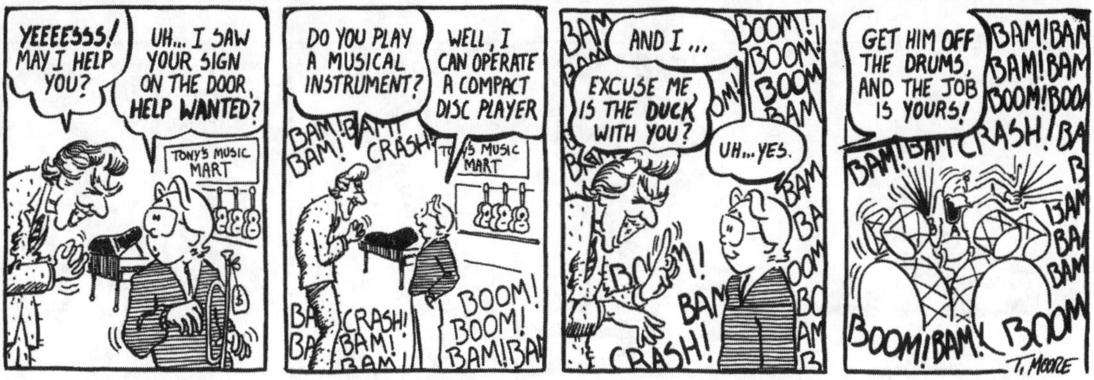
YEEEESSS! MAY I HELP YOU?
UH... I SAW YOUR SIGN ON THE DOOR, HELP WANTED?
TONY'S MUSIC MART
DO YOU PLAY A MUSICAL INSTRUMENT?
WELL, I CAN OPERATE A COMPACT DISC PLAYER
BAM! BAM! CRASH!
BOOM! BOOM! BAM!
AND I ...
EXCUSE ME, IS THE DUCK WITH YOU?
UH...YES.
CRASH!
GET HIM OFF THE DRUMS, AND THE JOB IS YOURS!
BAM! BAM! BAM! BOOM!
BOOM! BAM! BOOM
T. MOORE

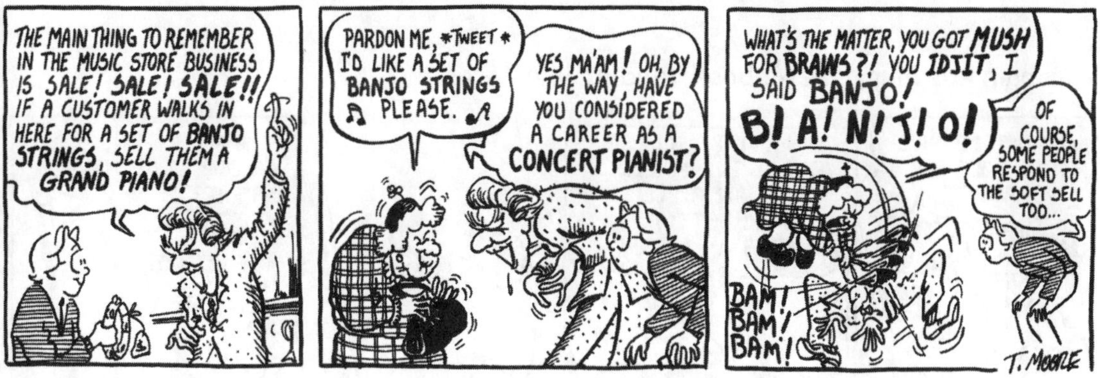
THE MAIN THING TO REMEMBER IN THE MUSIC STORE BUSINESS IS SALE! SALE! SALE!! IF A CUSTOMER WALKS IN HERE FOR A SET OF BANJO STRINGS, SELL THEM A GRAND PIANO!
PARDON ME, *TWEET* I'D LIKE A SET OF BANJO STRINGS PLEASE.
YES MA'AM! OH, BY THE WAY, HAVE YOU CONSIDERED A CAREER AS A CONCERT PIANIST?
WHAT'S THE MATTER, YOU GOT MUSH FOR BRAINS?! YOU IDJIT, I SAID BANJO! B! A! N! J! O!
OF COURSE, SOME PEOPLE RESPOND TO THE SOFT SELL TOO...
BAM! BAM! BAM!
T. MOORE

Somehow, Oliver ended up in a forest and Alex became a punk rabbit, while Katchoo morphed into a dark haired menace. Blame it on lack of sleep.

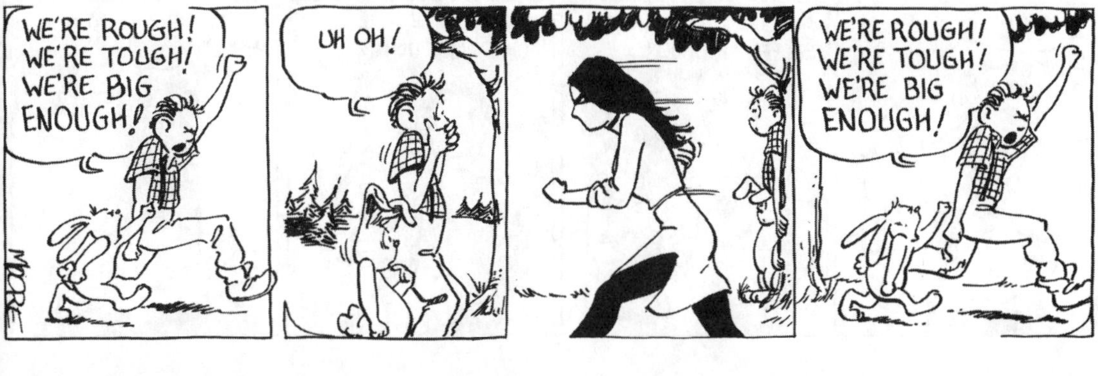
WE'RE ROUGH! WE'RE TOUGH! WE'RE BIG ENOUGH!
MOORE
UH OH!
WE'RE ROUGH! WE'RE TOUGH! WE'RE BIG ENOUGH!

I didn't do many like the ones below. I remember doing them in a hotel room in Albuquerque, New Mexico while eating fast food tacos and watching *Reanimator* on cable tv. Swear to God. I like to multi-task.

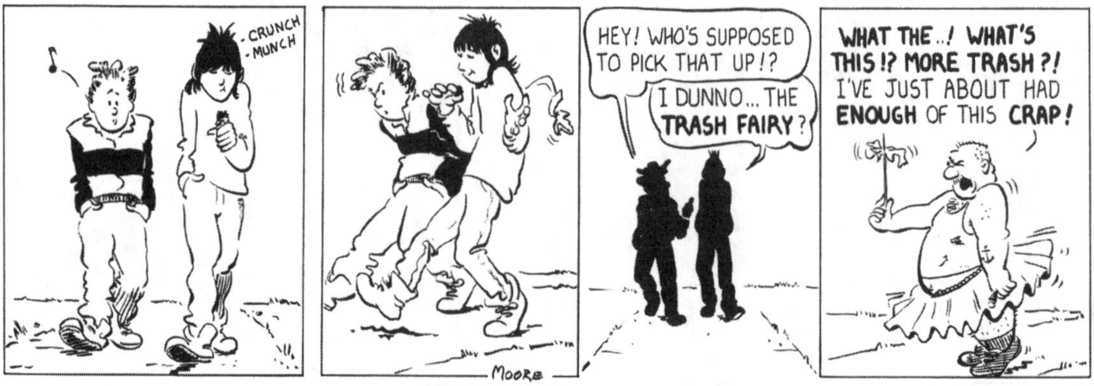
-CRUNCH
-MUNCH
HEY! WHO'S SUPPOSED TO PICK THAT UP!?
I DUNNO... THE TRASH FAIRY?
WHAT THE..! WHAT'S THIS!? MORE TRASH?! I'VE JUST ABOUT HAD ENOUGH OF THIS CRAP!
MOORE

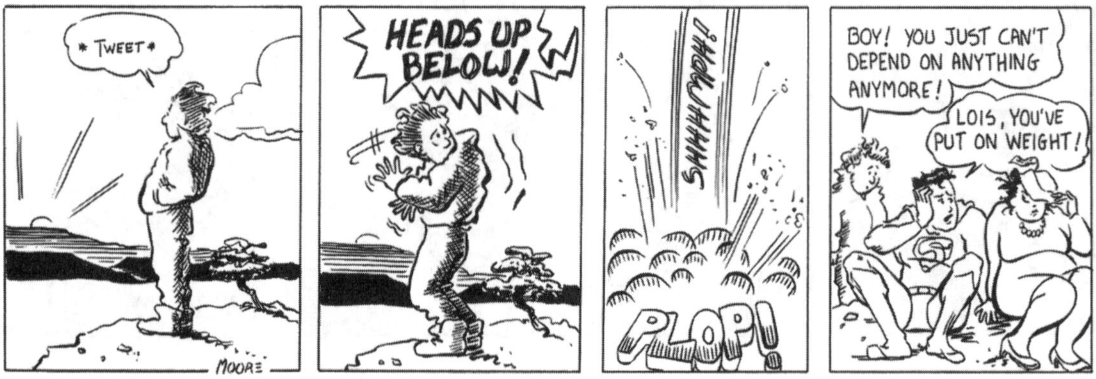
* TWEET *
HEADS UP BELOW!
SHHHHWHOOP!
PLOP!
BOY! YOU JUST CAN'T DEPEND ON ANYTHING ANYMORE!
LOIS, YOU'VE PUT ON WEIGHT!
MOORE

This pair was in my sketchbook, kind of like notes.

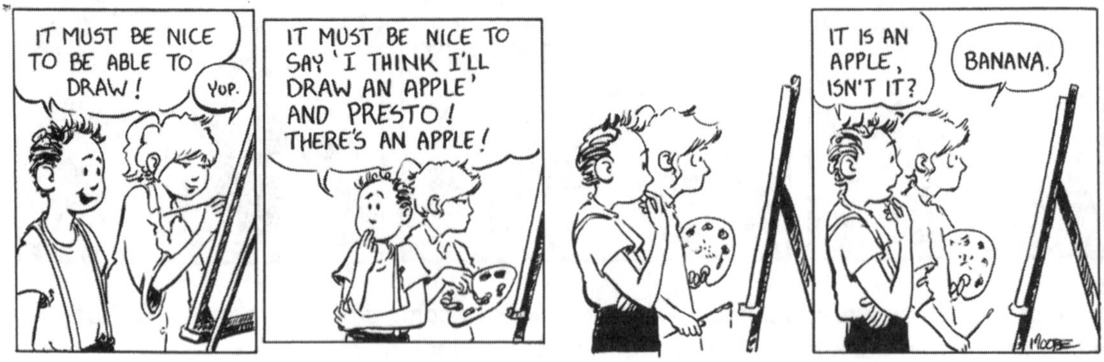
IT MUST BE NICE TO BE ABLE TO DRAW!
YUP.
IT MUST BE NICE TO SAY 'I THINK I'LL DRAW AN APPLE' AND PRESTO! THERE'S AN APPLE!
IT IS AN APPLE, ISN'T IT?
BANANA.
MOORE

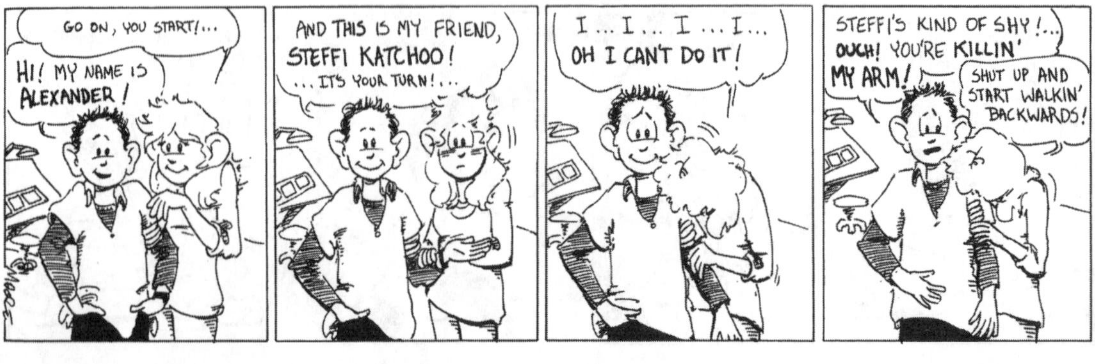
GO ON, YOU START!...
HI! MY NAME IS ALEXANDER!
AND THIS IS MY FRIEND, STEFFI KATCHOO!
... IT'S YOUR TURN!...
I... I... I... I...
OH I CAN'T DO IT!
STEFFI'S KIND OF SHY!...
OUCH! YOU'RE KILLIN' MY ARM!
SHUT UP AND START WALKIN' BACKWARDS!
MOORE

HOMER GURFICH

Homer Gurfich is a cigar smoking toad in plaid pants. What more do you need to know? That he was the star of countless demented underground comics drawn by me and my best friend in school? That he was the victim of every nasty thing a teenage boy can imagine on paper, from fiery car crashes to the Black Plague? I tried a severely domesticated version for the newspapers. I should have stuck with plagues.

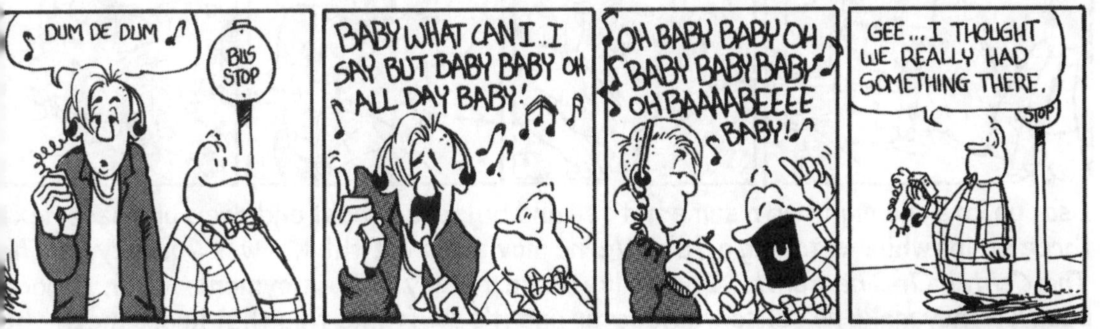
DUM DE DUM
BUS STOP
BABY WHAT CAN I..I SAY BUT BABY BABY OH ALL DAY BABY!
OH BABY BABY OH BABY BABY BABY OH BAAAABEEEE BABY!
GEE... I THOUGHT WE REALLY HAD SOMETHING THERE.
STOP

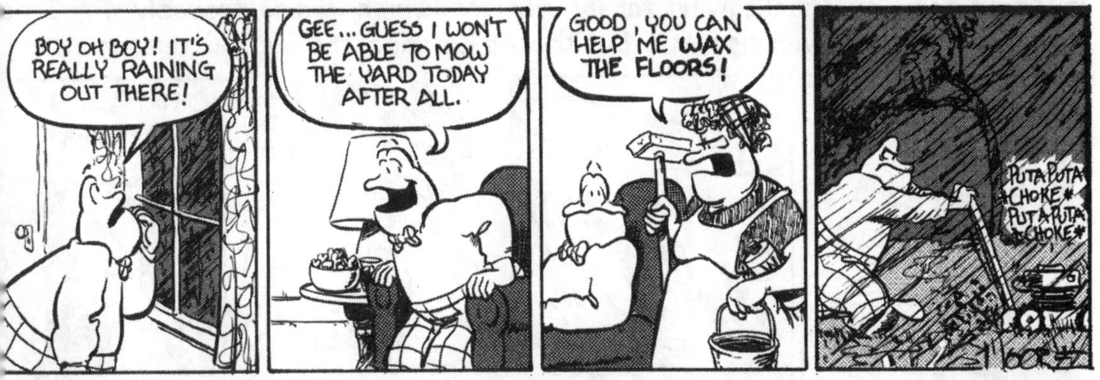
BOY OH BOY! IT'S REALLY RAINING OUT THERE!
GEE... GUESS I WON'T BE ABLE TO MOW THE YARD TODAY AFTER ALL.
GOOD, YOU CAN HELP ME WAX THE FLOORS!
PUTA PUTA *CHOKE* PUTA PUTA *CHOKE*

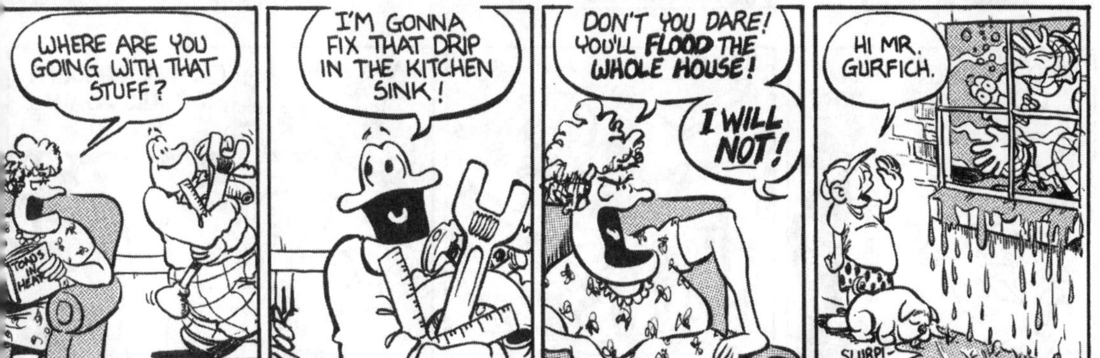
WHERE ARE YOU GOING WITH THAT STUFF?
I'M GONNA FIX THAT DRIP IN THE KITCHEN SINK!
DON'T YOU DARE! YOU'LL FLOOD THE WHOLE HOUSE!
I WILL NOT!
HI MR. GURFICH.
SLURP!

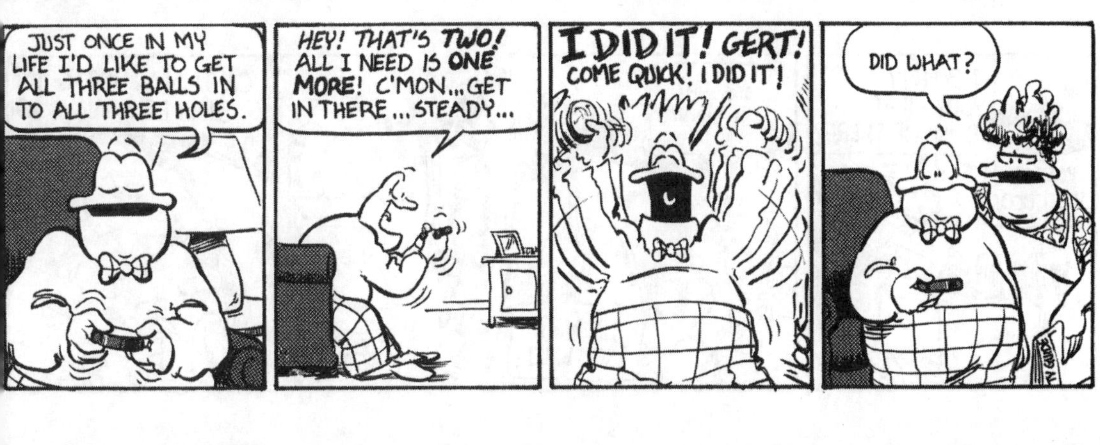
JUST ONCE IN MY LIFE I'D LIKE TO GET ALL THREE BALLS IN TO ALL THREE HOLES.
HEY! THAT'S TWO! ALL I NEED IS ONE MORE! C'MON...GET IN THERE... STEADY...
I DID IT! GERT! COME QUICK! I DID IT!
DID WHAT?

I love those Don Martin feet. I think that's where the *tweet*s come from, too.

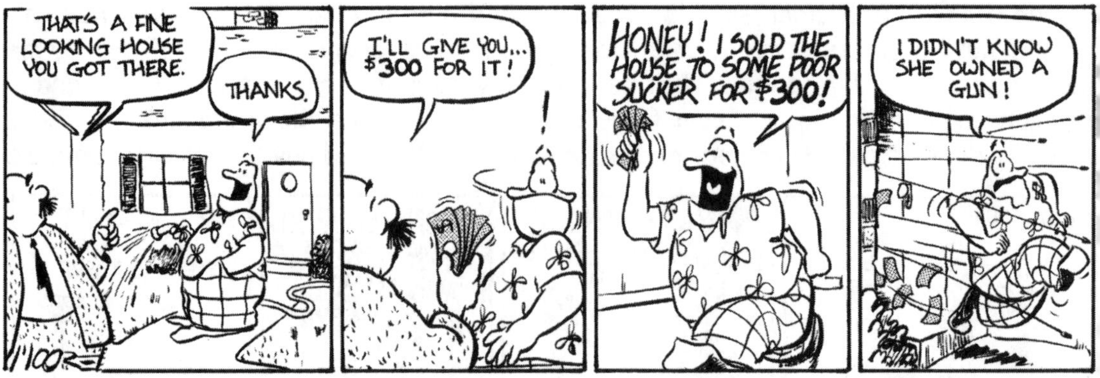
THAT'S A FINE LOOKING HOUSE YOU GOT THERE.
THANKS.
I'LL GIVE YOU... $300 FOR IT!
!
HONEY! I SOLD THE HOUSE TO SOME POOR SUCKER FOR $300!
I DIDN'T KNOW SHE OWNED A GUN!

I sat up late one night with some hot tea and buttered toast and drew up these next three strips while watching a Jules Verne movie on tv; I think it was *Journey To The The Center Of The Earth.* I just did these for my own enjoyment, which is good because they make no sense whatsoever and it's stuff like this that keeps me at the children's table at Thanksgiving family reunions, which is also probably why I do stuff like this. It's a vicious circle. But there's Katchoo, the wood kitten something.

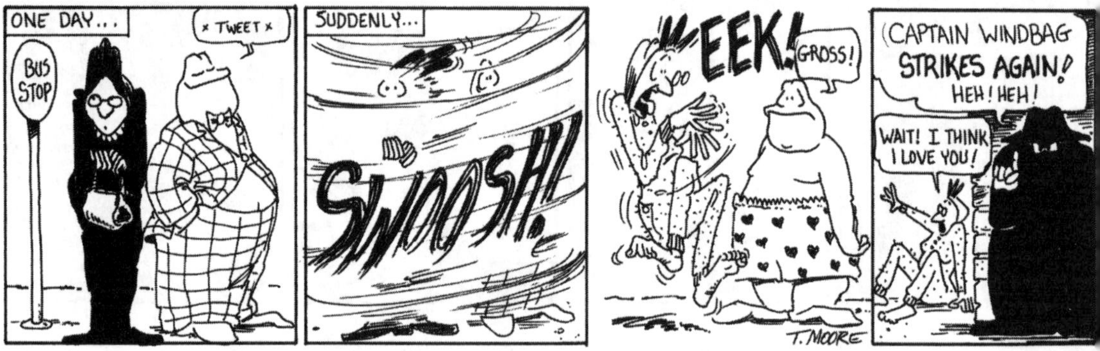
ONE DAY...
BUS STOP
× TWEET ×
SUDDENLY...
SWOOSH!
EEK!
GROSS!
CAPTAIN WINDBAG STRIKES AGAIN! HEH! HEH!
WAIT! I THINK I LOVE YOU!
T. MOORE

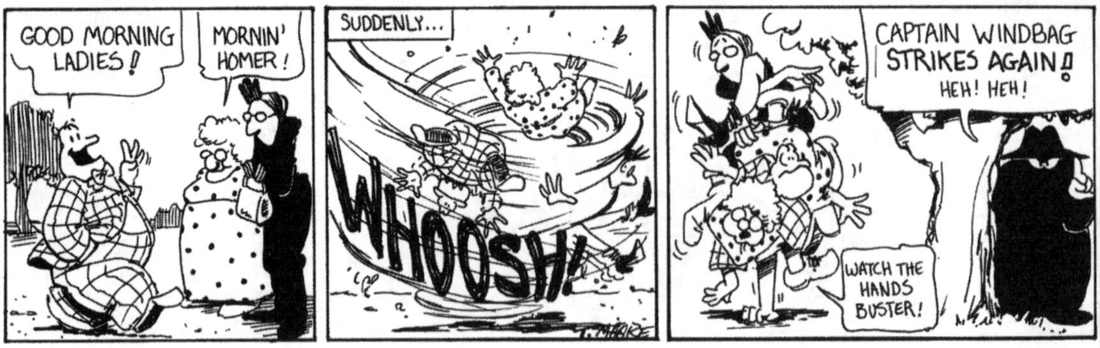
GOOD MORNING LADIES!
MORNIN' HOMER!
SUDDENLY...
WHOOSH!
CAPTAIN WINDBAG STRIKES AGAIN!! HEH! HEH!
WATCH THE HANDS BUSTER!

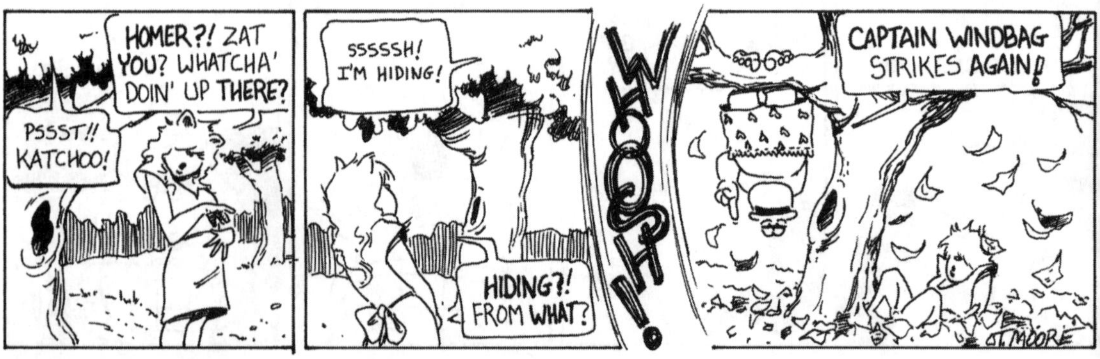
HOMER?! ZAT YOU? WHATCHA' DOIN' UP THERE?
PSSST!! KATCHOO!
SSSSSH! I'M HIDING!
HIDING?! FROM WHAT?
WHOOSH!
CAPTAIN WINDBAG STRIKES AGAIN!
T. MOORE

When I got Homer out of the house, I began to have a lot more fun.

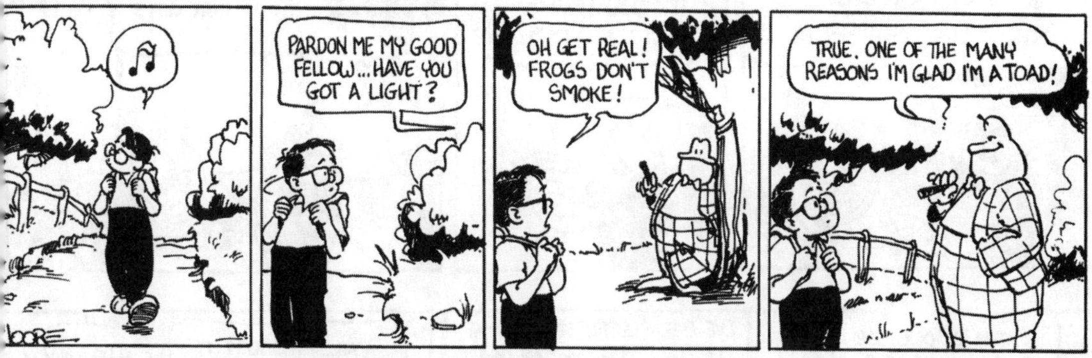
PARDON ME MY GOOD FELLOW...HAVE YOU GOT A LIGHT?
OH GET REAL! FROGS DON'T SMOKE!
TRUE. ONE OF THE MANY REASONS I'M GLAD I'M A TOAD!

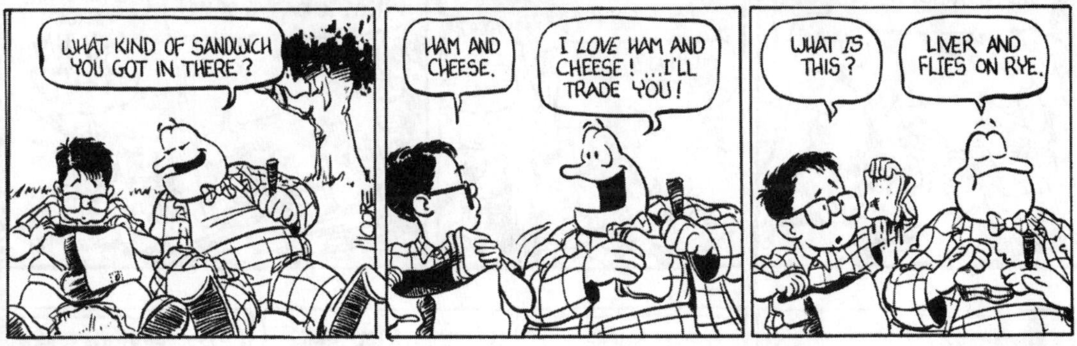
WHAT KIND OF SANDWICH YOU GOT IN THERE?
HAM AND CHEESE.
I *LOVE* HAM AND CHEESE! ...I'LL TRADE YOU!
WHAT *IS* THIS?
LIVER AND FLIES ON RYE.

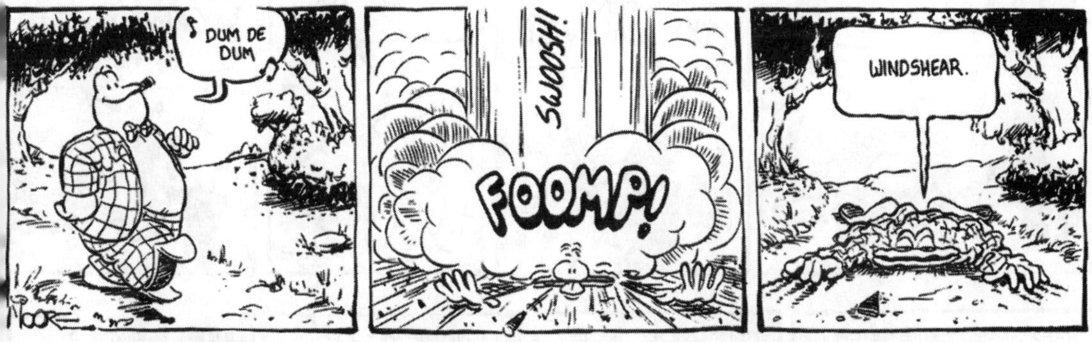
DUM DE DUM
SWOOSH!
FOOMP!
WINDSHEAR.

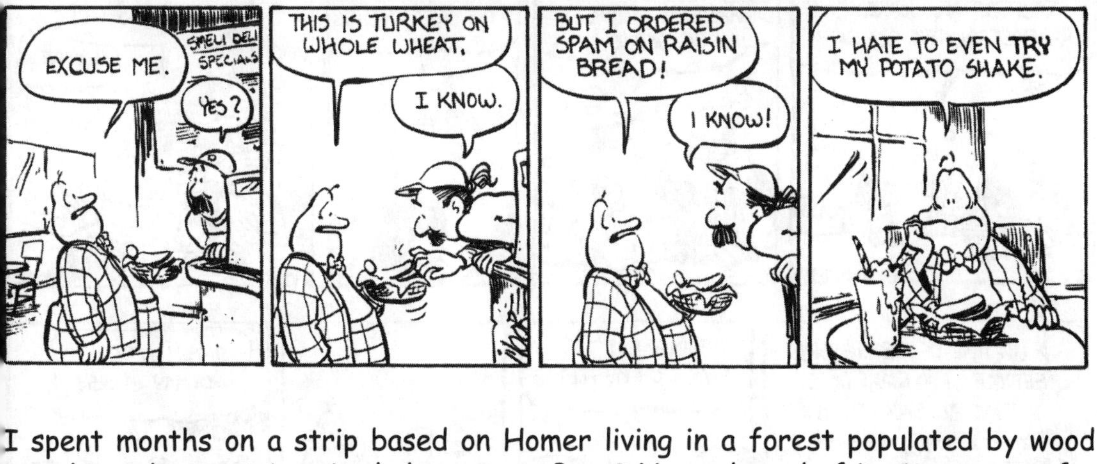
EXCUSE ME.
SMELI DELI SPECIALS
YES?
THIS IS TURKEY ON WHOLE WHEAT.
I KNOW.
BUT I ORDERED SPAM ON RAISIN BREAD!
I KNOW!
I HATE TO EVEN **TRY** MY POTATO SHAKE.

I spent months on a strip based on Homer living in a forest populated by wood nymphs and eccentric animal characters. Pogo? Never heard of it. Anyway, my favorite character was a bitter old owl they called Judge, because that's what he used to be, before the scandal. And remember, this was done before the Clinton administration, so it was hard to find a role model. Such ground breaking stuff here.

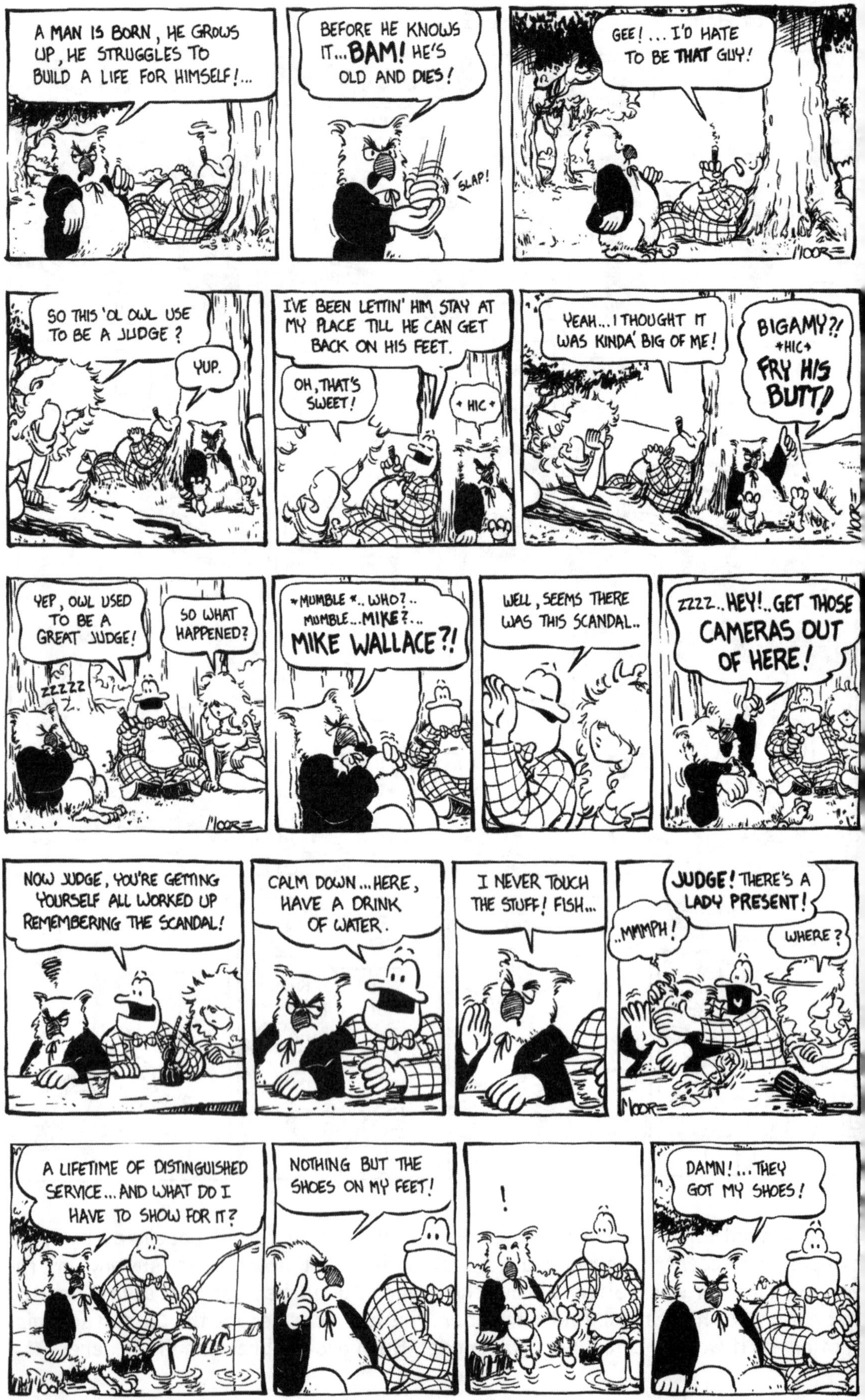
A MAN IS BORN, HE GROWS UP, HE STRUGGLES TO BUILD A LIFE FOR HIMSELF!...
BEFORE HE KNOWS IT...BAM! HE'S OLD AND DIES!
SLAP!
GEE!... I'D HATE TO BE THAT GUY!
SO THIS 'OL OWL USE TO BE A JUDGE?
YUP.
I'VE BEEN LETTIN' HIM STAY AT MY PLACE TILL HE CAN GET BACK ON HIS FEET.
OH, THAT'S SWEET!
HIC
YEAH... I THOUGHT IT WAS KINDA' BIG OF ME!
BIGAMY?! *HIC* FRY HIS BUTT!
YEP, OWL USED TO BE A GREAT JUDGE!
SO WHAT HAPPENED?
ZZZZZ
MUMBLE.. WHO?.. MUMBLE...MIKE?...
MIKE WALLACE?!
WELL, SEEMS THERE WAS THIS SCANDAL..
ZZZZ..HEY!..GET THOSE CAMERAS OUT OF HERE!
NOW JUDGE, YOU'RE GETTING YOURSELF ALL WORKED UP REMEMBERING THE SCANDAL!
CALM DOWN...HERE, HAVE A DRINK OF WATER.
I NEVER TOUCH THE STUFF! FISH...
JUDGE! THERE'S A LADY PRESENT!
..MMMPH!
WHERE?
A LIFETIME OF DISTINGUISHED SERVICE...AND WHAT DO I HAVE TO SHOW FOR IT?
NOTHING BUT THE SHOES ON MY FEET!
!
DAMN!... THEY GOT MY SHOES!

Little known fact here, Homer is the only one on the planet to actually see the King since his untimely departure. He made a donut run for him. This bit was the first time a syndicate editor responded with encouragement, advising me there was medication that could help people like me.

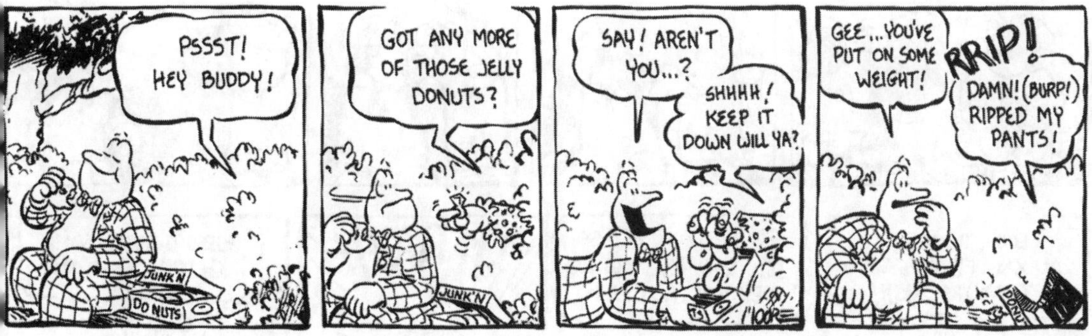
PSSST! HEY BUDDY!
JUNK'N DONUTS
GOT ANY MORE OF THOSE JELLY DONUTS?
SAY! AREN'T YOU...?
SHHHH! KEEP IT DOWN WILL YA?
GEE...YOU'VE PUT ON SOME WEIGHT!
RRIP!
DAMN! (BURP!) RIPPED MY PANTS!

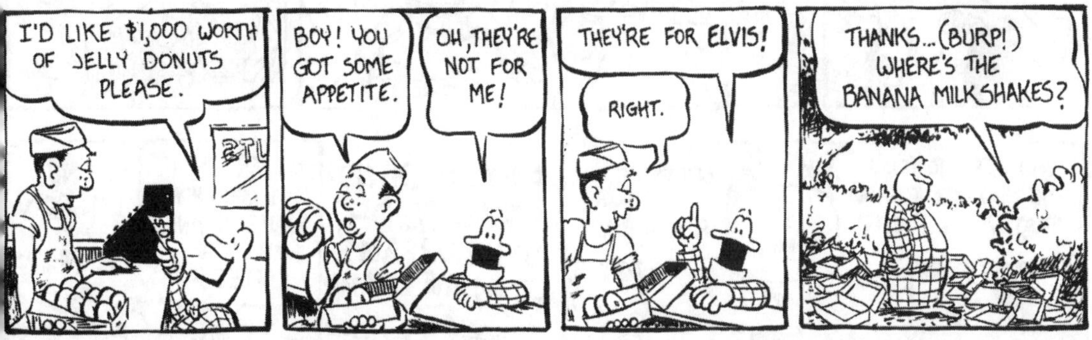
I'D LIKE $1,000 WORTH OF JELLY DONUTS PLEASE.
BOY! YOU GOT SOME APPETITE.
OH, THEY'RE NOT FOR ME!
THEY'RE FOR ELVIS!
RIGHT.
THANKS...(BURP!) WHERE'S THE BANANA MILKSHAKES?

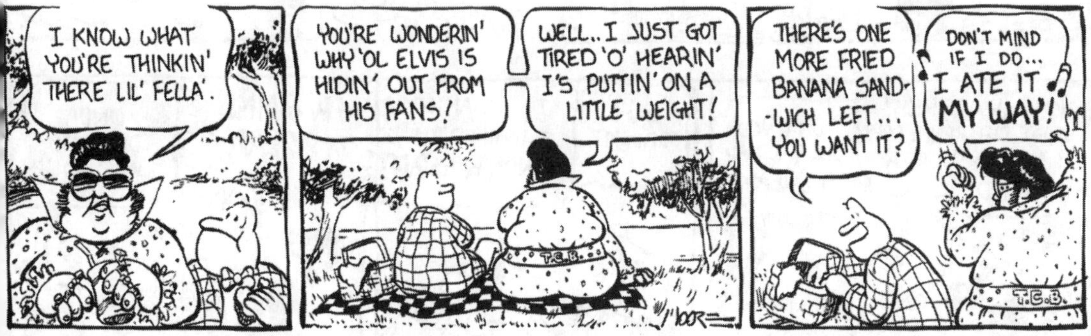
I KNOW WHAT YOU'RE THINKIN' THERE LIL' FELLA'.
YOU'RE WONDERIN' WHY 'OL ELVIS IS HIDIN' OUT FROM HIS FANS!
WELL.. I JUST GOT TIRED 'O' HEARIN' I'S PUTTIN' ON A LITTLE WEIGHT!
THERE'S ONE MORE FRIED BANANA SAND-WICH LEFT... YOU WANT IT?
DON'T MIND IF I DO... I ATE IT MY WAY!

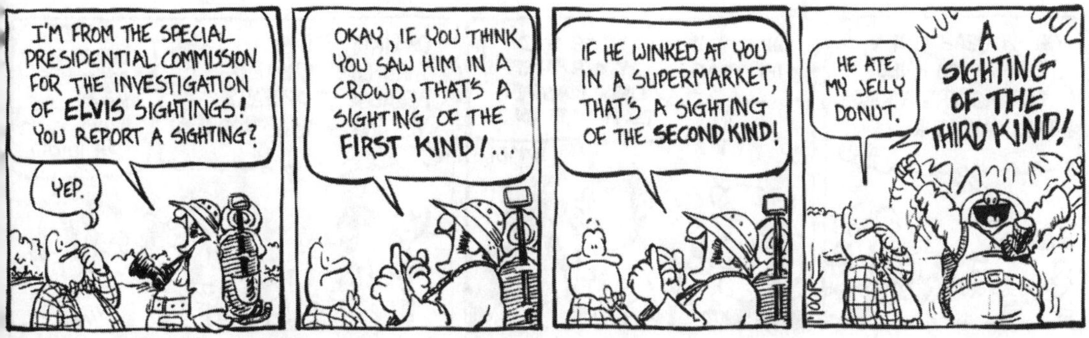
I'M FROM THE SPECIAL PRESIDENTIAL COMMISSION FOR THE INVESTIGATION OF ELVIS SIGHTINGS! YOU REPORT A SIGHTING?
YEP.
OKAY, IF YOU THINK YOU SAW HIM IN A CROWD, THAT'S A SIGHTING OF THE FIRST KIND!...
IF HE WINKED AT YOU IN A SUPERMARKET, THAT'S A SIGHTING OF THE SECOND KIND!
HE ATE MY JELLY DONUT.
A SIGHTING OF THE THIRD KIND!

Being poor, I naturally came to the conclusion that all rich people were toads.

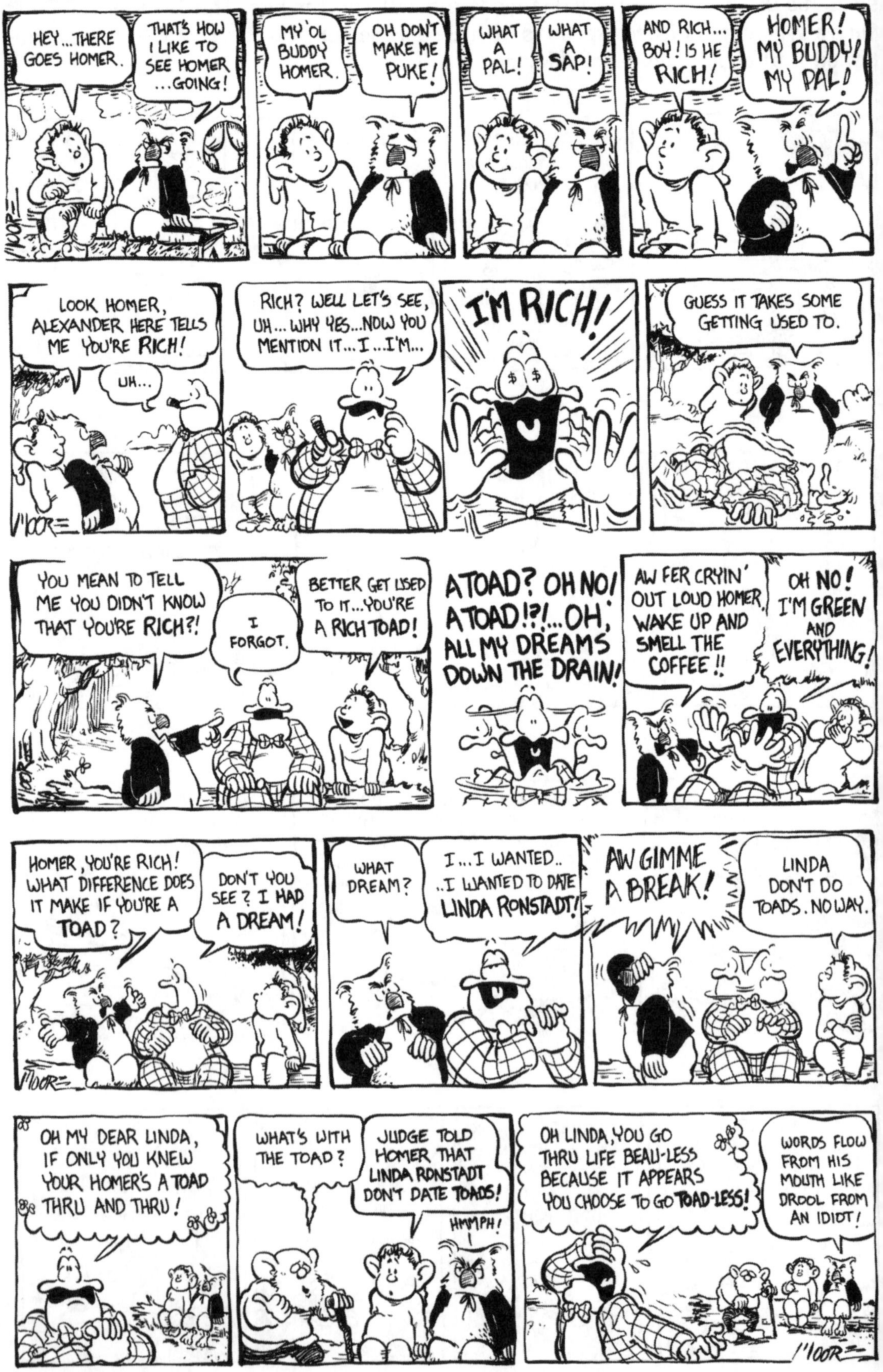
HEY...THERE GOES HOMER.
THAT'S HOW I LIKE TO SEE HOMER ...GOING!
MY 'OL BUDDY HOMER.
OH DON'T MAKE ME PUKE!
WHAT A PAL!
WHAT A SAP!
AND RICH... BOY! IS HE RICH!
HOMER! MY BUDDY! MY PAL!
LOOK HOMER, ALEXANDER HERE TELLS ME YOU'RE RICH!
UH...
RICH? WELL LET'S SEE, UH... WHY YES...NOW YOU MENTION IT...I...I'M...
I'M RICH!
GUESS IT TAKES SOME GETTING USED TO.
YOU MEAN TO TELL ME YOU DIDN'T KNOW THAT YOU'RE RICH?!
I FORGOT.
BETTER GET USED TO IT...YOU'RE A RICH TOAD!
A TOAD? OH NO! A TOAD!?!...OH, ALL MY DREAMS DOWN THE DRAIN!
AW FER CRYIN' OUT LOUD HOMER, WAKE UP AND SMELL THE COFFEE!!
OH NO! I'M GREEN AND EVERYTHING!
HOMER, YOU'RE RICH! WHAT DIFFERENCE DOES IT MAKE IF YOU'RE A TOAD?
DON'T YOU SEE? I HAD A DREAM!
WHAT DREAM?
I...I WANTED.. ..I WANTED TO DATE LINDA RONSTADT!
AW GIMME A BREAK!
LINDA DON'T DO TOADS. NO WAY.
OH MY DEAR LINDA, IF ONLY YOU KNEW YOUR HOMER'S A TOAD THRU AND THRU!
WHAT'S WITH THE TOAD?
JUDGE TOLD HOMER THAT LINDA RONSTADT DON'T DATE TOADS!
HMMPH!
OH LINDA, YOU GO THRU LIFE BEAU-LESS BECAUSE IT APPEARS YOU CHOOSE TO GO TOAD-LESS!
WORDS FLOW FROM HIS MOUTH LIKE DROOL FROM AN IDIOT!

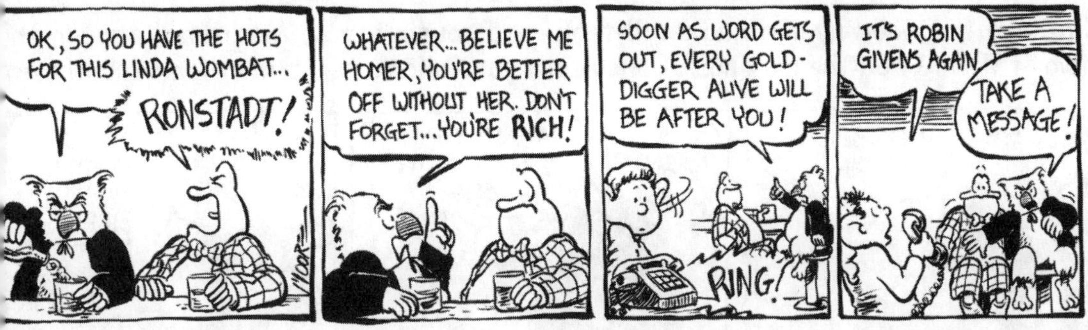
OK, SO YOU HAVE THE HOTS FOR THIS LINDA WOMBAT...
RONSTADT!
WHATEVER... BELIEVE ME HOMER, YOU'RE BETTER OFF WITHOUT HER. DON'T FORGET... YOU'RE RICH!
SOON AS WORD GETS OUT, EVERY GOLD-DIGGER ALIVE WILL BE AFTER YOU!
RING!
IT'S ROBIN GIVENS AGAIN
TAKE A MESSAGE!

I'm not prepared to discuss my crush on Linda Ronstadt, and neither should you. Let's move on to a lighter topic, liiiike... nuclear arms! Yaaaaay!

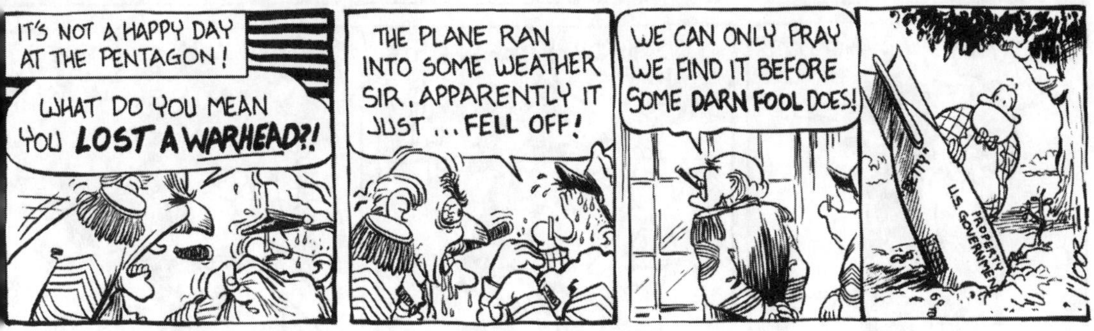
IT'S NOT A HAPPY DAY AT THE PENTAGON!
WHAT DO YOU MEAN YOU LOST A WARHEAD?!
THE PLANE RAN INTO SOME WEATHER SIR. APPARENTLY IT JUST... FELL OFF!
WE CAN ONLY PRAY WE FIND IT BEFORE SOME DARN FOOL DOES!
PROPERTY U.S. GOVERNMENT

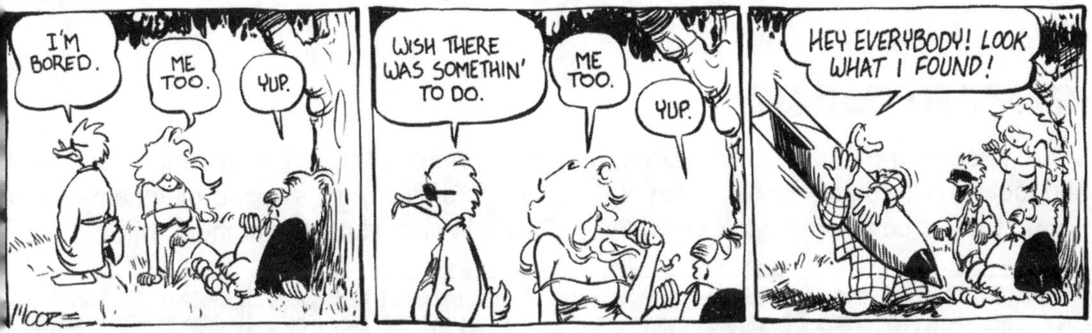
I'M BORED.
ME TOO.
YUP.
WISH THERE WAS SOMETHIN' TO DO.
ME TOO.
YUP.
HEY EVERYBODY! LOOK WHAT I FOUND!

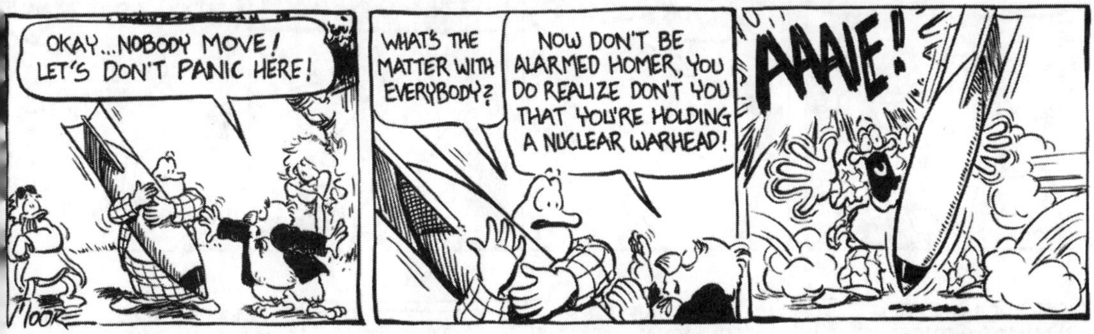
OKAY... NOBODY MOVE! LET'S DON'T PANIC HERE!
WHAT'S THE MATTER WITH EVERYBODY?
NOW DON'T BE ALARMED HOMER, YOU DO REALIZE DON'T YOU THAT YOU'RE HOLDING A NUCLEAR WARHEAD!
AAAIE!

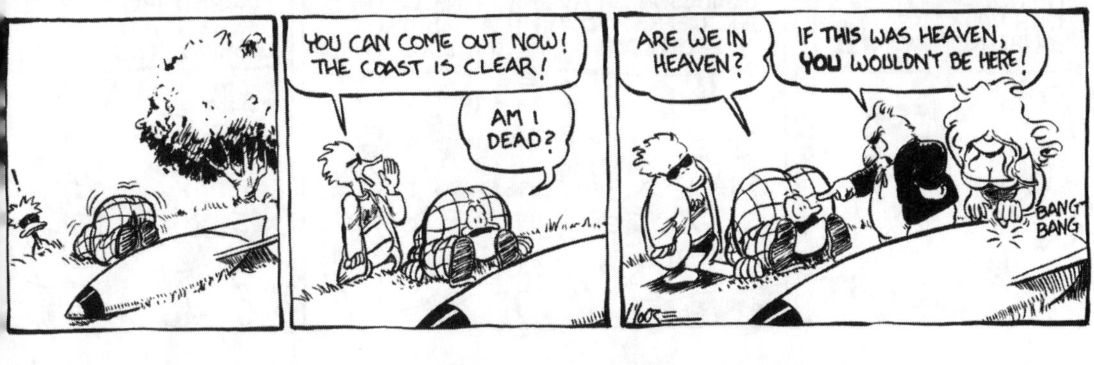
YOU CAN COME OUT NOW! THE COAST IS CLEAR!
AM I DEAD?
ARE WE IN HEAVEN?
IF THIS WAS HEAVEN, YOU WOULDN'T BE HERE!
BANG BANG

Katchoo the wood nymph had an ill-tempered cousin named Madison. Between the two of them I had the makings of one really good character, but I didn't know it yet.

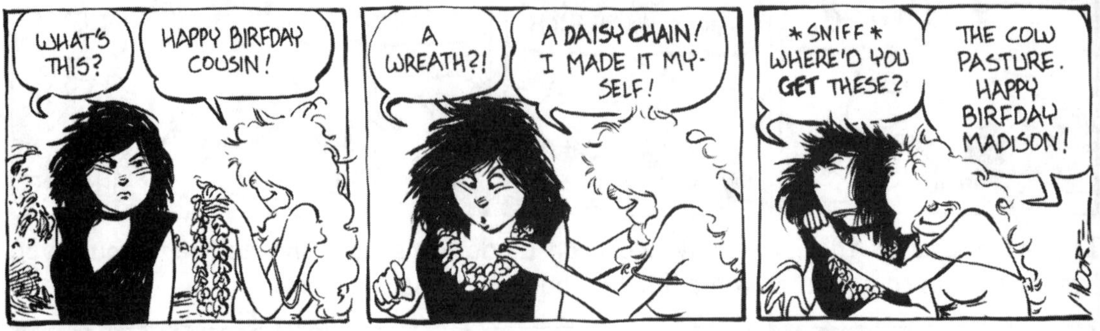
WHAT'S THIS?
HAPPY BIRFDAY COUSIN!
A WREATH?!
A DAISY CHAIN! I MADE IT MY-SELF!
SNIFF WHERE'D YOU GET THESE?
THE COW PASTURE. HAPPY BIRFDAY MADISON!
MOORE

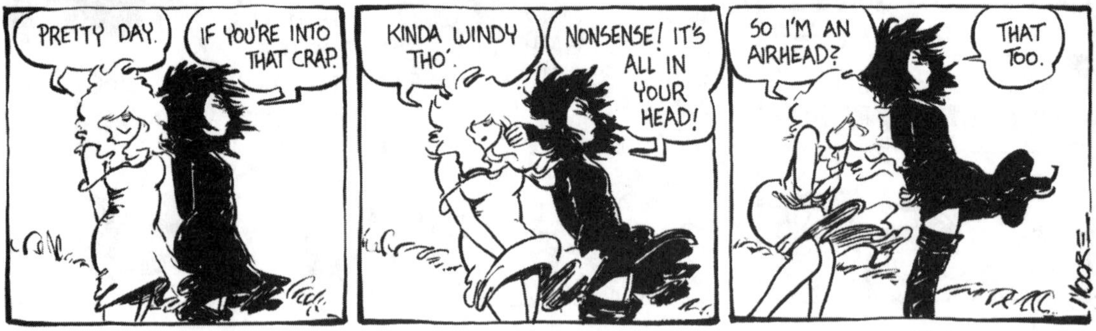
PRETTY DAY.
IF YOU'RE INTO THAT CRAP.
KINDA WINDY THO'.
NONSENSE! IT'S ALL IN YOUR HEAD!
SO I'M AN AIRHEAD?
THAT TOO.
MOORE

STEFFI KATCHOO

After receiving a couple of rejections on the forest strips, I went back to school. And look who I found there – Steffi Katchoo! Steffi's biggest problem seems to be a muciferous computer geek version of Oliver Wonderbee (remember him?).

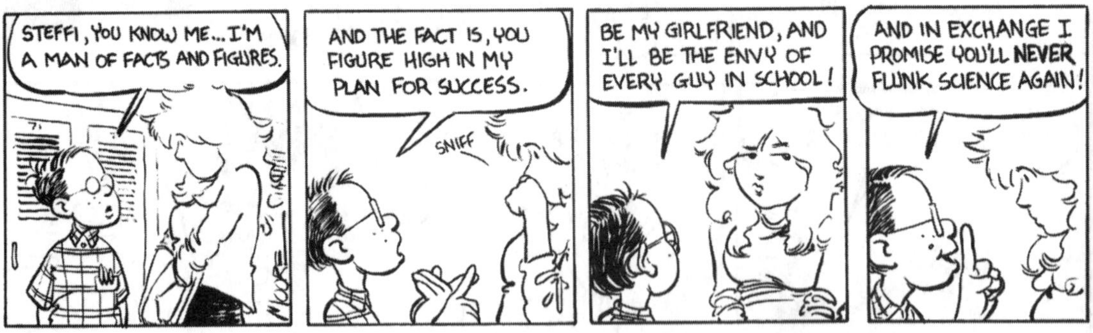
STEFFI, YOU KNOW ME...I'M A MAN OF FACTS AND FIGURES.
AND THE FACT IS, YOU FIGURE HIGH IN MY PLAN FOR SUCCESS.
SNIFF
BE MY GIRLFRIEND, AND I'LL BE THE ENVY OF EVERY GUY IN SCHOOL!
AND IN EXCHANGE I PROMISE YOU'LL NEVER FLUNK SCIENCE AGAIN!
MOORE

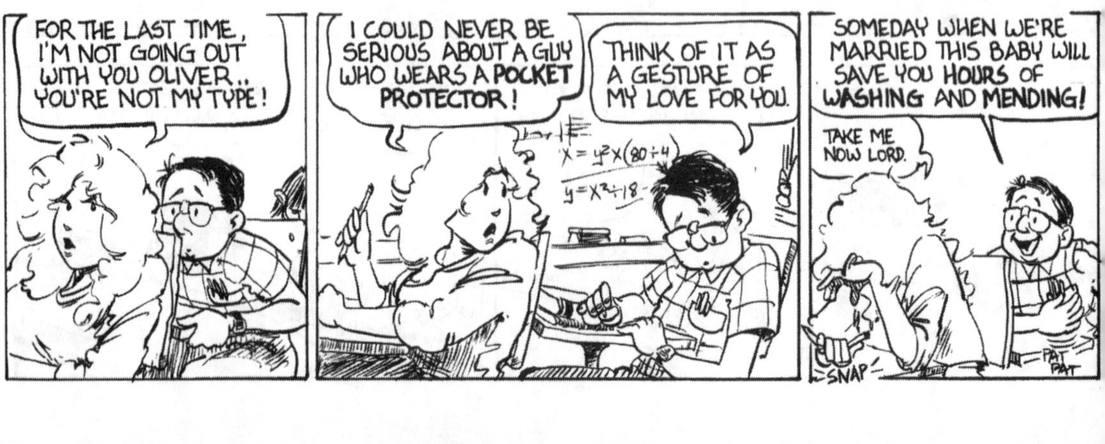
FOR THE LAST TIME, I'M NOT GOING OUT WITH YOU OLIVER.. YOU'RE NOT MY TYPE!
I COULD NEVER BE SERIOUS ABOUT A GUY WHO WEARS A POCKET PROTECTOR!
THINK OF IT AS A GESTURE OF MY LOVE FOR YOU.
SOMEDAY WHEN WE'RE MARRIED THIS BABY WILL SAVE YOU HOURS OF WASHING AND MENDING!
TAKE ME NOW LORD.
SNAP
PAT PAT
MOORE

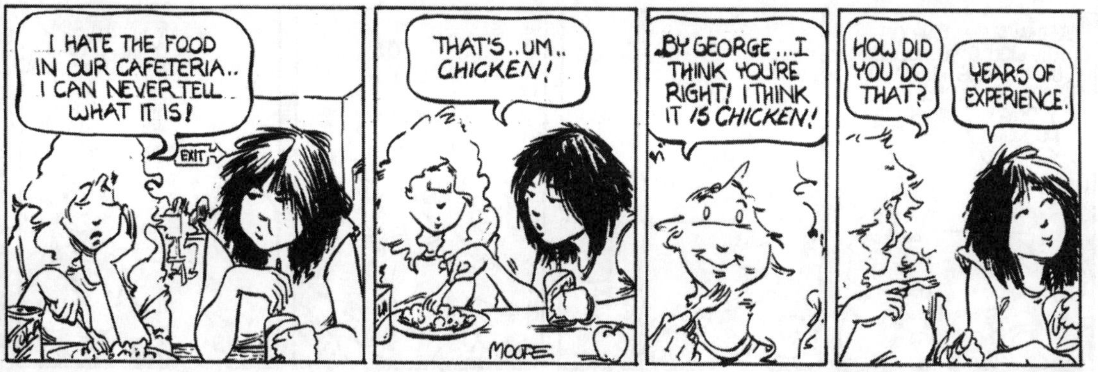
...I HATE THE FOOD IN OUR CAFETERIA.. I CAN NEVER TELL WHAT IT IS!
EXIT
THAT'S..UM.. CHICKEN!
MOORE
BY GEORGE...I THINK YOU'RE RIGHT! I THINK IT IS CHICKEN!
HOW DID YOU DO THAT?
YEARS OF EXPERIENCE.

This strip is the first time I paired the surly girl with the easy going guy, my David.

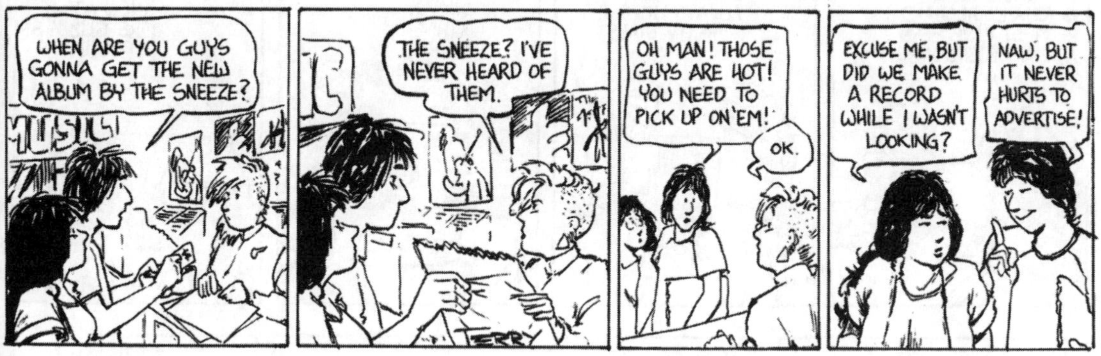
WHEN ARE YOU GUYS GONNA GET THE NEW ALBUM BY THE SNEEZE?
MUSIC
THE SNEEZE? I'VE NEVER HEARD OF THEM.
TERRY
OH MAN! THOSE GUYS ARE HOT! YOU NEED TO PICK UP ON 'EM!
OK.
EXCUSE ME, BUT DID WE MAKE A RECORD WHILE I WASN'T LOOKING?
NAW, BUT IT NEVER HURTS TO ADVERTISE!

Steffie Katchoo had a dingbat neighbor named Mrs. Maltsby who later became one of my favorite characters in SIP, Aunt Libby. In SIP, Uncle Maury talks about Aunt Libby's run-in with UFO's. Here's where all that came from.

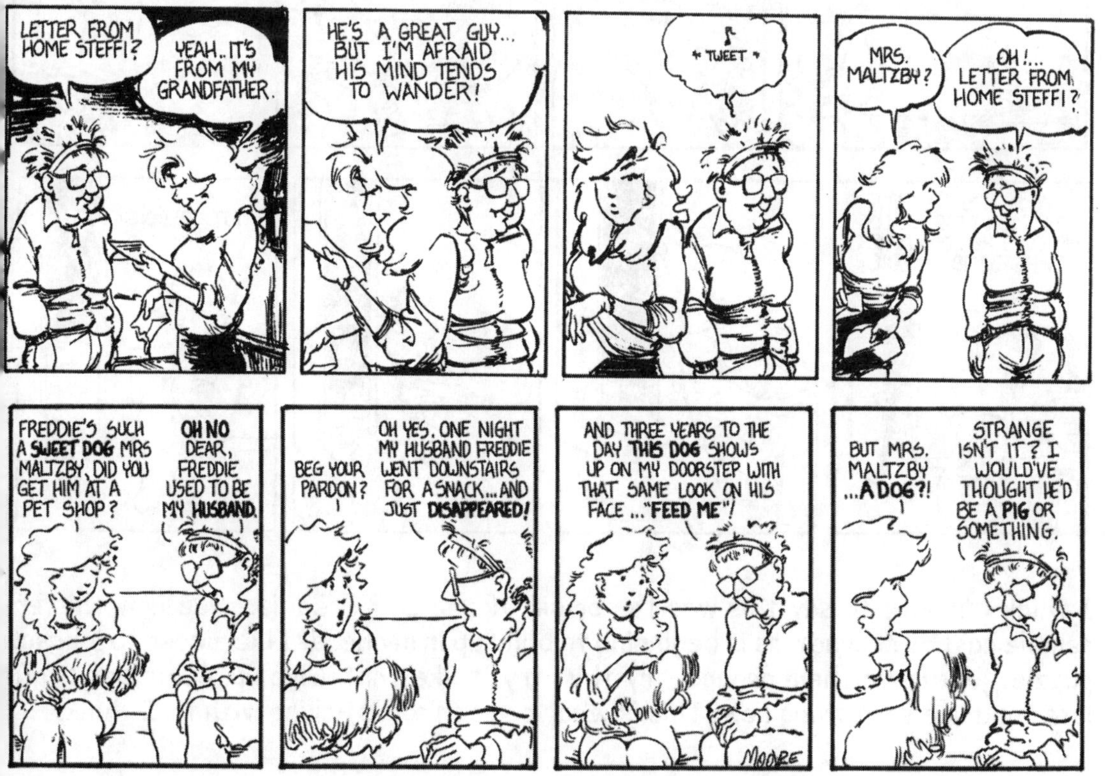
LETTER FROM HOME STEFFI?
YEAH.. IT'S FROM MY GRANDFATHER.
HE'S A GREAT GUY... BUT I'M AFRAID HIS MIND TENDS TO WANDER!
* TWEET *
MRS. MALTZBY?
OH!... LETTER FROM HOME STEFFI?
FREDDIE'S SUCH A SWEET DOG MRS MALTZBY, DID YOU GET HIM AT A PET SHOP?
OH NO DEAR, FREDDIE USED TO BE MY HUSBAND.
BEG YOUR PARDON?
OH YES, ONE NIGHT MY HUSBAND FREDDIE WENT DOWNSTAIRS FOR A SNACK...AND JUST DISAPPEARED!
AND THREE YEARS TO THE DAY THIS DOG SHOWS UP ON MY DOORSTEP WITH THAT SAME LOOK ON HIS FACE..."FEED ME"!
BUT MRS. MALTZBY ...A DOG?!
STRANGE ISN'T IT? I WOULD'VE THOUGHT HE'D BE A PIG OR SOMETHING.
MOORE

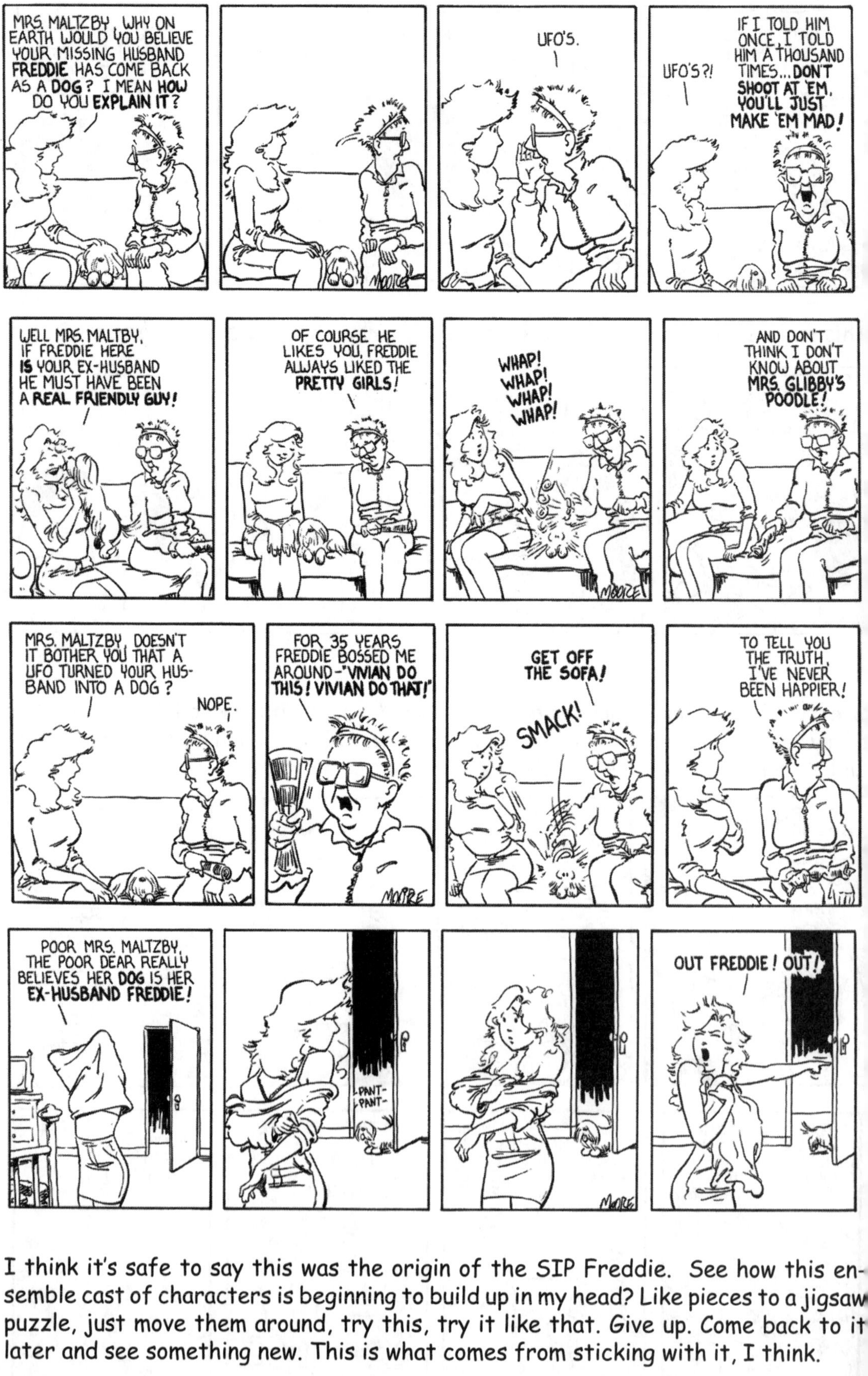
MRS. MALTZBY, WHY ON EARTH WOULD YOU BELIEVE YOUR MISSING HUSBAND FREDDIE HAS COME BACK AS A DOG? I MEAN HOW DO YOU EXPLAIN IT?
UFO'S.
UFO'S?!
IF I TOLD HIM ONCE, I TOLD HIM A THOUSAND TIMES... DON'T SHOOT AT 'EM, YOU'LL JUST MAKE 'EM MAD!
WELL MRS. MALTBY, IF FREDDIE HERE IS YOUR EX-HUSBAND HE MUST HAVE BEEN A REAL FRIENDLY GUY!
OF COURSE HE LIKES YOU, FREDDIE ALWAYS LIKED THE PRETTY GIRLS!
WHAP! WHAP! WHAP! WHAP!
AND DON'T THINK I DON'T KNOW ABOUT MRS. GLIBBY'S POODLE!
MRS. MALTZBY, DOESN'T IT BOTHER YOU THAT A UFO TURNED YOUR HUS-BAND INTO A DOG?
NOPE.
FOR 35 YEARS FREDDIE BOSSED ME AROUND -"VIVIAN DO THIS! VIVIAN DO THAT!"
GET OFF THE SOFA!
SMACK!
TO TELL YOU THE TRUTH, I'VE NEVER BEEN HAPPIER!
POOR MRS. MALTZBY, THE POOR DEAR REALLY BELIEVES HER DOG IS HER EX-HUSBAND FREDDIE!
PANT-PANT-
OUT FREDDIE! OUT!

I think it's safe to say this was the origin of the SIP Freddie. See how this ensemble cast of characters is beginning to build up in my head? Like pieces to a jigsaw puzzle, just move them around, try this, try it like that. Give up. Come back to it later and see something new. This is what comes from sticking with it, I think.

HOLLYWOOD

n the midst of my experiments, I drew up a few strips about a Hollywood movie tudio and the characters who made it sputter. Reappearing was my little geek guy nd a SIP-David prototype named Alton. Again, I was just playing around with ideas.

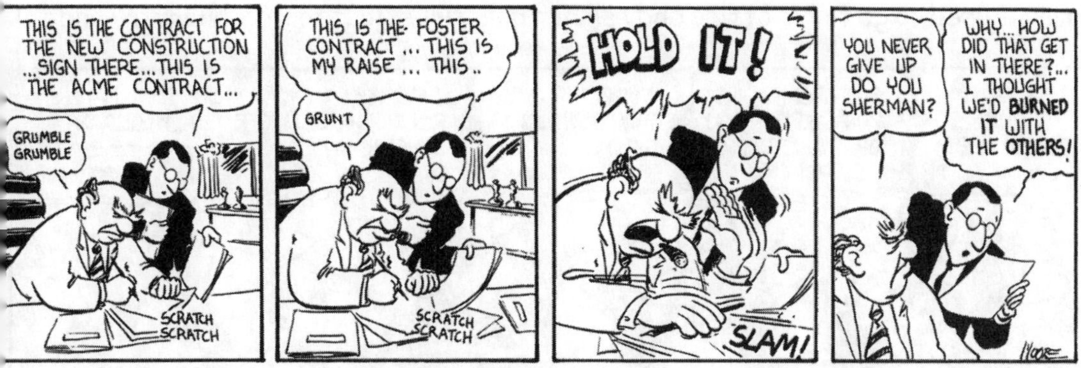
THIS IS THE CONTRACT FOR THE NEW CONSTRUCTION ...SIGN THERE... THIS IS THE ACME CONTRACT...
GRUMBLE GRUMBLE
SCRATCH SCRATCH
THIS IS THE FOSTER CONTRACT ... THIS IS MY RAISE ... THIS..
GRUNT
SCRATCH SCRATCH
HOLD IT!
SLAM!
YOU NEVER GIVE UP DO YOU SHERMAN?
WHY... HOW DID THAT GET IN THERE?... I THOUGHT WE'D BURNED IT WITH THE OTHERS!
MOORE

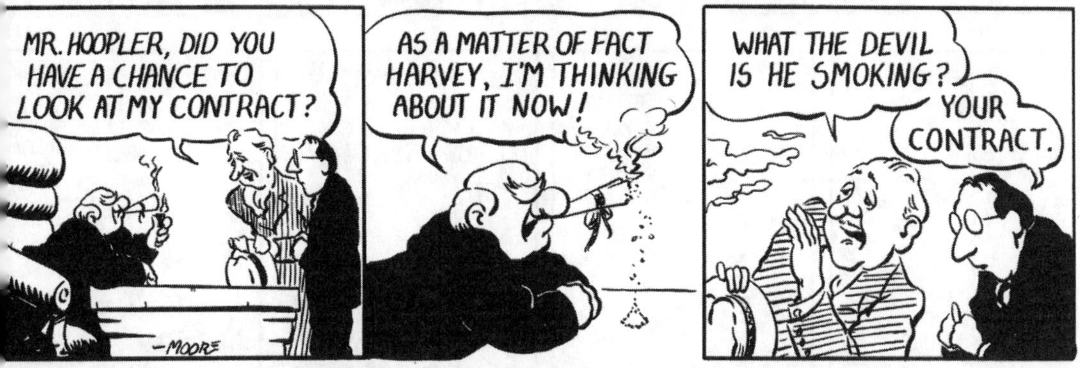
MR. HOOPLER, DID YOU HAVE A CHANCE TO LOOK AT MY CONTRACT?
MOORE
AS A MATTER OF FACT HARVEY, I'M THINKING ABOUT IT NOW!
WHAT THE DEVIL IS HE SMOKING?
YOUR CONTRACT.

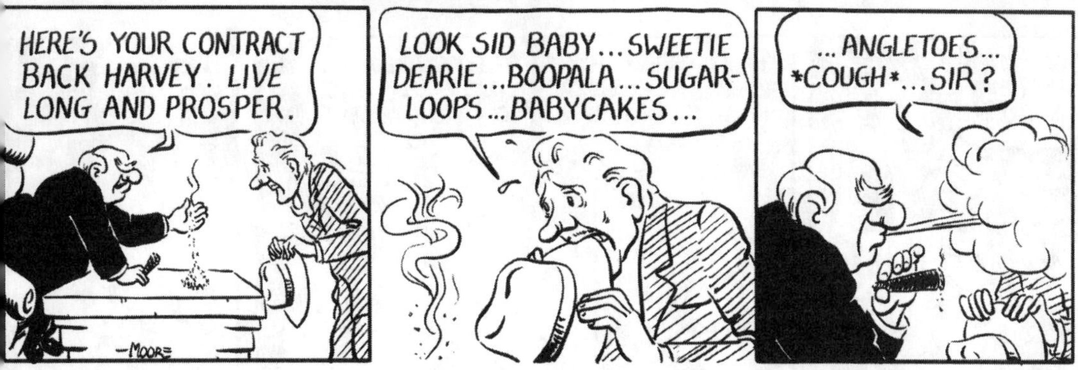
HERE'S YOUR CONTRACT BACK HARVEY. LIVE LONG AND PROSPER.
MOORE
LOOK SID BABY... SWEETIE DEARIE... BOOPALA... SUGAR-LOOPS... BABYCAKES...
... ANGLETOES... *COUGH*... SIR?

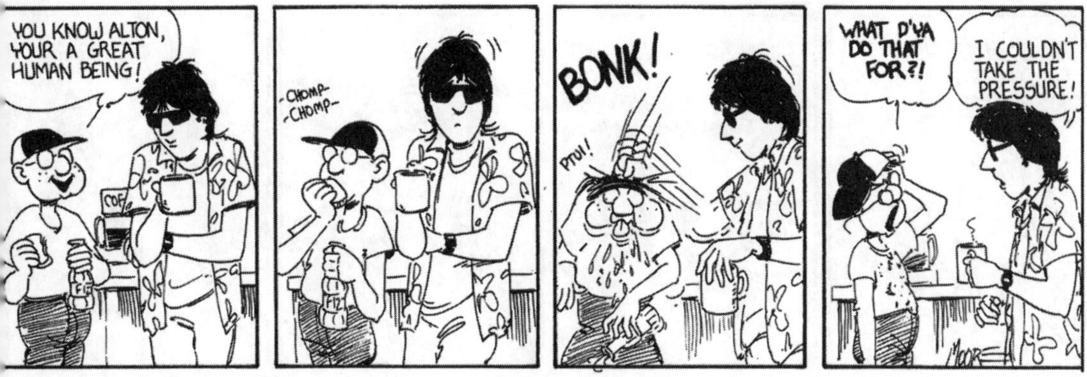
YOU KNOW ALTON, YOUR A GREAT HUMAN BEING!
CHOMP CHOMP
BONK!
PTUI!
WHAT D'YA DO THAT FOR?!
I COULDN'T TAKE THE PRESSURE!
MOORE

YUP YUP AND AWAY!

I decided Hollywood life might be too hard for people to relate to, so I reigned i back into the local neighborhood, with working stiffs like you and me. The coffe gag: I worked with a man who did this – drank coffee all morning and couldn't finis a sentence by mid-morning because he was dealing with an overload of, well... yo know. I used to go to his office and ask him questions, just to watch him try and talk

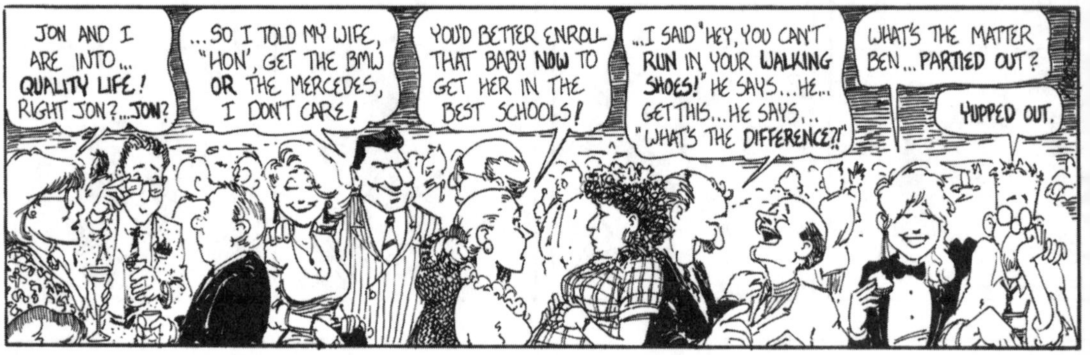
JON AND I ARE INTO... QUALITY LIFE! RIGHT JON?... JON?
...SO I TOLD MY WIFE, "HON', GET THE BMW OR THE MERCEDES, I DON'T CARE!
YOU'D BETTER ENROLL THAT BABY NOW TO GET HER IN THE BEST SCHOOLS!
...I SAID 'HEY, YOU CAN'T RUN IN YOUR WALKING SHOES!" HE SAYS... HE... GET THIS... HE SAYS... "WHAT'S THE DIFFERENCE?!"
WHAT'S THE MATTER BEN... PARTIED OUT?
YUPPED OUT.

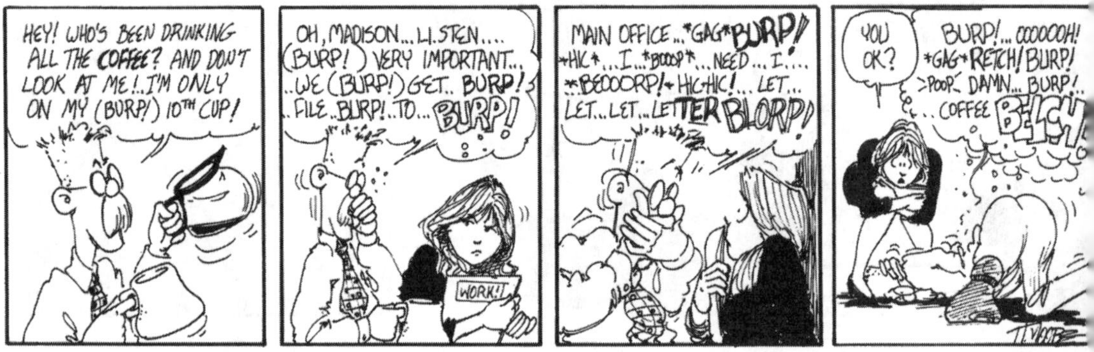
HEY! WHO'S BEEN DRINKING ALL THE COFFEE? AND DON'T LOOK AT ME!.. I'M ONLY ON MY (BURP!) 10TH CUP!
OH, MADISON... LI.STEN.... (BURP!) VERY IMPORTANT... ..WE (BURP!) GET.. BURP! ..FILE..BURP!...TO... BURP!
WORK!
MAIN OFFICE...*GAG* BURP! *HIC*...I...*BOOOP*...NEED...I... *BEOOORP!*HIC HIC!... LET... LET...LET...LETTER BLORP!
YOU OK?
BURP!... OOOOOOH! *GAG* RETCH! BURP! DAMN... BURP! ...COFFEE

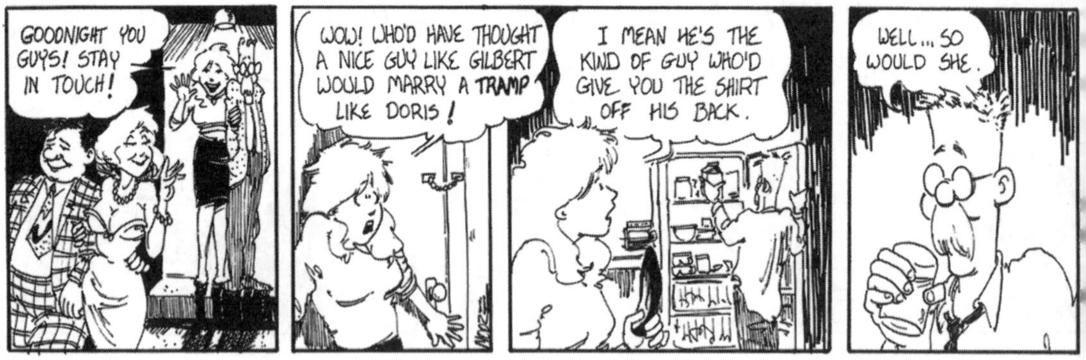
GOODNIGHT YOU GUYS! STAY IN TOUCH!
WOW! WHO'D HAVE THOUGHT A NICE GUY LIKE GILBERT WOULD MARRY A TRAMP LIKE DORIS!
I MEAN HE'S THE KIND OF GUY WHO'D GIVE YOU THE SHIRT OFF HIS BACK.
WELL... SO WOULD SHE.

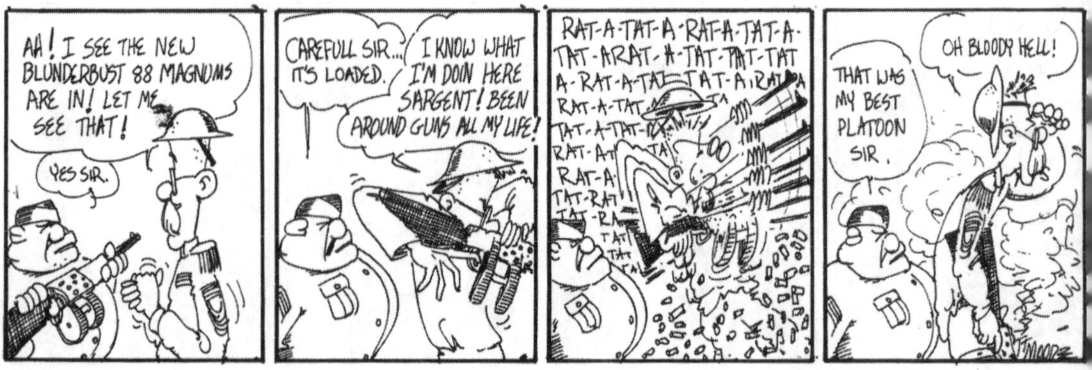
AH! I SEE THE NEW BLUNDERBUST 88 MAGNUMS ARE IN! LET ME SEE THAT!
YES SIR.
CAREFULL SIR... IT'S LOADED.
I KNOW WHAT I'M DOIN HERE SARGENT! BEEN AROUND GUNS ALL MY LIFE!
RAT-A-TAT-A-RAT-A-TAT-A-
THAT WAS MY BEST PLATOON SIR.
OH BLOODY HELL!

Steffi Katchoo fit into this yuppie world thing nicely, this time as an artist turning the table on male-female, artist-model stereotypes. Typical Katchoo, I discovered.

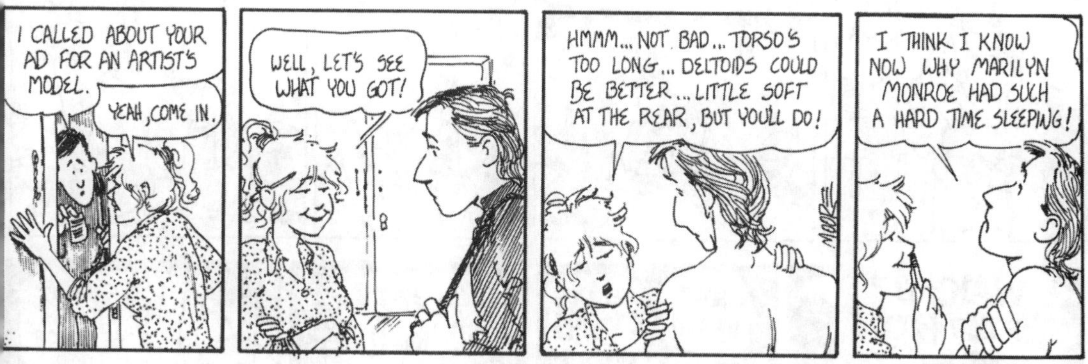
I CALLED ABOUT YOUR AD FOR AN ARTIST'S MODEL.
YEAH, COME IN.
WELL, LET'S SEE WHAT YOU GOT!
HMMM... NOT BAD... TORSO'S TOO LONG... DELTOIDS COULD BE BETTER... LITTLE SOFT AT THE REAR, BUT YOU'LL DO!
I THINK I KNOW NOW WHY MARILYN MONROE HAD SUCH A HARD TIME SLEEPING!

One night I ate too many Krispie Treats and came up with this pair of weirdos.

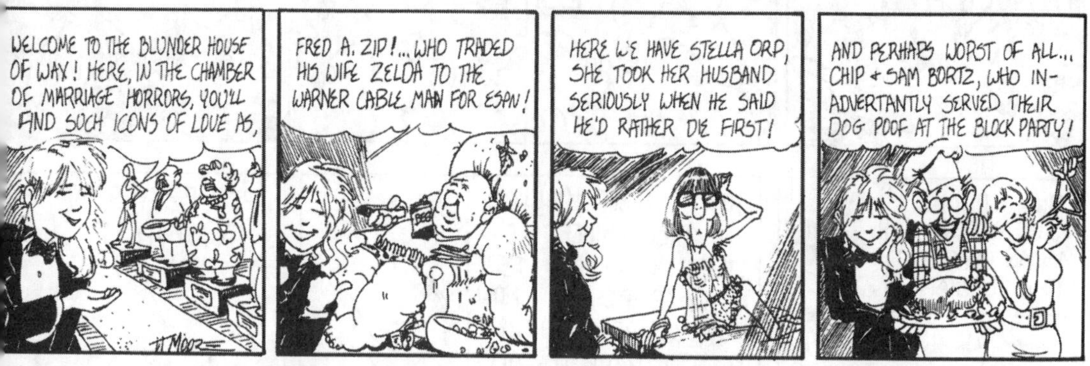
WELCOME TO THE BLUNDER HOUSE OF WAX! HERE, IN THE CHAMBER OF MARRIAGE HORRORS, YOU'LL FIND SUCH ICONS OF LOVE AS,
FRED A. ZIP!... WHO TRADED HIS WIFE ZELDA TO THE WARNER CABLE MAN FOR ESPN!
HERE WE HAVE STELLA ORP, SHE TOOK HER HUSBAND SERIOUSLY WHEN HE SAID HE'D RATHER DIE FIRST!
AND PERHAPS WORST OF ALL... CHIP + SAM BORTZ, WHO INADVERTANTLY SERVED THEIR DOG POOP AT THE BLOCK PARTY!

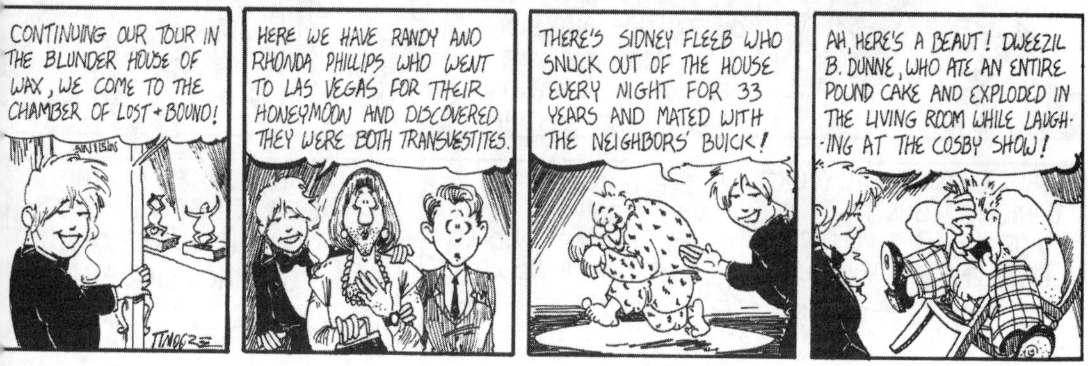
CONTINUING OUR TOUR IN THE BLUNDER HOUSE OF WAX, WE COME TO THE CHAMBER OF LOST + BOUND!
HERE WE HAVE RANDY AND RHONDA PHILLIPS WHO WENT TO LAS VEGAS FOR THEIR HONEYMOON AND DISCOVERED THEY WERE BOTH TRANSVESTITES.
THERE'S SIDNEY FLEEB WHO SNUCK OUT OF THE HOUSE EVERY NIGHT FOR 33 YEARS AND MATED WITH THE NEIGHBORS' BUICK!
AH, HERE'S A BEAUT! DWEEZIL B. DUNNE, WHO ATE AN ENTIRE POUND CAKE AND EXPLODED IN THE LIVING ROOM WHILE LAUGH-ING AT THE COSBY SHOW!

Right around this time I lost all focus and began sketching out various ideas, like kings and queens and all the things in between, but I came back to Steffi Katchoo.

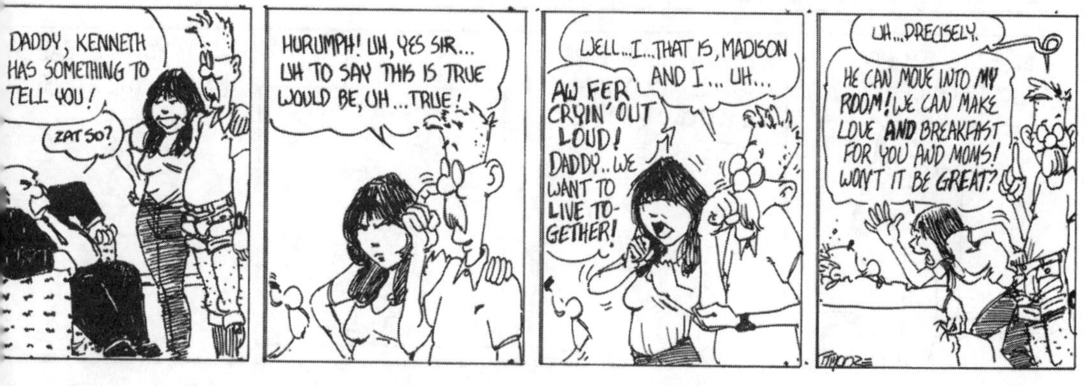
DADDY, KENNETH HAS SOMETHING TO TELL YOU!
ZAT SO?
HURUMPH! UH, YES SIR... UH TO SAY THIS IS TRUE WOULD BE, UH... TRUE!
WELL... I... THAT IS, MADISON AND I... UH...
AW FER CRYIN' OUT LOUD! DADDY.. WE WANT TO LIVE TO-GETHER!
UH... PRECISELY.
HE CAN MOVE INTO MY ROOM! WE CAN MAKE LOVE AND BREAKFAST FOR YOU AND MOMS! WON'T IT BE GREAT?

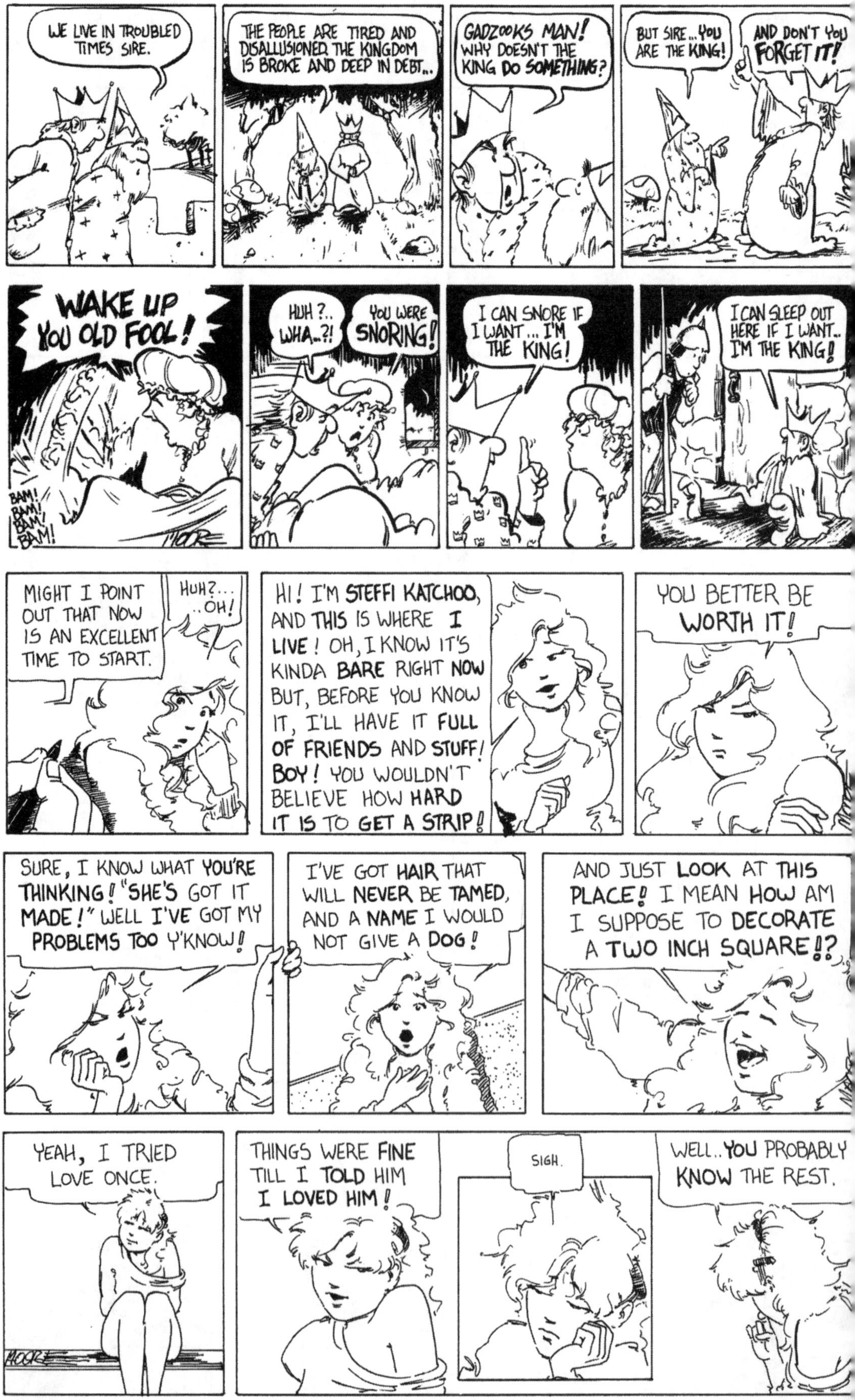
WE LIVE IN TROUBLED TIMES SIRE.
THE PEOPLE ARE TIRED AND DISALLUSIONED. THE KINGDOM IS BROKE AND DEEP IN DEBT...
GADZOOKS MAN! WHY DOESN'T THE KING DO SOMETHING?
BUT SIRE...YOU ARE THE KING!
AND DON'T YOU FORGET IT!
WAKE UP YOU OLD FOOL!
BAM! BAM! BAM! BAM!
HUH?.. WHA..?!
YOU WERE SNORING!
I CAN SNORE IF I WANT... I'M THE KING!
I CAN SLEEP OUT HERE IF I WANT.. I'M THE KING!
MIGHT I POINT OUT THAT NOW IS AN EXCELLENT TIME TO START.
HUH?... ...OH!
HI! I'M STEFFI KATCHOO, AND THIS IS WHERE I LIVE! OH, I KNOW IT'S KINDA BARE RIGHT NOW BUT, BEFORE YOU KNOW IT, I'LL HAVE IT FULL OF FRIENDS AND STUFF! BOY! YOU WOULDN'T BELIEVE HOW HARD IT IS TO GET A STRIP!
YOU BETTER BE WORTH IT!
SURE, I KNOW WHAT YOU'RE THINKING! "SHE'S GOT IT MADE!" WELL I'VE GOT MY PROBLEMS TOO Y'KNOW!
I'VE GOT HAIR THAT WILL NEVER BE TAMED, AND A NAME I WOULD NOT GIVE A DOG!
AND JUST LOOK AT THIS PLACE! I MEAN HOW AM I SUPPOSE TO DECORATE A TWO INCH SQUARE!?
YEAH, I TRIED LOVE ONCE.
MOORE
THINGS WERE FINE TILL I TOLD HIM I LOVED HIM!
SIGH.
WELL..YOU PROBABLY KNOW THE REST.

RANCINE

liked Steffi Katchoo a lot, but I couldn't figure out what to do with her exactly. ly instincts told me I'd be more comfortable with a down to earth setting, like a amily. So I developed a normal thinking, girl-next-door and built a family around er. The important thing to me was that she be somebody I could meet in real life.

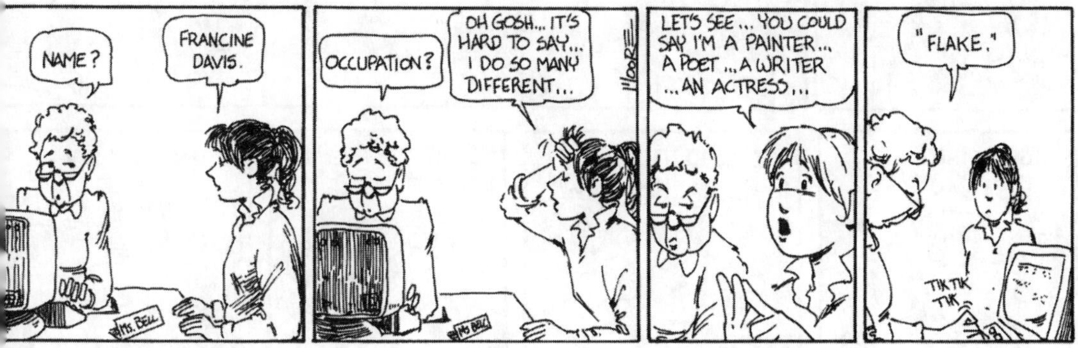

NAME?
FRANCINE DAVIS.
MS. BELL
OCCUPATION?
OH GOSH... IT'S HARD TO SAY... I DO SO MANY DIFFERENT...
MS. BELL
LET'S SEE... YOU COULD SAY I'M A PAINTER... A POET... A WRITER ... AN ACTRESS...
"FLAKE."
TIKTIK TIK

tried her as a wife...

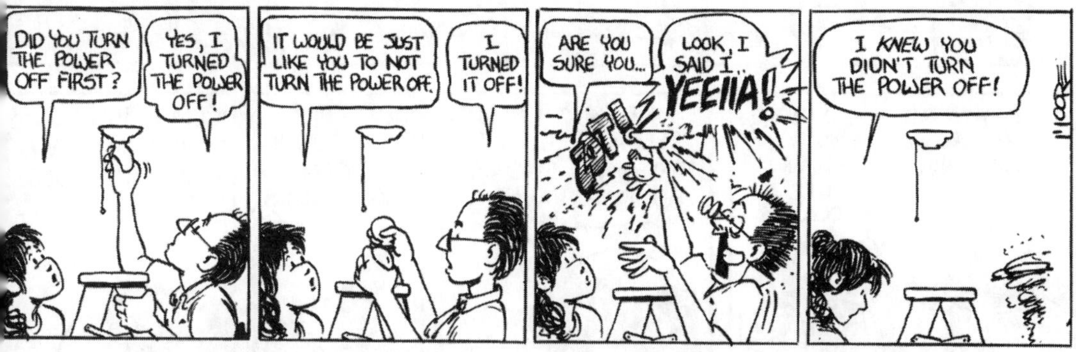

DID YOU TURN THE POWER OFF FIRST?
YES, I TURNED THE POWER OFF!
IT WOULD BE JUST LIKE YOU TO NOT TURN THE POWER OFF.
I TURNED IT OFF!
ARE YOU SURE YOU...
LOOK, I SAID I...
YEEIIA!
ZOT!
I KNEW YOU DIDN'T TURN THE POWER OFF!

tried her as a middle-aged mother, a teenage daughter. I tried everything. Agh!

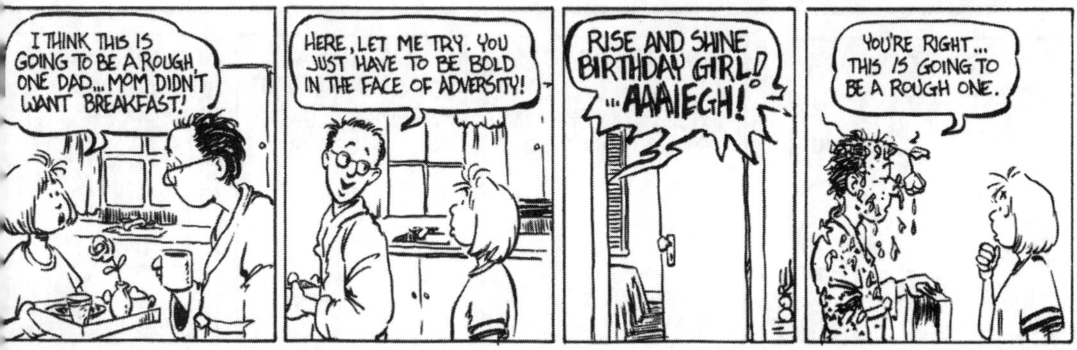

I THINK THIS IS GOING TO BE A ROUGH ONE DAD... MOM DIDN'T WANT BREAKFAST!
HERE, LET ME TRY. YOU JUST HAVE TO BE BOLD IN THE FACE OF ADVERSITY!
RISE AND SHINE BIRTHDAY GIRL!
... AAAIEGH!
YOU'RE RIGHT... THIS IS GOING TO BE A ROUGH ONE.

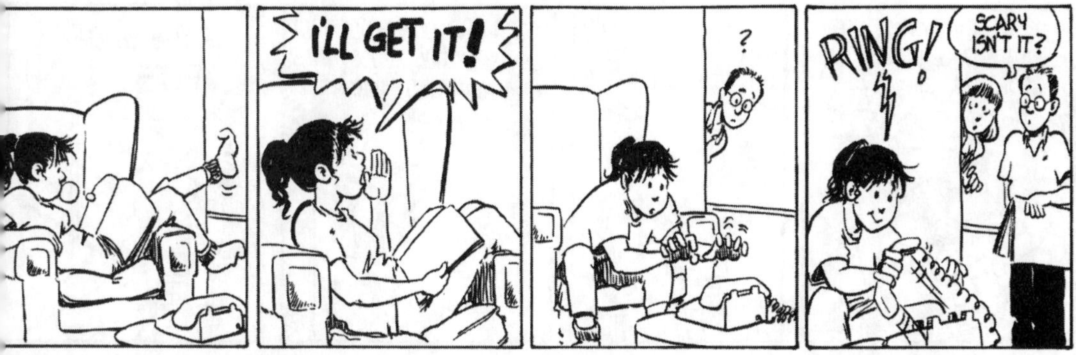

I'LL GET IT!
?
RING!
SCARY ISN'T IT?

AAAAGH! LOOK AT THIS BATHTUB!

HOW CAN I LOSE THIS MUCH HAIR *EVERY* DAY...

... AND STILL HAVE ANY *LEFT ON MY HEAD*?!

WELL ... YOU CAN'T.
SHEESH!

MOORE

TURN THAT TV DOWN!
SIGH

I SAID TURN THAT RACKET DOWN!
CLICK!

I STILL HEAR IT!
I TURNED THE BLASTED THING OFF!

THEN **UNPLUG IT!**
CRUNCH!

I FEEL A HEADACHE COMING ON...DO WE HAVE ANY ASPIRIN?
YOU DON'T NEED ANY ASPIRIN! YOU'RE A HYPOCHONDRIAC!

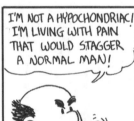

I'M NOT A HYPOCHONDRIAC! I'M LIVING WITH PAIN THAT WOULD STAGGER A NORMAL MAN!

WELL, THAT WOULD EXPLAIN THAT GOOFY WALK OF YOURS.

CONGRATULATIONS! YOU'VE JUST GIVEN BIRTH TO A 10LB. MIGRANE!

MOORE

DICK, HAVE YOU SEEN WEEZY? I CAN'T FIND HER ANYWHERE.
NO.

DID YOU CHECK THE CLOTHES BASKET? YOU KNOW SHE LOVES TO SLEEP IN THERE.

I'VE BEEN DOING LAUNDRY ALL MORNING, I DIDN'T SEE HER IN THERE.

CHUG-A-CHUG-A-CHUG-A-CHUG!

MOORE

TURN THAT GAME OFF AND TAKE WEEZY FOR HER WALK!

I DON'T WANT TO BE SEEN IN PUBLIC WITH THIS ☆€!! MUTT!
PANT-PANT

GO! AND DON'T USE THAT WORD IN THIS HOUSE! IT'S A MEANINGLESS INTENSIVE!

IF THE SHOE FITS...!

MOORE

Francine didn't seem to be interesting enough to carry the strip by herself, so I made her the companion to a Walter Mitty day dreaming Oliver Wonderbee who now resembled a mad bomber I used to draw in high school, but who would know? Shhh. This bed gag was done before Trainspotting came out, by the way. Maybe I'll sue.

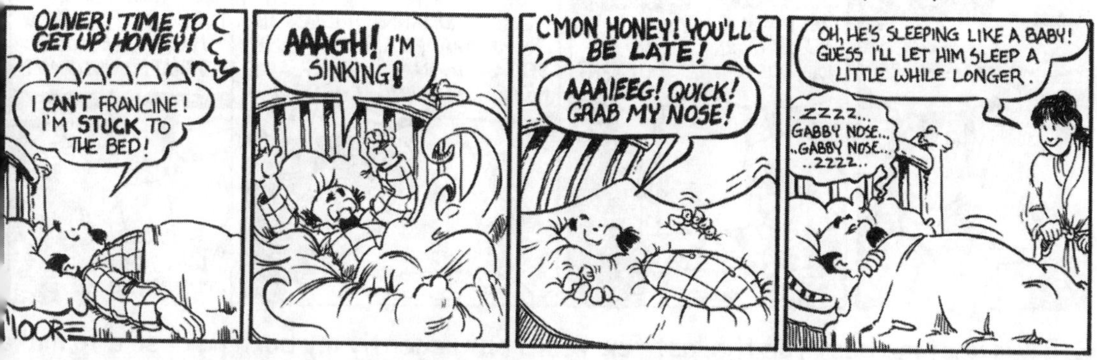
OLIVER! TIME TO GET UP HONEY!
I CAN'T FRANCINE! I'M STUCK TO THE BED!
AAAGH! I'M SINKING!
C'MON HONEY! YOU'LL BE LATE!
AAAIEEG! QUICK! GRAB MY NOSE!
OH, HE'S SLEEPING LIKE A BABY! GUESS I'LL LET HIM SLEEP A LITTLE WHILE LONGER.
..ZZZZ... GABBY NOSE... ..GABBY NOSE... ..ZZZZ..

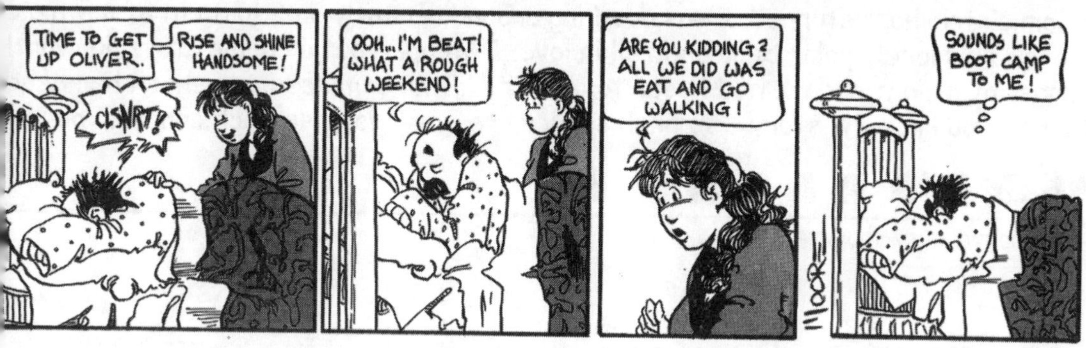
TIME TO GET UP OLIVER.
RISE AND SHINE HANDSOME!
OOH...I'M BEAT! WHAT A ROUGH WEEKEND!
ARE YOU KIDDING? ALL WE DID WAS EAT AND GO WALKING!
SOUNDS LIKE BOOT CAMP TO ME!

I hate going to the dentist, don't you? They know that, that's why they're a bit odd.

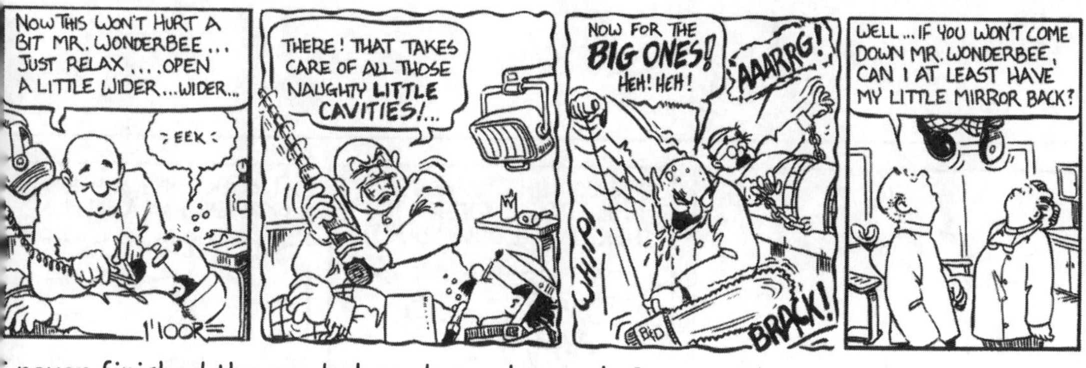
NOW THIS WON'T HURT A BIT MR. WONDERBEE... JUST RELAX....OPEN A LITTLE WIDER...WIDER...
EEK
THERE! THAT TAKES CARE OF ALL THOSE NAUGHTY LITTLE CAVITIES!...
NOW FOR THE BIG ONES! HEH! HEH!
AAARRG!
WHIP!
BRACK!
WELL...IF YOU WON'T COME DOWN MR. WONDERBEE, CAN I AT LEAST HAVE MY LITTLE MIRROR BACK?

I never finished the gag below, do you know why?

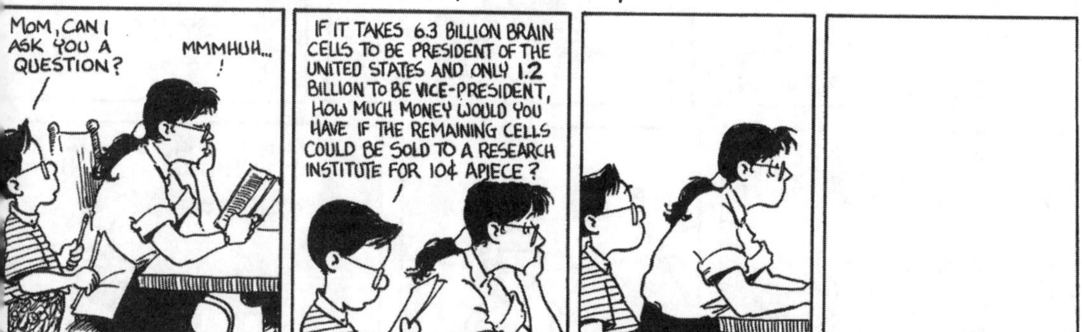
MOM, CAN I ASK YOU A QUESTION?
MMMHUH...
IF IT TAKES 6.3 BILLION BRAIN CELLS TO BE PRESIDENT OF THE UNITED STATES AND ONLY 1.2 BILLION TO BE VICE-PRESIDENT, HOW MUCH MONEY WOULD YOU HAVE IF THE REMAINING CELLS COULD BE SOLD TO A RESEARCH INSTITUTE FOR 10¢ APIECE?

ecause it's not a new idea, it's a comic strip cliche - have a provocative youngster sk a question, pause a beat in the third panel for reaction, the adult mutters her hilosophical dismay in the fourth. Now I'm trying too hard to make a comic strip.

The strip below was done during my SIP days, and it shows. In contrast to the previous strip, this one is honest and original. I'm happy with it. If I took SIP to the strips, this is probably what it would look like.

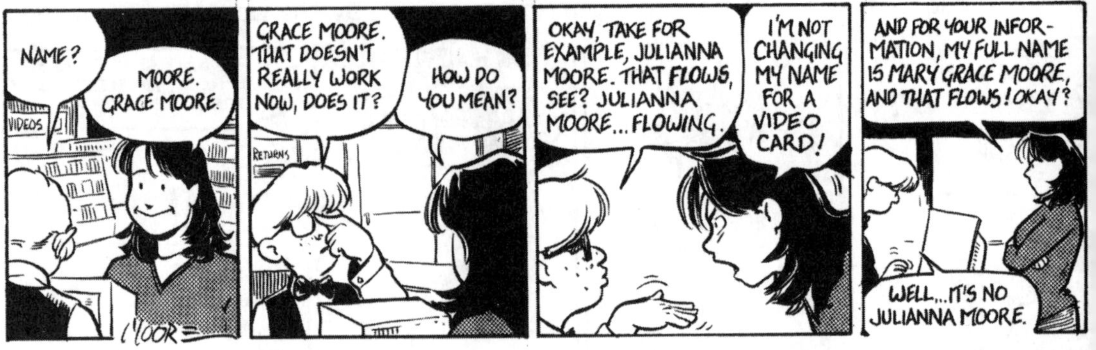
NAME?
MOORE. GRACE MOORE.
VIDEOS
GRACE MOORE. THAT DOESN'T REALLY WORK NOW, DOES IT?
HOW DO YOU MEAN?
RETURNS
OKAY, TAKE FOR EXAMPLE, JULIANNA MOORE. THAT FLOWS, SEE? JULIANNA MOORE... FLOWING.
I'M NOT CHANGING MY NAME FOR A VIDEO CARD!
AND FOR YOUR INFORMATION, MY FULL NAME IS MARY GRACE MOORE, AND THAT FLOWS! OKAY?
WELL,...IT'S NO JULIANNA MOORE.
MOOR

SIP has kept me busy for the last few years but recently my burning desire to make a comic strip has returned. I was doodling around recently and, just out of nowhere I drew this lonely polar bear and fell in love. I whipped out a couple of weeks worth almost overnight and rushed it off to a friend... who grimaced and shook her head So now you know my story - six inch comics are easy, good six inch comics... hard.

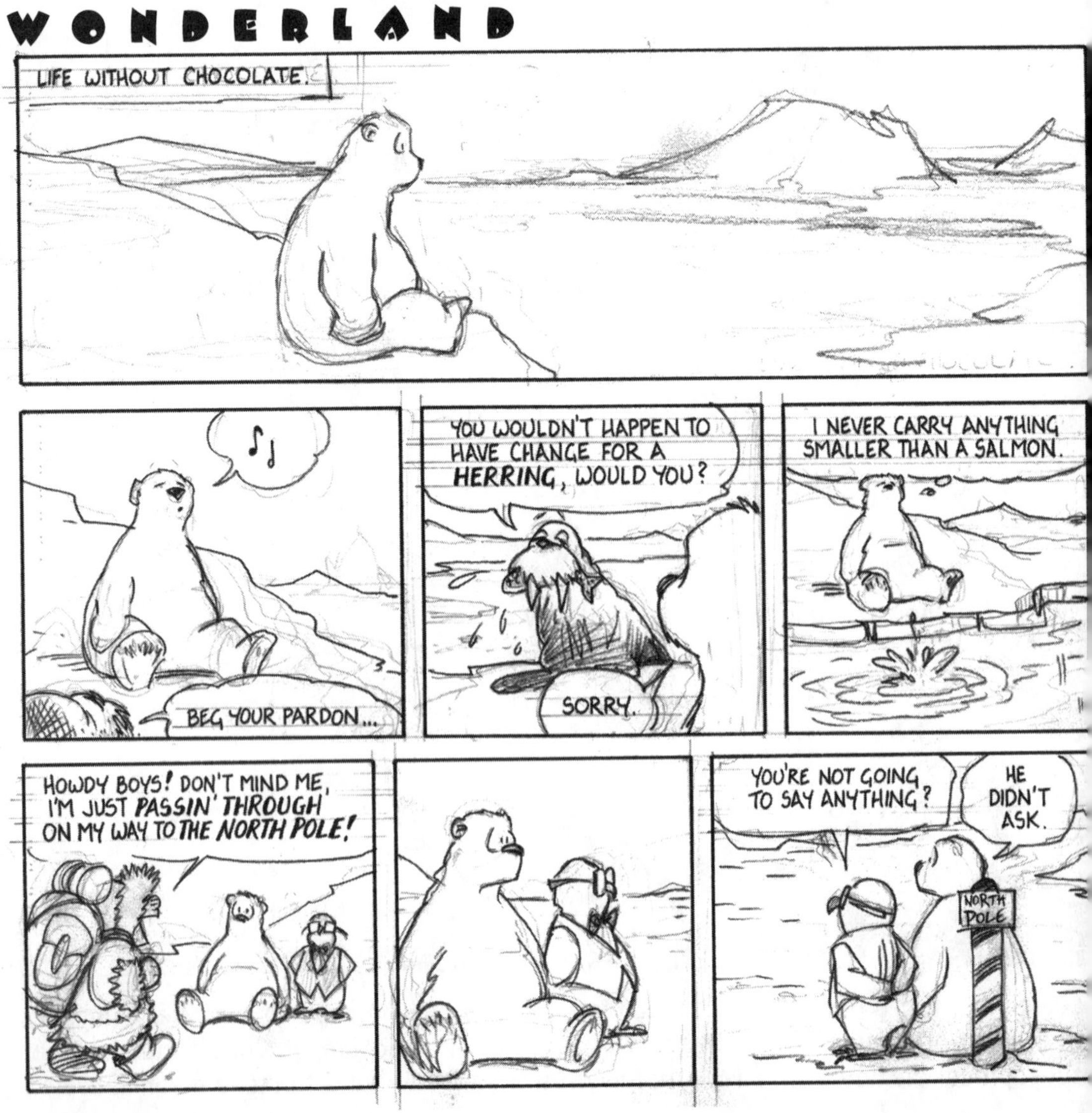
WONDERLAND
LIFE WITHOUT CHOCOLATE.
BEG YOUR PARDON...
YOU WOULDN'T HAPPEN TO HAVE CHANGE FOR A HERRING, WOULD YOU?
SORRY.
I NEVER CARRY ANYTHING SMALLER THAN A SALMON.
HOWDY BOYS! DON'T MIND ME, I'M JUST PASSIN' THROUGH ON MY WAY TO THE NORTH POLE!
YOU'RE NOT GOING TO SAY ANYTHING?
HE DIDN'T ASK.
NORTH POLE

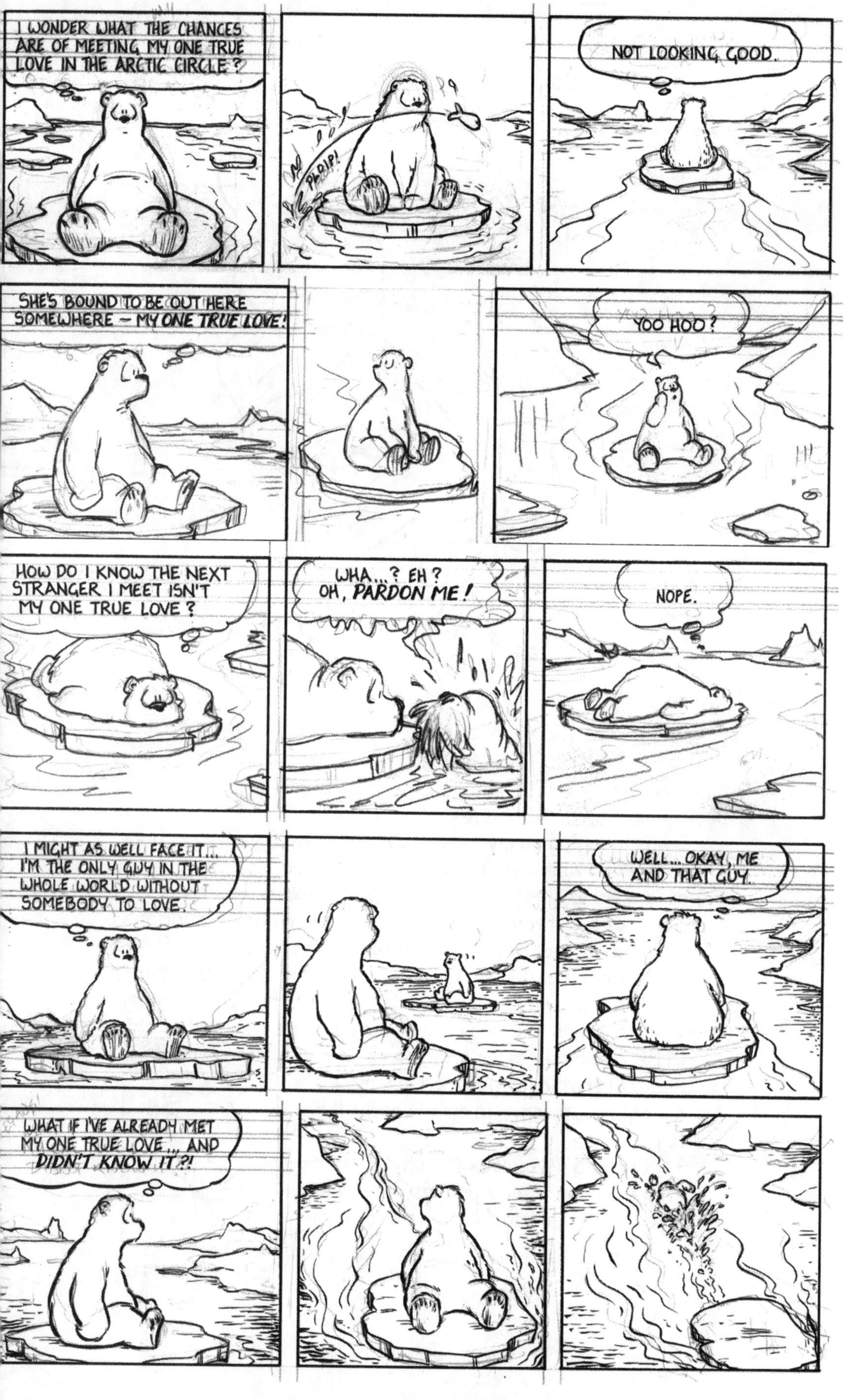
I WONDER WHAT THE CHANCES ARE OF MEETING MY ONE TRUE LOVE IN THE ARCTIC CIRCLE?
PLOIP!
NOT LOOKING GOOD.
SHE'S BOUND TO BE OUT HERE SOMEWHERE — MY ONE TRUE LOVE!
YOO HOO?
HOW DO I KNOW THE NEXT STRANGER I MEET ISN'T MY ONE TRUE LOVE?
WHA...? EH? OH, PARDON ME!
NOPE.
I MIGHT AS WELL FACE IT... I'M THE ONLY GUY IN THE WHOLE WORLD WITHOUT SOMEBODY TO LOVE.
WELL... OKAY, ME AND THAT GUY.
WHAT IF I'VE ALREADY MET MY ONE TRUE LOVE... AND DIDN'T KNOW IT?!

I was lounging on my favorite homemade futon, a garbage bag filled with syndicate rejection slips, not doing much of anything, just twiddling with an atomic string model I'd crafted from some stray pasta, when it suddenly dawned on me that I had cartooning in my blood. If this sounds painful don't despair, I've learned to live with it. But the truth is, I'm living with cartoons that would cripple a normal man. To prove my point I have assembled this little book collecting the voices in my head. I'm not looking for sympathy, just a giggle every once in awhile and I'll be happy.

Oh, and if you look for any of these strips in the funny papers, you won't find them. I wasn't kidding about the futon.

—Terry Moore

AVING GRACE

s you are probably all too aware, I have been living with an insatiable desire to have
y own comic strip. And I'm not talking about worldwide syndication, I'm just talking
bout a strip to call my own. That's all, just one little strip, perfect in every way —
apable of achieving world peace and a cure for most diseases. Oh sure, you may say
'm a dreamer, that I expect too much from this funny blue ball we call home, but
've learned nothing if not this... that... tha... oh crap, there's the phone. Excuse me.

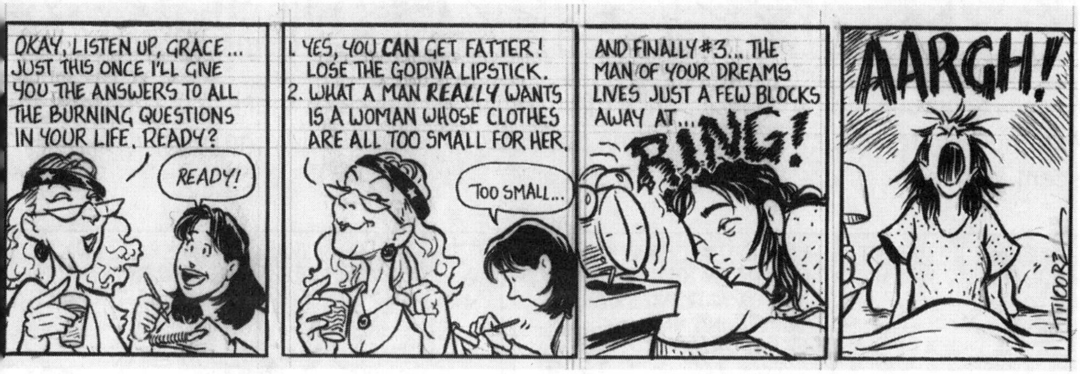

OKAY, LISTEN UP, GRACE... JUST THIS ONCE I'LL GIVE YOU THE ANSWERS TO ALL THE BURNING QUESTIONS IN YOUR LIFE. READY?
READY!
1. YES, YOU CAN GET FATTER! LOSE THE GODIVA LIPSTICK.
2. WHAT A MAN REALLY WANTS IS A WOMAN WHOSE CLOTHES ARE ALL TOO SMALL FOR HER.
TOO SMALL...
AND FINALLY #3... THE MAN OF YOUR DREAMS LIVES JUST A FEW BLOCKS AWAY AT...
RING!
AARGH!

o, when we left off last issue (Paradise Too!, the debut issue... last year, remem-
er?), I introduced you to Grace, a young working woman who bears a remarkable
esemblance to somebody... I can't quite put my finger on it though... anyway, I had
n idea to do a strip about this young woman with a single life, weight problems, self-
steem issues... I swear, this sounds so familiar to me but I just can't quite place it...
ut here are a few ideas I bounced around, trying to get a feel for what life with
race would be like.

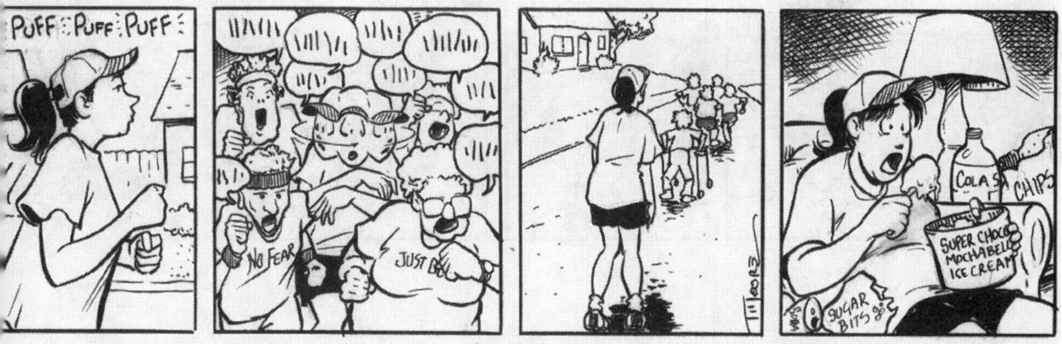

PUFF PUFF PUFF
NO FEAR
COLA
CHIPS
SUPER CHOCO MOCHABELLO ICE CREAM
SUGAR BITS

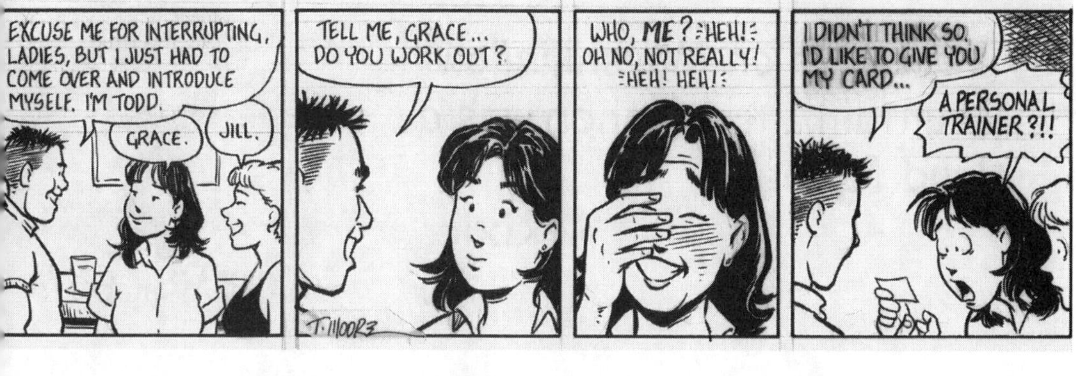

EXCUSE ME FOR INTERRUPTING, LADIES, BUT I JUST HAD TO COME OVER AND INTRODUCE MYSELF. I'M TODD.
GRACE.
JILL.
TELL ME, GRACE... DO YOU WORK OUT?
WHO, ME? HEH! OH NO, NOT REALLY! HEH! HEH!
I DIDN'T THINK SO. I'D LIKE TO GIVE YOU MY CARD...
A PERSONAL TRAINER?!!

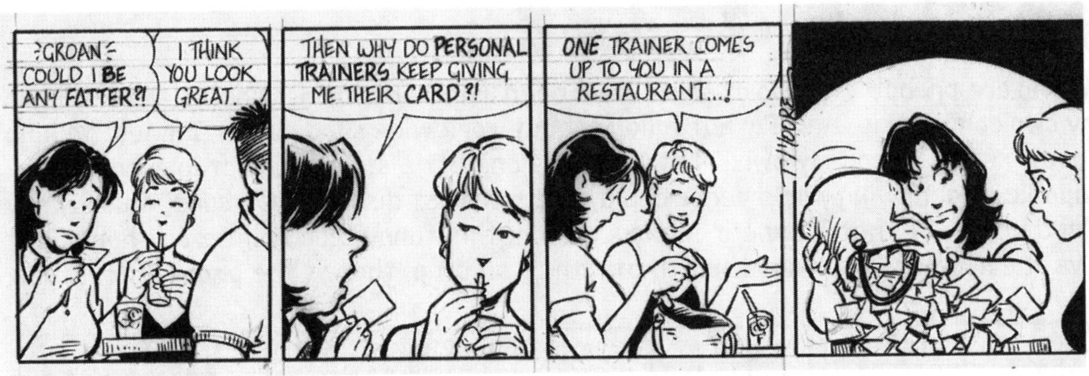
GROAN
COULD I BE ANY FATTER?!
I THINK YOU LOOK GREAT.
THEN WHY DO PERSONAL TRAINERS KEEP GIVING ME THEIR CARD?!
ONE TRAINER COMES UP TO YOU IN A RESTAURANT...!
T. MOORE

Grace is surrounded by a swell bunch of fellas at work: a sexist jerk and a pantaphobic. Men have often questioned my harsh satires of men... but I've noticed women don't seem to mind.

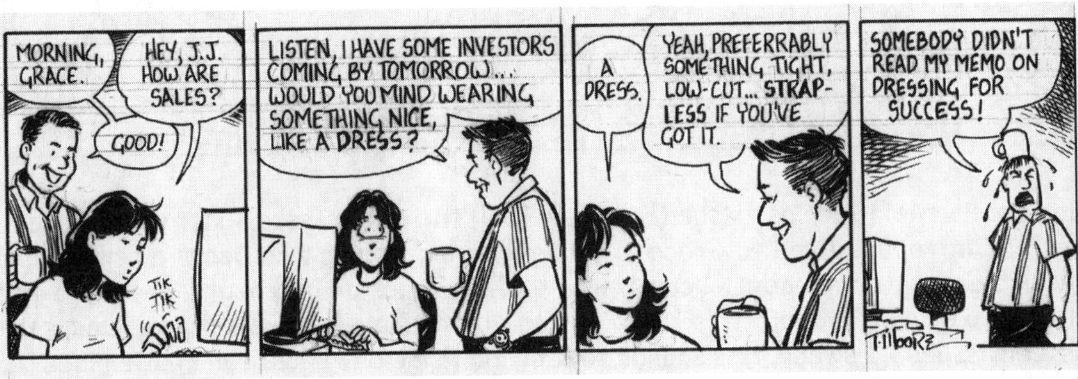
MORNING, GRACE.
HEY, J.J. HOW ARE SALES?
GOOD!
TIK TIK
LISTEN, I HAVE SOME INVESTORS COMING BY TOMORROW... WOULD YOU MIND WEARING SOMETHING NICE, LIKE A DRESS?
A DRESS.
YEAH, PREFERRABLY SOMETHING TIGHT, LOW-CUT... STRAPLESS IF YOU'VE GOT IT.
SOMEBODY DIDN'T READ MY MEMO ON DRESSING FOR SUCCESS!
T. MOORE

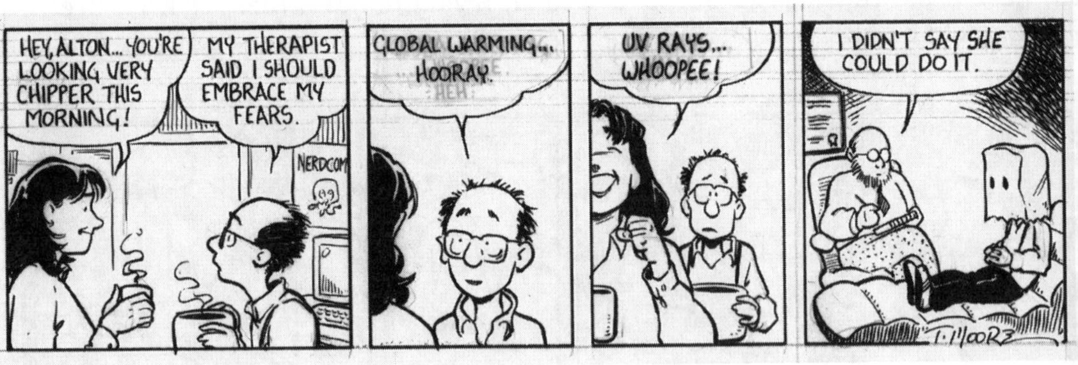
HEY, ALTON... YOU'RE LOOKING VERY CHIPPER THIS MORNING!
MY THERAPIST SAID I SHOULD EMBRACE MY FEARS.
NERDCOM
GLOBAL WARMING... HOORAY.
UV RAYS... WHOOPEE!
I DIDN'T SAY SHE COULD DO IT.
T. MOORE

"I grew up on Marshmallow Mountain... my father was a cloud farmer."

—Kixie

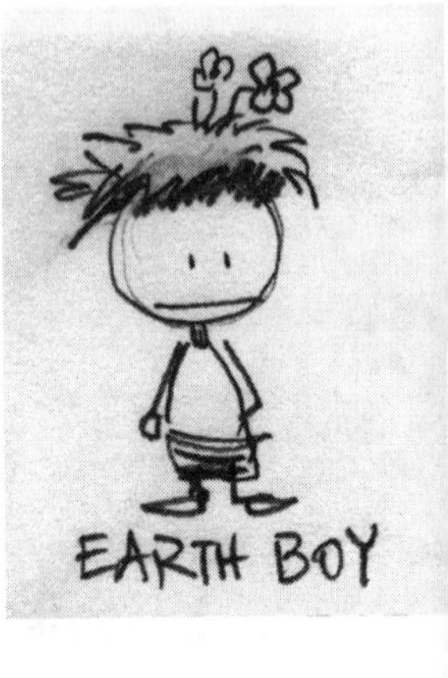
EARTH BOY

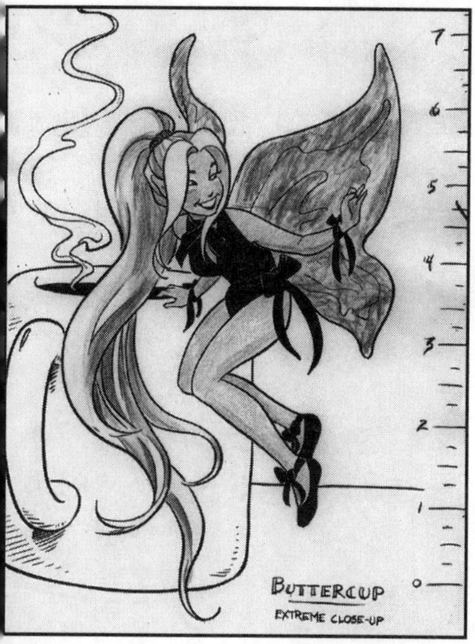
7
6
5
4
3
2
1
0
BUTTERCUP
EXTREME CLOSE-UP

KIXIE & GRACE

Suppose you woke up one morning to find a faerie on your pillow. Think about it.

Suppose you woke up and discovered the house you just bought was lousy with faeries. In fact, they tell you that they've lived in the house for quite some time and they're rather ticked at you for moving into THEIR house uninvited.

That's what I was thinking when I drew up this little scenario with a blonde Grace.

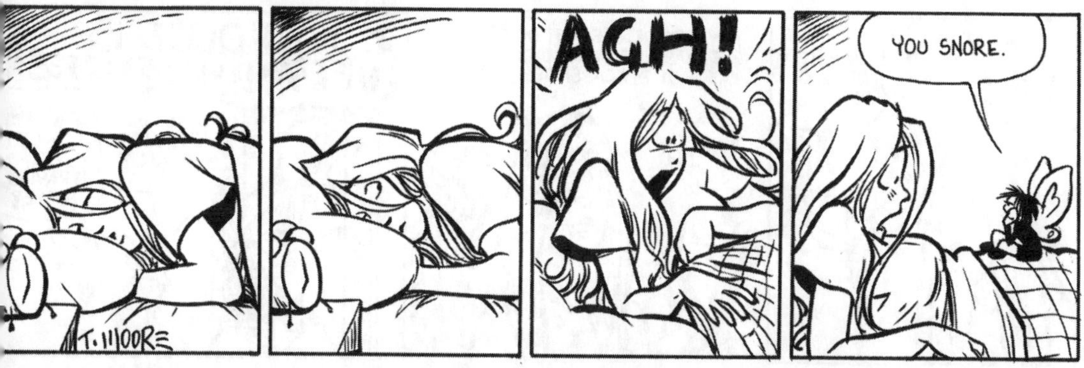
T. MOORE
AGH!
YOU SNORE.

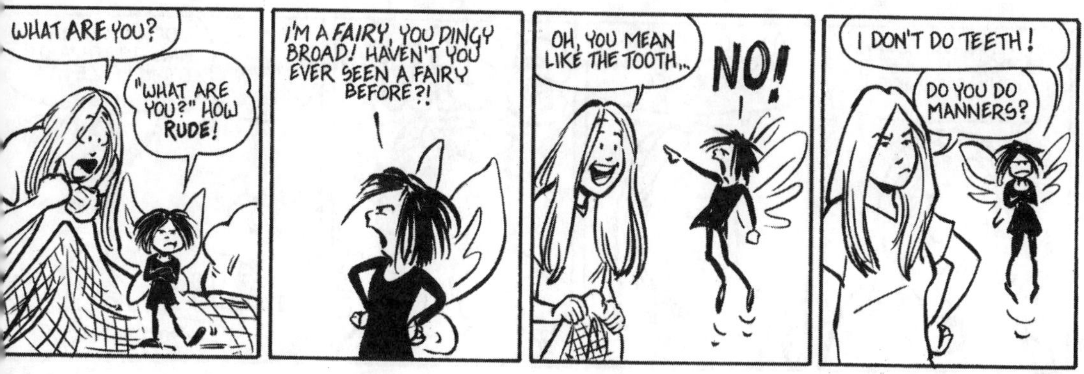
WHAT ARE YOU?
"WHAT ARE YOU?" HOW RUDE!
I'M A FAIRY, YOU DINGY BROAD! HAVEN'T YOU EVER SEEN A FAIRY BEFORE?!
OH, YOU MEAN LIKE THE TOOTH...
NO!
I DON'T DO TEETH!
DO YOU DO MANNERS?

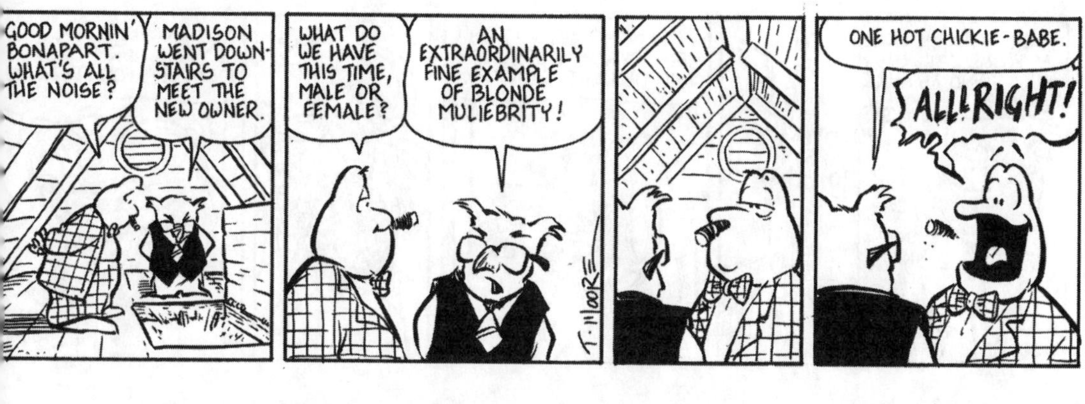
GOOD MORNIN' BONAPART. WHAT'S ALL THE NOISE?
MADISON WENT DOWN-STAIRS TO MEET THE NEW OWNER.
WHAT DO WE HAVE THIS TIME, MALE OR FEMALE?
AN EXTRAORDINARILY FINE EXAMPLE OF BLONDE MULIEBRITY!
T. MOORE
ONE HOT CHICKIE-BABE.
ALL RIGHT!

Grace & Kixie

"I live at the bottom of the sky, just to the left of time."

— Kixie

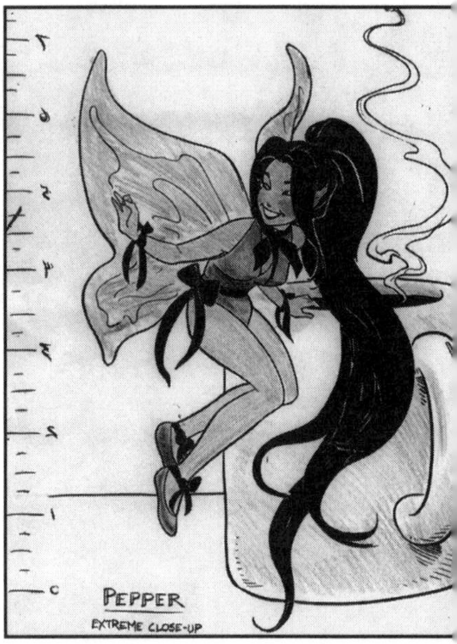
PEPPER
EXTREME CLOSE-UP

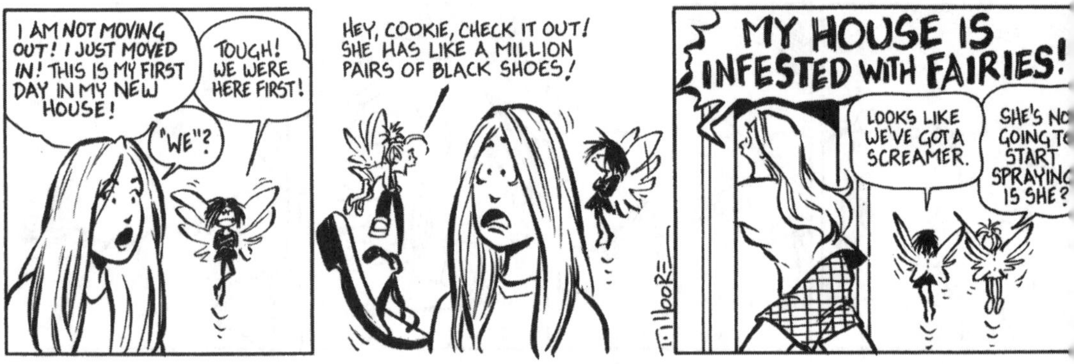
I AM NOT MOVING OUT! I JUST MOVED IN! THIS IS MY FIRST DAY IN MY NEW HOUSE!
TOUGH! WE WERE HERE FIRST!
"WE"?
HEY, COOKIE, CHECK IT OUT! SHE HAS LIKE A MILLION PAIRS OF BLACK SHOES!
MY HOUSE IS INFESTED WITH FAIRIES!
LOOKS LIKE WE'VE GOT A SCREAMER.
SHE'S NO GOING T START SPRAYIN IS SHE?

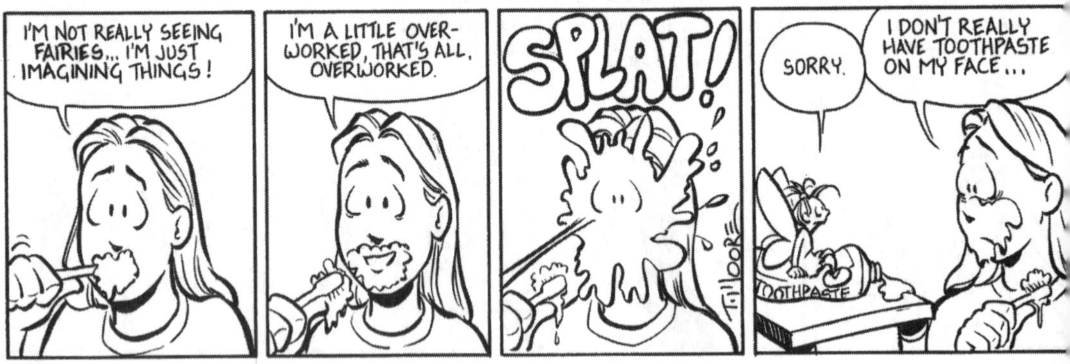
I'M NOT REALLY SEEING FAIRIES... I'M JUST IMAGINING THINGS!
I'M A LITTLE OVER-WORKED, THAT'S ALL. OVERWORKED.
SPLAT!
SORRY.
I DON'T REALLY HAVE TOOTHPASTE ON MY FACE...
TOOTHPASTE

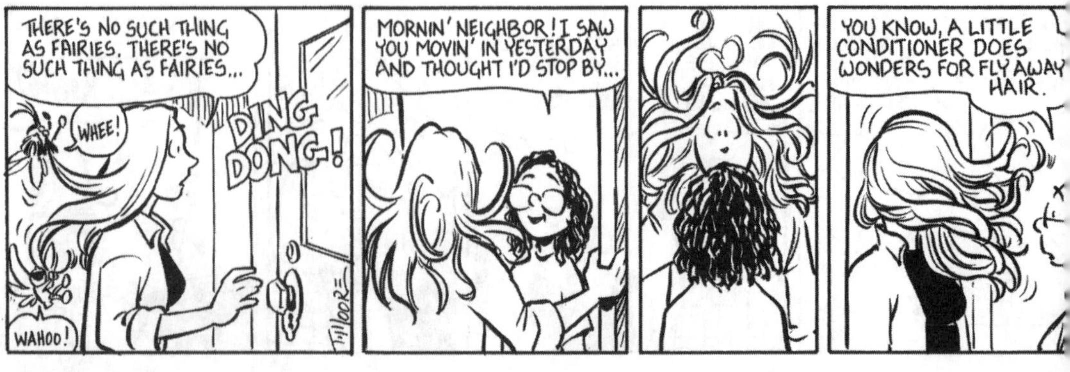
THERE'S NO SUCH THING AS FAIRIES. THERE'S NO SUCH THING AS FAIRIES...
WHEE!
DING DONG!
WAHOO!
MORNIN' NEIGHBOR! I SAW YOU MOVIN' IN YESTERDAY AND THOUGHT I'D STOP BY...
YOU KNOW, A LITTLE CONDITIONER DOES WONDERS FOR FLY AWAY HAIR.

WONDERVILLE

Every now and then I'll get the fool idea that I'm the best candidate for a cartoon character. I certainly look the part. This idea most recently struck me one night over a bag of Burger Boo-Boos. I grabbed a pen and scribbled the following four strips on the back of a speeding ticket. The rest has nothing to do with history.

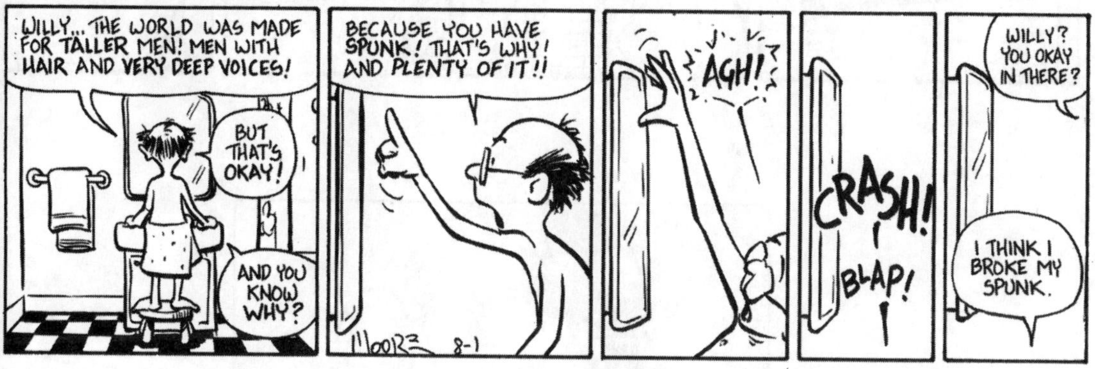
WILLY... THE WORLD WAS MADE FOR TALLER MEN! MEN WITH HAIR AND VERY DEEP VOICES!
BUT THAT'S OKAY!
AND YOU KNOW WHY?
BECAUSE YOU HAVE SPUNK! THAT'S WHY! AND PLENTY OF IT!!
MOORE 8-1
AGH!
CRASH!
BLAP!
WILLY? YOU OKAY IN THERE?
I THINK I BROKE MY SPUNK.

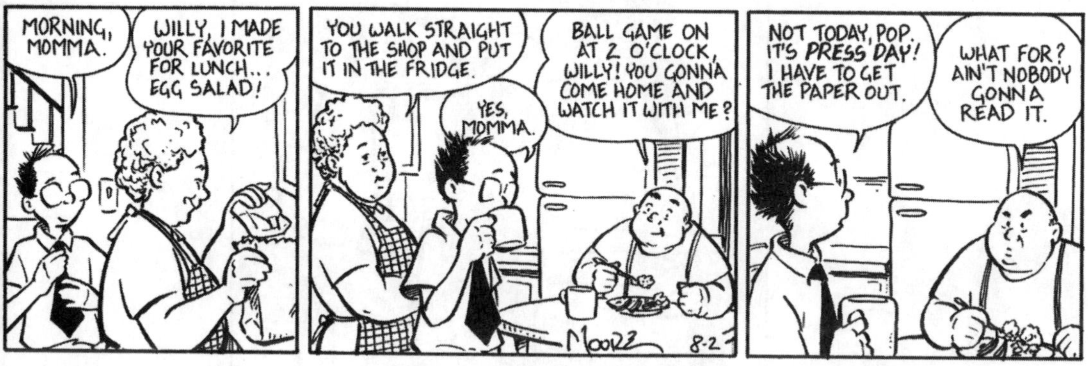
MORNING, MOMMA.
WILLY, I MADE YOUR FAVORITE FOR LUNCH... EGG SALAD!
YOU WALK STRAIGHT TO THE SHOP AND PUT IT IN THE FRIDGE.
YES, MOMMA.
BALL GAME ON AT 2 O'CLOCK, WILLY! YOU GONNA COME HOME AND WATCH IT WITH ME?
MOORE 8-2
NOT TODAY, POP. IT'S PRESS DAY! I HAVE TO GET THE PAPER OUT.
WHAT FOR? AIN'T NOBODY GONNA READ IT.

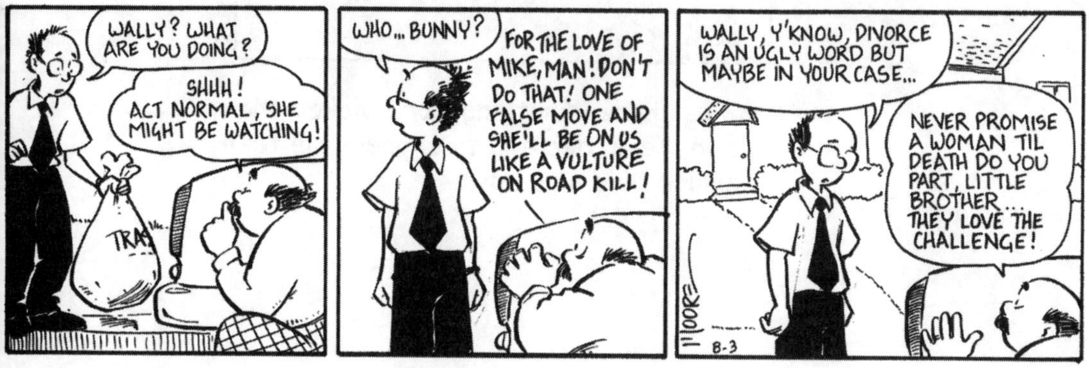
WALLY? WHAT ARE YOU DOING?
SHHH! ACT NORMAL, SHE MIGHT BE WATCHING!
WHO... BUNNY?
FOR THE LOVE OF MIKE, MAN! DON'T DO THAT! ONE FALSE MOVE AND SHE'LL BE ON US LIKE A VULTURE ON ROAD KILL!
WALLY, Y'KNOW, DIVORCE IS AN UGLY WORD BUT MAYBE IN YOUR CASE...
NEVER PROMISE A WOMAN TIL DEATH DO YOU PART, LITTLE BROTHER... THEY LOVE THE CHALLENGE!
MOORE 8-3

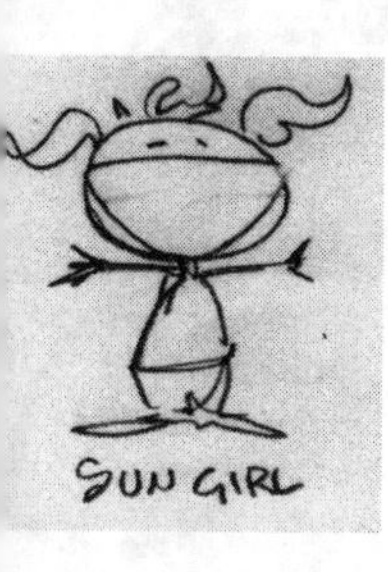
SUN GIRL

"Now's not good for me. How about half past now... say, now-thirty?"

—Kixie

WILLY... YOU FORGOT YOUR LUNCH.
THANKS, MOM.
OH, AND WALLY... BUNNY CALLED. SHE'S LOOKING FOR YOU.
THANKS, MOMMA.
MOORE 8-4

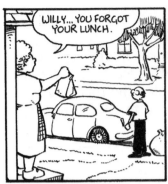

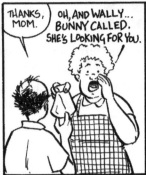

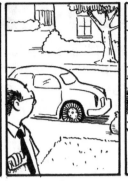

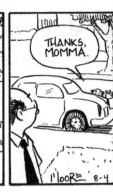

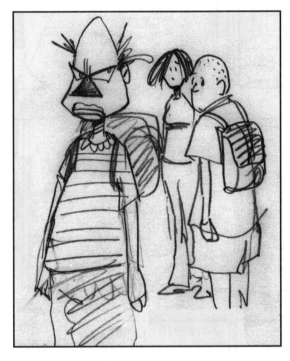

Knowing there is nothing more wicked than a clown, Kevin decided to express his teen anger in a bold new way.

"She's so plastine. She doesn't care who she gets thrown out of."
— Madison

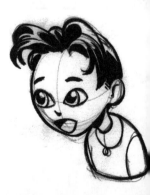

KIXIE AND GRACE ROUGHS

After the Wonderville fiasco I crawled back to Kixie and Grace on my knees and begged for another chance. They returned to the studio on two conditions: that I take them seriously and I allow Ringo to play the drums his way. I'm fine with the drum thing, but I keep forgeting that first part.

Anyway, we sat down and came up with the idea of just letting the girls be natural (Don't B sharp, don't B flat, just B natural). Kixie kept changing her name in the scripts, from Kimmi to Mika and... well, the whole thing felt shakey to me, so I only penciled up their ideas. I hope you can read the lettering, Grace insisted on doing it herself. That's what happens when you create by committee. Oh, and please ignore the little numbers. Kixie can't count worth beans.

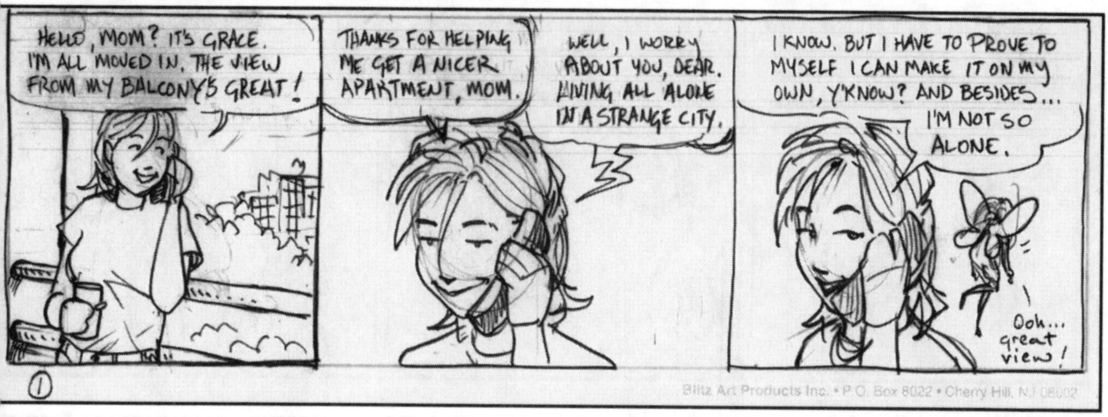
HELLO, MOM? IT'S GRACE. I'M ALL MOVED IN. THE VIEW FROM MY BALCONY'S GREAT!
THANKS FOR HELPING ME GET A NICER APARTMENT, MOM.
WELL, I WORRY ABOUT YOU, DEAR. LIVING ALL ALONE IN A STRANGE CITY.
I KNOW. BUT I HAVE TO PROVE TO MYSELF I CAN MAKE IT ON MY OWN, Y'KNOW? AND BESIDES...
I'M NOT SO ALONE.
Ooh... great view!
Blitz Art Products Inc. • P.O. Box 8022 • Cherry Hill, NJ 08002

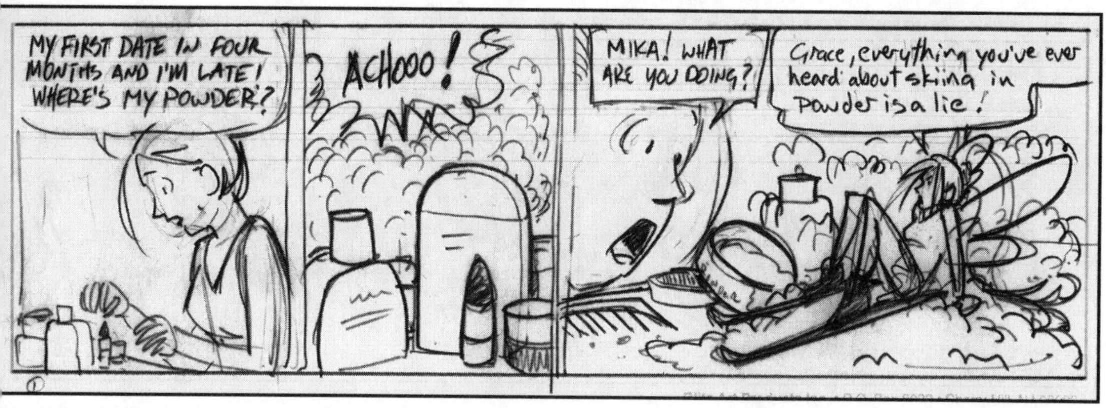
MY FIRST DATE IN FOUR MONTHS AND I'M LATE! WHERE'S MY POWDER?
ACHOOO!
MIKA! WHAT ARE YOU DOING?
Grace, everything you've ever heard about skiing in powder is a lie!

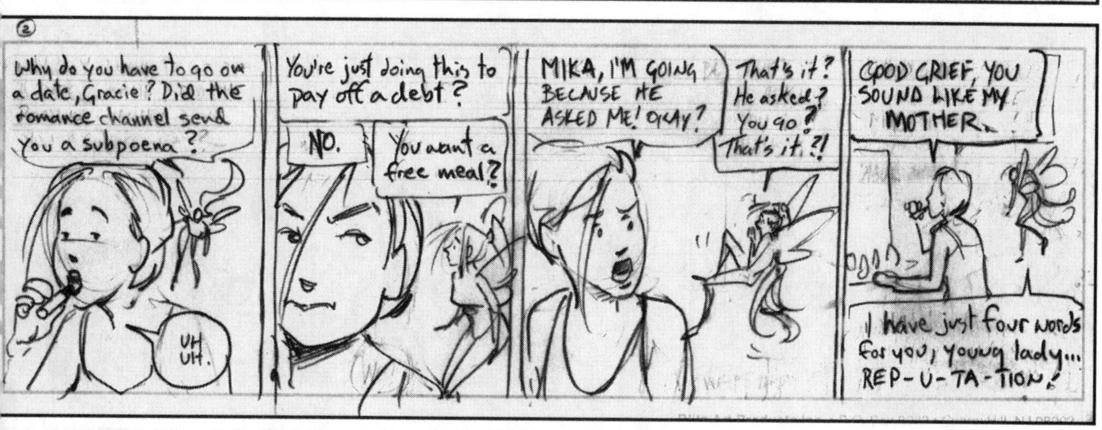
Why do you have to go on a date, Gracie? Did the romance channel send you a subpoena?
UH UH.
You're just doing this to pay off a debt?
NO.
You want a free meal?
MIKA, I'M GOING BECAUSE HE ASKED ME! OKAY?
That's it? He asked? You go? That's it?!
GOOD GRIEF, YOU SOUND LIKE MY MOTHER.
I have just four words for you, young lady... REP-U-TA-TION!

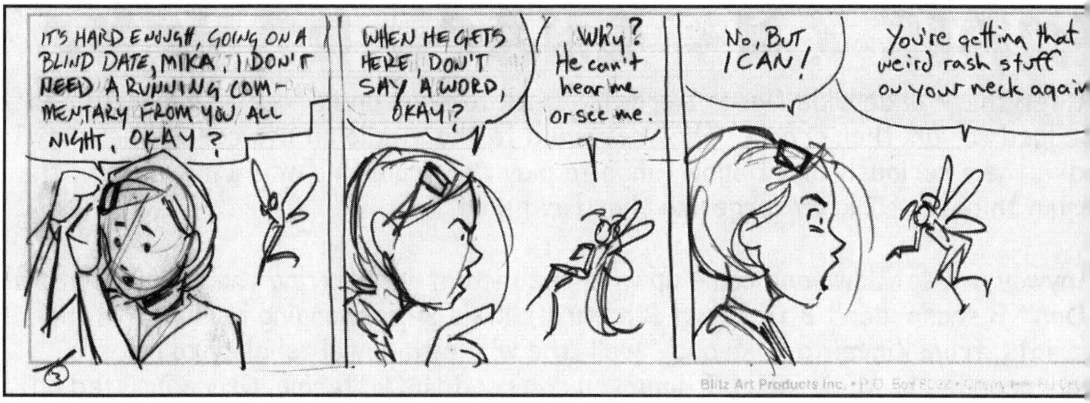
IT'S HARD ENOUGH, GOING ON A BLIND DATE, MIKA, I DON'T NEED A RUNNING COMMENTARY FROM YOU ALL NIGHT, OKAY?
3
WHEN HE GETS HERE, DON'T SAY A WORD, OKAY?
Why? He can't hear me or see me.
No, BUT I CAN!
You're getting that weird rash stuff on your neck again

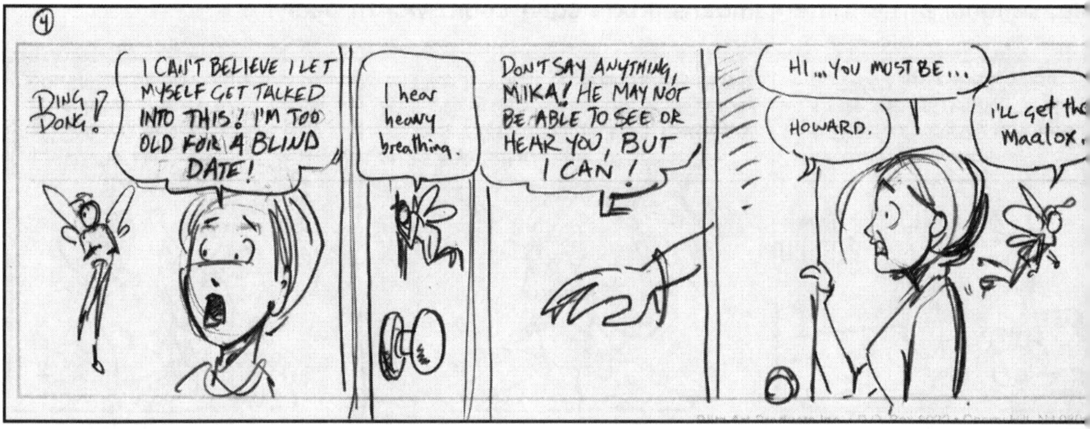
4
DING DONG!
I CAN'T BELIEVE I LET MYSELF GET TALKED INTO THIS! I'M TOO OLD FOR A BLIND DATE!
I hear heavy breathing.
DON'T SAY ANYTHING, MIKA! HE MAY NOT BE ABLE TO SEE OR HEAR YOU, BUT I CAN!
HI... YOU MUST BE...
HOWARD.
I'll get the Maalox.

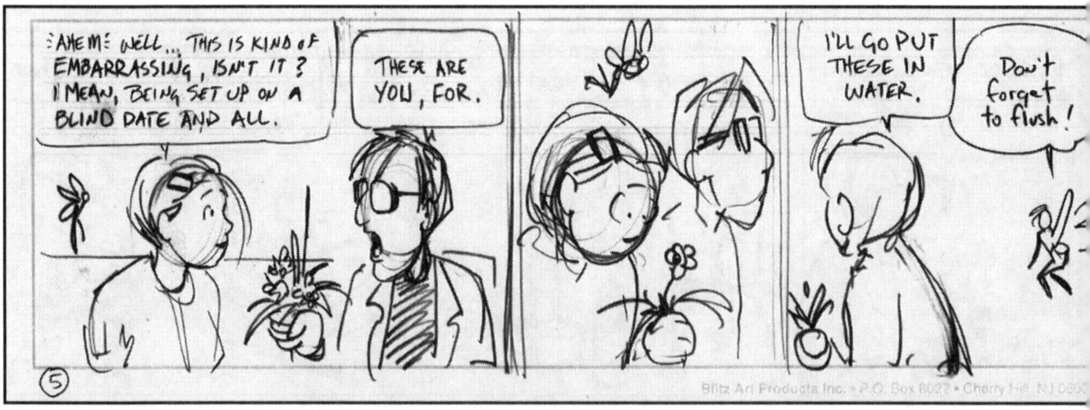
AHEM WELL... THIS IS KIND OF EMBARRASSING, ISN'T IT? I MEAN, BEING SET UP ON A BLIND DATE AND ALL.
THESE ARE YOU, FOR.
I'LL GO PUT THESE IN WATER.
Don't forget to flush!
5

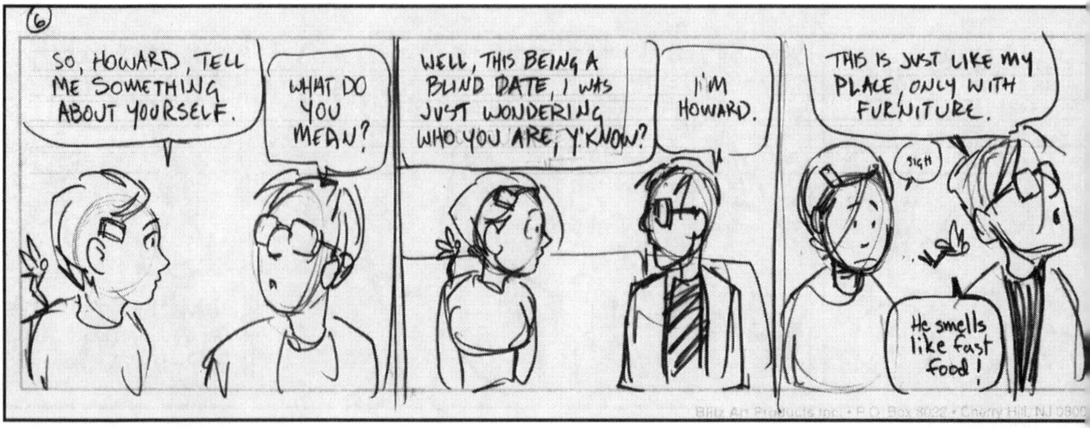
6
SO, HOWARD, TELL ME SOMETHING ABOUT YOURSELF.
WHAT DO YOU MEAN?
WELL, THIS BEING A BLIND DATE, I WAS JUST WONDERING WHO YOU ARE, Y'KNOW?
I'M HOWARD.
THIS IS JUST LIKE MY PLACE, ONLY WITH FURNITURE.
SIGH
He smells like fast food!

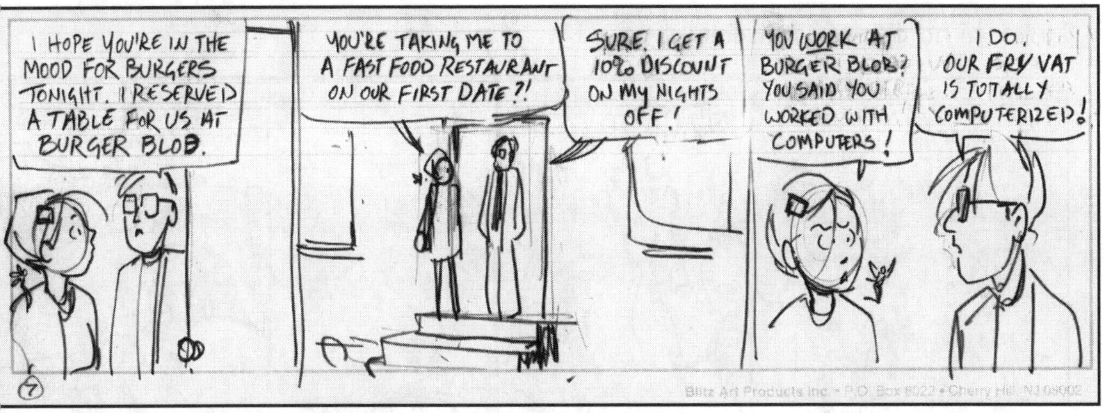
7
I HOPE YOU'RE IN THE MOOD FOR BURGERS TONIGHT. I RESERVED A TABLE FOR US AT BURGER BLOB.
YOU'RE TAKING ME TO A FAST FOOD RESTAURANT ON OUR FIRST DATE?!
SURE. I GET A 10% DISCOUNT ON MY NIGHTS OFF!
YOU WORK AT BURGER BLOB? YOU SAID YOU WORKED WITH COMPUTERS!
I DO. OUR FRY VAT IS TOTALLY COMPUTERIZED!
Blitz Art Products Inc. • P.O. Box 8022 • Cherry Hill, NJ 08002

I couldn't hear what Kixie 's punchline was on this next one, and she wouldn't repeat it.

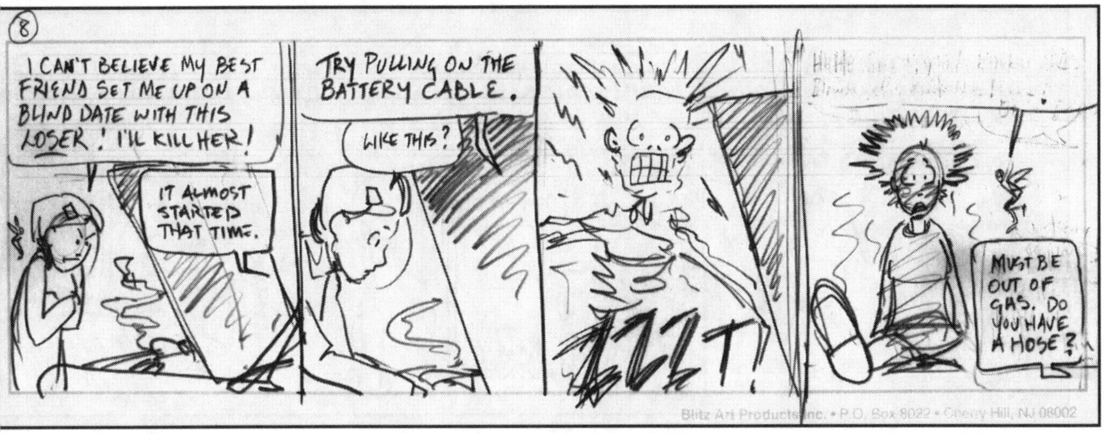
8
I CAN'T BELIEVE MY BEST FRIEND SET ME UP ON A BLIND DATE WITH THIS LOSER! I'LL KILL HER!
IT ALMOST STARTED THAT TIME.
TRY PULLING ON THE BATTERY CABLE.
LIKE THIS?
ZZZT!
MUST BE OUT OF GAS. DO YOU HAVE A HOSE?
Blitz Art Products Inc. • P.O. Box 8022 • Cherry Hill, NJ 08002

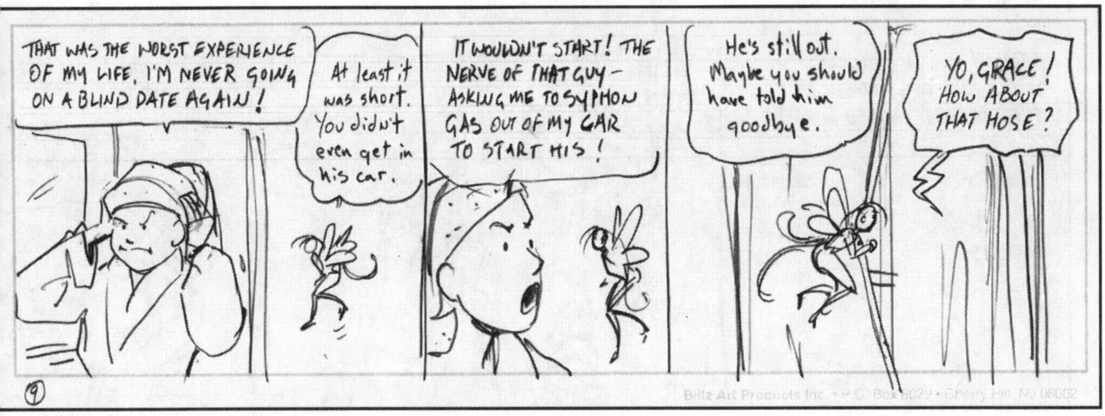
THAT WAS THE WORST EXPERIENCE OF MY LIFE. I'M NEVER GOING ON A BLIND DATE AGAIN!
At least it was short. You didn't even get in his car.
IT WOULDN'T START! THE NERVE OF THAT GUY— ASKING ME TO SYPHON GAS OUT OF MY CAR TO START HIS!
He's still out. Maybe you should have told him goodbye.
YO, GRACE! HOW ABOUT THAT HOSE?
9
Blitz Art Products Inc. • P.O. Box 8022 • Cherry Hill, NJ 08002

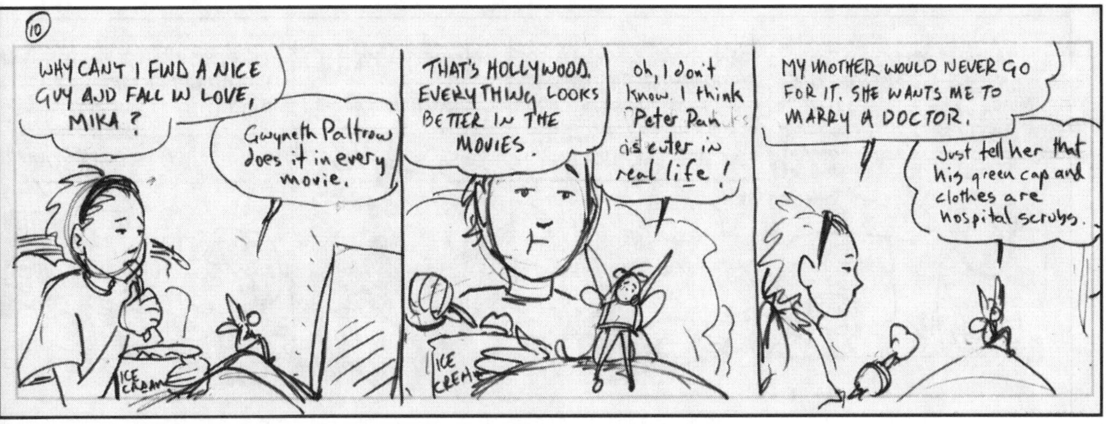
10
WHY CAN'T I FIND A NICE GUY AND FALL IN LOVE, MIKA?
Gwyneth Paltrow does it in every movie.
ICE CREAM
THAT'S HOLLYWOOD. EVERYTHING LOOKS BETTER IN THE MOVIES.
Oh, I don't know. I think "Peter Pan" is cuter in real life!
ICE CREAM
MY MOTHER WOULD NEVER GO FOR IT. SHE WANTS ME TO MARRY A DOCTOR.
Just tell her that his green cap and clothes are hospital scrubs.

Hi ho, hi ho, it's off to work we go.

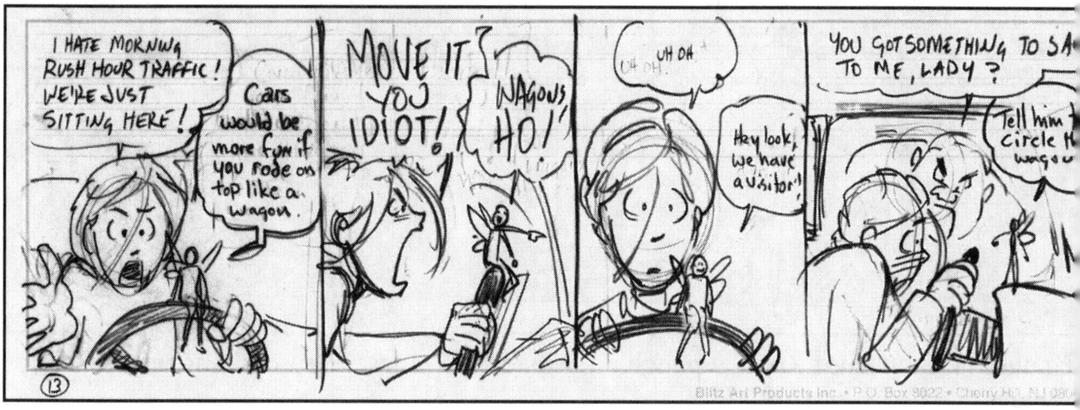
I HATE MORNING RUSH HOUR TRAFFIC! WE'RE JUST SITTING HERE!
Cars would be more fun if you rode on top like a wagon.
MOVE IT YOU IDIOT!
WAGONS HO!
UH OH.
Hey look, we have a visitor!
YOU GOT SOMETHING TO SA TO ME, LADY?
Tell him t circle th wagon
13

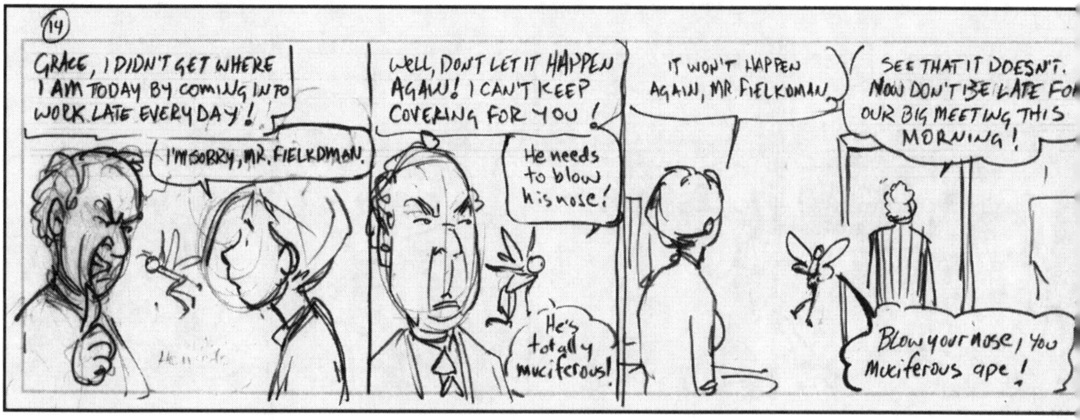
14
GRACE, I DIDN'T GET WHERE I AM TODAY BY COMING INTO WORK LATE EVERY DAY!
I'M SORRY, MR. FIELKDMAN.
WELL, DON'T LET IT HAPPEN AGAIN! I CAN'T KEEP COVERING FOR YOU!
He needs to blow his nose!
He's totally muciferous!
IT WON'T HAPPEN AGAIN, MR FIELKDMAN.
SEE THAT IT DOESN'T. NOW DON'T BE LATE FO OUR BIG MEETING THIS MORNING!
Blow your nose, you muciferous ape!

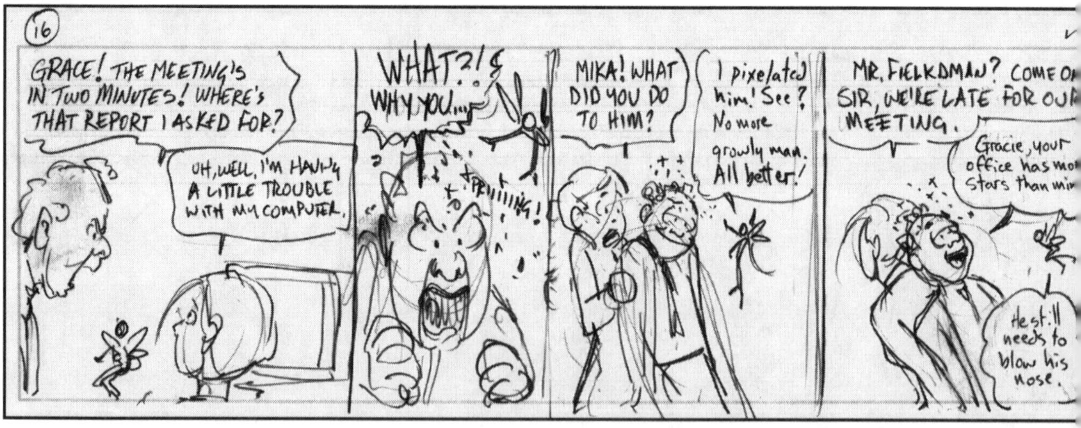
16
GRACE! THE MEETING'S IN TWO MINUTES! WHERE'S THAT REPORT I ASKED FOR?
UH, WELL, I'M HAVING A LITTLE TROUBLE WITH MY COMPUTER.
WHAT?!$ WHY YOU...
PRIIIING!
MIKA! WHAT DID YOU DO TO HIM?
I pixelated him! See? No more growly man. All better!
MR. FIELKDMAN? COME O SIR, WE'RE LATE FOR OUR MEETING.
Gracie, your office has mo stars than mi
He still needs to blow his nose.

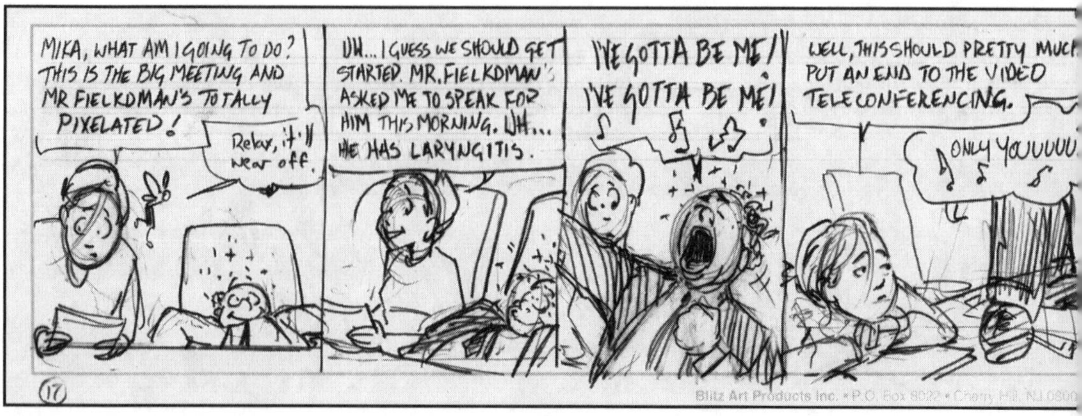
MIKA, WHAT AM I GOING TO DO? THIS IS THE BIG MEETING AND MR FIELKDMAN'S TOTALLY PIXELATED!
Relax, it'll wear off.
UH... I GUESS WE SHOULD GET STARTED. MR. FIELKDMAN'S ASKED ME TO SPEAK FOR HIM THIS MORNING. UH... HE HAS LARYNGITIS.
I'VE GOTTA BE ME! I'VE GOTTA BE ME!
WELL, THIS SHOULD PRETTY MUC PUT AN END TO THE VIDEO TELECONFERENCING.
ONLY YOUUUUU.
17

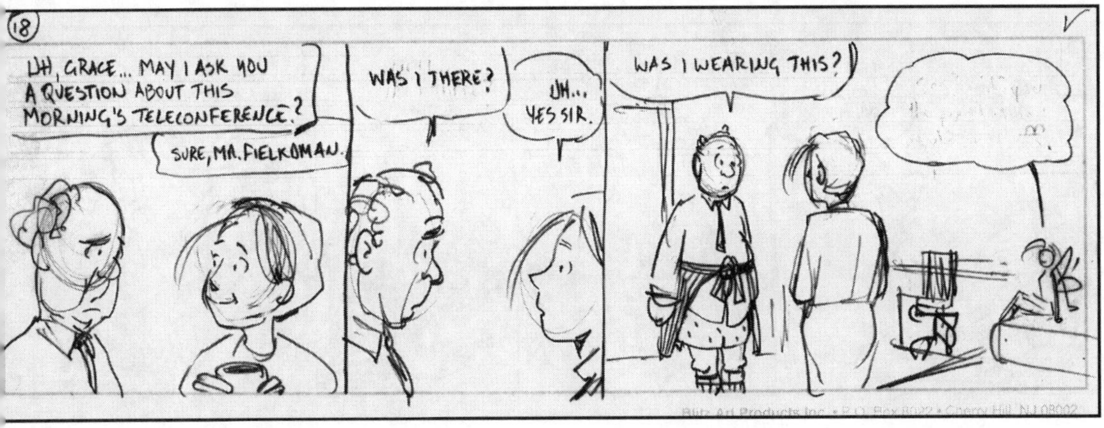
18
UH, GRACE... MAY I ASK YOU A QUESTION ABOUT THIS MORNING'S TELECONFERENCE?
SURE, MR. FIELKOMAN.
WAS I THERE?
UH... YES SIR.
WAS I WEARING THIS?
Blitz Art Products Inc. • P.O. Box 8022 • Cherry Hill, NJ 08002

"Only after we made you put something on", Kixie replied. But what you see is the censored version. "Too racy!" cried the San Muey Herald editor.

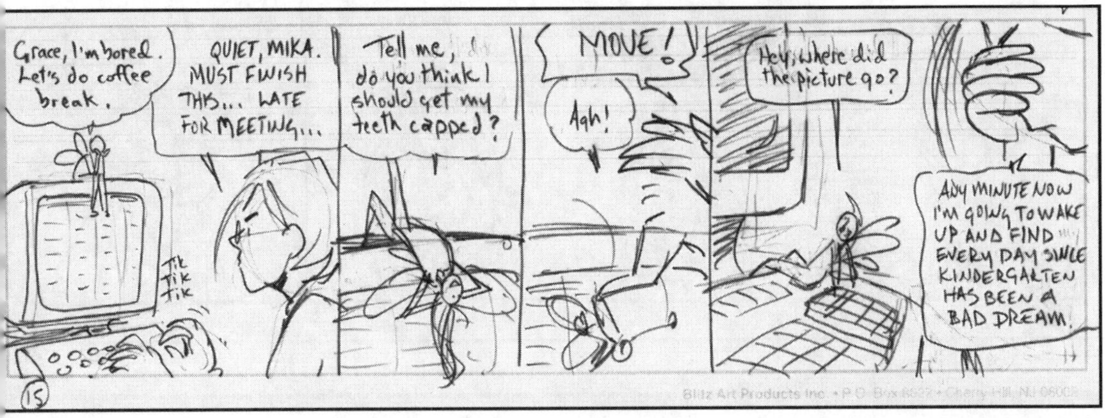
Grace, I'm bored. Let's do coffee break.
QUIET, MIKA. MUST FINISH THIS... LATE FOR MEETING...
Tik Tik Tik
Tell me, do you think I should get my teeth capped?
MOVE!
Aah!
Hey, where did the picture go?
ANY MINUTE NOW I'M GOING TO WAKE UP AND FIND EVERY DAY SINCE KINDERGARTEN HAS BEEN A BAD DREAM.
15
Blitz Art Products Inc. • P.O. Box 8022 • Cherry Hill, NJ 08002

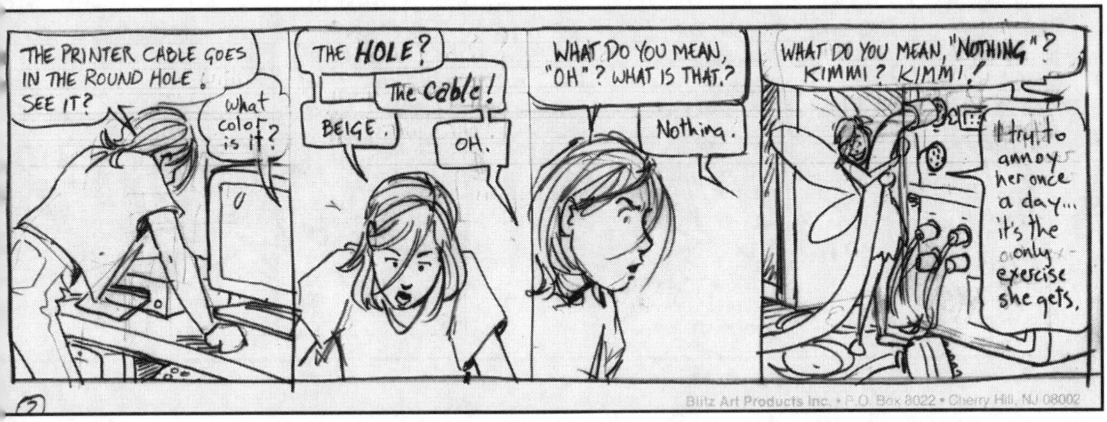
THE PRINTER CABLE GOES IN THE ROUND HOLE. SEE IT?
What color is it?
THE HOLE?
The Cable!
BEIGE.
OH.
WHAT DO YOU MEAN, "OH"? WHAT IS THAT?
Nothing.
WHAT DO YOU MEAN, "NOTHING"? KIMMI? KIMMI!
I try to annoy her once a day... it's the only exercise she gets.
Blitz Art Products Inc. • P.O. Box 8022 • Cherry Hill, NJ 08002

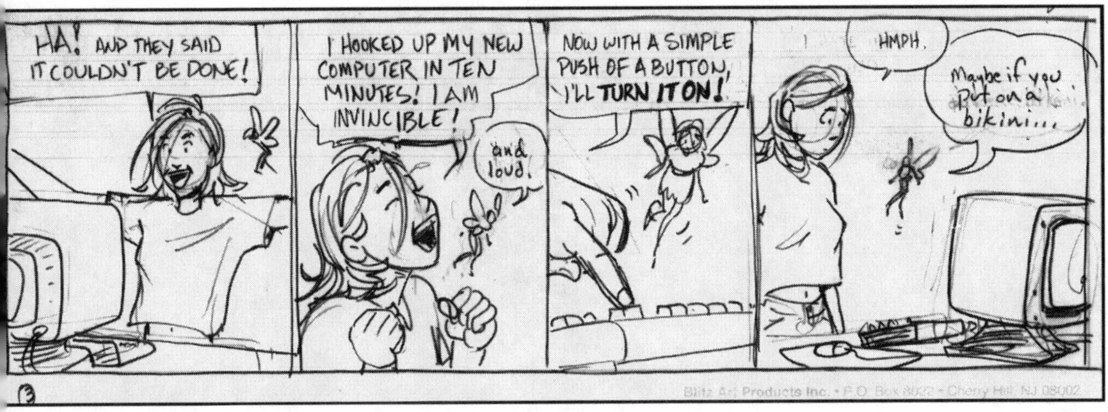
HA! AND THEY SAID IT COULDN'T BE DONE!
I HOOKED UP MY NEW COMPUTER IN TEN MINUTES! I AM INVINCIBLE!
and loud.
NOW WITH A SIMPLE PUSH OF A BUTTON, I'LL TURN IT ON!
HMPH.
Maybe if you put on a bikini...
13
Blitz Art Products Inc. • P.O. Box 8022 • Cherry Hill, NJ 08002

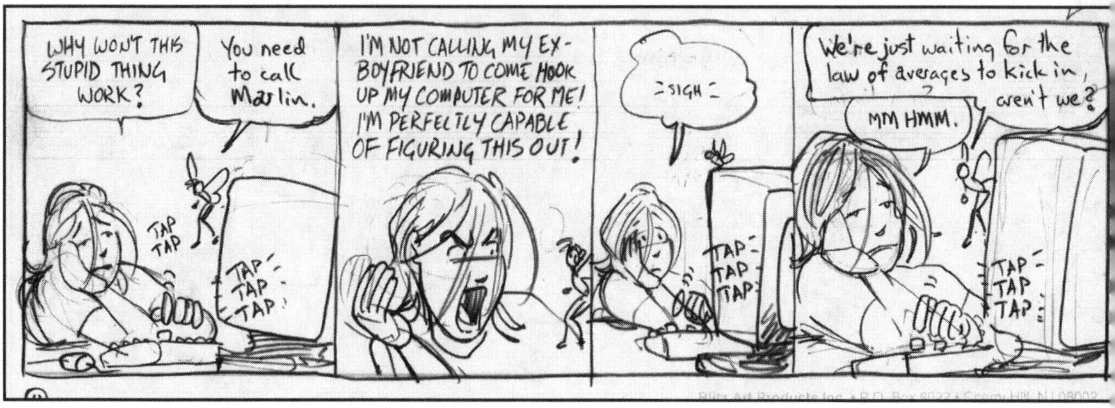
WHY WON'T THIS STUPID THING WORK?
You need to call Marlin.
TAP TAP
TAP TAP TAP
I'M NOT CALLING MY EX-BOYFRIEND TO COME HOOK UP MY COMPUTER FOR ME! I'M PERFECTLY CAPABLE OF FIGURING THIS OUT!
SIGH
TAP TAP TAP
We're just waiting for the law of averages to kick in, aren't we?
MM HMM.
TAP TAP TAP

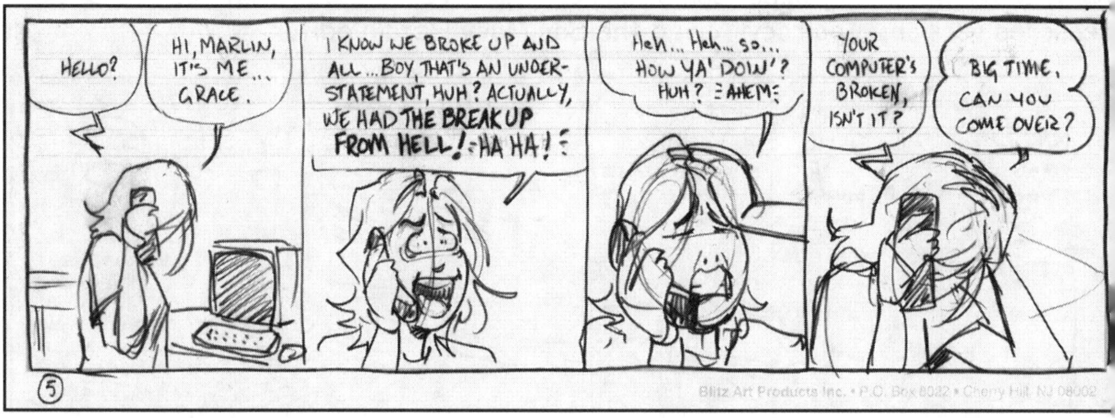
HELLO?
HI, MARLIN, IT'S ME... GRACE.
I KNOW WE BROKE UP AND ALL... BOY, THAT'S AN UNDER-STATEMENT, HUH? ACTUALLY, WE HAD THE BREAKUP FROM HELL! HA HA!
Heh... Heh... so... HOW YA' DOIN'? HUH? AHEM
YOUR COMPUTER'S BROKEN, ISN'T IT?
BIG TIME. CAN YOU COME OVER?
5
Blitz Art Products Inc. • P.O. Box 8022 • Cherry Hill, NJ 08002

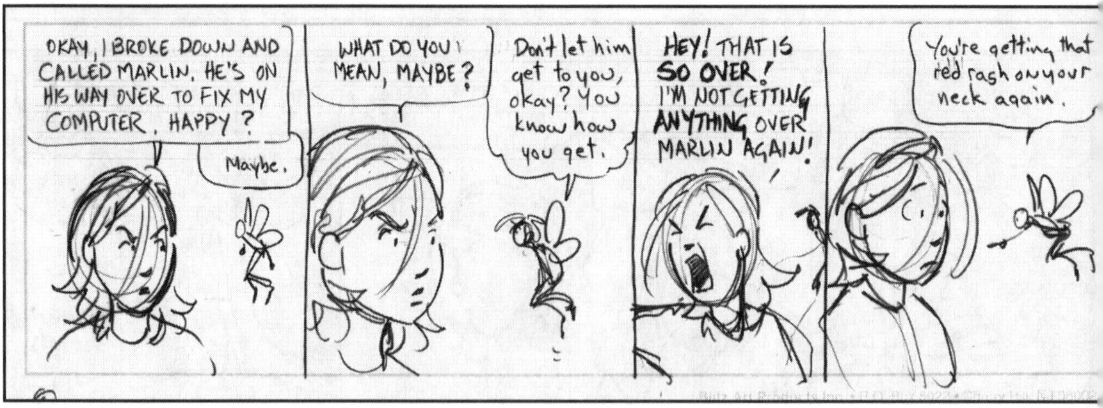
OKAY, I BROKE DOWN AND CALLED MARLIN. HE'S ON HIS WAY OVER TO FIX MY COMPUTER. HAPPY?
Maybe.
WHAT DO YOU MEAN, MAYBE?
Don't let him get to you, okay? You know how you get.
HEY! THAT IS SO OVER! I'M NOT GETTING ANYTHING OVER MARLIN AGAIN!
You're getting that red rash on your neck again.

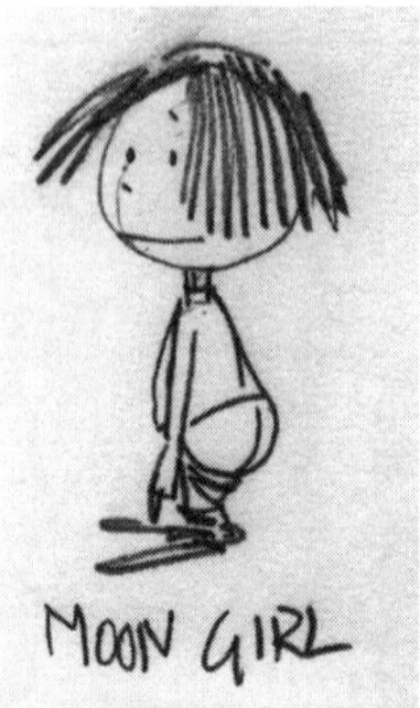
MOON GIRL

KIXIE

ne day I decided to focus on Kixie. Grace the Normal Girl took a back seat and y only plan was to follow Kixie around the house. If she's worth having her own trip, she must be worth following around the house, right? It's a really lame-o dea, but I got pretty excited when the ideas began to flow and something new appened... the strip I was drawing made me happy. Not creator agenda happy, ust happy. This little Kixie won my heart. When I posted these strips on the trangers In Paradise website, fans came out of the woodwork. Instantly I was looded with email from around the world and it was official... Kixie had arrived.

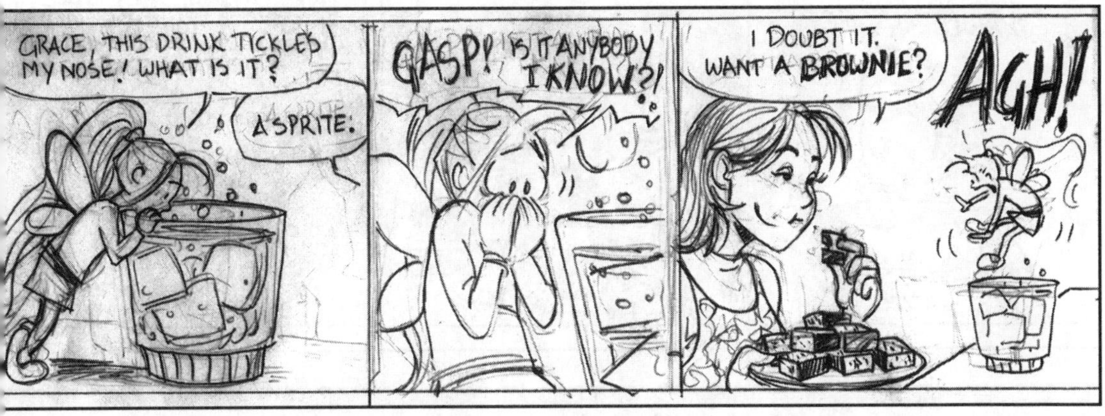
GRACE, THIS DRINK TICKLES MY NOSE! WHAT IS IT?
A SPRITE.
GASP! IS IT ANYBODY I KNOW?!
I DOUBT IT. WANT A BROWNIE?
AGH!

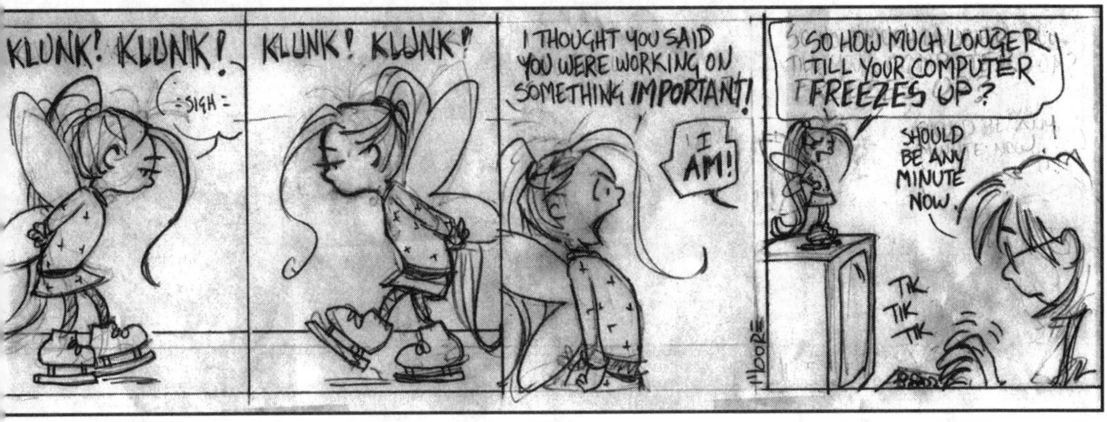
KLUNK! KLUNK!
=SIGH=
KLUNK! KLUNK!
I THOUGHT YOU SAID YOU WERE WORKING ON SOMETHING IMPORTANT!
I AM!
SO HOW MUCH LONGER TILL YOUR COMPUTER FREEZES UP?
SHOULD BE ANY MINUTE NOW.
TIK TIK TIK
MOORE

id I mention that faeries like strawberry cake?

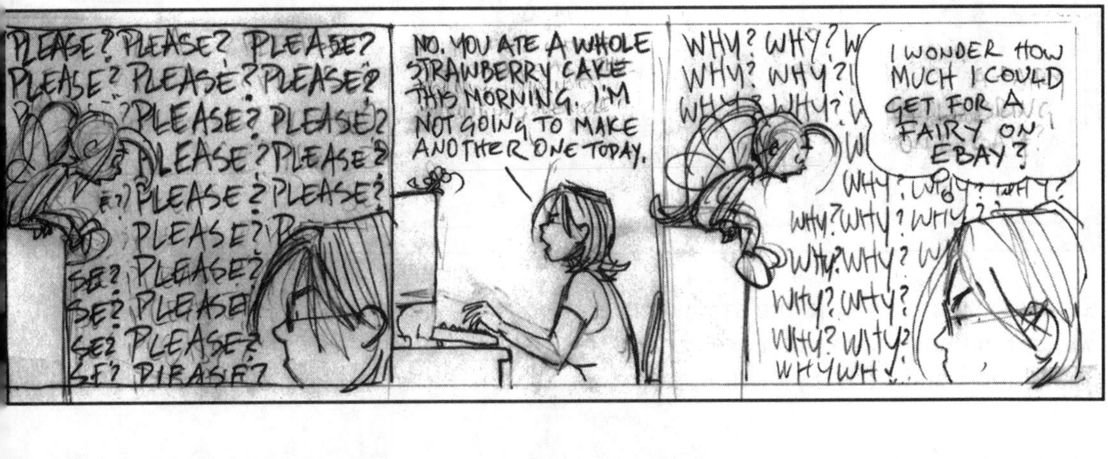
PLEASE? PLEASE? PLEASE? PLEASE? PLEASE? PLEASE? PLEASE? PLEASE? PLEASE? PLEASE? PLEASE? PLEASE? PLEASE? PLEASE? PLEASE? PLEASE?
NO. YOU ATE A WHOLE STRAWBERRY CAKE THIS MORNING. I'M NOT GOING TO MAKE ANOTHER ONE TODAY.
WHY? WHY? WHY? WHY? WHY? WHY? WHY? WHY? WHY? WHY? WHY? WHY? WHY? WHY?
I WONDER HOW MUCH I COULD GET FOR A FAIRY ON EBAY?

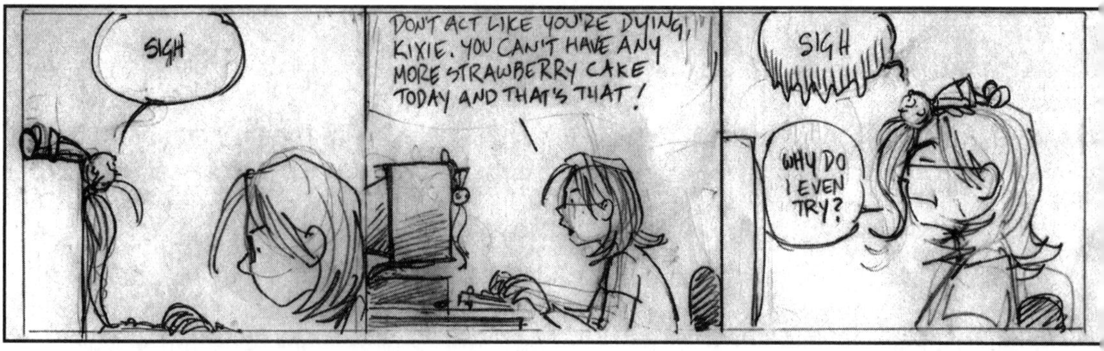
SIGH
DON'T ACT LIKE YOU'RE DYING, KIXIE. YOU CAN'T HAVE ANY MORE STRAWBERRY CAKE TODAY AND THAT'S THAT!
SIGH
WHY DO I EVEN TRY?

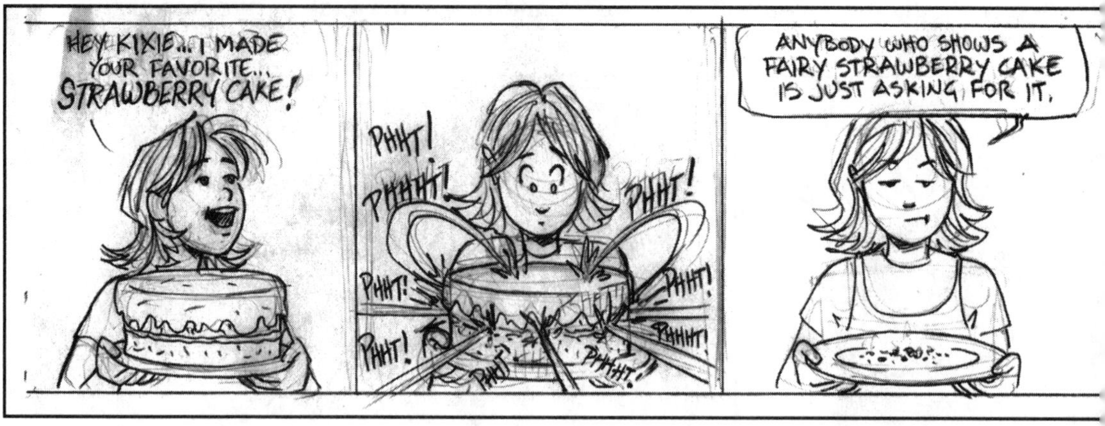
HEY KIXIE... I MADE YOUR FAVORITE... STRAWBERRY CAKE!
PHHT!
PHHHT!
PHHT!
PHHT!
PHHHT!
PHHT!
PHHHT!
PHHHT!
PHHT!
ANYBODY WHO SHOWS A FAIRY STRAWBERRY CAKE IS JUST ASKING FOR IT.

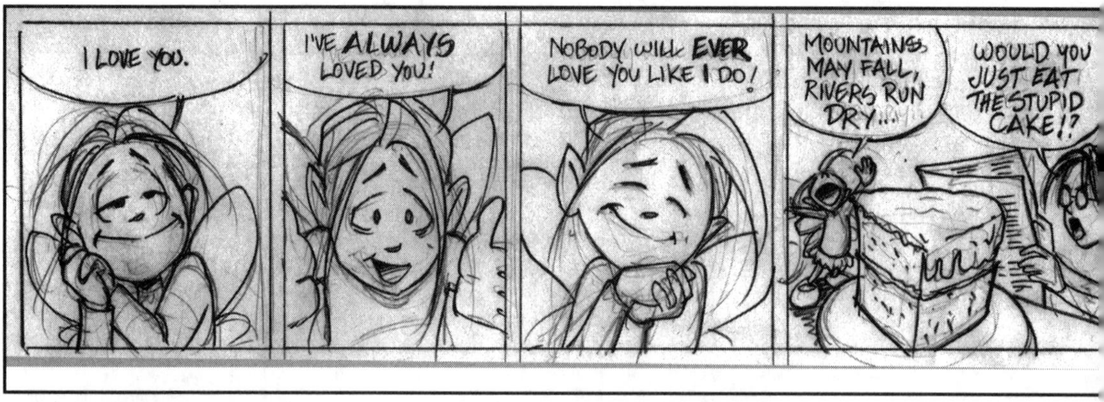
I LOVE YOU.
I'VE ALWAYS LOVED YOU!
NOBODY WILL EVER LOVE YOU LIKE I DO!
MOUNTAINS MAY FALL, RIVERS RUN DRY...
WOULD YOU JUST EAT THE STUPID CAKE!?

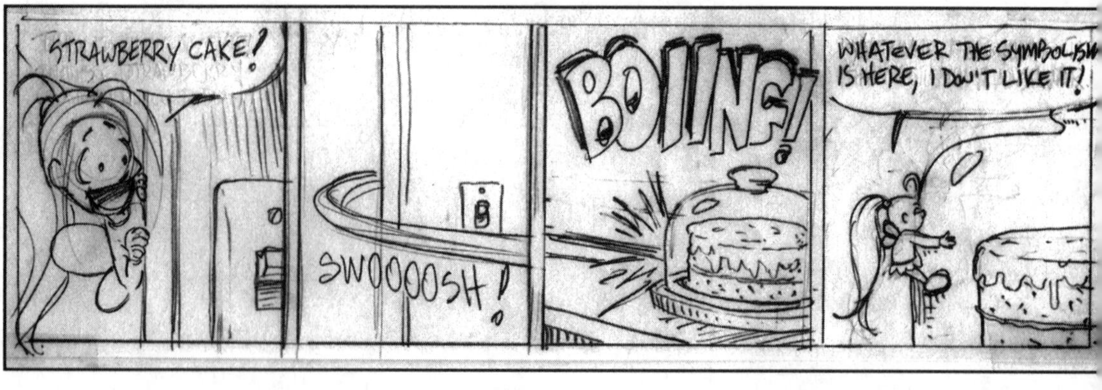
STRAWBERRY CAKE!
SWOOOOSH!
BOIING!
WHATEVER THE SYMBOLISM IS HERE, I DON'T LIKE IT!

If I seem to be stuck in a strawberry cake mode here, it's on purpose. I was wondering how much mileage I could get out of the simplest thing. I take the same approach with my brain.

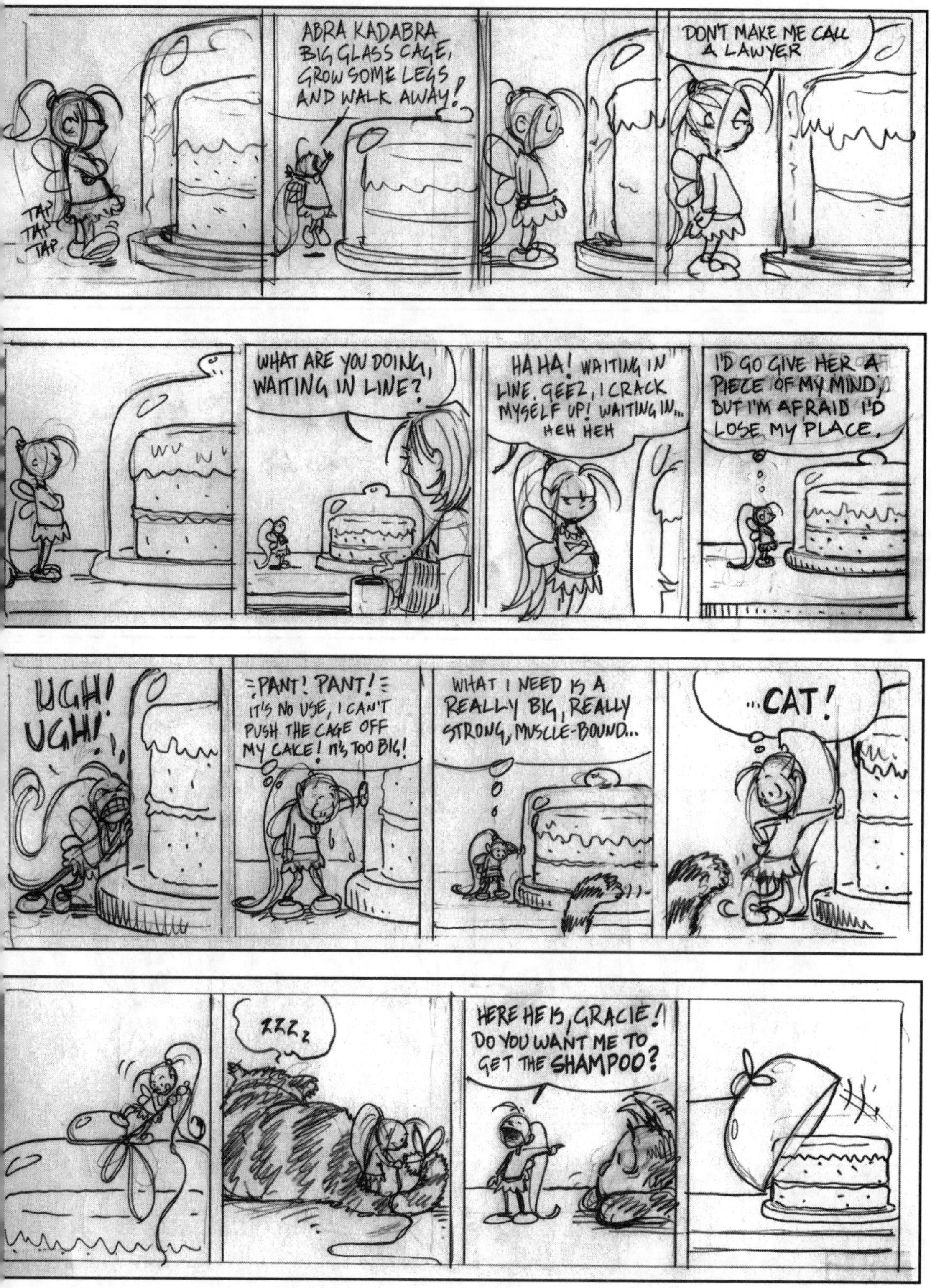
TAP TAP TAP
ABRA KADABRA BIG GLASS CAGE, GROW SOME LEGS AND WALK AWAY!
DON'T MAKE ME CALL A LAWYER
WHAT ARE YOU DOING, WAITING IN LINE?
HA HA! WAITING IN LINE. GEEZ, I CRACK MYSELF UP! WAITING IN... HEH HEH
I'D GO GIVE HER A PIECE OF MY MIND, BUT I'M AFRAID I'D LOSE MY PLACE.
UGH! UGH!
PANT! PANT! IT'S NO USE, I CAN'T PUSH THE CAGE OFF MY CAKE! IT'S TOO BIG!
WHAT I NEED IS A REALLY BIG, REALLY STRONG, MUSCLE-BOUND...
...CAT!
ZZZz
HERE HE IS, GRACIE! DO YOU WANT ME TO GET THE SHAMPOO?

"I am a symphony, a melancholy symphony, Oliver. Such is the melody of my discontent. I have not been overburdened with happiness or charm."

— Mother Wonderbee

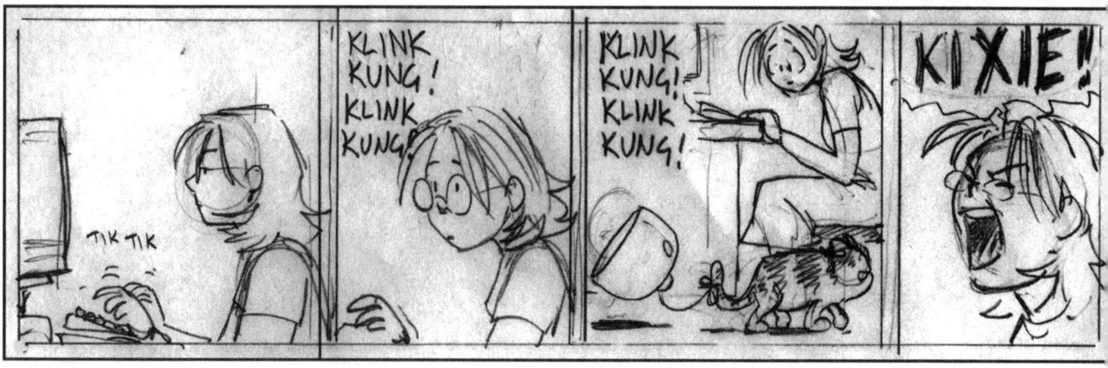
TIK TIK
KLINK KUNG! KLINK KUNG!
KLINK KUNG! KLINK KUNG!
KIXIE!

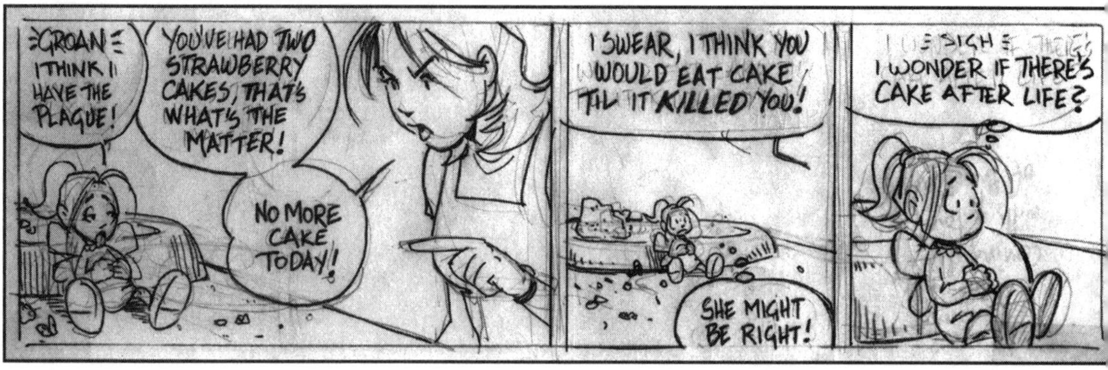
GROAN I THINK I HAVE THE PLAGUE!
YOU'VE HAD TWO STRAWBERRY CAKES, THAT'S WHAT'S THE MATTER!
NO MORE CAKE TODAY!
I SWEAR, I THINK YOU WOULD EAT CAKE TIL IT KILLED YOU!
SHE MIGHT BE RIGHT!
SIGH
I WONDER IF THERE'S CAKE AFTER LIFE?

Well, I think we've pretty much run that idea into the ground and backed over it a few times. Have you ever tried explaining makeup to a faerie?

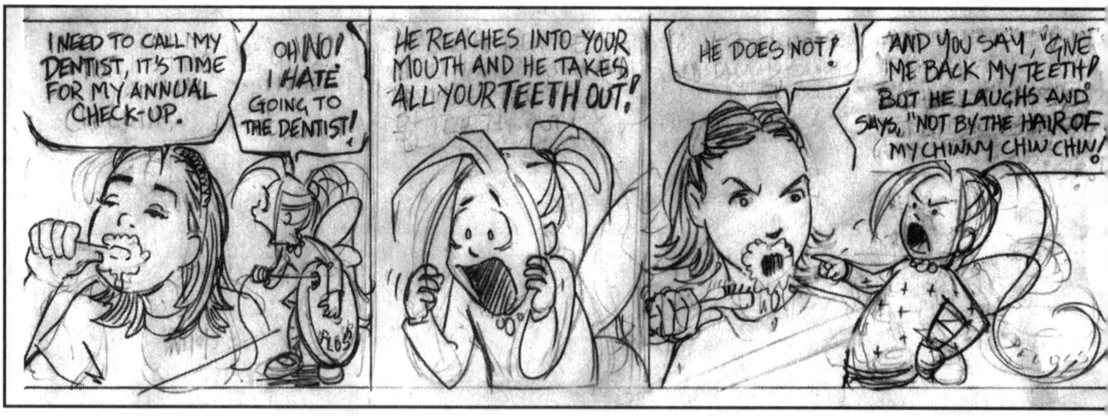
I NEED TO CALL MY DENTIST, IT'S TIME FOR MY ANNUAL CHECK-UP.
OH NO! I HATE GOING TO THE DENTIST!
HE REACHES INTO YOUR MOUTH AND HE TAKES ALL YOUR TEETH OUT!
HE DOES NOT!
AND YOU SAY, "GIVE ME BACK MY TEETH!" BUT HE LAUGHS AND SAYS, "NOT BY THE HAIR OF MY CHINNY CHIN CHIN!"

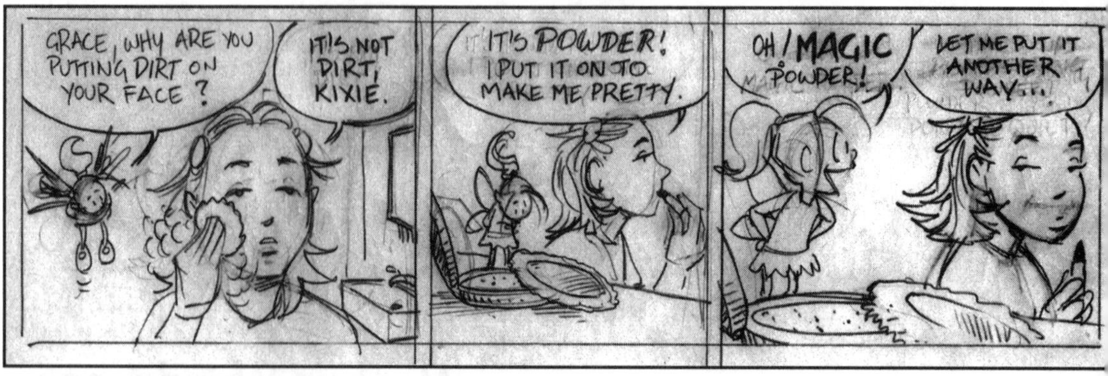
GRACE, WHY ARE YOU PUTTING DIRT ON YOUR FACE?
IT'S NOT DIRT, KIXIE.
IT'S POWDER! I PUT IT ON TO MAKE ME PRETTY.
OH! MAGIC POWDER!
LET ME PUT IT ANOTHER WAY...

Faeries are incredibly vain. Don't let them tell you any different.

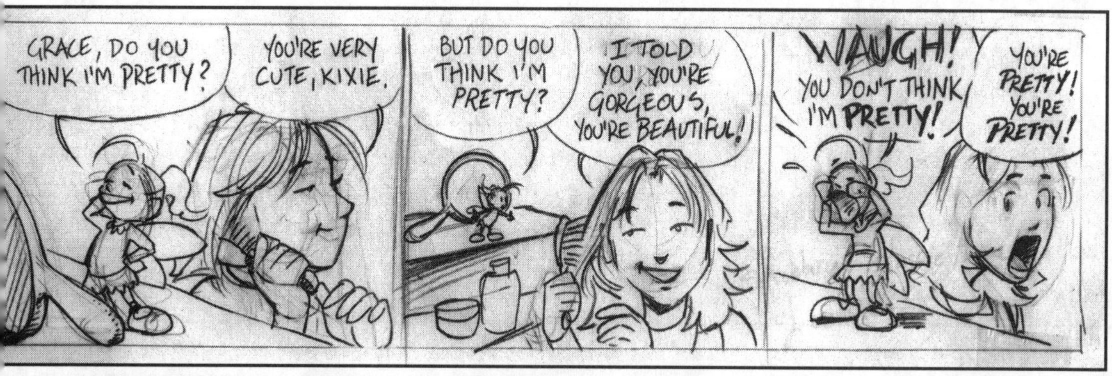
GRACE, DO YOU THINK I'M PRETTY?
YOU'RE VERY CUTE, KIXIE.
BUT DO YOU THINK I'M PRETTY?
I TOLD YOU, YOU'RE GORGEOUS, YOU'RE BEAUTIFUL!
WAUGH! YOU DON'T THINK I'M PRETTY!
YOU'RE PRETTY! YOU'RE PRETTY!

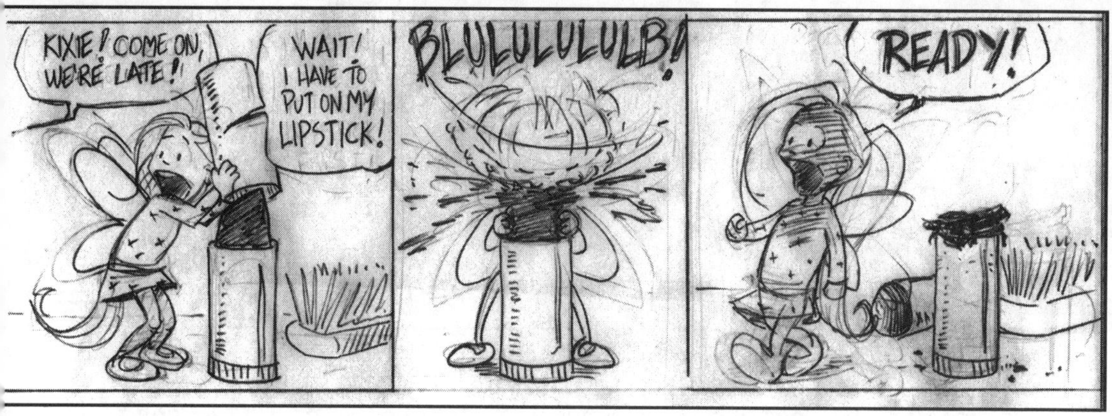
KIXIE! COME ON, WE'RE LATE!
WAIT! I HAVE TO PUT ON MY LIPSTICK!
BLULULULULB!
READY!

Faeries are only visible if they want to be. This helps with things like getting into the movies free of charge.

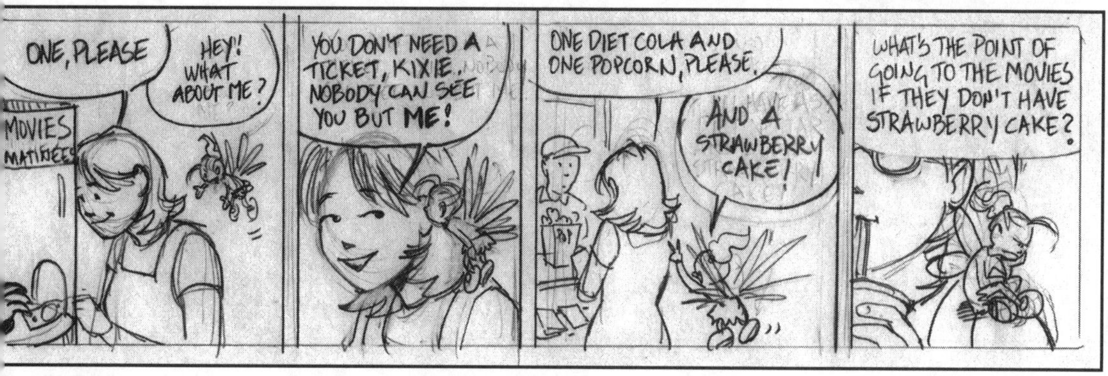
ONE, PLEASE
HEY! WHAT ABOUT ME?
MOVIES
MATINEES
YOU DON'T NEED A TICKET, KIXIE. NOBODY CAN SEE YOU BUT ME!
ONE DIET COLA AND ONE POPCORN, PLEASE.
AND A STRAWBERRY CAKE!
WHAT'S THE POINT OF GOING TO THE MOVIES IF THEY DON'T HAVE STRAWBERRY CAKE?

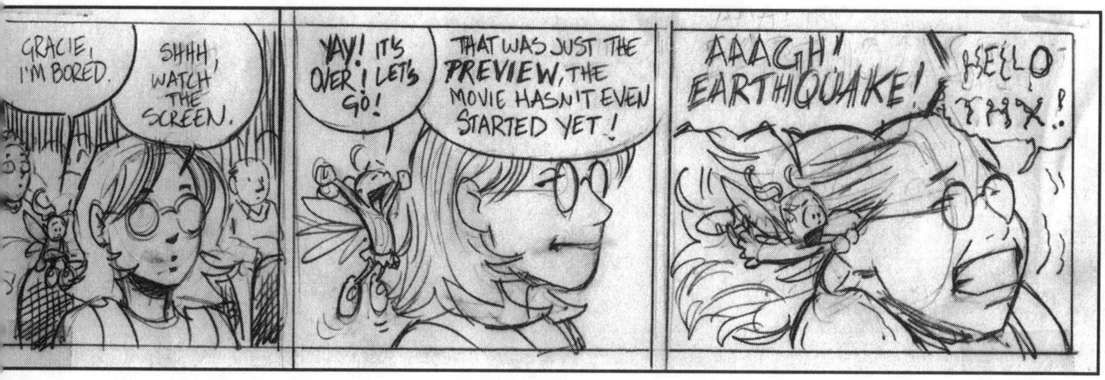
GRACIE, I'M BORED.
SHHH, WATCH THE SCREEN.
YAY! IT'S OVER! LET'S GO!
THAT WAS JUST THE PREVIEW, THE MOVIE HASN'T EVEN STARTED YET!
AAAGH! EARTHQUAKE!

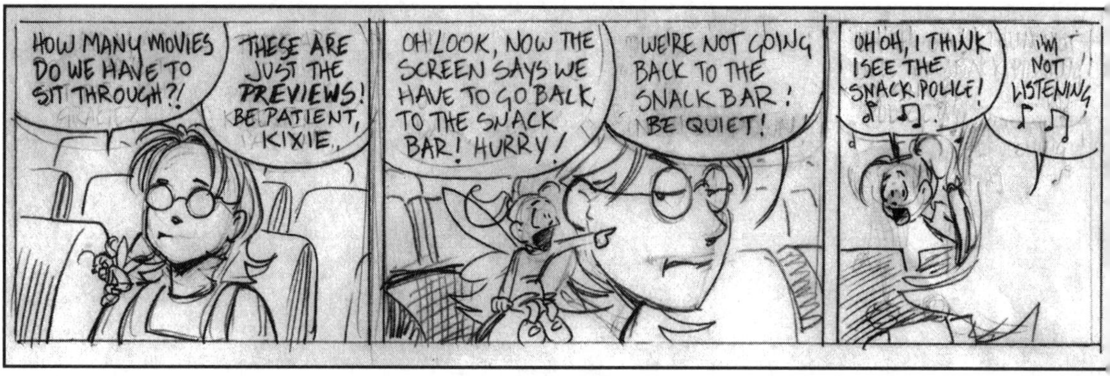
HOW MANY MOVIES DO WE HAVE TO SIT THROUGH?!
THESE ARE JUST THE PREVIEWS! BE PATIENT, KIXIE.
OH LOOK, NOW THE SCREEN SAYS WE HAVE TO GO BACK TO THE SNACK BAR! HURRY!
WE'RE NOT GOING BACK TO THE SNACK BAR! BE QUIET!
OH OH, I THINK I SEE THE SNACK POLICE!
I'M NOT LISTENING

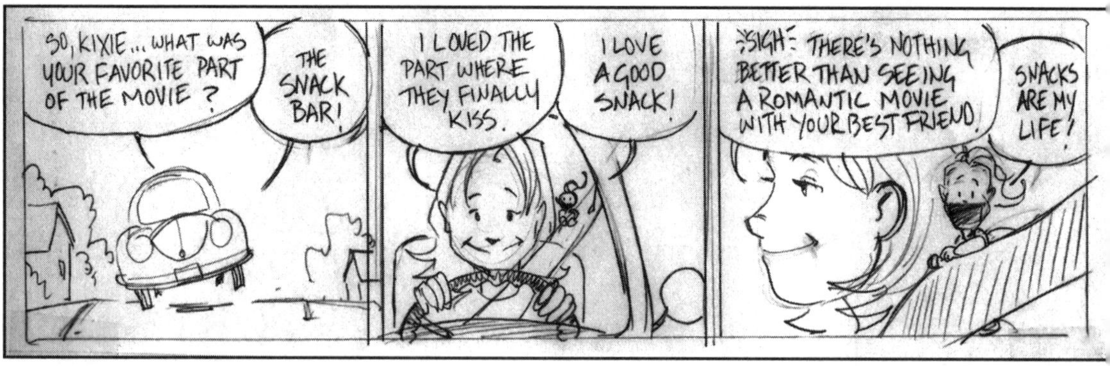
SO, KIXIE... WHAT WAS YOUR FAVORITE PART OF THE MOVIE?
THE SNACK BAR!
I LOVED THE PART WHERE THEY FINALLY KISS.
I LOVE A GOOD SNACK!
SIGH THERE'S NOTHING BETTER THAN SEEING A ROMANTIC MOVIE WITH YOUR BEST FRIEND.
SNACKS ARE MY LIFE!

Faeries also don't like getting their wings wet, it makes them dizzy. Poor Kixie doesn't understand why Grace insists on this cruel ritual every week.

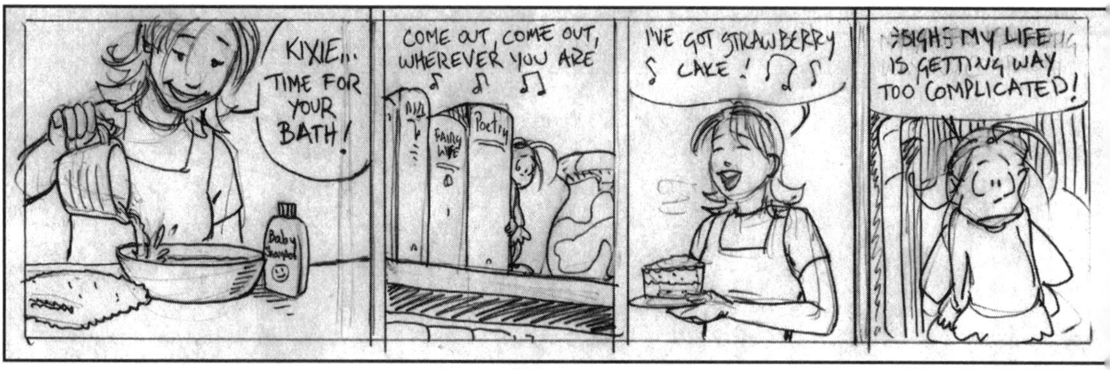
KIXIE... TIME FOR YOUR BATH!
COME OUT, COME OUT, WHEREVER YOU ARE
Poetry
I'VE GOT STRAWBERRY CAKE!
SIGH MY LIFE IS GETTING WAY TOO COMPLICATED!

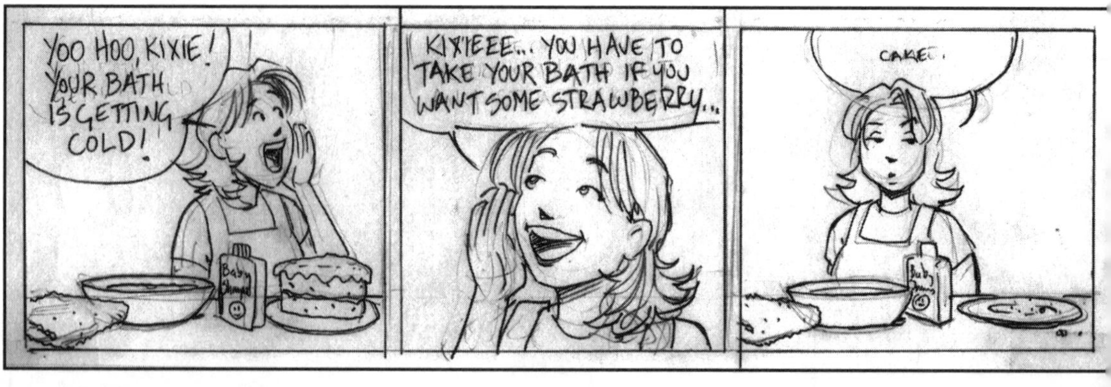
YOO HOO, KIXIE! YOUR BATH IS GETTING COLD!
KIXIEEE... YOU HAVE TO TAKE YOUR BATH IF YOU WANT SOME STRAWBERRY...
CAKE.

ike all faeries, Kixie has an insatiable sweet tooth. Getting her to eat her vegtables is next to impossible. Being the good person that she is though, Grace ives it her best.

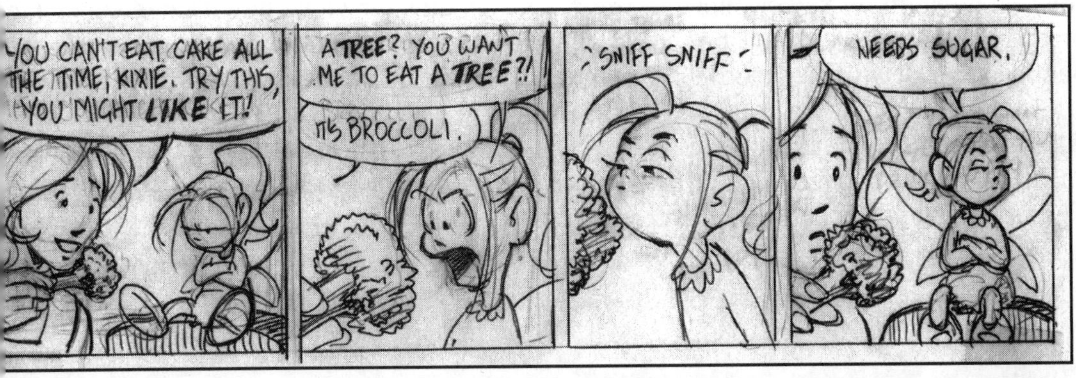
YOU CAN'T EAT CAKE ALL THE TIME, KIXIE. TRY THIS, YOU MIGHT LIKE IT!
A TREE? YOU WANT ME TO EAT A TREE?!
IT'S BROCCOLI.
SNIFF SNIFF
NEEDS SUGAR.

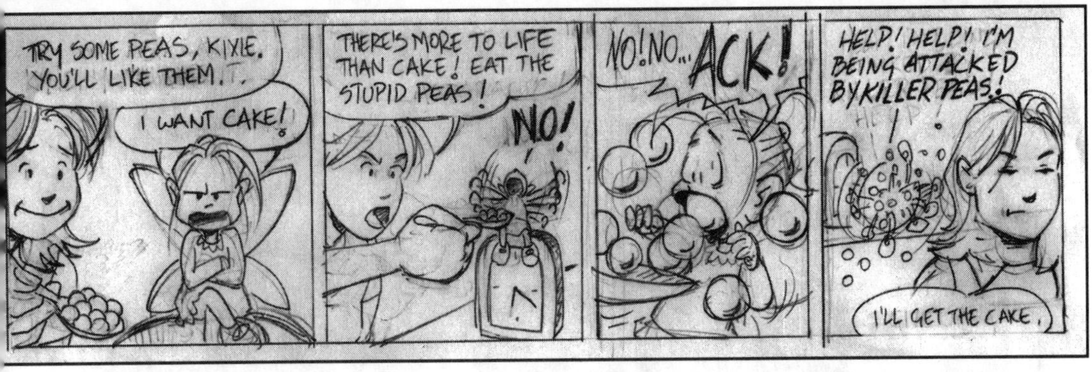
TRY SOME PEAS, KIXIE. YOU'LL LIKE THEM.
I WANT CAKE!
THERE'S MORE TO LIFE THAN CAKE! EAT THE STUPID PEAS!
NO!
NO! NO... ACK!
HELP! HELP! I'M BEING ATTACKED BY KILLER PEAS!
I'LL GET THE CAKE.

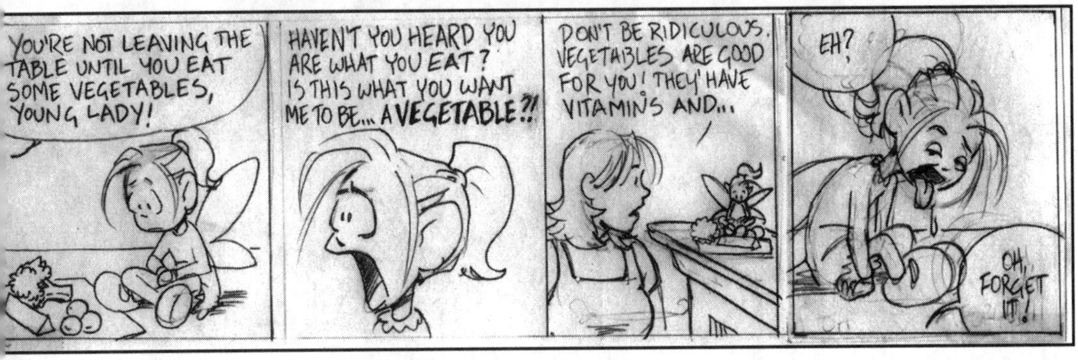
YOU'RE NOT LEAVING THE TABLE UNTIL YOU EAT SOME VEGETABLES, YOUNG LADY!
HAVEN'T YOU HEARD YOU ARE WHAT YOU EAT? IS THIS WHAT YOU WANT ME TO BE... A VEGETABLE?!
DON'T BE RIDICULOUS. VEGETABLES ARE GOOD FOR YOU! THEY HAVE VITAMINS AND...
EH?
OH, FORGET IT!

/ep, I like this Kixie. Even quiet time with her has its moments.

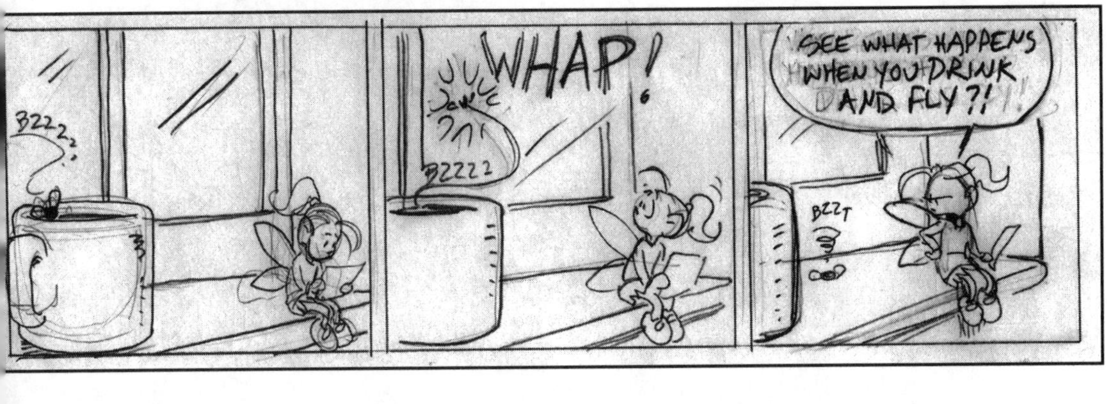
BZZ
WHAP!
BZZZZ
SEE WHAT HAPPENS WHEN YOU DRINK AND FLY?!
BZZT

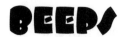

BEEPS

Kixie strips were laying all over the studio when I took a flight to somewhere I can't remember. After swallowing the faux turkey sandwich they always serve me at the back of the plane, I began doodling on the drink napkin, humming "Beep, beep, wiggle down the street." No wonder nobody will sit next to me.

I can't describe Beeps for you. When I have more to show you in future issues of Paradise Too, I suggest you put on some Miles Davis and read them all together. That's the closest connection I can offer.

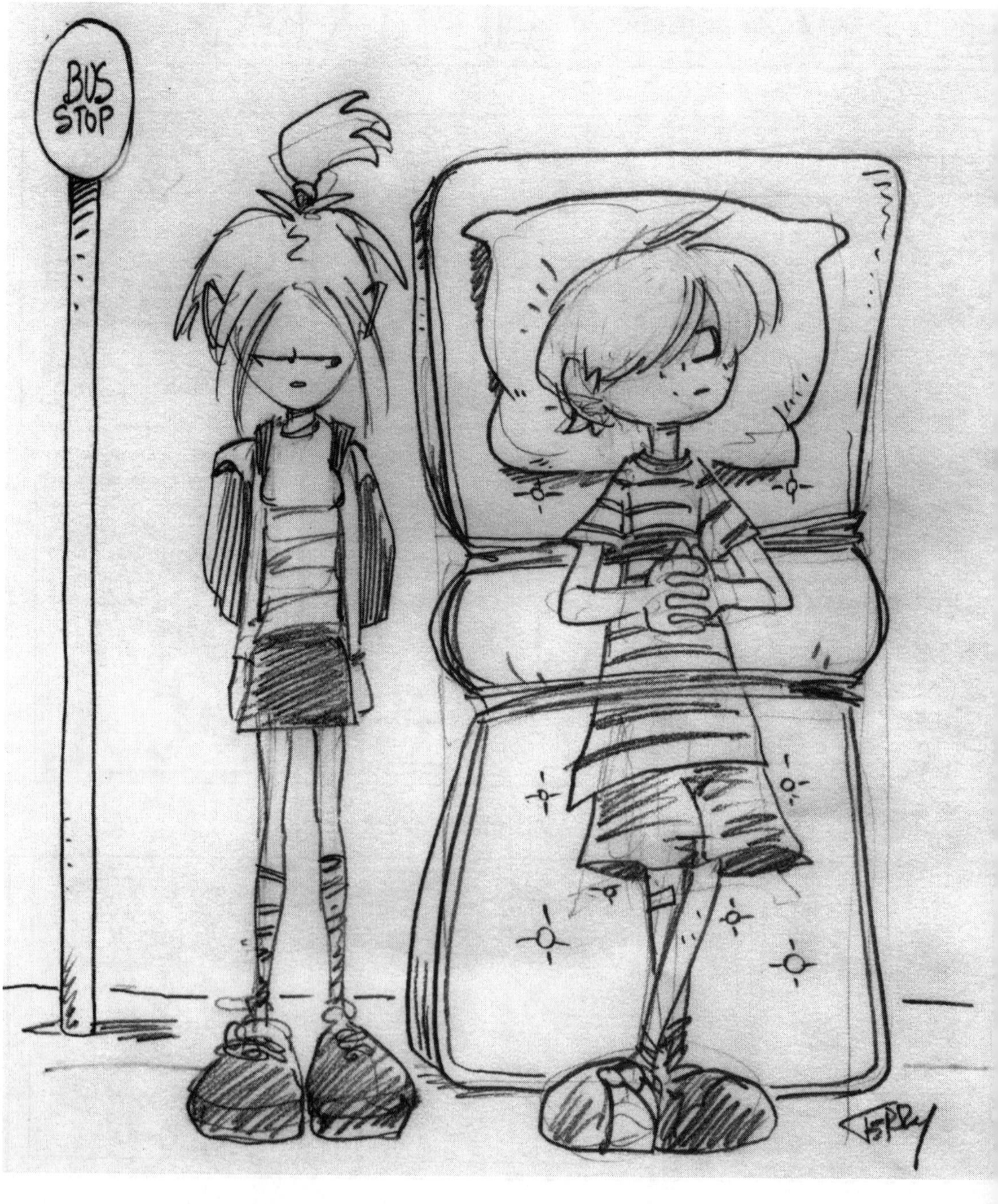
BUS STOP

BEEPS

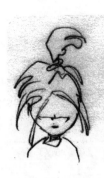

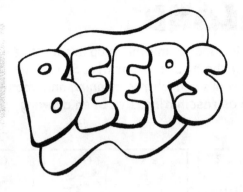

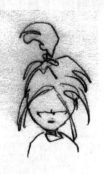

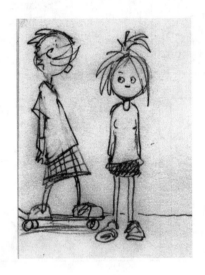

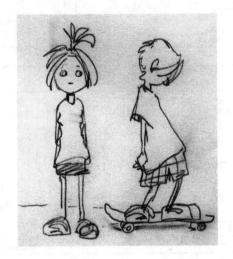

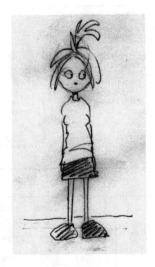

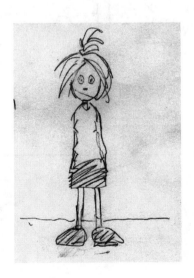

WONDERLAND

And then there is Wonderland. Somewhere up around the North Pole is a lovesick polar bear contemplating the mysteries of life. Set in the frozen tundra of the arctic circle, one lonely soul's search for meaning and happiness in a cold and barren world struck me as fascinating. I've been drawing the bear ever since.

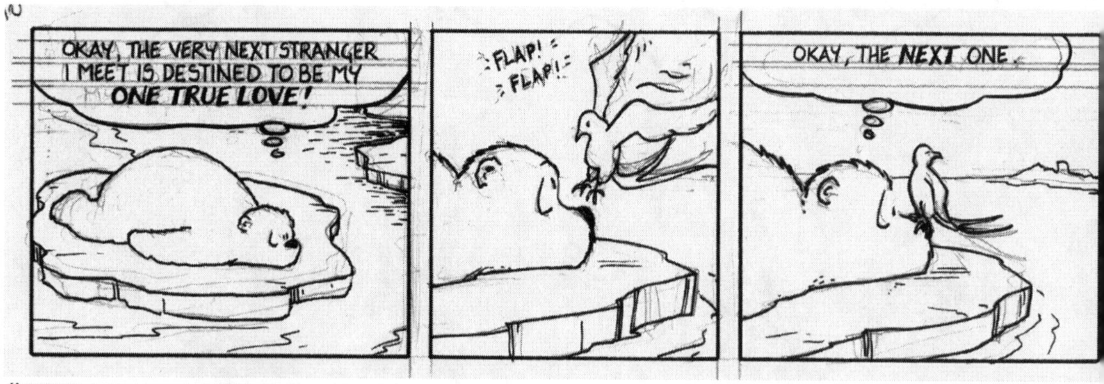

OKAY, THE VERY NEXT STRANGER I MEET IS DESTINED TO BE MY **ONE TRUE LOVE!**
FLAP! FLAP!
OKAY, THE **NEXT** ONE.

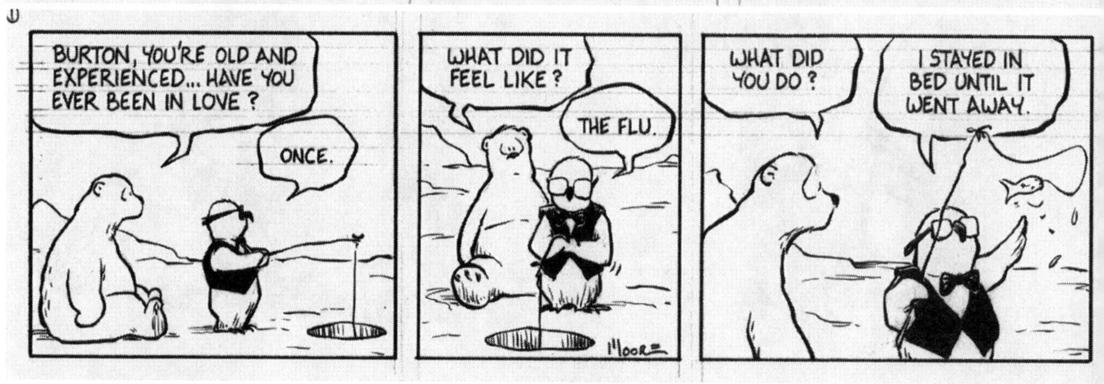

BURTON, YOU'RE OLD AND EXPERIENCED... HAVE YOU EVER BEEN IN LOVE?
ONCE.
WHAT DID IT FEEL LIKE?
THE FLU.
MOORE
WHAT DID YOU DO?
I STAYED IN BED UNTIL IT WENT AWAY.

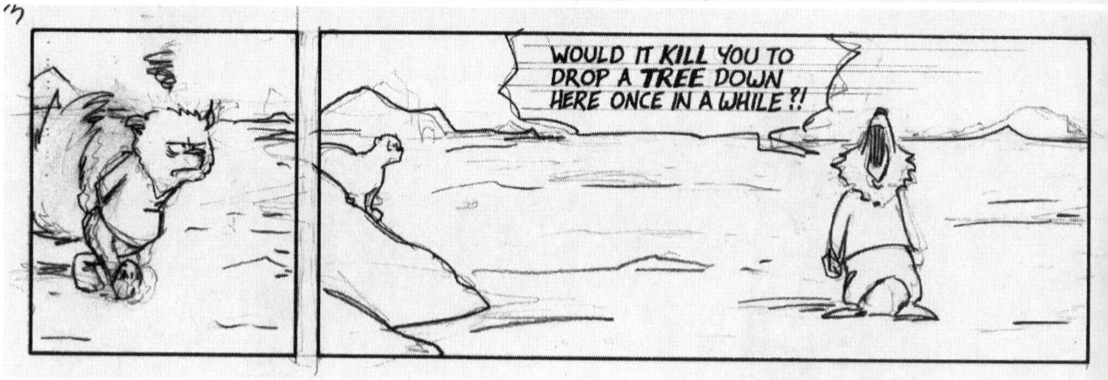

WOULD IT **KILL** YOU TO DROP A **TREE** DOWN HERE ONCE IN A WHILE?!

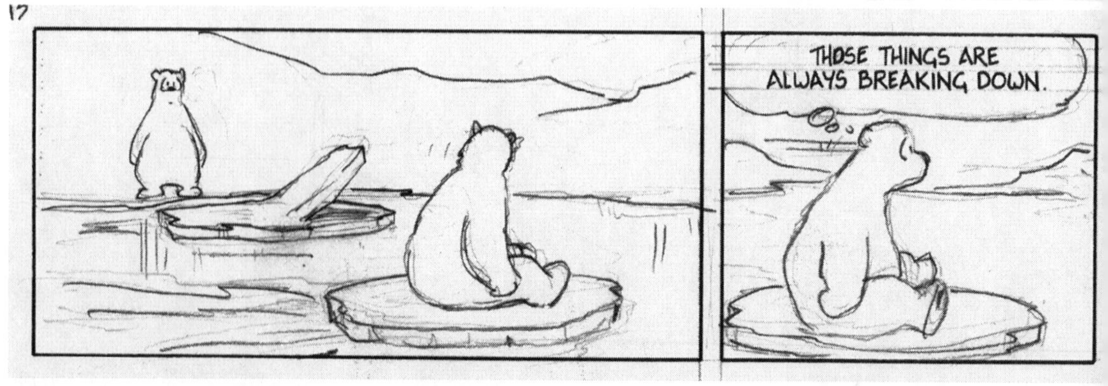

THOSE THINGS ARE ALWAYS BREAKING DOWN.

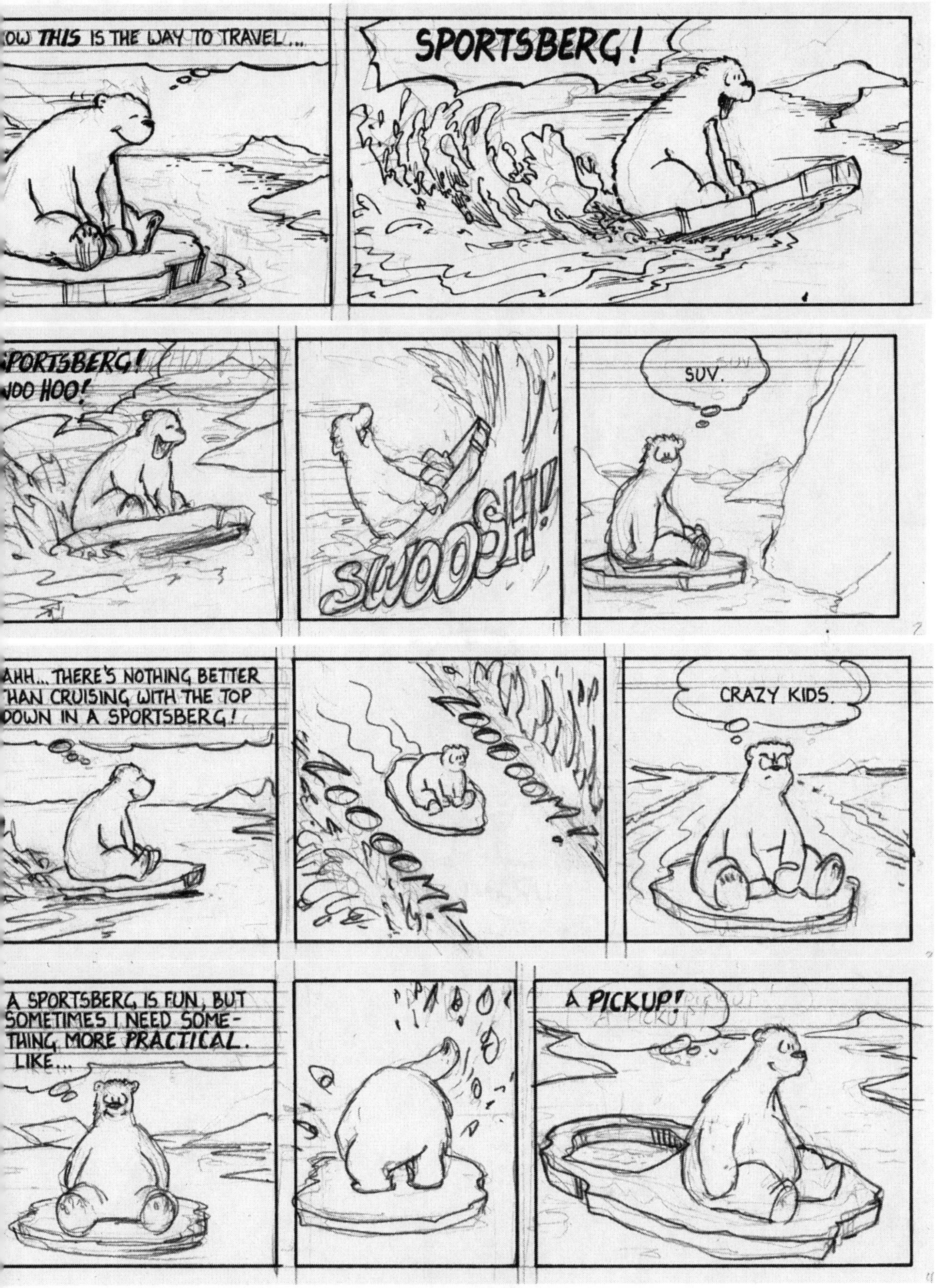
OW THIS IS THE WAY TO TRAVEL...
SPORTSBERG!
SPORTSBERG! WOO HOO!
SWOOSH!
SUV.
AHH... THERE'S NOTHING BETTER THAN CRUISING WITH THE TOP DOWN IN A SPORTSBERG!
CRAZY KIDS.
A SPORTSBERG IS FUN, BUT SOMETIMES I NEED SOME-THING MORE PRACTICAL. LIKE...
A PICKUP!

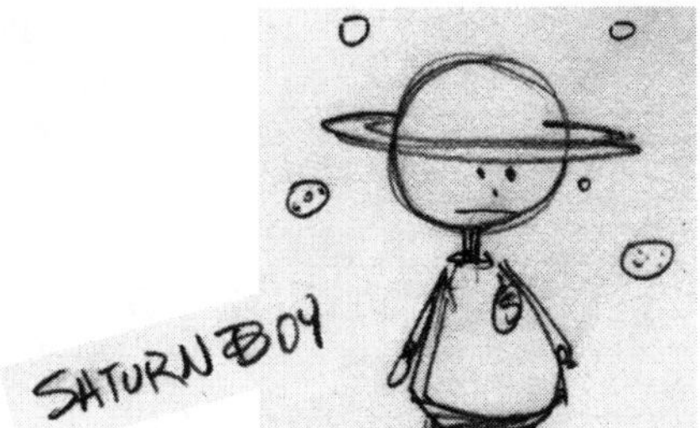
SATURN BOY

URANUS LAD

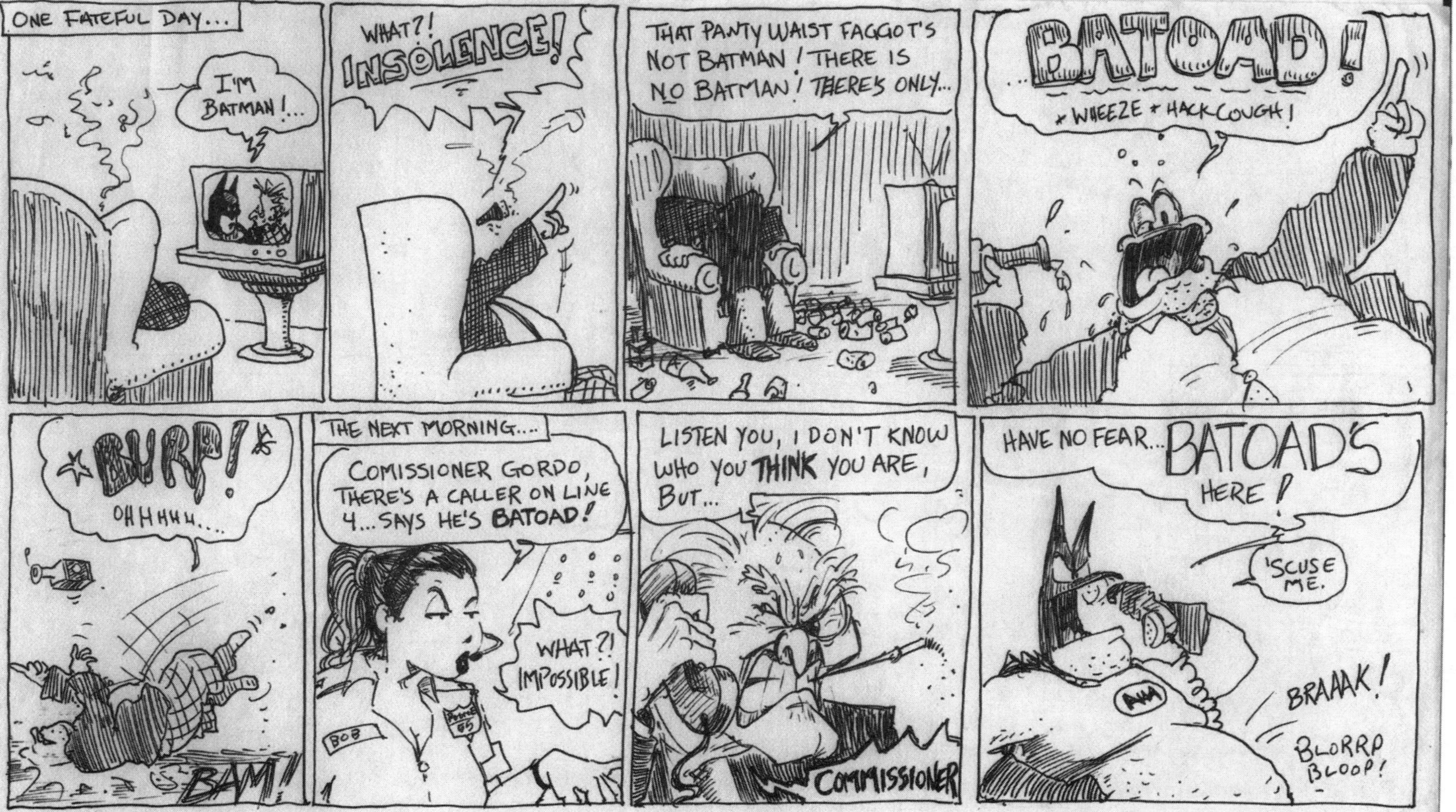
ONE FATEFUL DAY....
I'M BATMAN!...
WHAT?! INSOLENCE!
THAT PANTY WAIST FAGGOT'S NOT BATMAN! THERE IS NO BATMAN! THERE'S ONLY...
...BATOAD!
* WHEEZE * HACK COUGH!
BURP!
OHHHHH....
BAM!
THE NEXT MORNING....
COMISSIONER GORDO, THERE'S A CALLER ON LINE 4... SAYS HE'S BATOAD!
BOB
WHAT?! IMPOSSIBLE!
LISTEN YOU, I DON'T KNOW WHO YOU THINK YOU ARE, BUT...
COMMISSIONER
HAVE NO FEAR... BATOAD'S HERE!
'SCUSE ME.
BRAAAK!
BLORRP BLOOP!

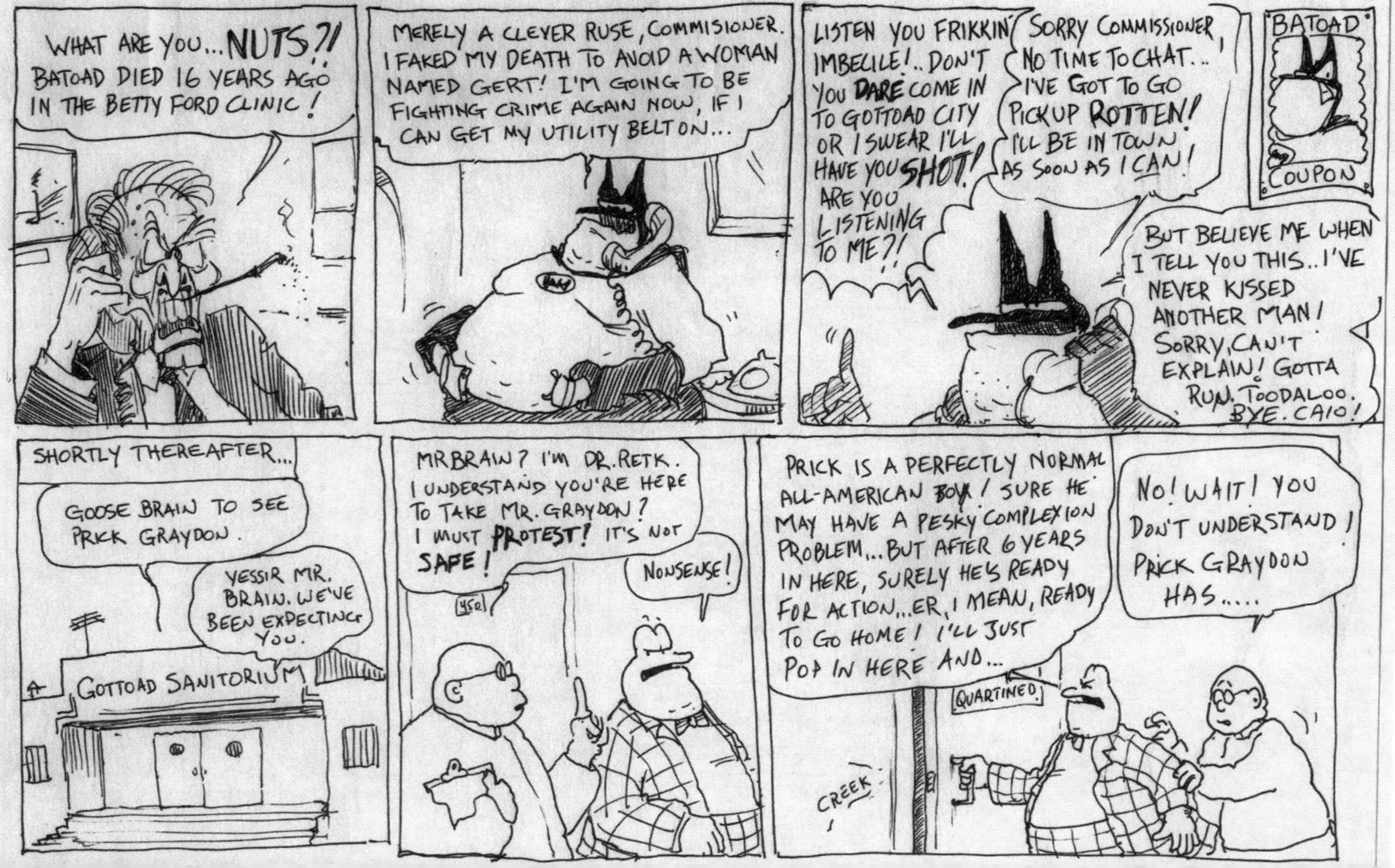
WHAT ARE YOU...NUTS?!
BATOAD DIED 16 YEARS AGO IN THE BETTY FORD CLINIC!
MERELY A CLEVER RUSE, COMMISIONER. I FAKED MY DEATH TO AVOID A WOMAN NAMED GERT! I'M GOING TO BE FIGHTING CRIME AGAIN NOW, IF I CAN GET MY UTILITY BELT ON...
LISTEN YOU FRIKKIN' IMBECILE!.. DON'T YOU DARE COME IN TO GOTTOAD CITY OR I SWEAR I'LL HAVE YOU SHOT! ARE YOU LISTENING TO ME?!
SORRY COMMISSIONER, NO TIME TO CHAT... I'VE GOT TO GO PICKUP ROTTEN! I'LL BE IN TOWN AS SOON AS I CAN!
BATOAD
COUPON
BUT BELIEVE ME WHEN I TELL YOU THIS.. I'VE NEVER KISSED ANOTHER MAN! SORRY, CAN'T EXPLAIN! GOTTA RUN. TOODALOO. BYE. CAIO!
SHORTLY THEREAFTER...
GOOSE BRAIN TO SEE PRICK GRAYDON.
YESSIR MR. BRAIN. WE'VE BEEN EXPECTING YOU.
GOTTOAD SANITORIUM
MR BRAIN? I'M DR. RETK. I UNDERSTAND YOU'RE HERE TO TAKE MR. GRAYDON? I MUST PROTEST! IT'S NOT SAFE!
NONSENSE!
PRICK IS A PERFECTLY NORMAL ALL-AMERICAN BOY! SURE HE MAY HAVE A PESKY COMPLEXION PROBLEM... BUT AFTER 6 YEARS IN HERE, SURELY HE'S READY FOR ACTION...ER, I MEAN, READY TO GO HOME! I'LL JUST POP IN HERE AND...
CREEK
QUARTINED
NO! WAIT! YOU DON'T UNDERSTAND! PRICK GRAYDON HAS.....

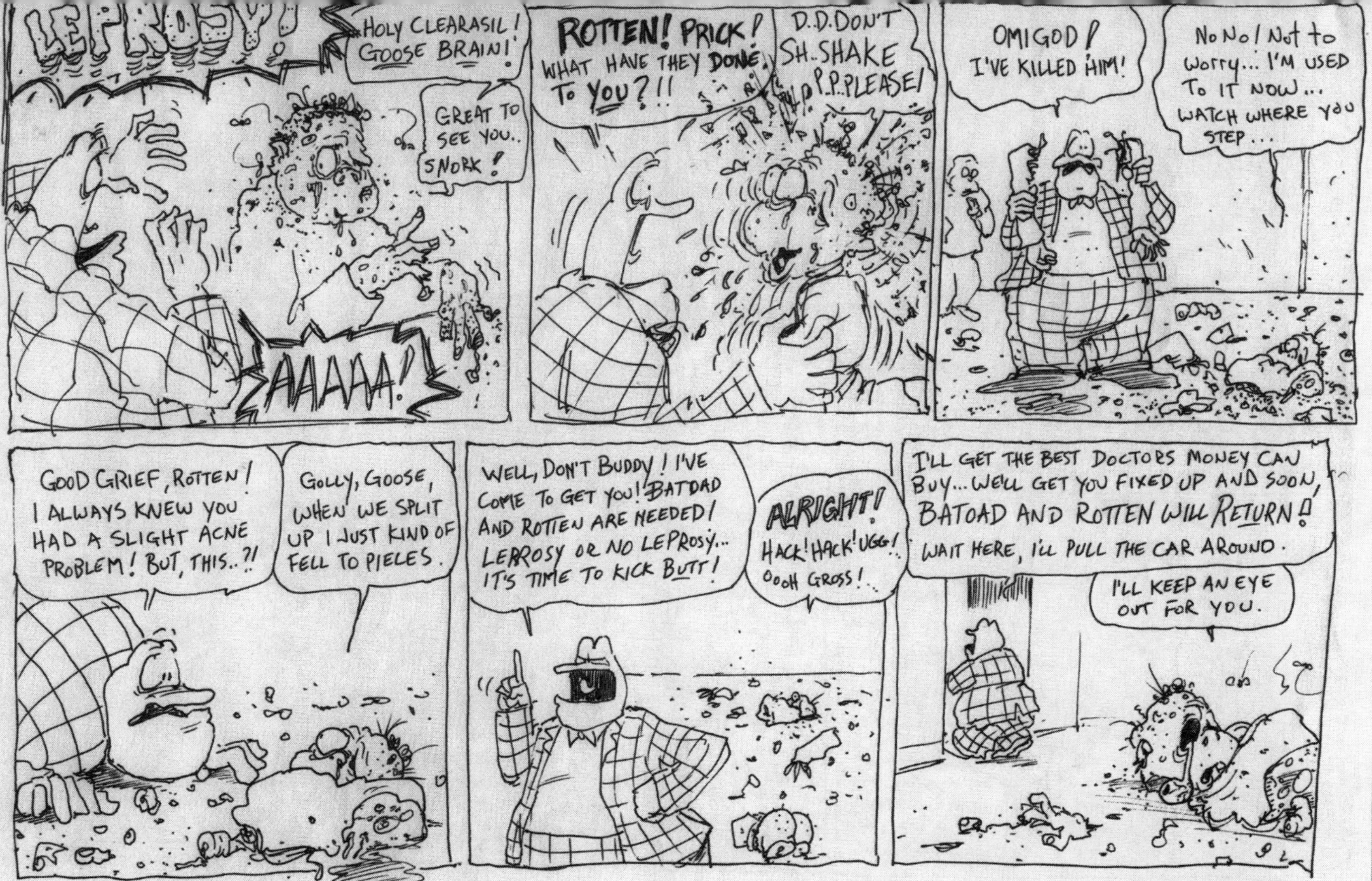
LEPROSY!
HOLY CLEARASIL! GOOSE BRAIN!
GREAT TO SEE YOU.. SNORK!
AAAAA!
ROTTEN! PRICK! WHAT HAVE THEY DONE TO YOU?!!
D.D.DON'T SH..SHAKE P.P.P.PLEASE!
OMIGOD! I'VE KILLED HIM!
NO NO! NOT TO WORRY... I'M USED TO IT NOW... WATCH WHERE YOU STEP...
GOOD GRIEF, ROTTEN! I ALWAYS KNEW YOU HAD A SLIGHT ACNE PROBLEM! BUT, THIS..?!
GOLLY, GOOSE, WHEN WE SPLIT UP I JUST KIND OF FELL TO PIECES.
WELL, DON'T BUDDY! I'VE COME TO GET YOU! BATOAD AND ROTTEN ARE NEEDED! LEPROSY OR NO LEPROSY... IT'S TIME TO KICK BUTT!
ALRIGHT! HACK! HACK! UGG! OOOH GROSS!
I'LL GET THE BEST DOCTORS MONEY CAN BUY... WE'LL GET YOU FIXED UP AND SOON, BATOAD AND ROTTEN WILL RETURN! WAIT HERE, I'LL PULL THE CAR AROUND.
I'LL KEEP AN EYE OUT FOR YOU.

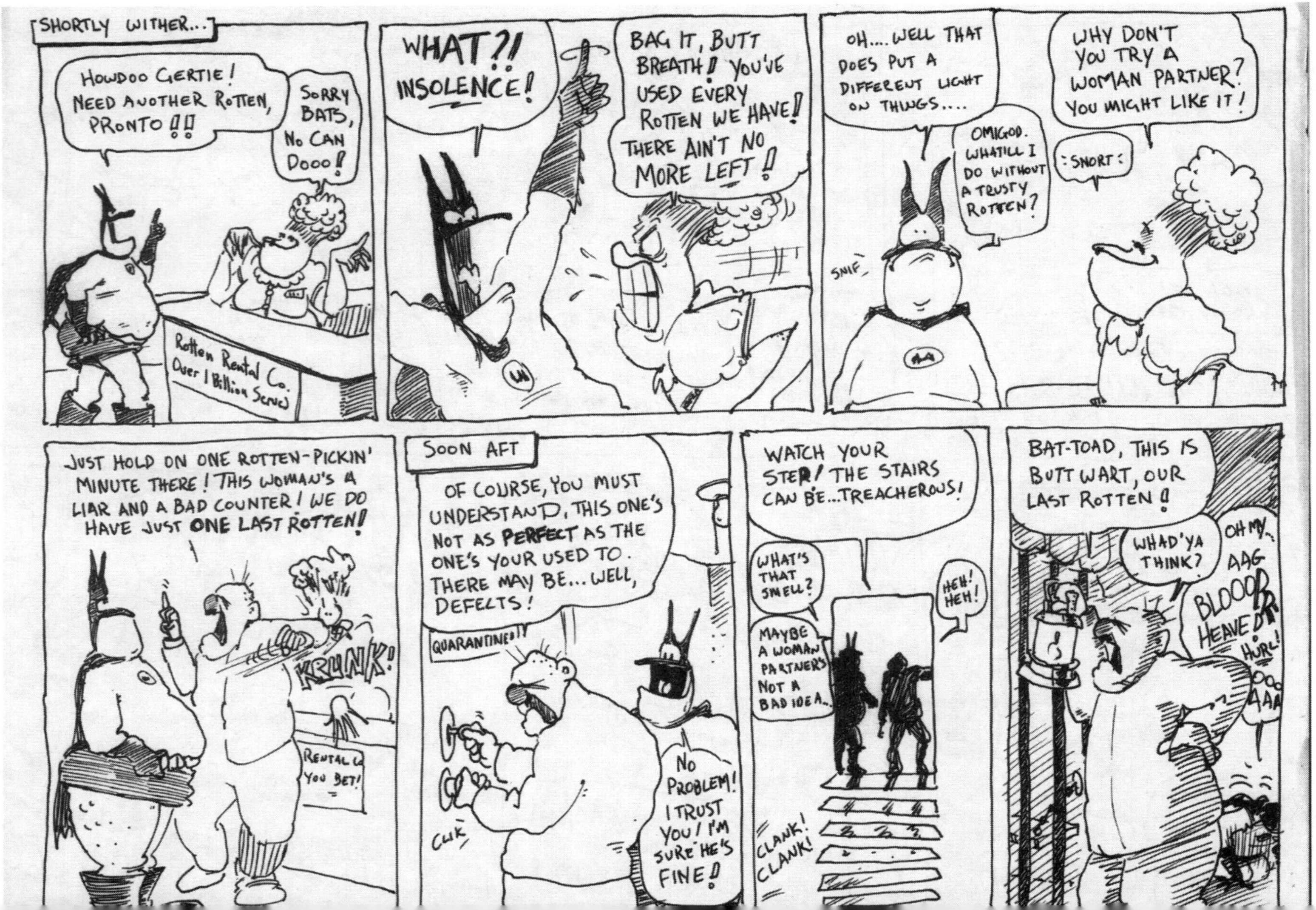
SHORTLY WITHER...
HOWDOO GERTIE! NEED ANOTHER ROTTEN, PRONTO!!!
SORRY BATS, NO CAN DOOO!
Rotten Rental Co. Over 1 Billion Served
WHAT?! INSOLENCE!
BAG IT, BUTT BREATH! YOU'VE USED EVERY ROTTEN WE HAVE! THERE AIN'T NO MORE LEFT!
OH.... WELL THAT DOES PUT A DIFFERENT LIGHT ON THINGS....
OMIGOD. WHATILL I DO WITHOUT A TRUSTY ROTTEN?
SNIF
WHY DON'T YOU TRY A WOMAN PARTNER? YOU MIGHT LIKE IT!
:SNORT:
JUST HOLD ON ONE ROTTEN-PICKIN' MINUTE THERE! THIS WOMAN'S A LIAR AND A BAD COUNTER! WE DO HAVE JUST ONE LAST ROTTEN!
KRUNK!
RENTAL C YOU BET!
SOON AFT
OF COURSE, YOU MUST UNDERSTAND, THIS ONE'S NOT AS PERFECT AS THE ONE'S YOUR USED TO. THERE MAY BE... WELL, DEFECTS!
QUARANTINE!!
NO PROBLEM! I TRUST YOU! I'M SURE HE'S FINE!
CLIK
WATCH YOUR STEP! THE STAIRS CAN BE...TREACHEROUS!
WHAT'S THAT SMELL?
MAYBE A WOMAN PARTNER'S NOT A BAD IDEA...
HEH! HEH!
CLANK! CLANK!
BAT-TOAD, THIS IS BUTT WART, OUR LAST ROTTEN!
WHAD'YA THINK?
OH MY... AAG BLOOORR HEAVE!R HURL! OOO AAA

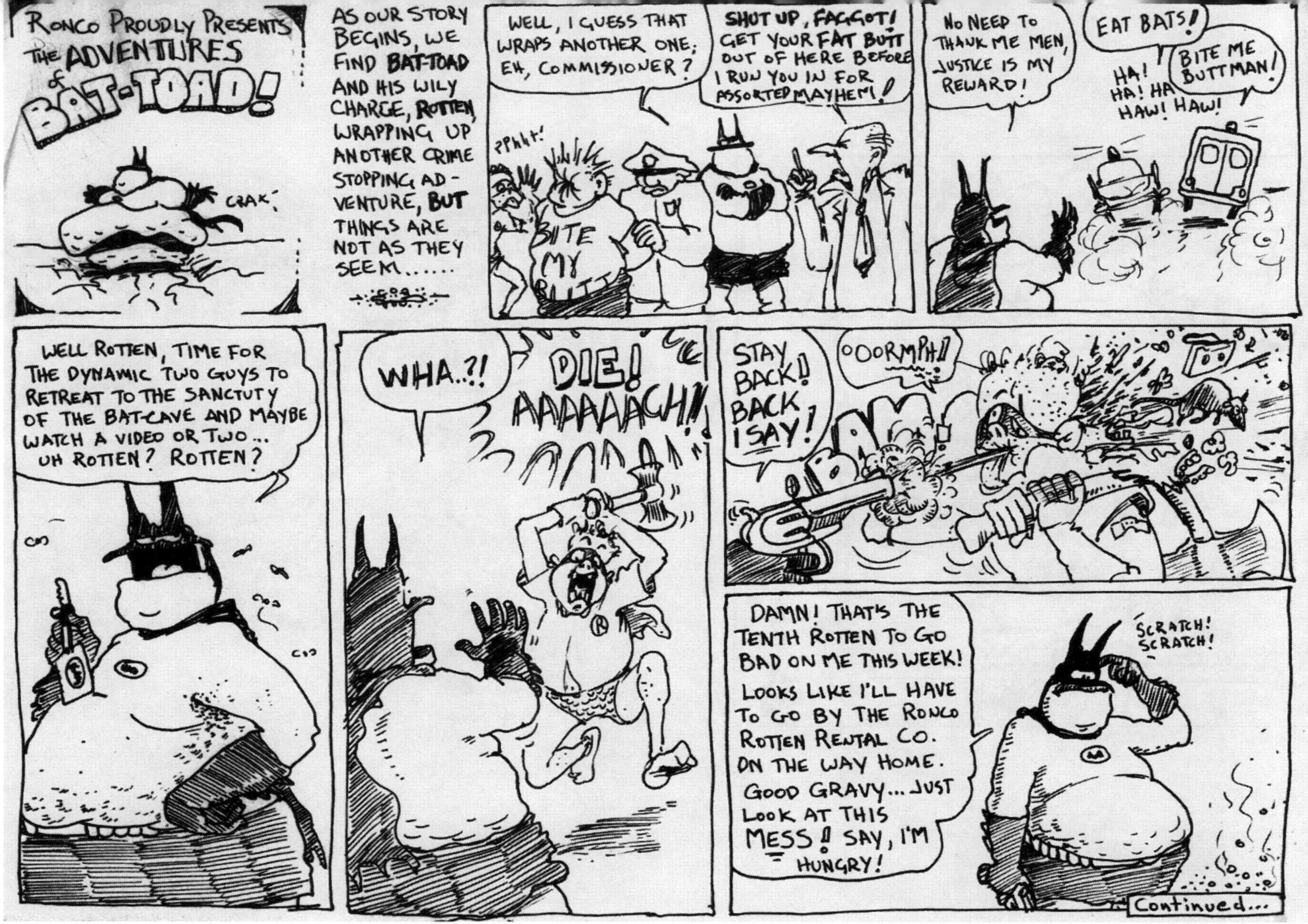

RONCO PROUDLY PRESENTS THE ADVENTURES of BAT-TOAD!
CRAK!
AS OUR STORY BEGINS, WE FIND BAT-TOAD AND HIS WILY CHARGE, ROTTEN, WRAPPING UP ANOTHER CRIME STOPPING ADVENTURE, BUT THINGS ARE NOT AS THEY SEEM......
WELL, I GUESS THAT WRAPS ANOTHER ONE; EH, COMMISSIONER?
SHUT UP, FAGGOT! GET YOUR FAT BUTT OUT OF HERE BEFORE I RUN YOU IN FOR ASSORTED MAYHEM!
PPhht!
BITE MY BUTT
NO NEED TO THANK ME MEN, JUSTICE IS MY REWARD!
EAT BATS!
BITE ME BUTTMAN!
HA! HA! HA HAW! HAW!
WELL ROTTEN, TIME FOR THE DYNAMIC TWO GUYS TO RETREAT TO THE SANCTUTY OF THE BAT-CAVE AND MAYBE WATCH A VIDEO OR TWO... UH ROTTEN? ROTTEN?
WHA..?!
DIE! AAAAAACH!!
STAY BACK! BACK I SAY!
OOORMPH!
BAM
DAMN! THAT'S THE TENTH ROTTEN TO GO BAD ON ME THIS WEEK! LOOKS LIKE I'LL HAVE TO GO BY THE RONCO ROTTEN RENTAL CO. ON THE WAY HOME. GOOD GRAVY... JUST LOOK AT THIS MESS! SAY, I'M HUNGRY!
SCRATCH! SCRATCH!
Continued...

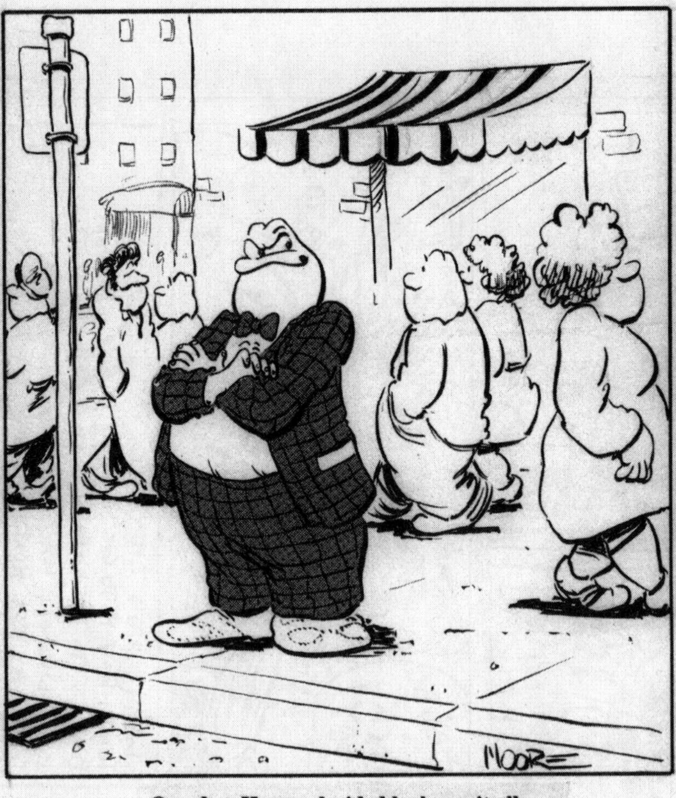

One day, Homer decided he knew it all.

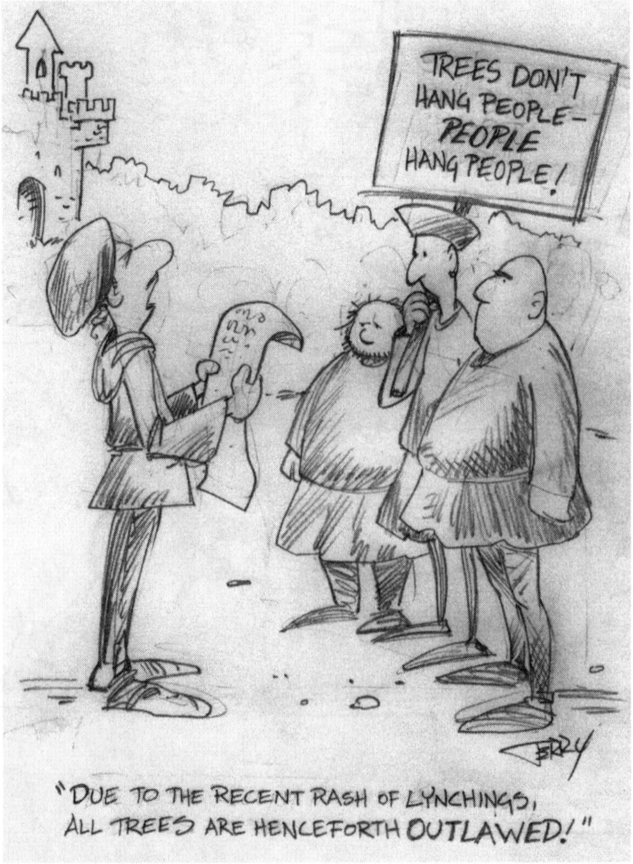
TREES DON'T HANG PEOPLE— PEOPLE HANG PEOPLE!

"DUE TO THE RECENT RASH OF LYNCHINGS, ALL TREES ARE HENCEFORTH OUTLAWED!"

am not a political man, I think politics are silly and the parties are ridiculous. 'hen our recent election went awry I couldn't help but laugh. It's the funniest ing we've done since disco. During that month long ordeal I made these records.

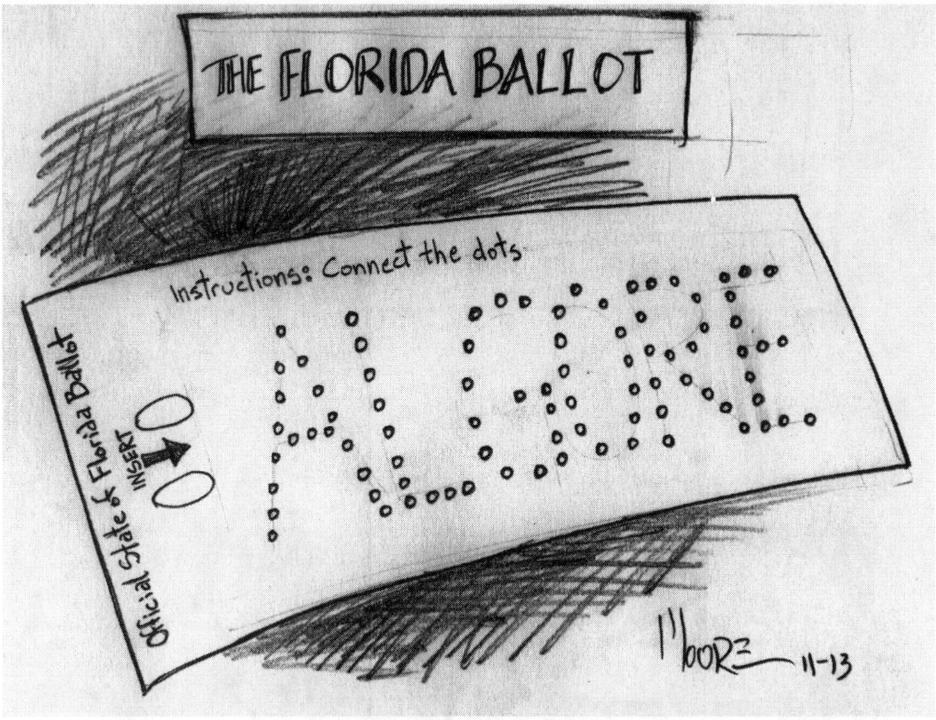
THE FLORIDA BALLOT
Instructions: Connect the dots
Official State of Florida Ballot
INSERT
M'OORE 11-13

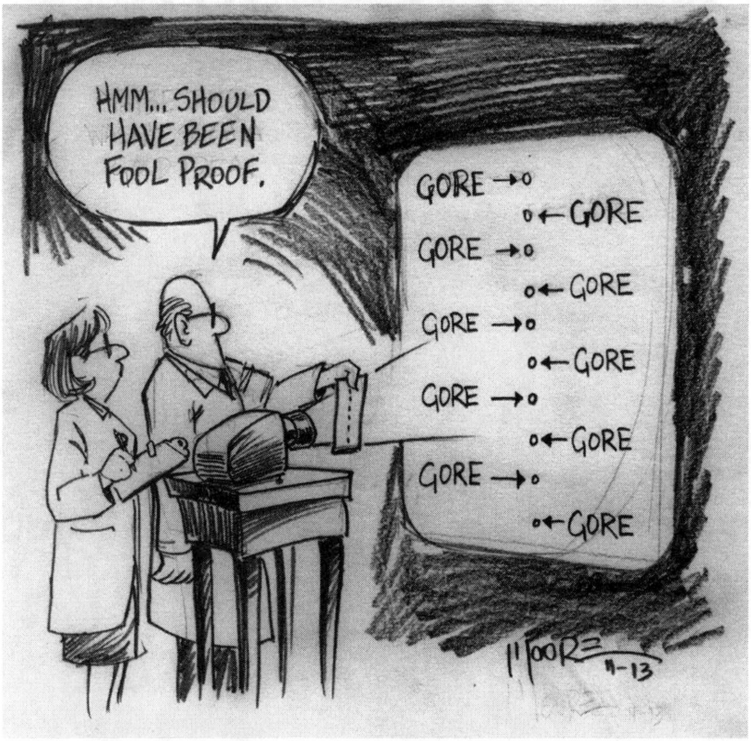
HMM... SHOULD HAVE BEEN FOOL PROOF.
GORE →o
o← GORE
GORE →o
o← GORE
GORE →o
o← GORE
GORE →o
o← GORE
GORE →o
o← GORE
M'OORE 11-13

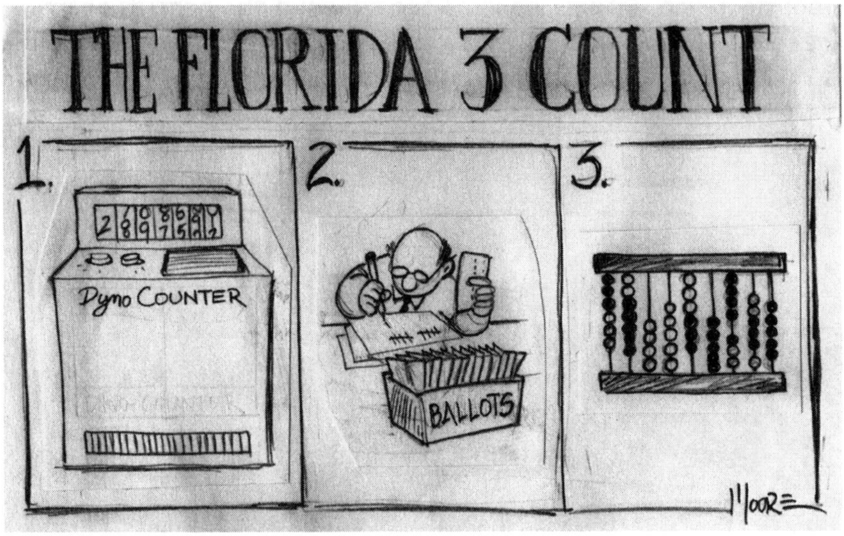
THE FLORIDA 3 COUNT
1.
Dyno COUNTER
2.
BALLOTS
3.
MOORE

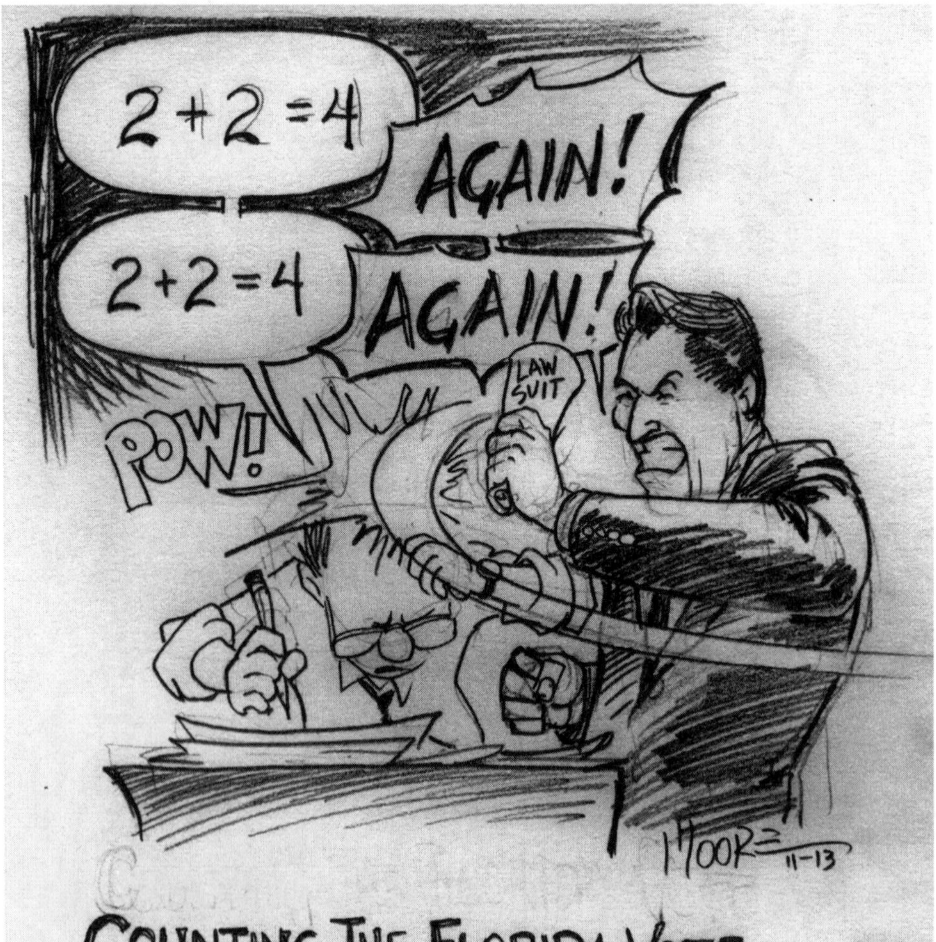
2+2=4
AGAIN!
2+2=4
AGAIN!
LAW SUIT
POW!
MOORE 11-13
COUNTING THE FLORIDA VOTE

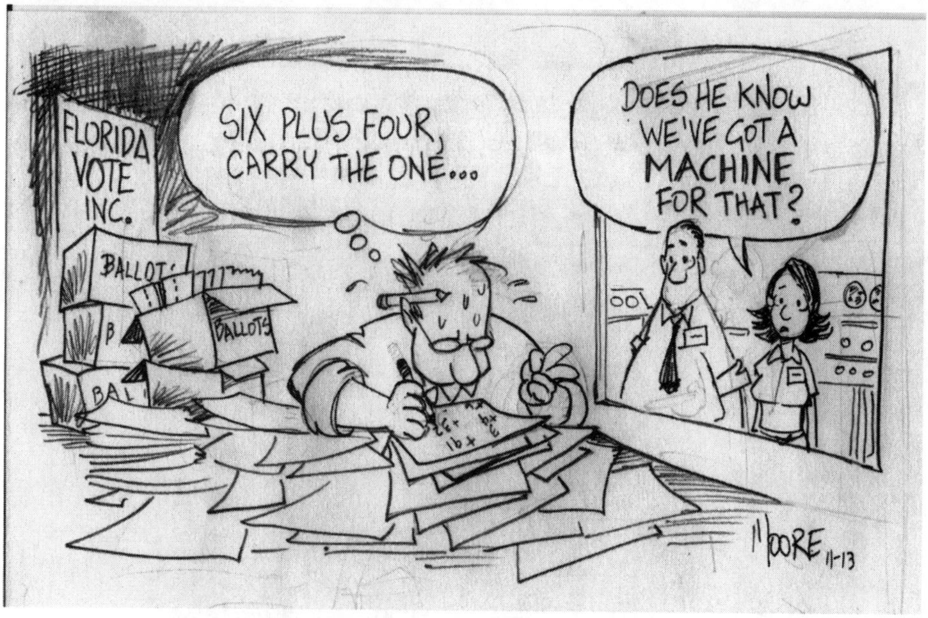
FLORIDA VOTE INC.
BALLOT
BALLOTS
SIX PLUS FOUR, CARRY THE ONE...
DOES HE KNOW WE'VE GOT A MACHINE FOR THAT?
MOORE 11-13

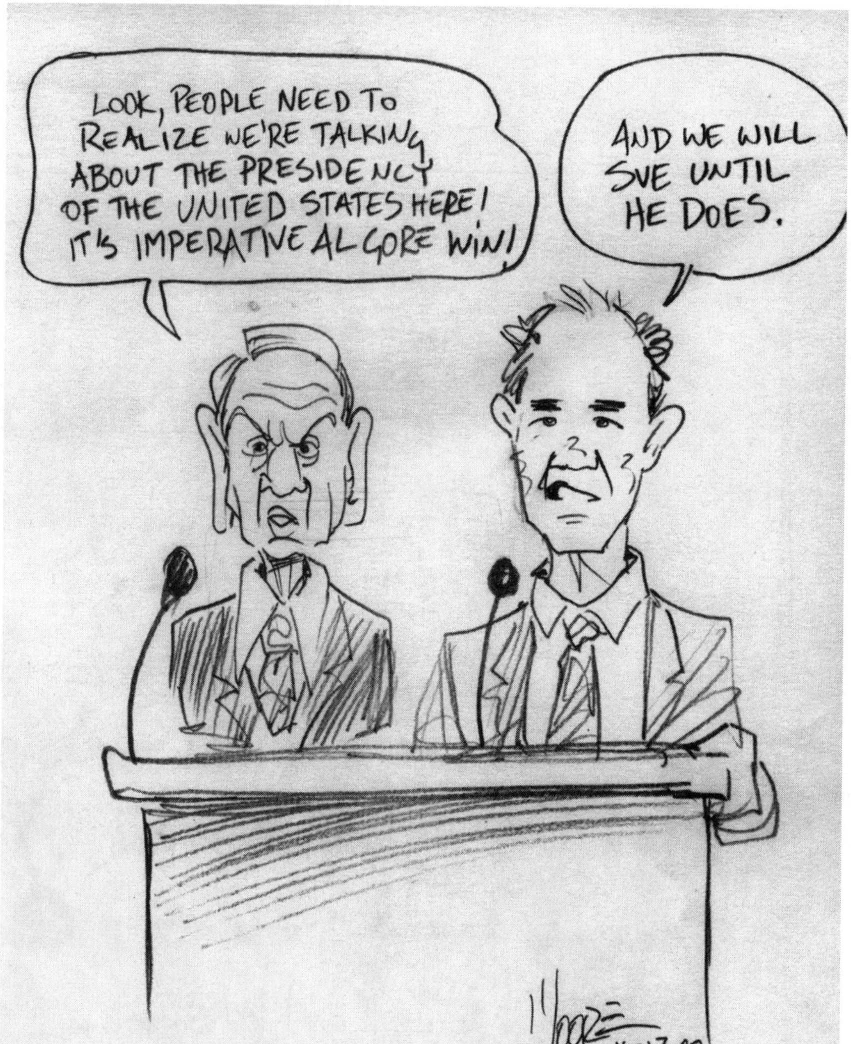
LOOK, PEOPLE NEED TO REALIZE WE'RE TALKING ABOUT THE PRESIDENCY OF THE UNITED STATES HERE! IT'S IMPERATIVE AL GORE WIN!
AND WE WILL SUE UNTIL HE DOES.
MOORE 11-17-00

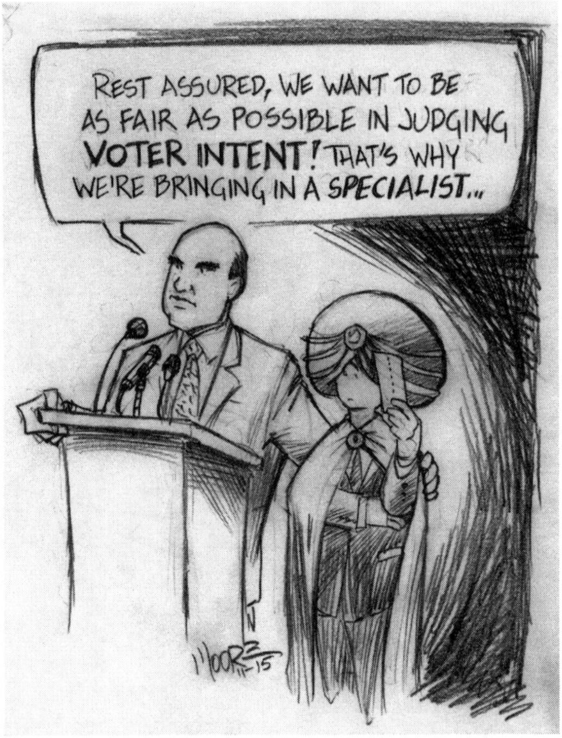
REST ASSURED, WE WANT TO BE AS FAIR AS POSSIBLE IN JUDGING VOTER INTENT! THAT'S WHY WE'RE BRINGING IN A SPECIALIST...

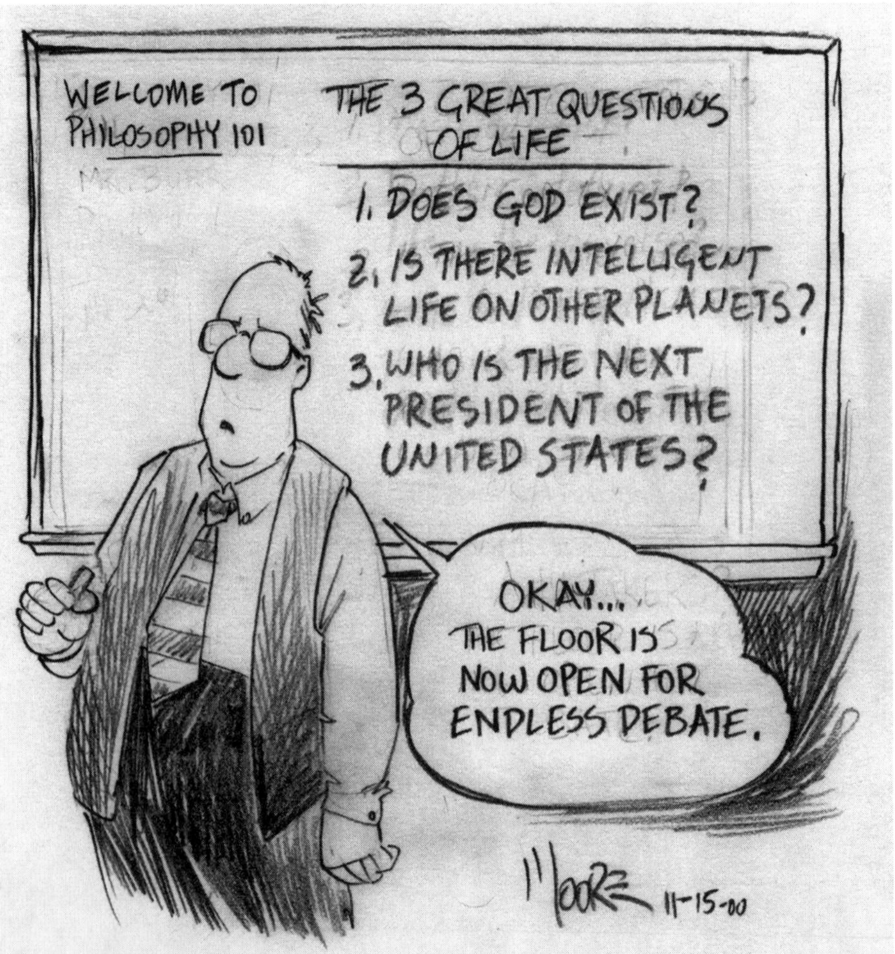
WELCOME TO PHILOSOPHY 101
THE 3 GREAT QUESTIONS OF LIFE
1. DOES GOD EXIST?
2. IS THERE INTELLIGENT LIFE ON OTHER PLANETS?
3. WHO IS THE NEXT PRESIDENT OF THE UNITED STATES?
OKAY... THE FLOOR IS NOW OPEN FOR ENDLESS DEBATE.
MOORE 11-15-00

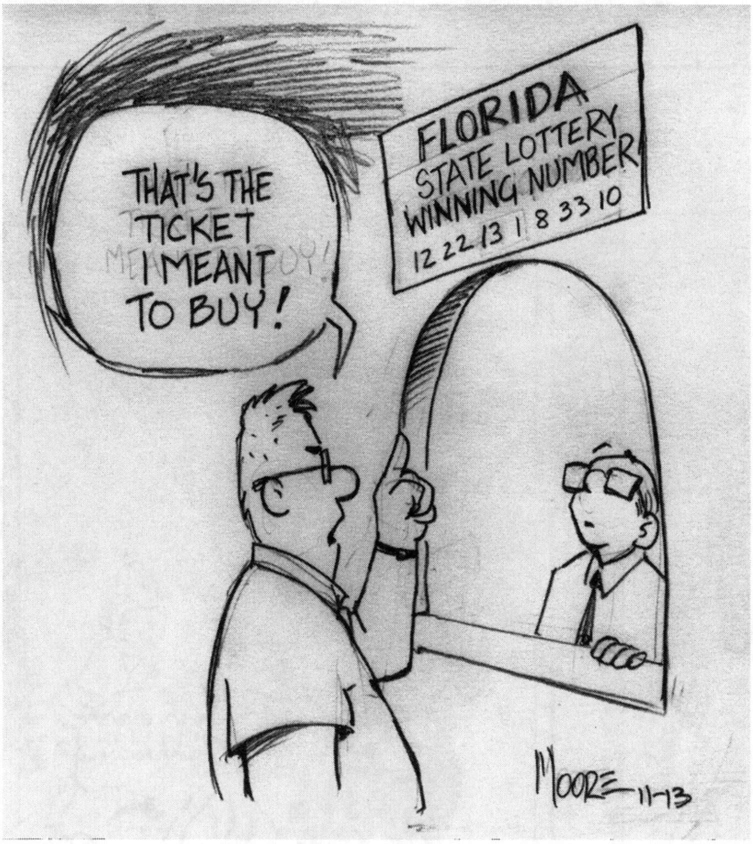
THAT'S THE TICKET I MEANT TO BUY!
FLORIDA STATE LOTTERY WINNING NUMBER
12 22 13 1 8 33 10
MOORE 11-13

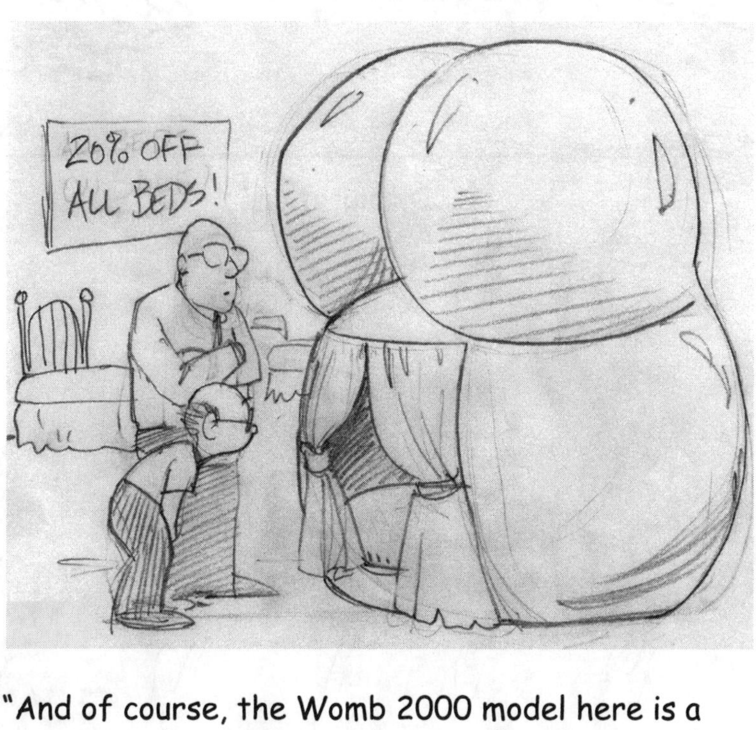
20% OFF ALL BEDS!

"And of course, the Womb 2000 model here is a consistent best seller with our male customers."

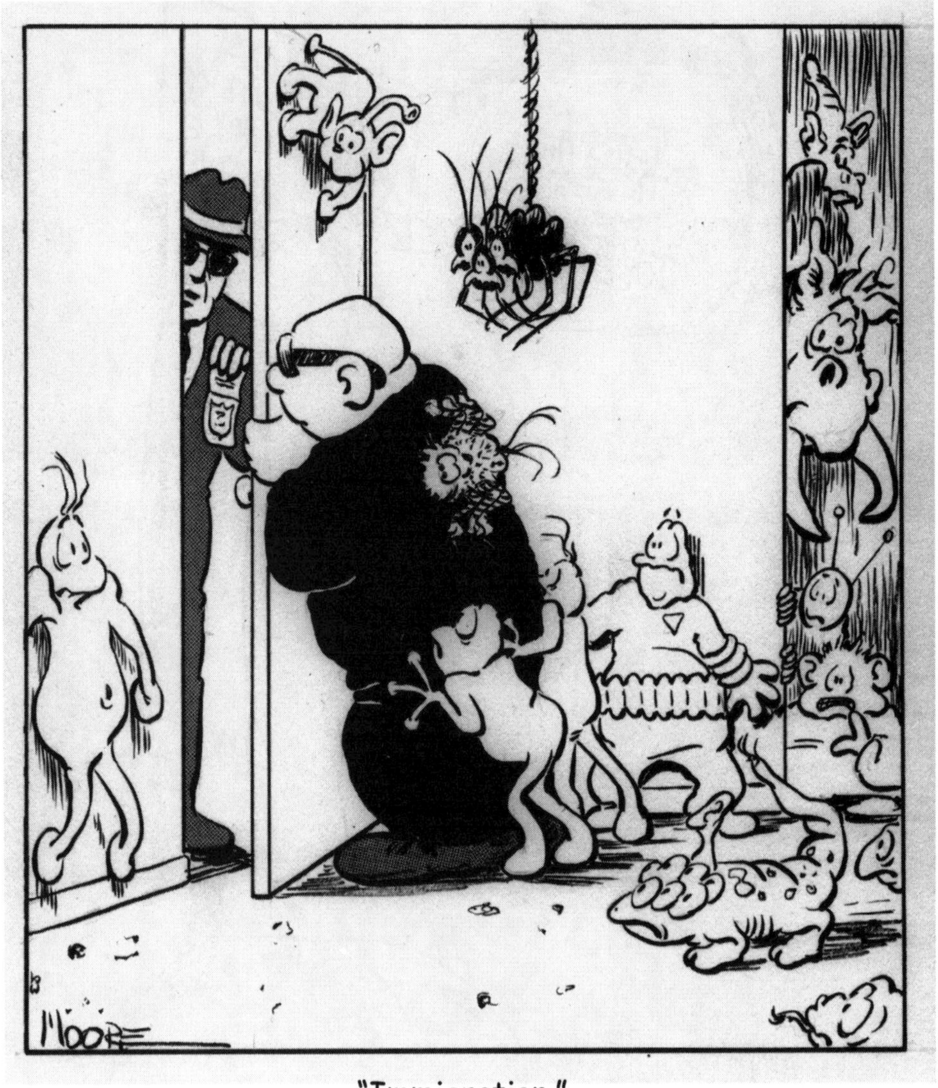
MOORE

"Immigration."

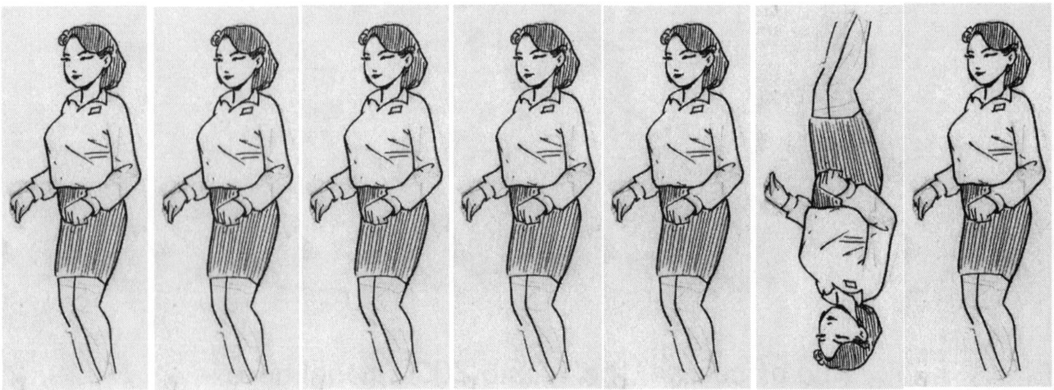

Every Saturday Mina liked to get looped.

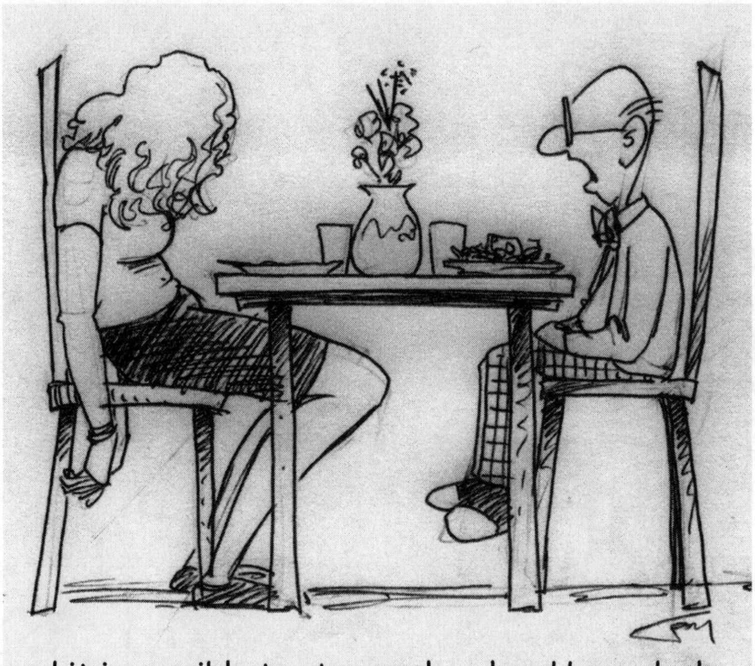

Marilyn found it impossible to stay awake when Howard, aka screen name "Studbucket", began the counter argument to his personal string theory. "No more computer dates," she slurred, then blacked out.

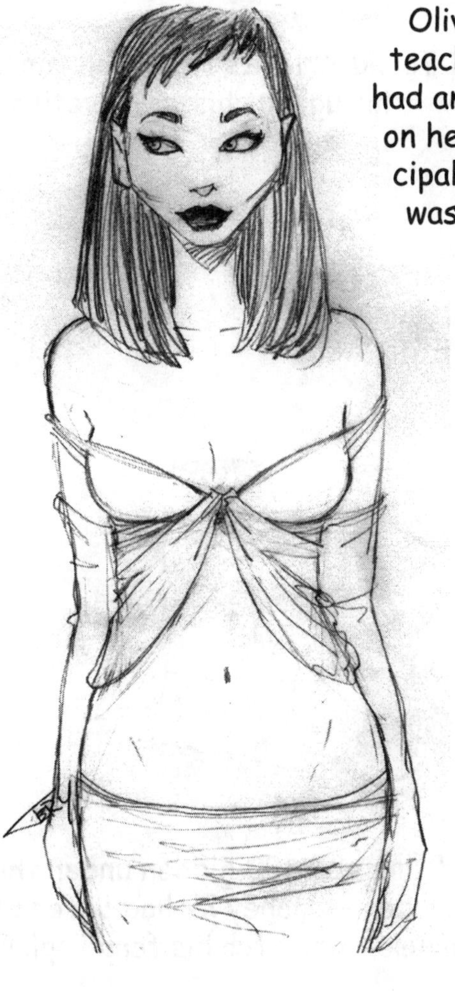

Olivia, the new drama teacher at Porkpie High, had anticipated a few looks on her first day, but Principal Hathaway's drooling was totally unexpected.

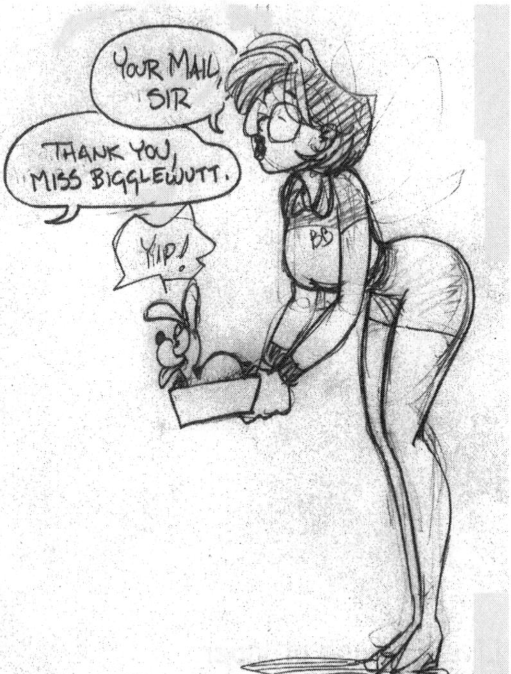

YOUR MAIL, SIR
THANK YOU, MISS BIGGLEWUTT.
YIP!
BB

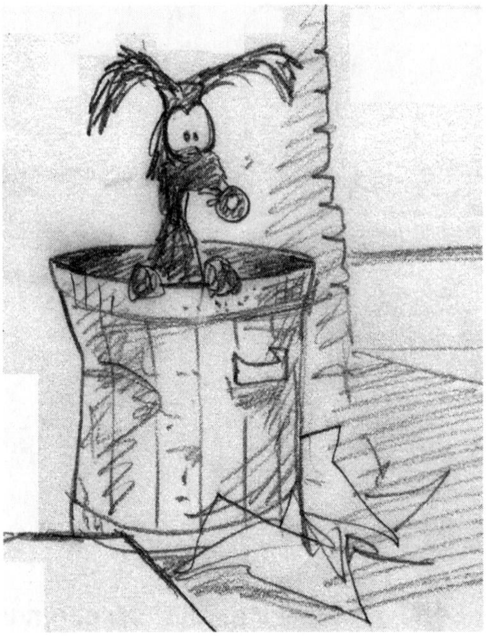

Morris loved to drink from the toilet
but the blackouts were hell.

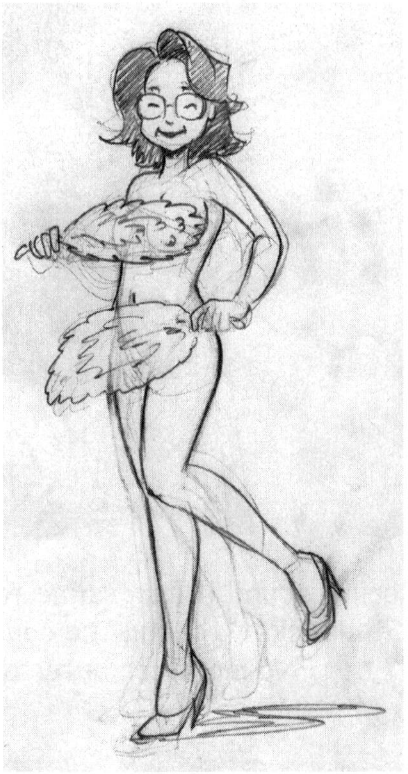

I found Arlene's report on fan gir
throughout history riveting.

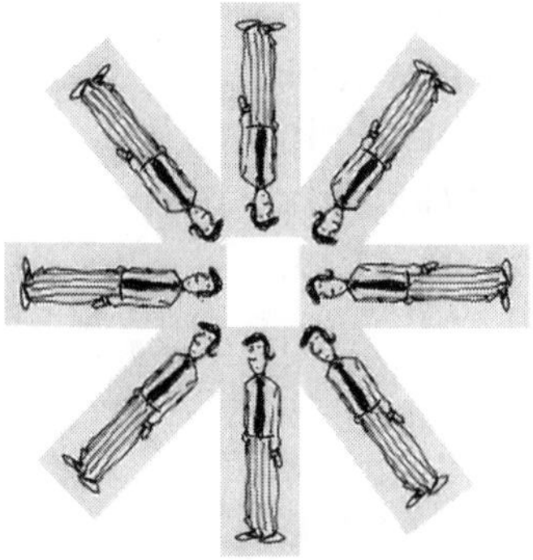

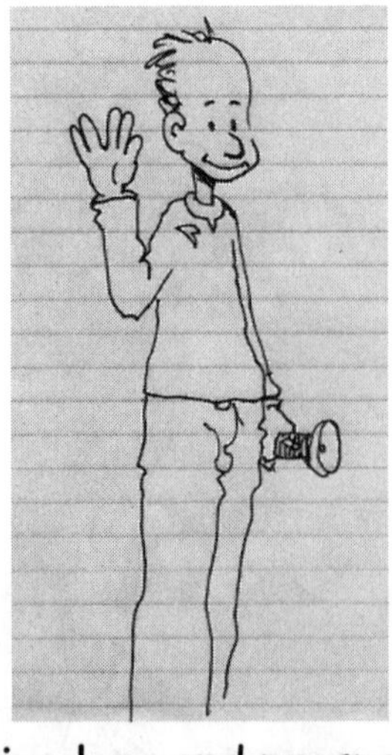

Live long and prosper

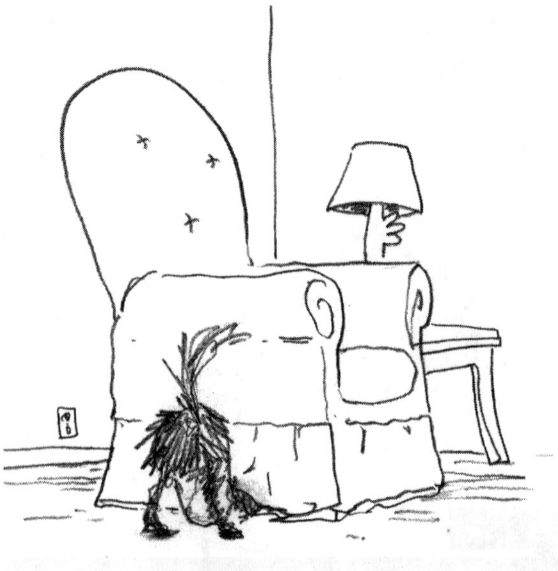

Morris had almost $400 hidden under the
chair in the den — money he had pilfered
around the house to pay for his fang implants

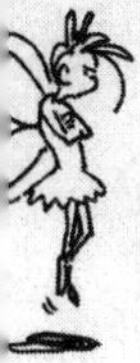

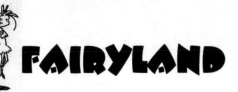

FAIRYLAND

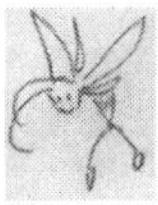

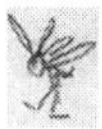

Von't you come along to a fairyland with me,
place where magic rains up from the green and purple seas?
Vhere little baby clouds kiss the top of baby trees,
nd forty pretty maids keep a cottage just for me.

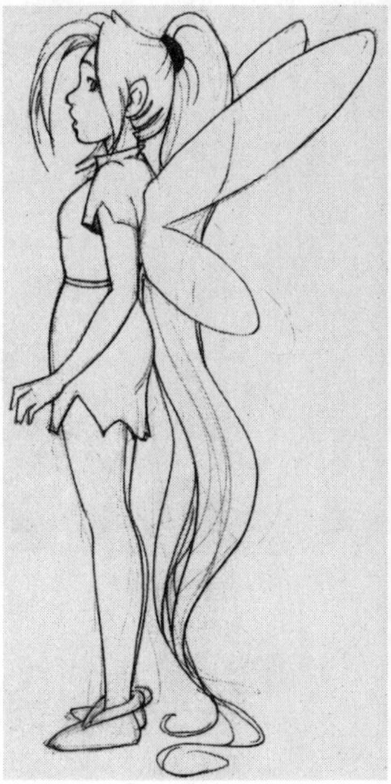

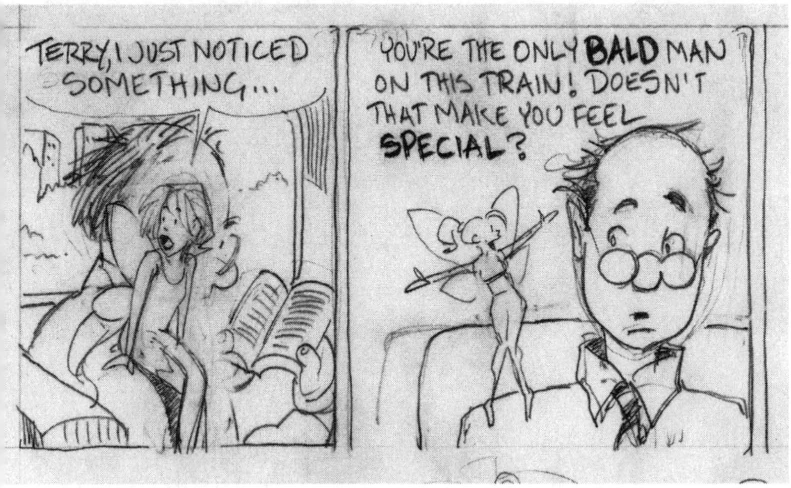
TERRY, I JUST NOTICED SOMETHING...
YOU'RE THE ONLY BALD MAN ON THIS TRAIN! DOESN'T THAT MAKE YOU FEEL SPECIAL?

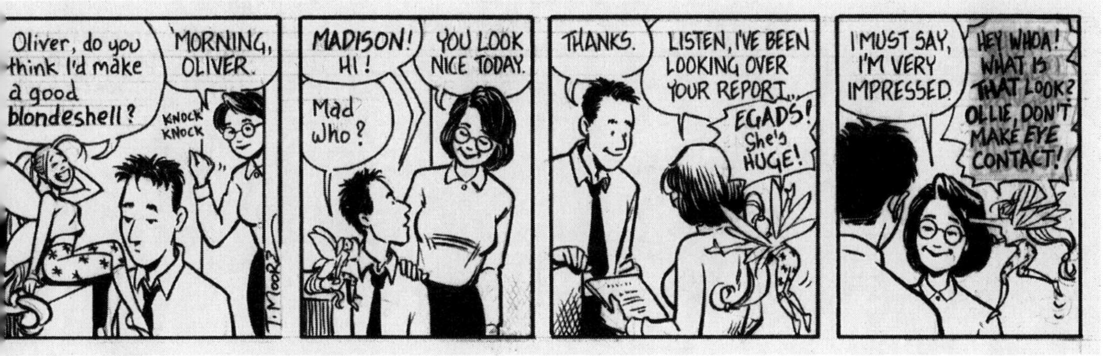
Oliver, do you think I'd make a good blondeshell?
'MORNING, OLIVER.
KNOCK KNOCK
T. MOORE
MADISON! HI!
YOU LOOK NICE TODAY.
Mad who?
THANKS.
LISTEN, I'VE BEEN LOOKING OVER YOUR REPORT...
EGADS! She's HUGE!
I MUST SAY, I'M VERY IMPRESSED.
HEY WHOA! WHAT IS THAT LOOK? OLLIE, DON'T MAKE EYE CONTACT!

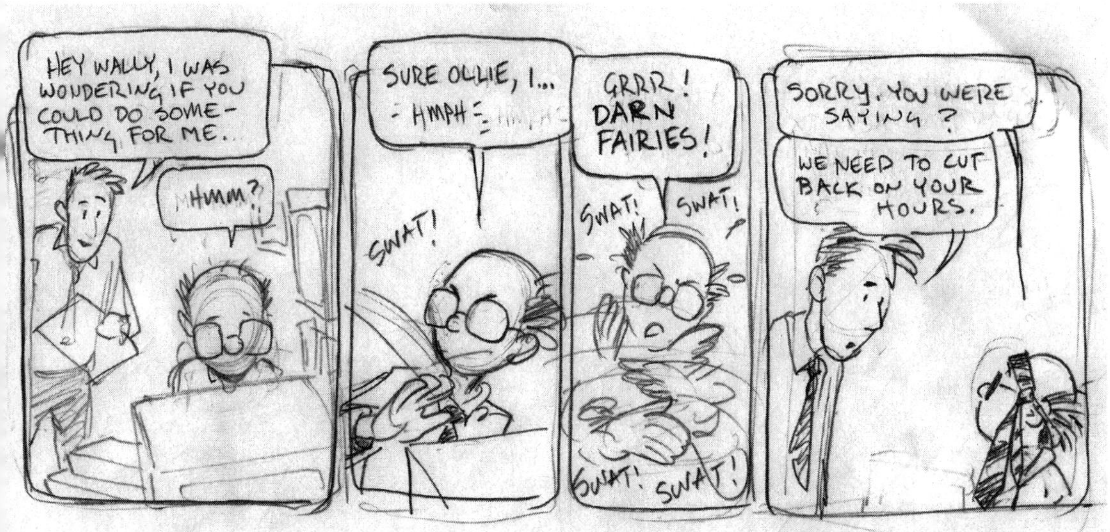
HEY WALLY, I WAS WONDERING IF YOU COULD DO SOME-THING FOR ME...
MHMM?
SURE OLLIE, I... HMPH
SWAT!
GRRR! DARN FAIRIES!
SWAT!
SWAT!
SWAT!
SWAT!
SORRY. YOU WERE SAYING?
WE NEED TO CUT BACK ON YOUR HOURS.

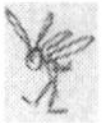

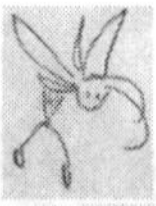

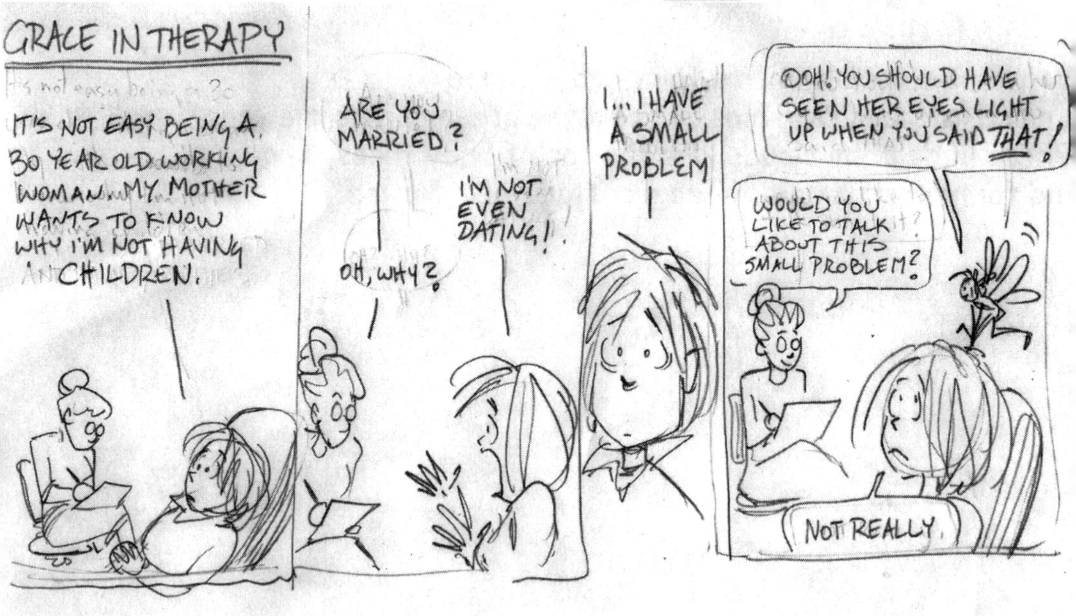
GRACE IN THERAPY
IT'S NOT EASY BEING A 30 YEAR OLD WORKING WOMAN... MY MOTHER WANTS TO KNOW WHY I'M NOT HAVING CHILDREN.
ARE YOU MARRIED?
I'M NOT EVEN DATING!
OH, WHY?
I... I HAVE A SMALL PROBLEM
OOH! YOU SHOULD HAVE SEEN HER EYES LIGHT UP WHEN YOU SAID THAT!
WOULD YOU LIKE TO TALK ABOUT THIS SMALL PROBLEM?
NOT REALLY

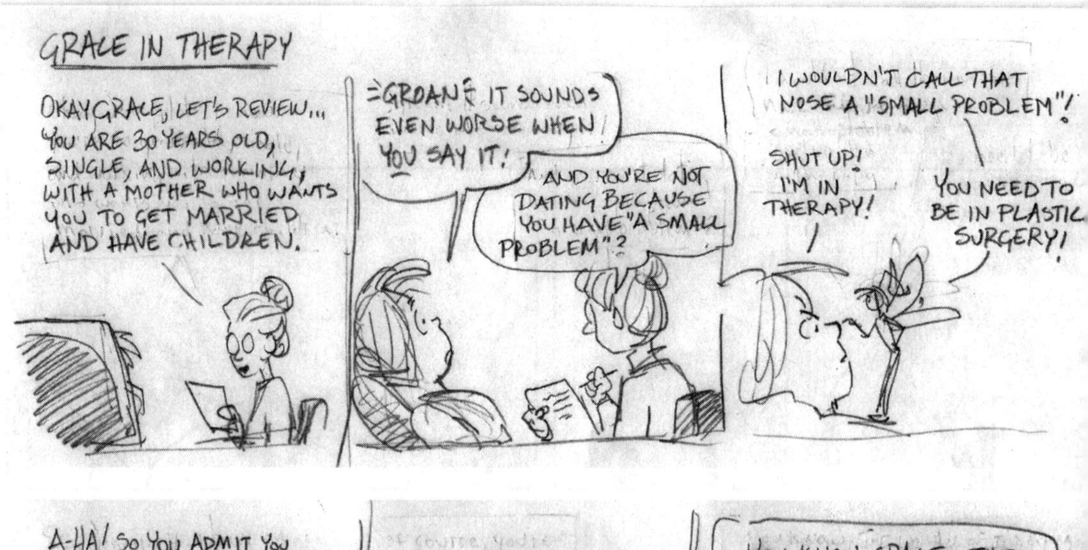
GRACE IN THERAPY
OKAY GRACE, LET'S REVIEW... YOU ARE 30 YEARS OLD, SINGLE, AND WORKING, WITH A MOTHER WHO WANTS YOU TO GET MARRIED AND HAVE CHILDREN.
=GROAN= IT SOUNDS EVEN WORSE WHEN YOU SAY IT!
AND YOU'RE NOT DATING BECAUSE YOU HAVE "A SMALL PROBLEM"?
I WOULDN'T CALL THAT NOSE A "SMALL PROBLEM"!
SHUT UP! I'M IN THERAPY!
YOU NEED TO BE IN PLASTIC SURGERY!

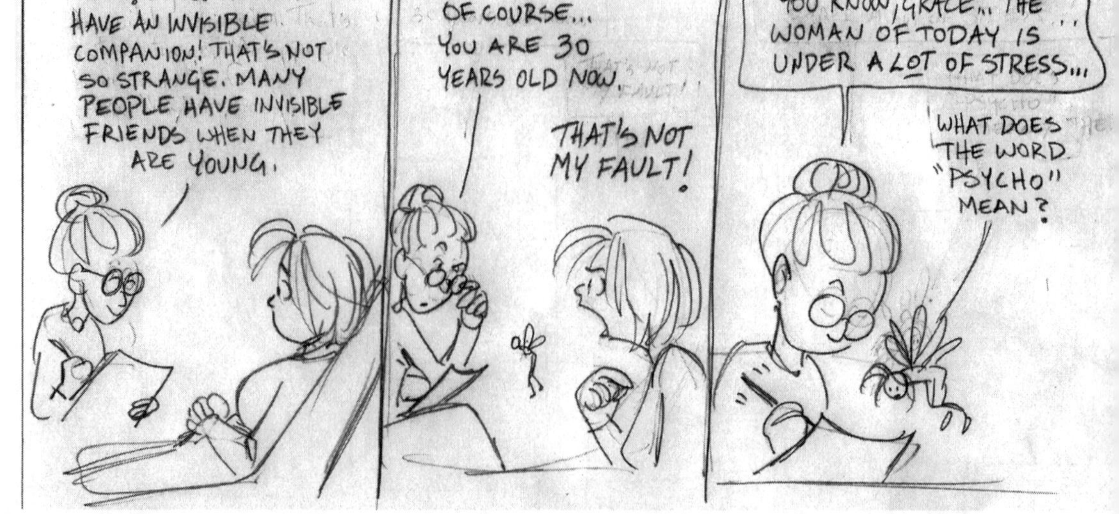
A-HA! SO YOU ADMIT YOU HAVE AN INVISIBLE COMPANION! THAT'S NOT SO STRANGE. MANY PEOPLE HAVE INVISIBLE FRIENDS WHEN THEY ARE YOUNG.
OF COURSE... YOU ARE 30 YEARS OLD NOW.
THAT'S NOT MY FAULT!
YOU KNOW, GRACE... THE WOMAN OF TODAY IS UNDER A LOT OF STRESS...
WHAT DOES THE WORD "PSYCHO" MEAN?

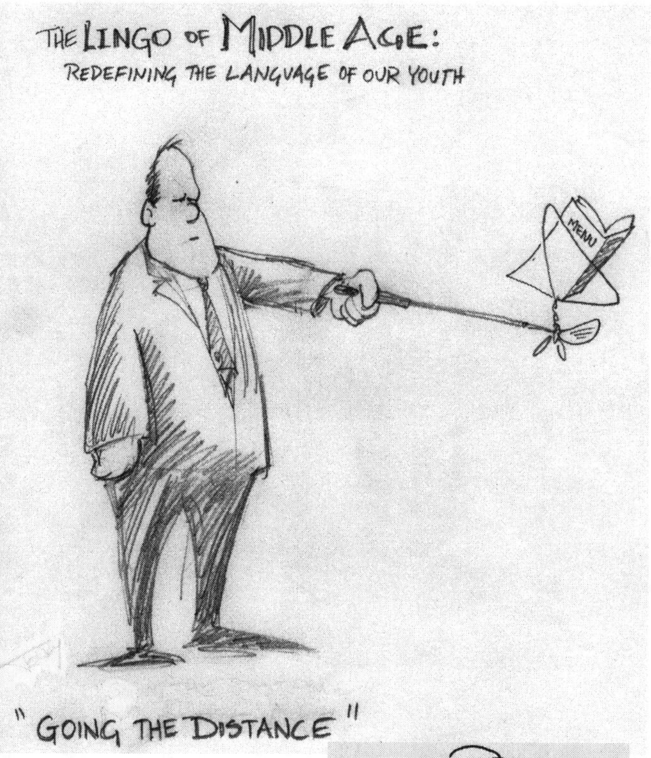
THE LINGO OF MIDDLE AGE:
REDEFINING THE LANGUAGE OF OUR YOUTH
MENU
"GOING THE DISTANCE"

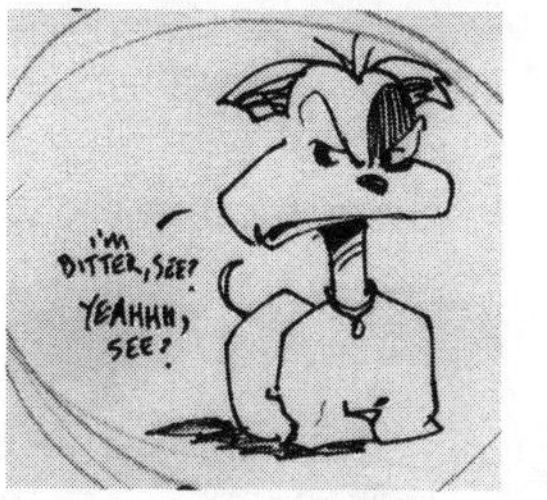
I'm BITTER, SEE?
YEAHHH, SEE?

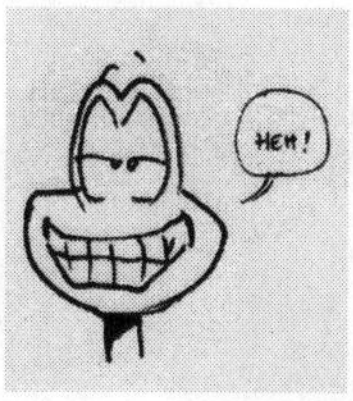
HEH!

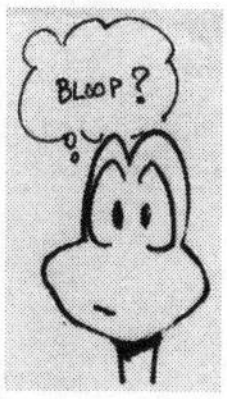
BLOOP?

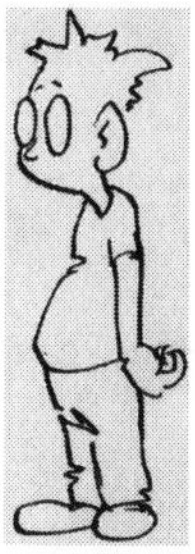

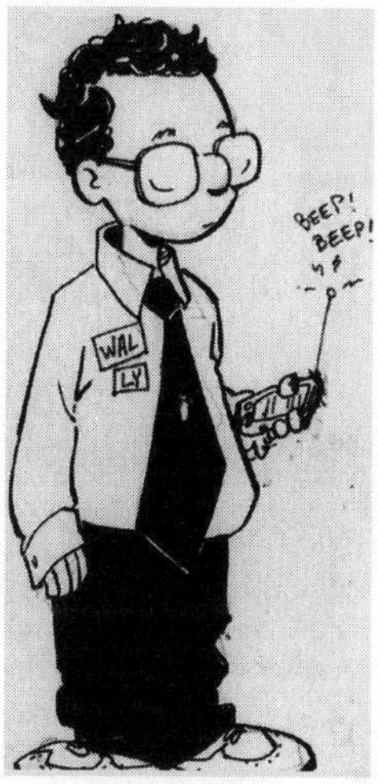
BEEP! BEEP!
WAL
LY

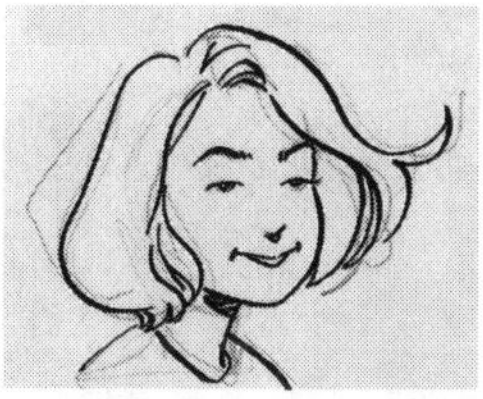

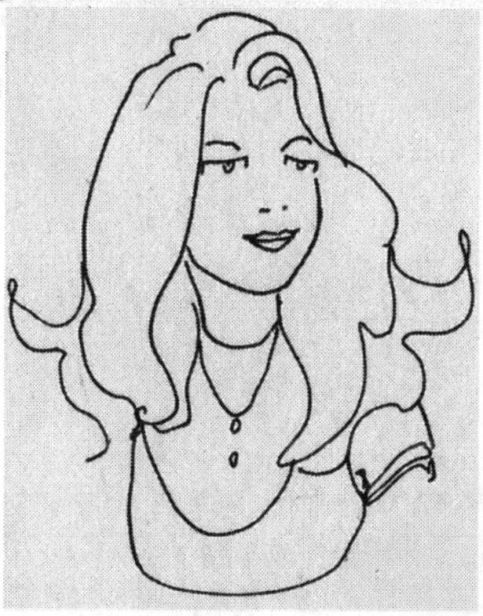

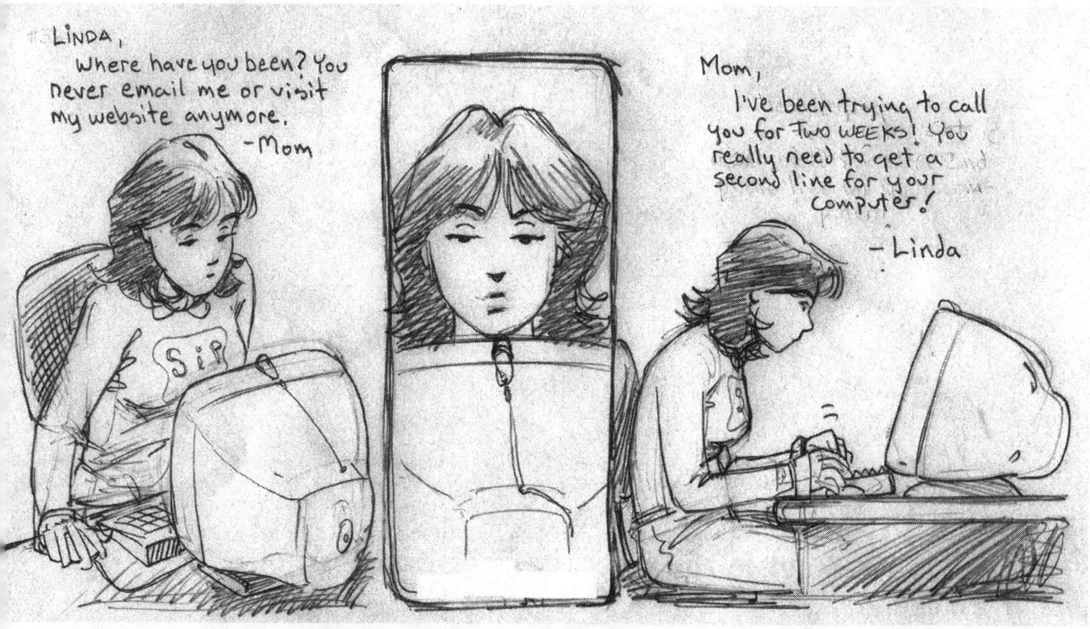
Linda,
Where have you been? You never email me or visit my website anymore.
-Mom
Mom,
I've been trying to call you for TWO WEEKS! You really need to get a second line for your computer!
-Linda
SiP

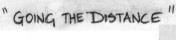

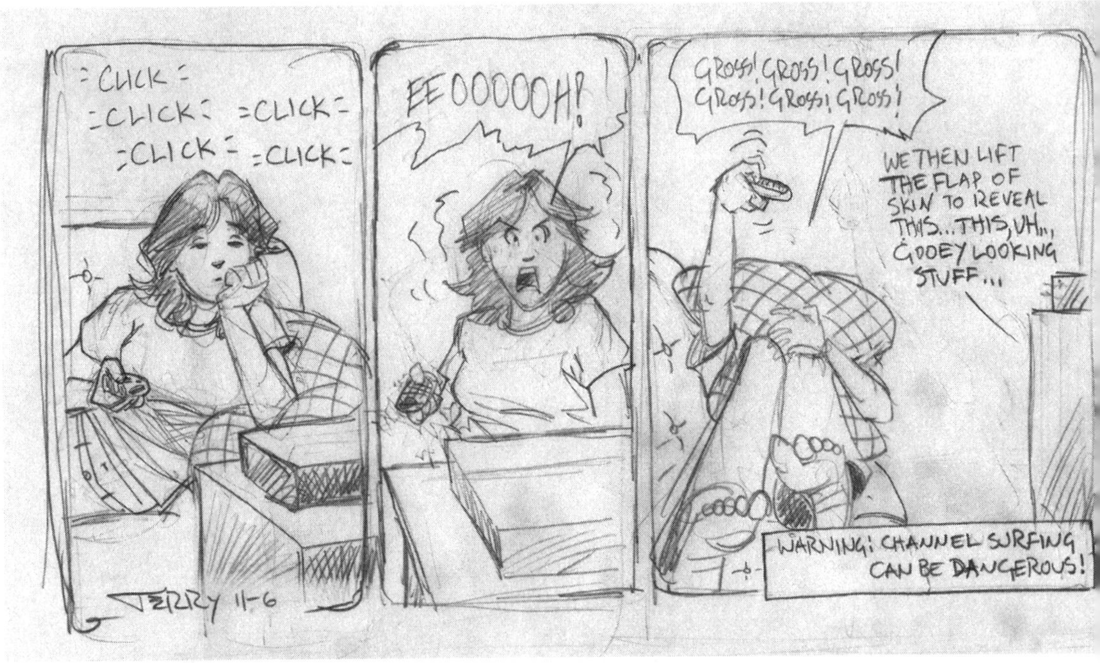

CLICK
CLICK
CLICK
CLICK
CLICK
TERRY 11-6
EEOOOOOH!
GROSS! GROSS! GROSS! GROSS! GROSS! GROSS!
WE THEN LIFT THE FLAP OF SKIN TO REVEAL THIS...THIS, UH... GOOEY LOOKING STUFF...
WARNING: CHANNEL SURFING CAN BE DANGEROUS!

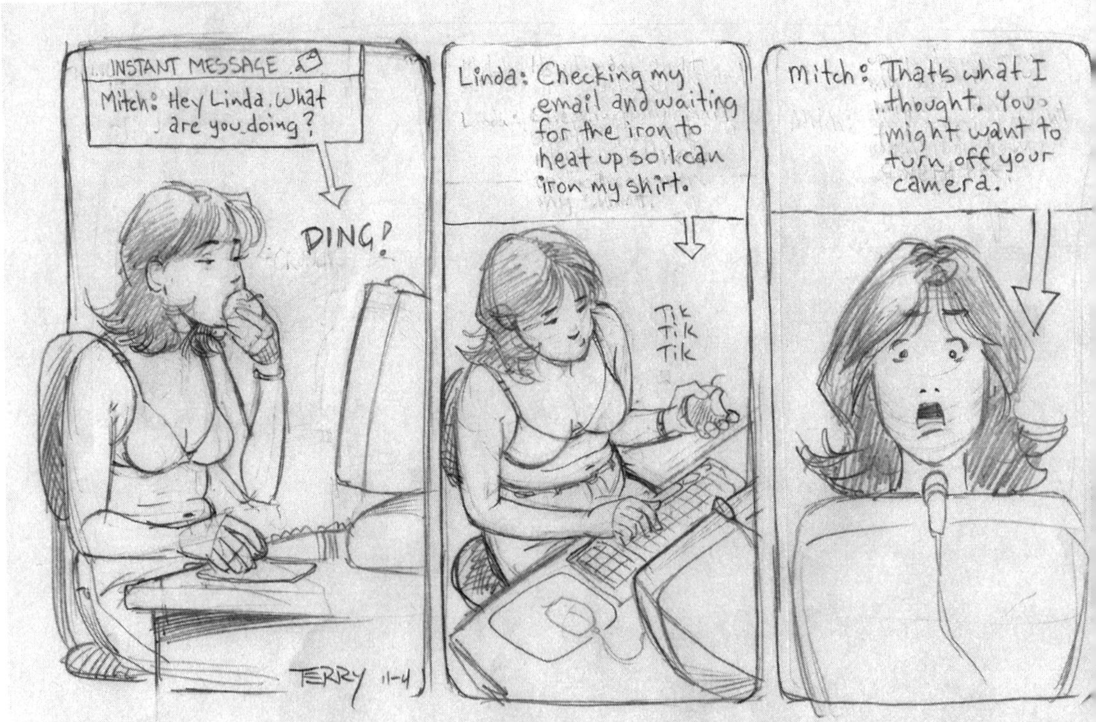

INSTANT MESSAGE
Mitch: Hey Linda. What are you doing?
DING!
TERRY 11-4
Linda: Checking my email and waiting for the iron to heat up so I can iron my shirt.
Tik
Tik
Tik
mitch: That's what I thought. You might want to turn off your camera.

The problem with Shih Tzus is you tend to give the doggie treat to the wrong end.

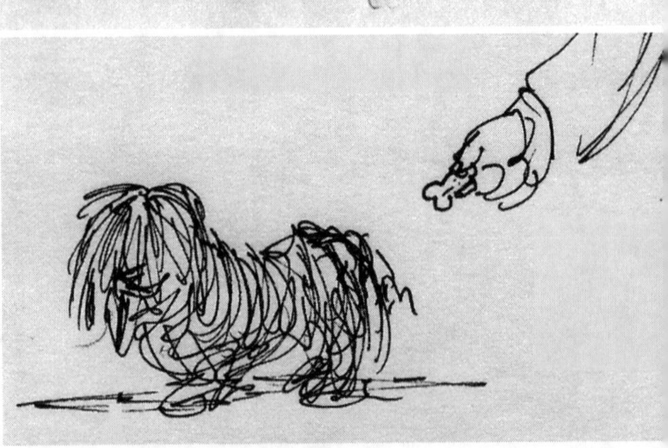

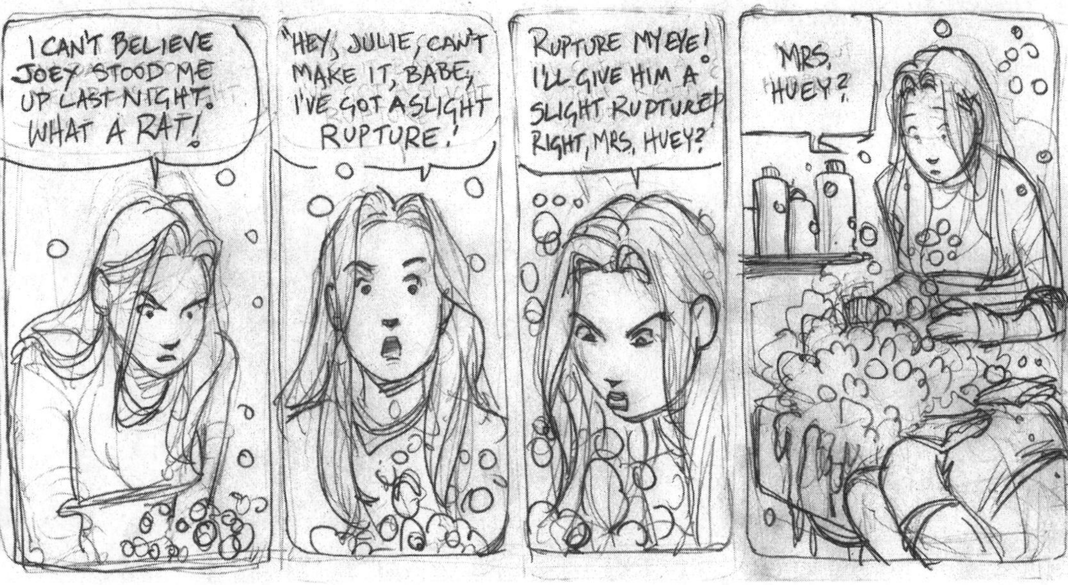
I CAN'T BELIEVE JOEY STOOD ME UP LAST NIGHT. WHAT A RAT!
"HEY, JULIE, CAN'T MAKE IT, BABE, I'VE GOT A SLIGHT RUPTURE."
RUPTURE MY EYE! I'LL GIVE HIM A SLIGHT RUPTURE! RIGHT, MRS. HUEY?
MRS. HUEY?

MORRIS

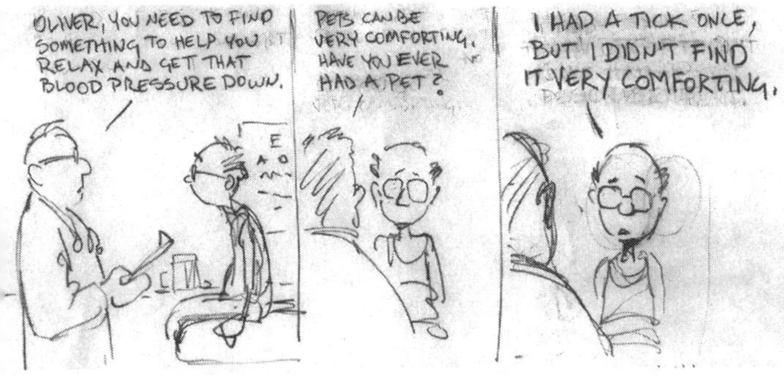
OLIVER, YOU NEED TO FIND SOMETHING TO HELP YOU RELAX AND GET THAT BLOOD PRESSURE DOWN.
PETS CAN BE VERY COMFORTING. HAVE YOU EVER HAD A PET?
I HAD A TICK ONCE, BUT I DIDN'T FIND IT VERY COMFORTING.

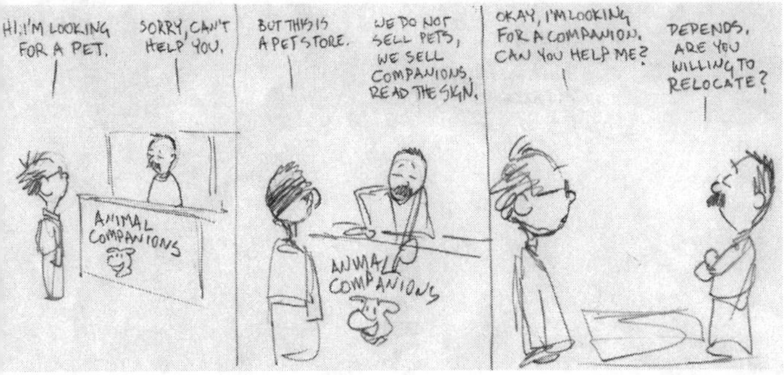
HI. I'M LOOKING FOR A PET.
SORRY, CAN'T HELP YOU.
ANIMAL COMPANIONS
BUT THIS IS A PET STORE.
WE DO NOT SELL PETS, WE SELL COMPANIONS. READ THE SIGN.
ANIMAL COMPANIONS
OKAY, I'M LOOKING FOR A COMPANION. CAN YOU HELP ME?
DEPENDS. ARE YOU WILLING TO RELOCATE?

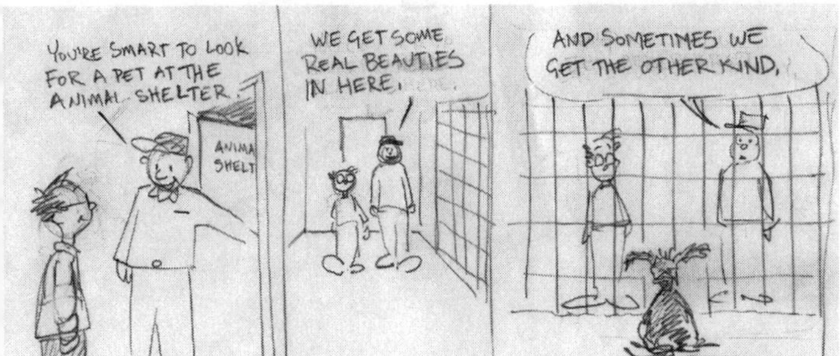
YOU'RE SMART TO LOOK FOR A PET AT THE ANIMAL SHELTER.
WE GET SOME REAL BEAUTIES IN HERE.
AND SOMETIMES WE GET THE OTHER KIND.

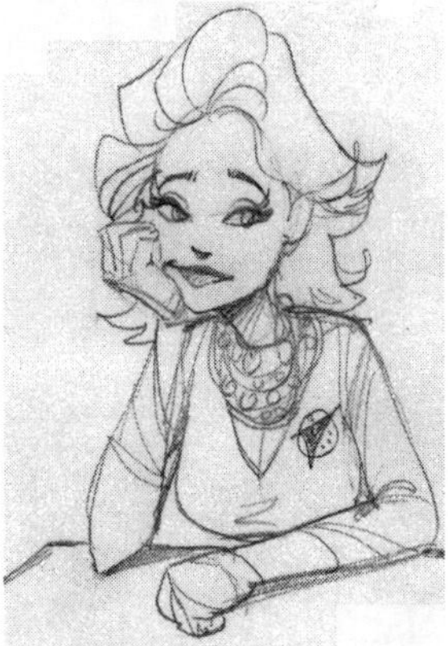

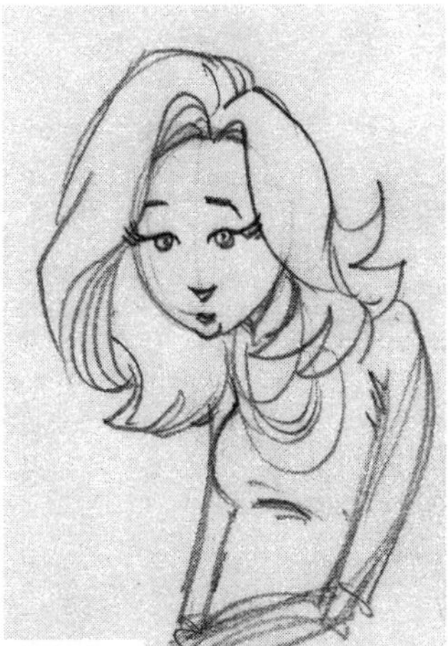

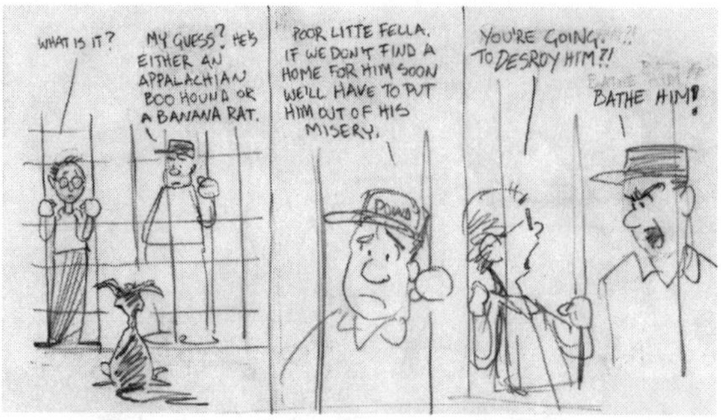
WHAT IS IT?
MY GUESS? HE'S EITHER AN APPALACHIAN BOO HOUND OR A BANANA RAT.
POOR LITTE FELLA. IF WE DON'T FIND A HOME FOR HIM SOON WE'LL HAVE TO PUT HIM OUT OF HIS MISERY.
YOU'RE GOING TO DESROY HIM?!
BATHE HIM!

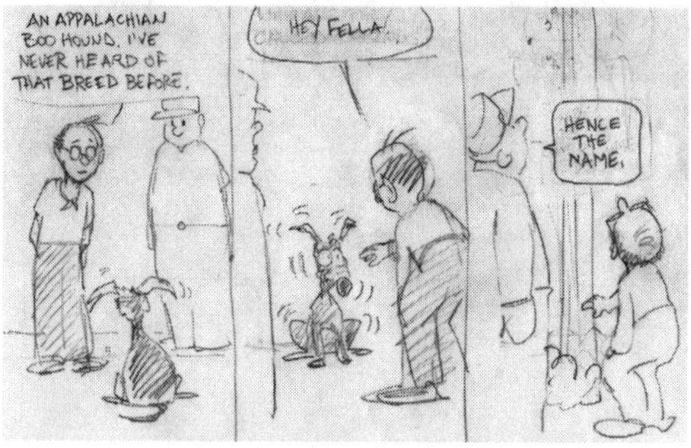
AN APPALACHIAN BOO HOUND. I'VE NEVER HEARD OF THAT BREED BEFORE.
HEY FELLA.
HENCE THE NAME.

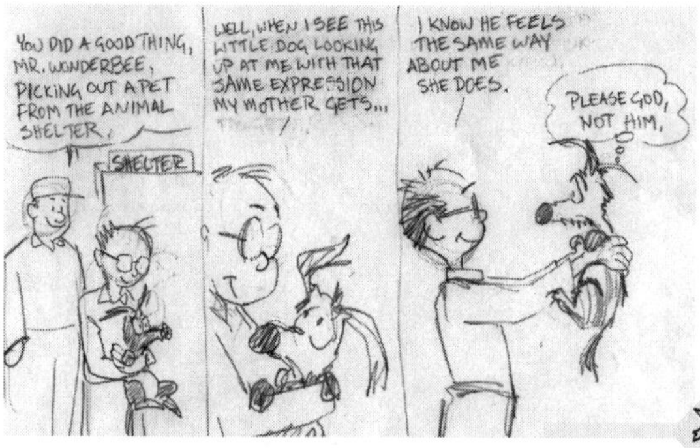
YOU DID A GOOD THING, MR. WONDERBEE, PICKING OUT A PET FROM THE ANIMAL SHELTER.
SHELTER
WELL, WHEN I SEE THIS LITTLE DOG LOOKING UP AT ME WITH THAT SAME EXPRESSION MY MOTHER GETS...
I KNOW HE FEELS THE SAME WAY ABOUT ME SHE DOES.
PLEASE GOD, NOT HIM.

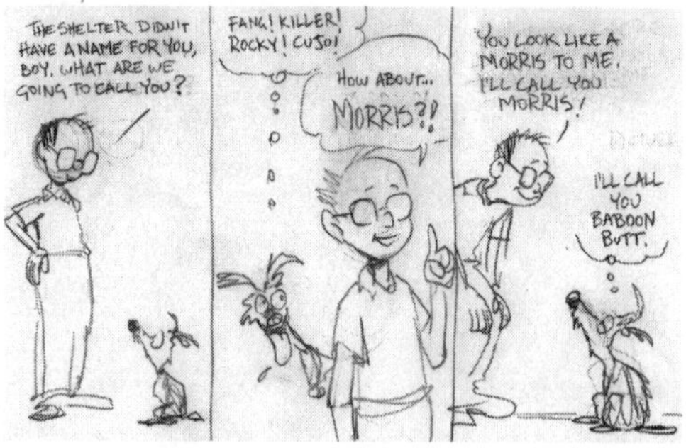
THE SHELTER DIDN'T HAVE A NAME FOR YOU, BOY. WHAT ARE WE GOING TO CALL YOU?
FANG! KILLER! ROCKY! CUJO!
HOW ABOUT... MORRIS?!
YOU LOOK LIKE A MORRIS TO ME. I'LL CALL YOU MORRIS!
I'LL CALL YOU BABOON BUTT.

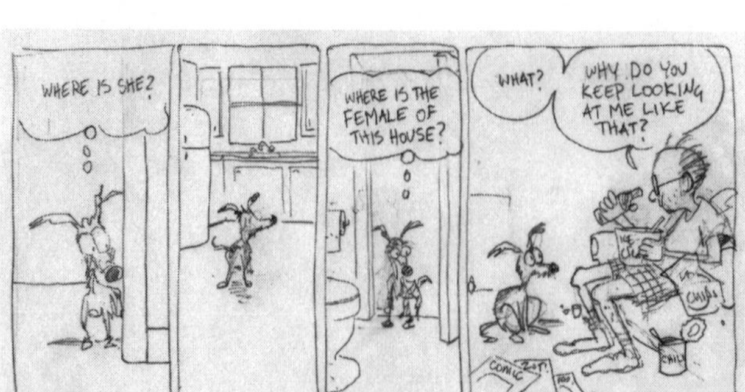
WHERE IS SHE?
WHERE IS THE FEMALE OF THIS HOUSE?
WHAT?
WHY DO YOU KEEP LOOKING AT ME LIKE THAT?

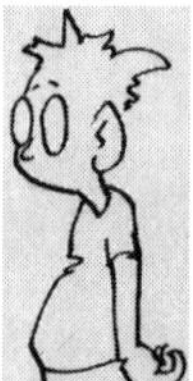

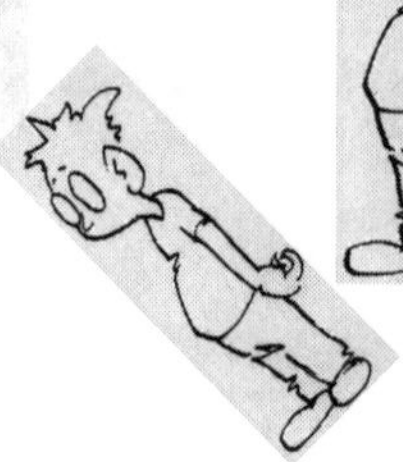

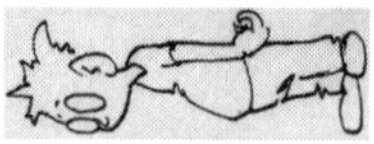

IN HIS SERVICE

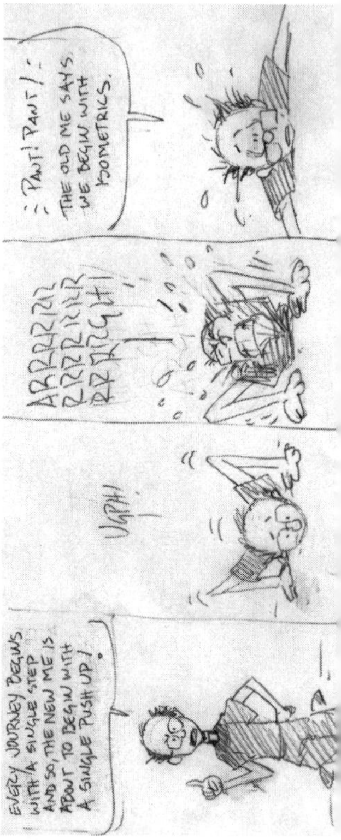
EVERY JOURNEY BEGINS WITH A SINGLE STEP AND SO, THE NEW ME IS ABOUT TO BEGIN WITH A SINGLE PUSH UP!
UGH!
ARRRRRRR RRRRRRRR RRRRGH!!
PANT! PANT! THE OLD ME SAYS WE BEGIN WITH ISOMETRICS.

IN HIS SERVICE

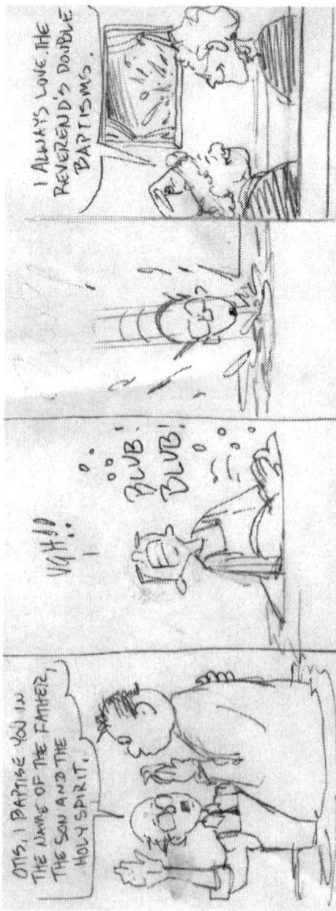
OTIS, I BAPTISE YOU IN THE NAME OF THE FATHER, THE SON AND THE HOLY SPIRIT.
UGH!!
BLUB! BLUB!
I ALWAYS LOVE THE REVEREND'S DOUBLE BAPTISMS.

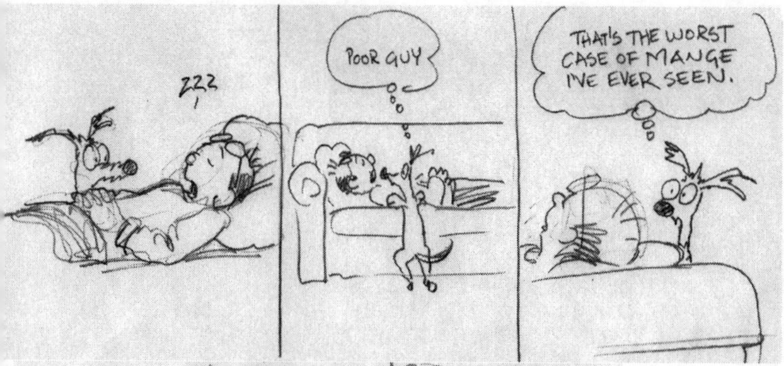
ZZZ
POOR GUY
THAT'S THE WORST CASE OF MANGE I'VE EVER SEEN.

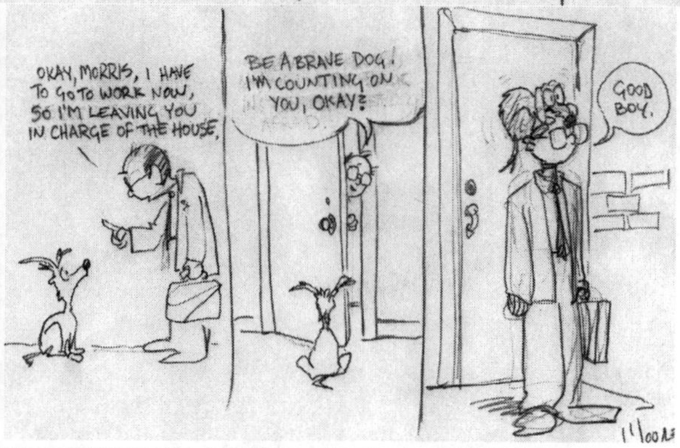
OKAY, MORRIS, I HAVE TO GO TO WORK NOW, SO I'M LEAVING YOU IN CHARGE OF THE HOUSE.
BE A BRAVE DOG! I'M COUNTING ON YOU, OKAY?
GOOD BOY.

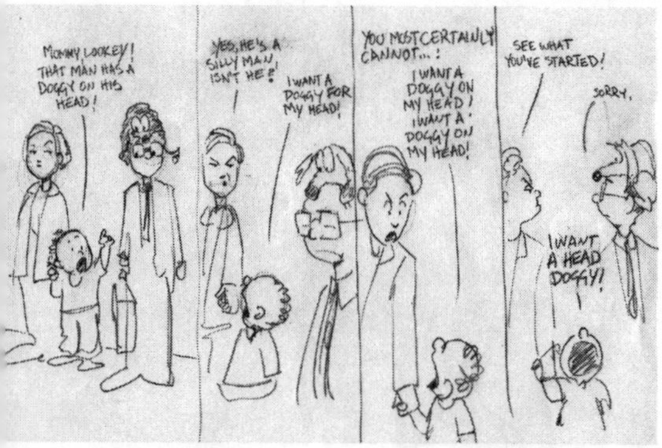
MOMMY LOOKEY! THAT MAN HAS A DOGGY ON HIS HEAD!
YES, HE'S A SILLY MAN, ISN'T HE?
I WANT A DOGGY FOR MY HEAD!
YOU MOST CERTAINLY CANNOT...!
I WANT A DOGGY ON MY HEAD! I WANT A DOGGY ON MY HEAD!
SEE WHAT YOU'VE STARTED!
SORRY.
I WANT A HEAD DOGGY!

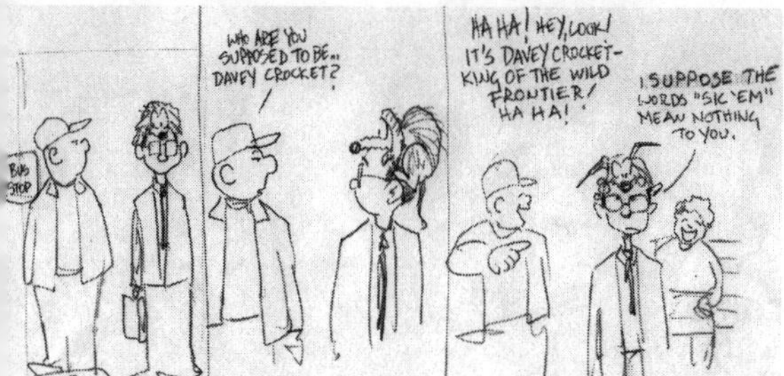
BUS STOP
WHO ARE YOU SUPPOSED TO BE.. DAVEY CROCKET?
HA HA! HEY, LOOK! IT'S DAVEY CROCKET-KING OF THE WILD FRONTIER! HA HA!
I SUPPOSE THE WORDS "SIC 'EM" MEAN NOTHING TO YOU.

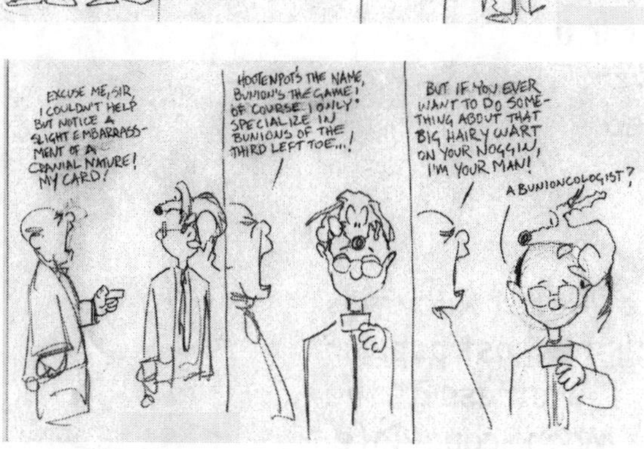
EXCUSE ME, SIR, I COULDN'T HELP BUT NOTICE A SLIGHT EMBARRASS-MENT OF A CRANIAL NATURE! MY CARD!
HOOTENPOT'S THE NAME, BUNIONS THE GAME! OF COURSE, I ONLY SPECIALIZE IN BUNIONS OF THE THIRD LEFT TOE...!
BUT IF YOU EVER WANT TO DO SOME-THING ABOUT THAT BIG HAIRY WART ON YOUR NOGGIN, I'M YOUR MAN!
A BUNIONCOLOGIST?

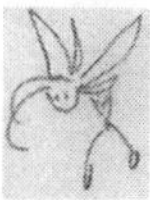

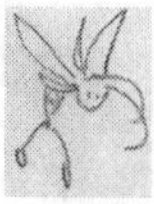

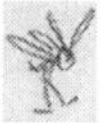

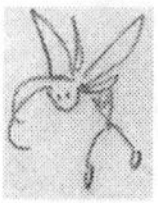

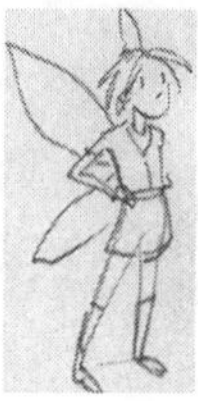

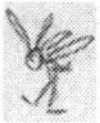

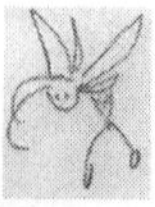

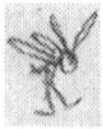

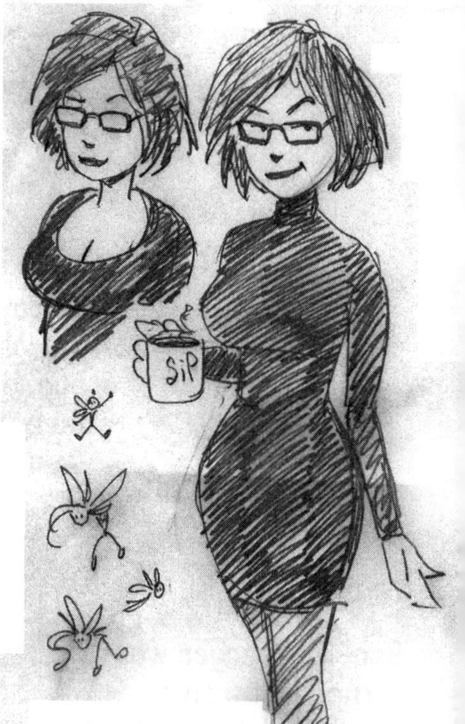
SIP

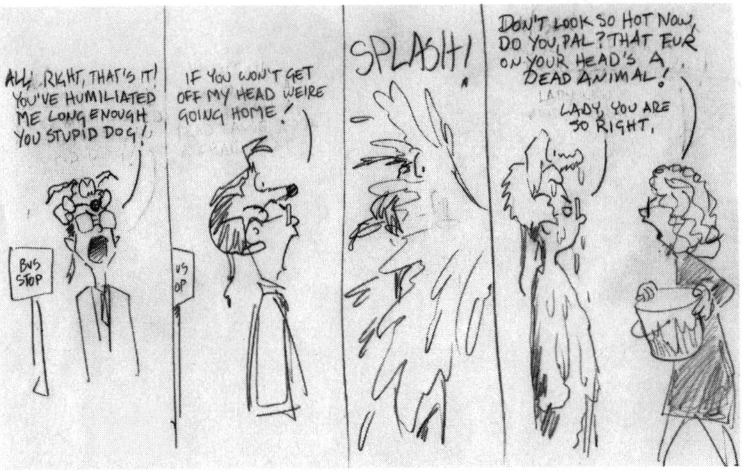
ALL RIGHT, THAT'S IT! YOU'VE HUMILIATED ME LONG ENOUGH YOU STUPID DOG!
BUS STOP
IF YOU WON'T GET OFF MY HEAD WEIRE GOING HOME!
SPLASH!
DON'T LOOK SO HOT NOW, DO YOU, PAL? THAT FUR ON YOUR HEAD'S A DEAD ANIMAL!
LADY, YOU ARE SO RIGHT.

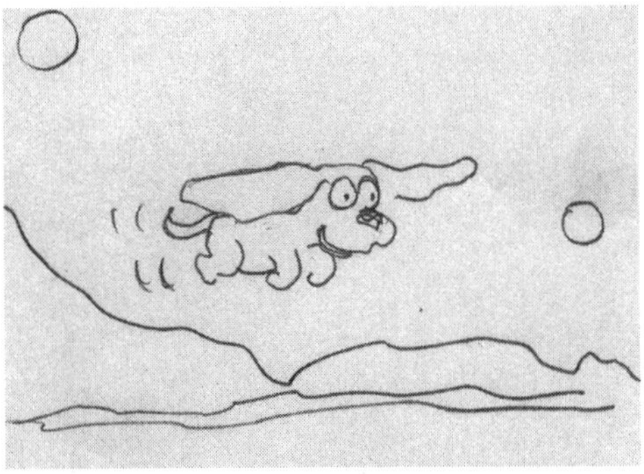

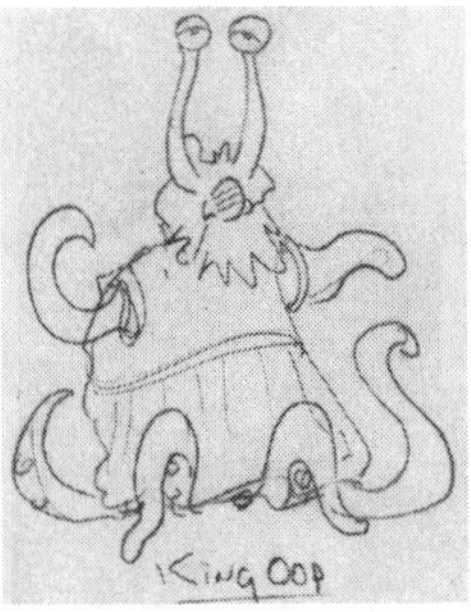
King Oop

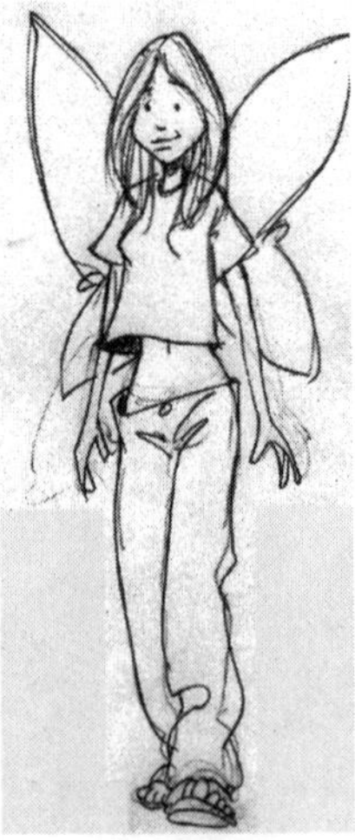

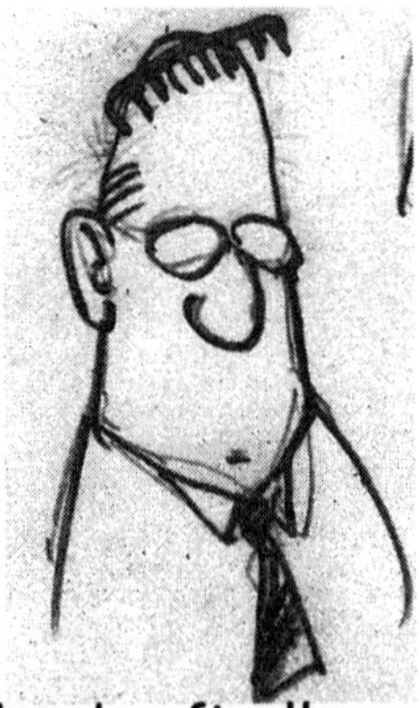

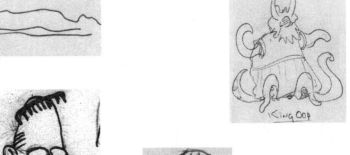

The day finally came when Harvis didn't have enough hair left for a decent comb over, so he improvised.

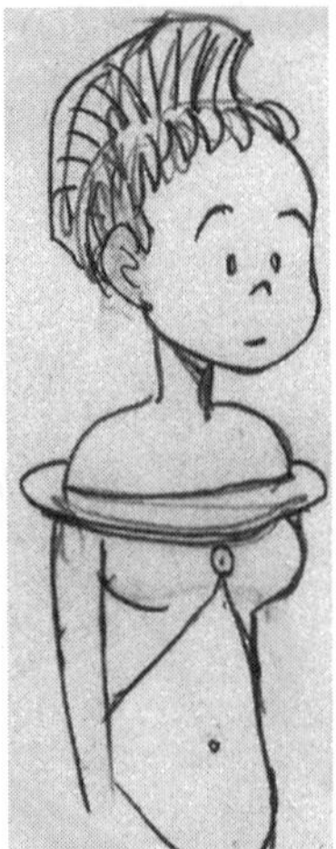

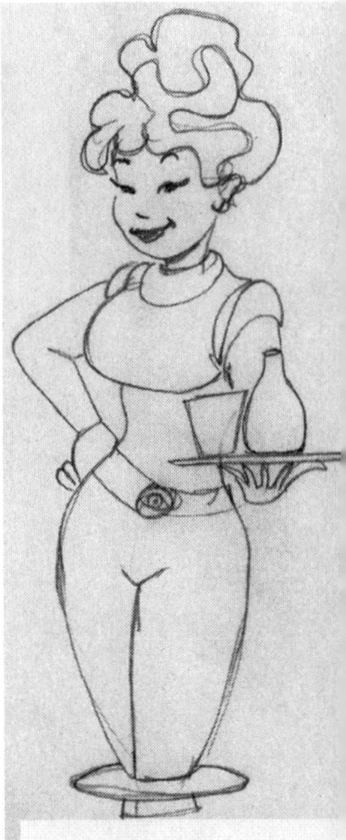

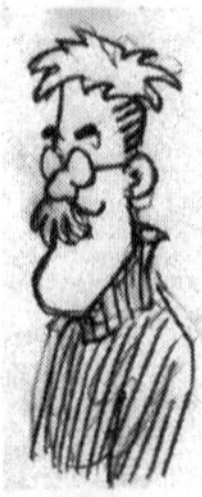

Ben Turdnergen was the first man to scale Mt. Everest in high heels.

Jet Cadet Riley was the most popular waitress at the MoonScape Cafe.

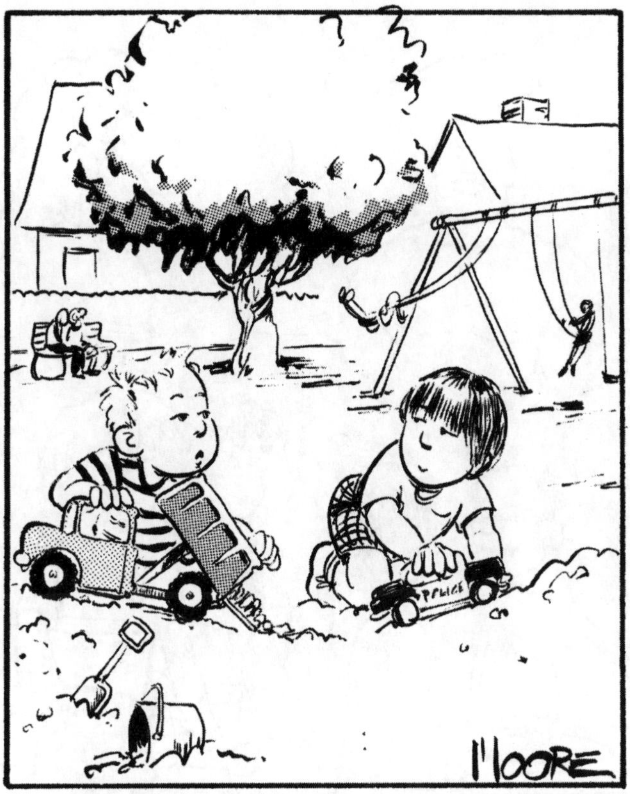
MOORE

Personally, I don't believe in spanking.

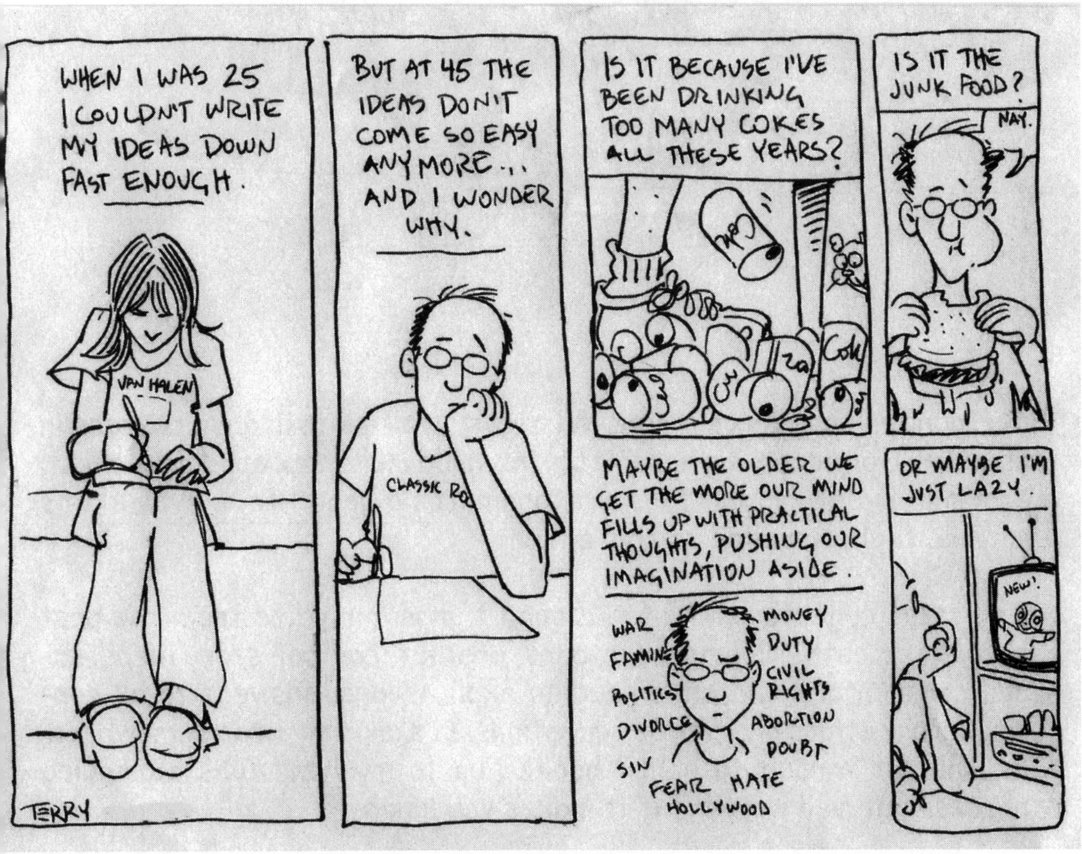
WHEN I WAS 25 I COULDN'T WRITE MY IDEAS DOWN FAST ENOUGH.
VAN HALEN
TERRY
BUT AT 45 THE IDEAS DON'T COME SO EASY ANY MORE... AND I WONDER WHY.
CLASSIC RO
IS IT BECAUSE I'VE BEEN DRINKING TOO MANY COKES ALL THESE YEARS?
IS IT THE JUNK FOOD?
NAY.
MAYBE THE OLDER WE GET THE MORE OUR MIND FILLS UP WITH PRACTICAL THOUGHTS, PUSHING OUR IMAGINATION ASIDE.
WAR
FAMINE
POLITICS
DIVORCE
SIN
MONEY
DUTY
CIVIL RIGHTS
ABORTION
DOUBT
FEAR HATE
HOLLYWOOD
OR MAYBE I'M JUST LAZY.
NEW!

Cartoonists have a great life. Whatever we lack in life we possess in abundance on paper. Things like brains, good looks, sex appeal... a chest. I've said it before and I'll say it again, it's a good life. Maybe that's why we feel compelled to share it.

This issue collects some of the good things in my life from the past couple of months. Political cartoons, doodles, cartoon story ideas, social commentary, blatant Freudian explorations, answers to all contemporary ethics and physics questions. It's all in my head somewhere, leaking out through a pencil hooked up to my hand. It's a grueling process but well worth it if it makes you laugh.

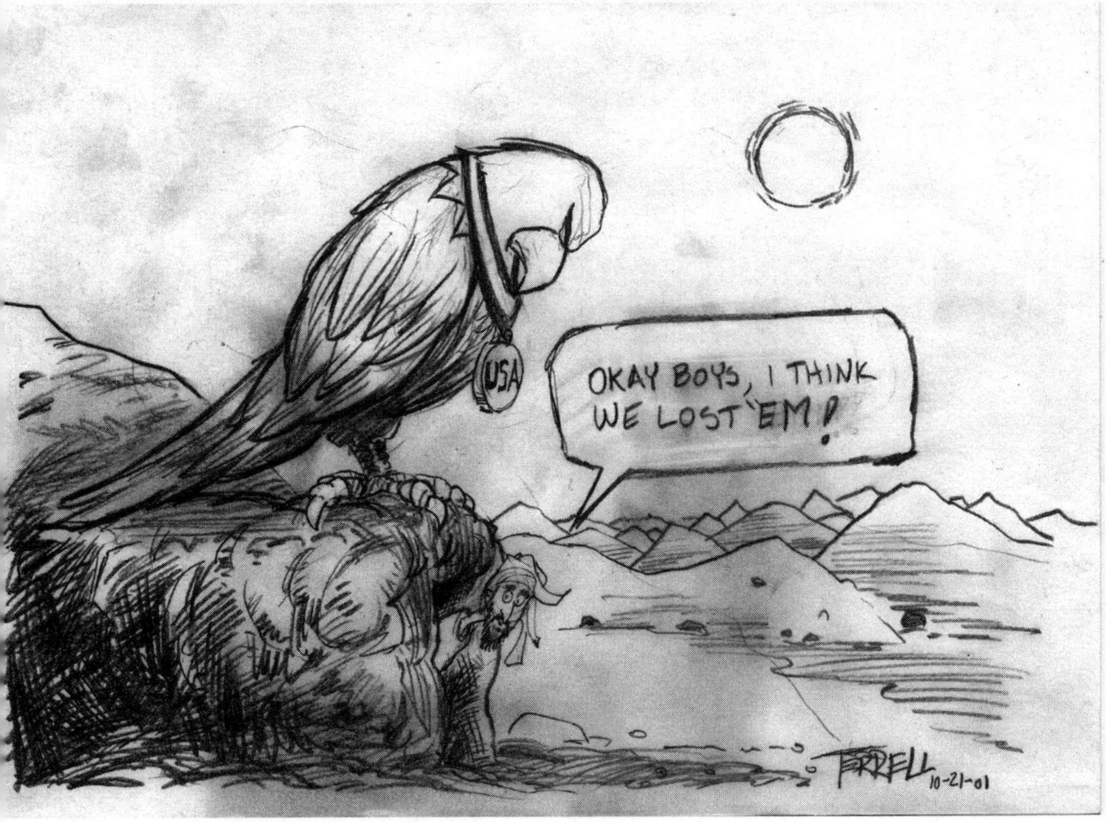
USA
OKAY BOYS, I THINK WE LOST 'EM!
FERRELL 10-21-01

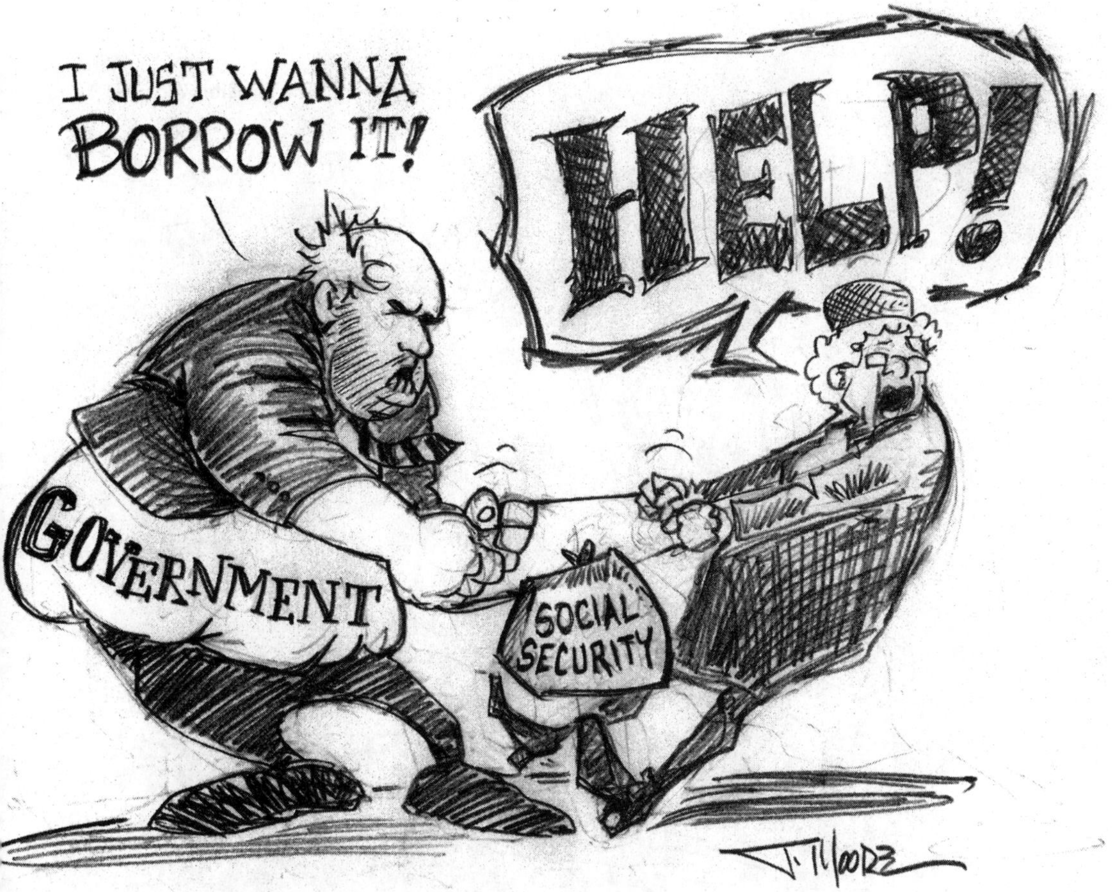
I JUST WANNA BORROW IT!
HELP!
GOVERNMENT
SOCIAL SECURITY
J. MOORE

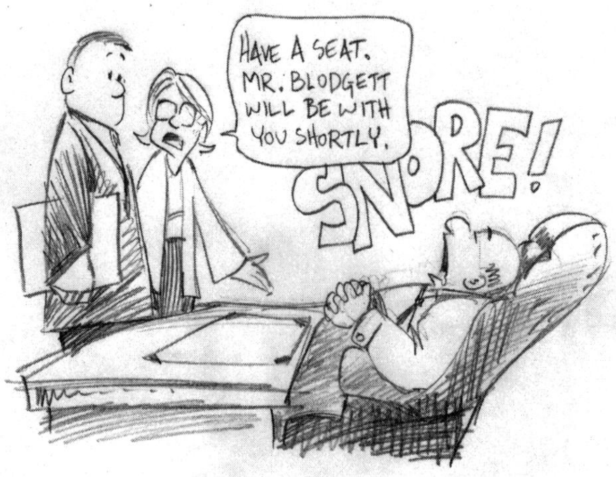
HAVE A SEAT. MR. BLODGETT WILL BE WITH YOU SHORTLY.
SNORE!

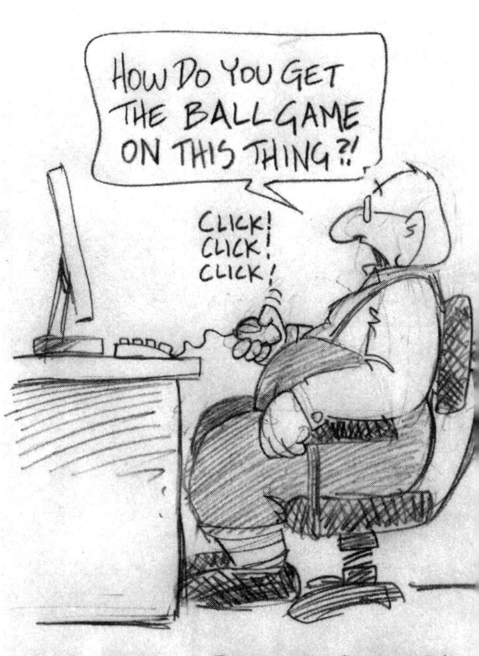
HOW DO YOU GET THE BALLGAME ON THIS THING?!
CLICK! CLICK! CLICK!
WE REALLY PREFER GRANDPA STAY OFF THE COMPUTER.

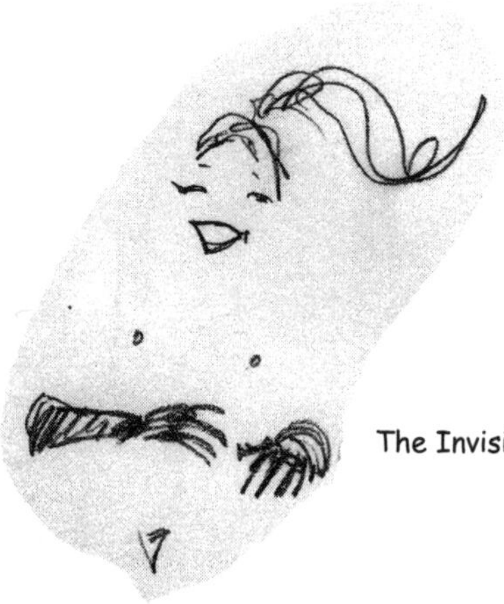
The Invisible Woman

The Invisible Man

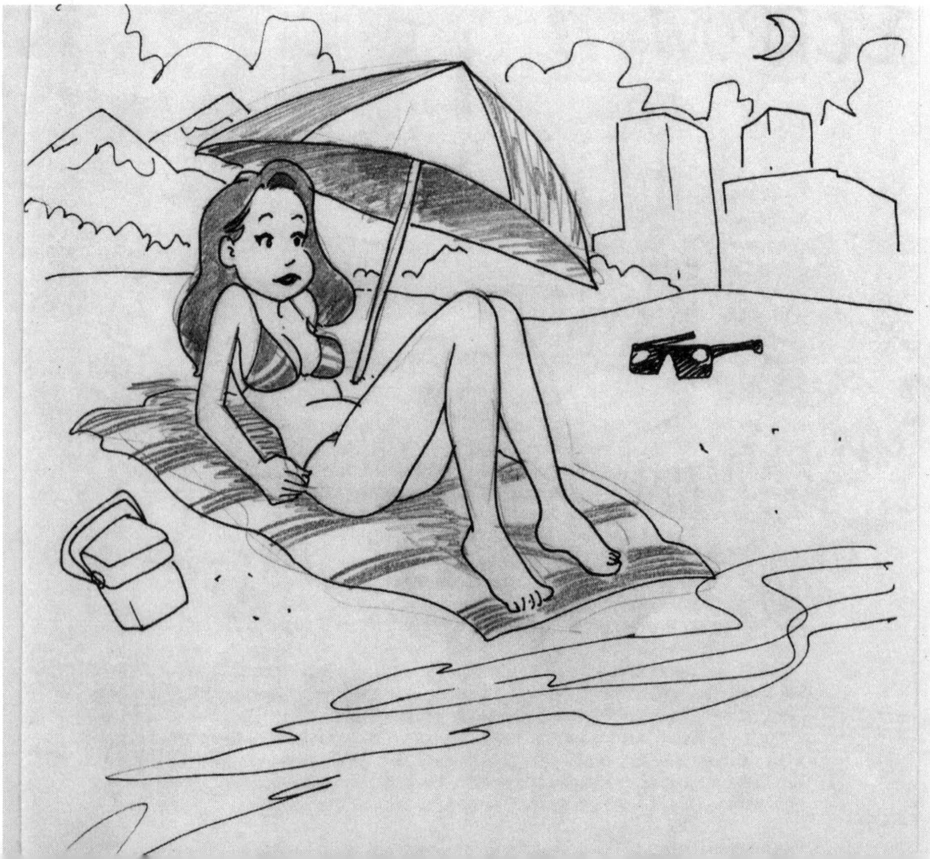

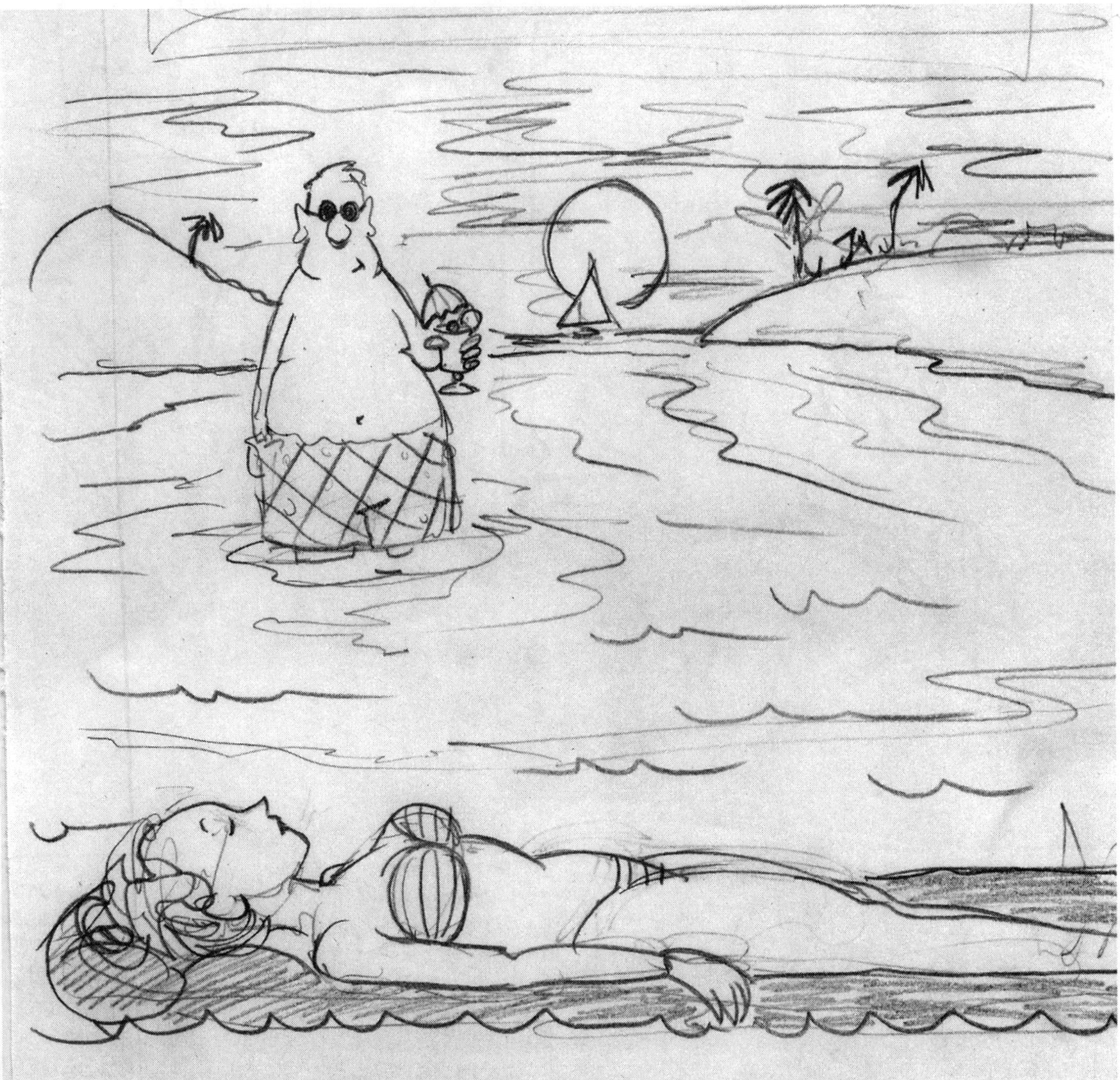

HOWARD'S MOST EXCELLENT VACATION

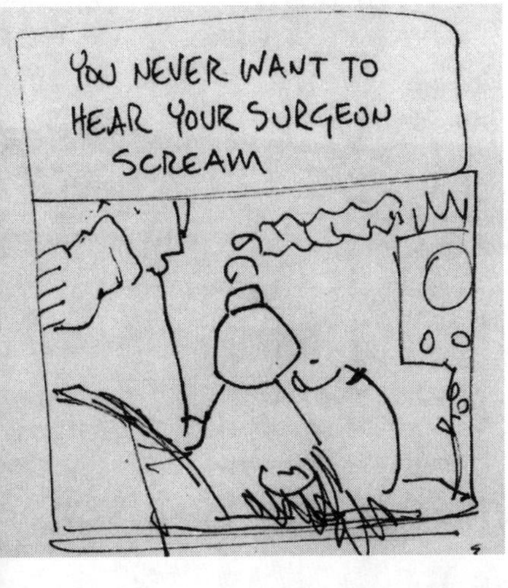
YOU NEVER WANT TO HEAR YOUR SURGEON SCREAM

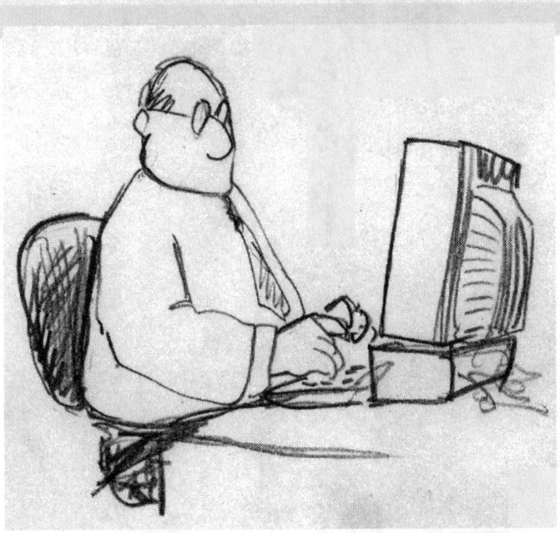

"DEAR MARTY,
ACTUALLY, I AM NEITHER A REPUBLICAN NOR A DEMOCRAT... I PREFER TO THINK OF MYSELF AS A REPUBLICRAT."

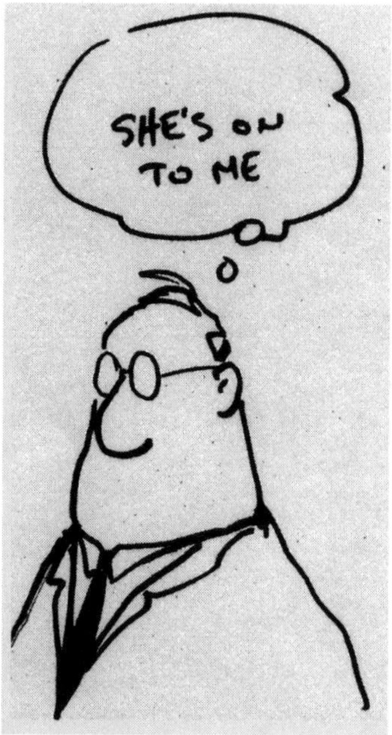
SHE'S ON TO ME

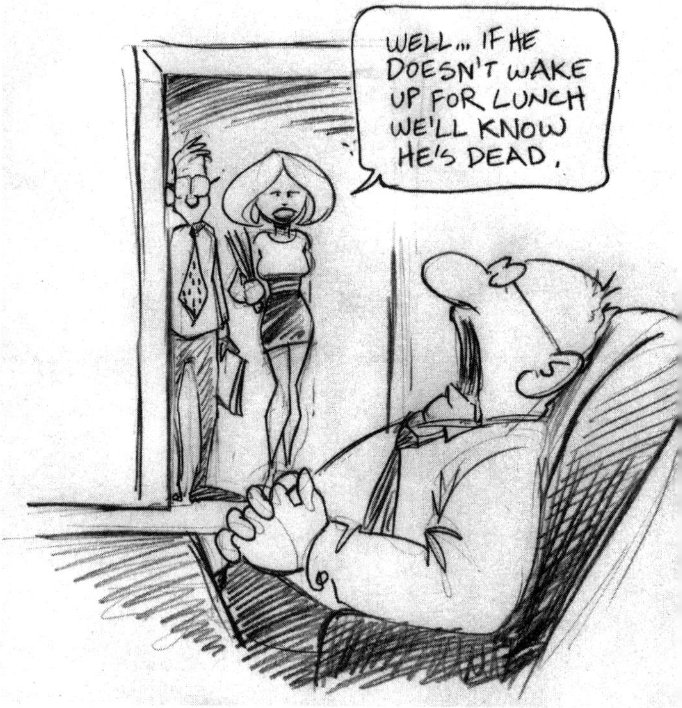
WELL... IF HE DOESN'T WAKE UP FOR LUNCH WE'LL KNOW HE'S DEAD.

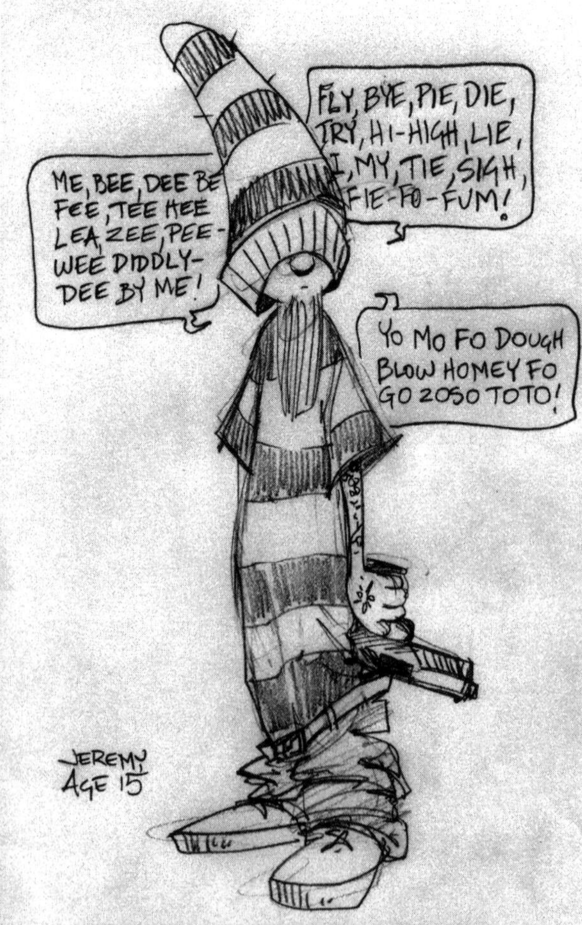
ME, BEE, DEE BE FEE, TEE HEE LEA, ZEE, PEE-WEE DIDDLY-DEE BY ME!
FLY, BYE, PIE, DIE, TRY, HI-HIGH, LIE, I, MY, TIE, SIGH, FIE-FO-FUM!
YO MO FO DOUGH BLOW HOMEY FO GO 2OSO TOTO!
JEREMY AGE 15

WHERE IT'S ALL HEADING

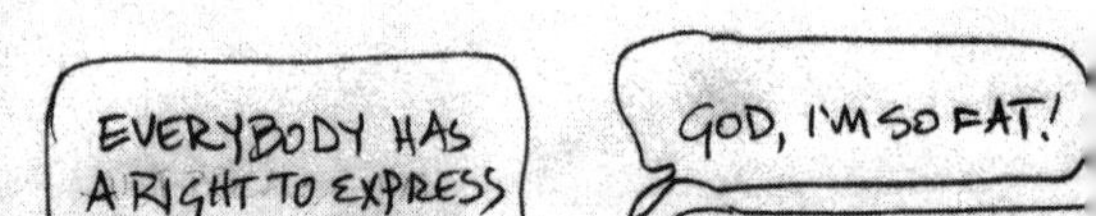
EVERYBODY HAS A RIGHT TO EXPRESS THEIR SEXUALITY IN THEIR OWN WAY – I LIKE BRITTANY SPEAR'S WAY!
GOD, I'M SO FAT!
I GOT THE BOOBS & LI
FOR MY BIRTHDAY. THEY'RE NOT AS BIG AS BRITTA
SPEARS, BUT I HAVE MORE TATTOO'S!
DRUGS, PARENTS GUNS, TATTOO'S, VIOLENCE BRITTANY BRITTANY BRITTANY RAP, DRIVEBY'S SEX, DRUGS, PUKING UP EVER MEAL AND SEX
MY PARENTS ARE LIKE, "YOU CAN'T GO OUT DRESSED LIKE THAT!" AND I'M LIKE, "WHO ARE YOU TO TELL ME WHAT TO DO?!" Y'KNOW? GOD, THEY'RE SO PATHETIC.
BRIFFANY AGE 15

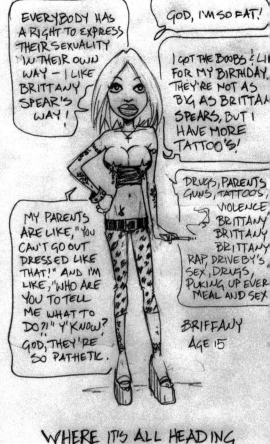

WHERE IT'S ALL HEADING

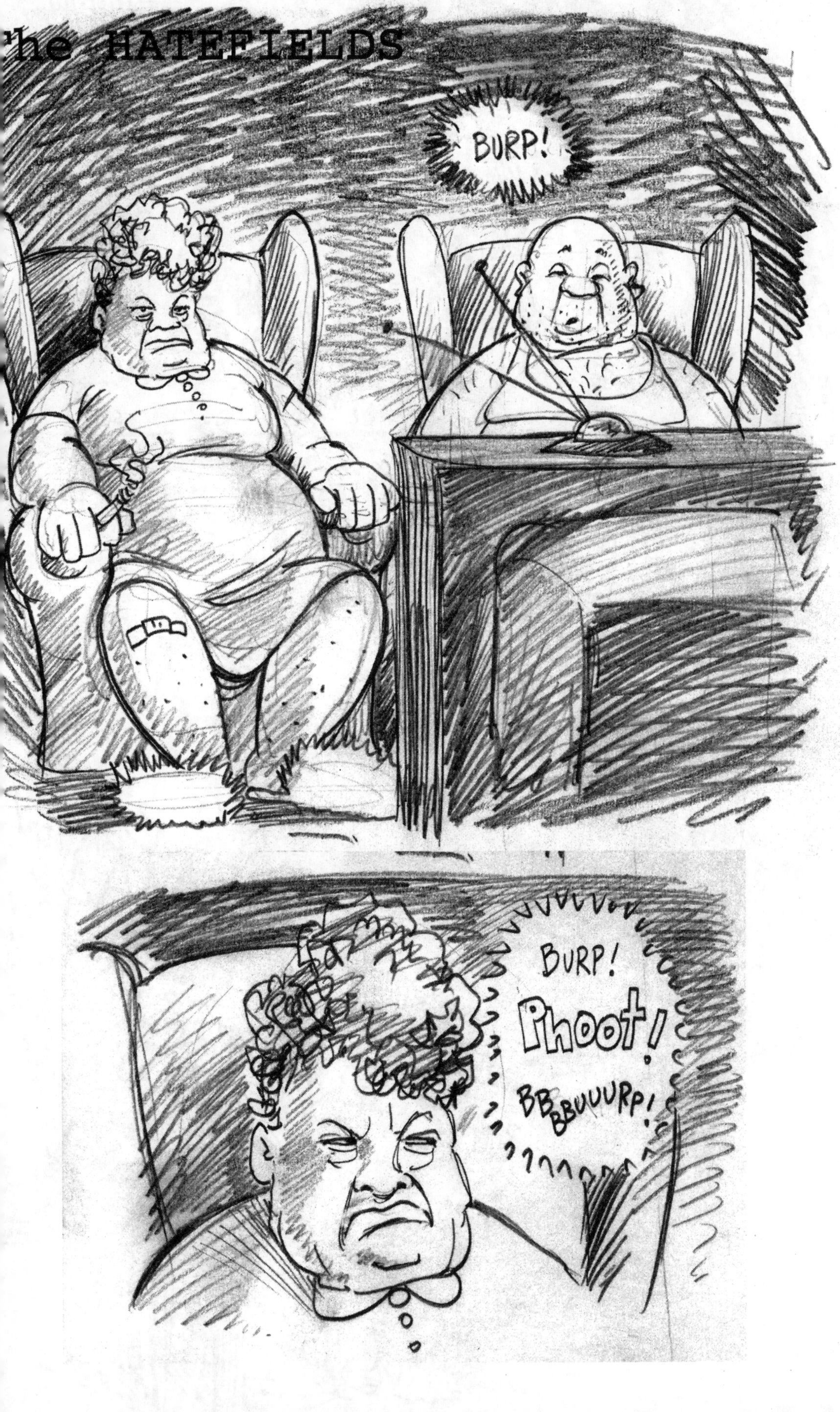
'he HATEFIELDS
BURP!
BURP!
Phoot!
BBBBUUURP!

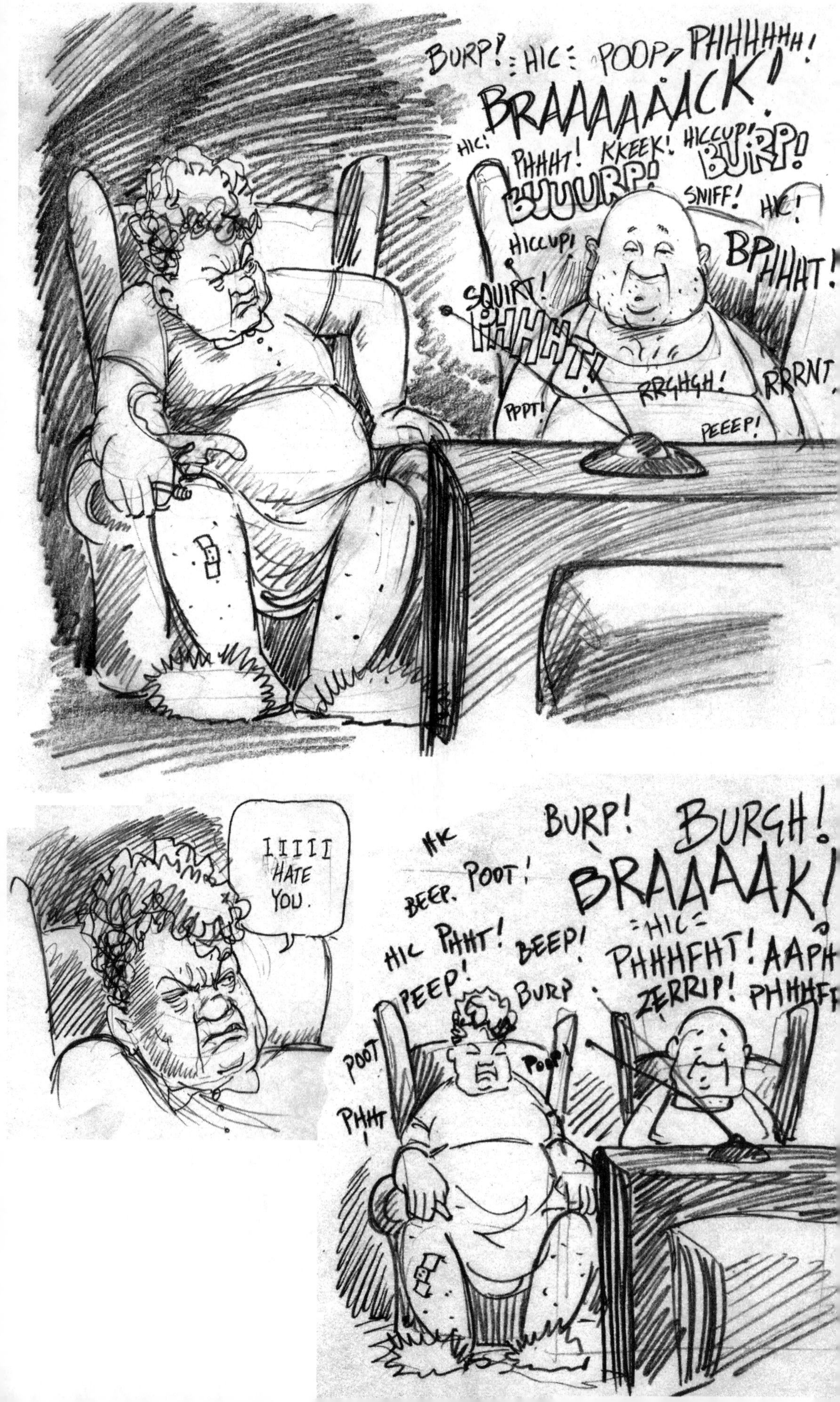
BURP! HIC POOP! PHHHHHH!
BRAAAAAACK!
HIC! PHHHT! KKEEK! HICCUP! BURP!
BUUURP! SNIFF! HIC!
HICCUP!
BPHHAT!
SQUIRT!
PHHHT!
RRGHGH! RRRNT!
PPPT!
PEEEP!
IIIII HATE YOU.
BURP! BURGH!
HK
BEEP. POOT!
BRAAAAK!
HIC PHHT! BEEP! HIC
PHHHFHT! AAPH
PEEP! BURP ZERRIP! PHHHF
POOT
POOT
PHHT!

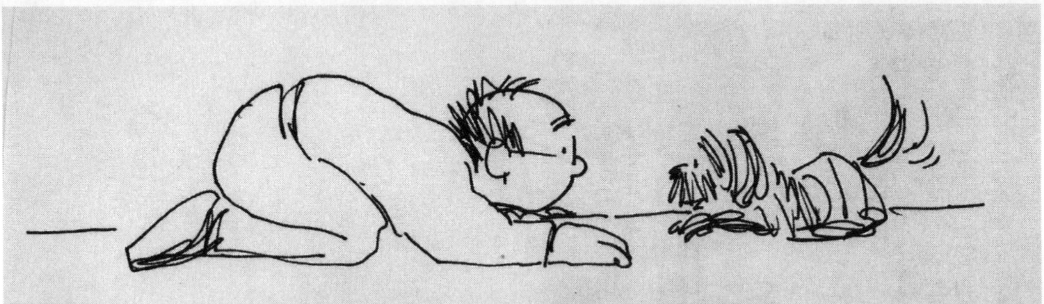

THE DOG WHISPERER

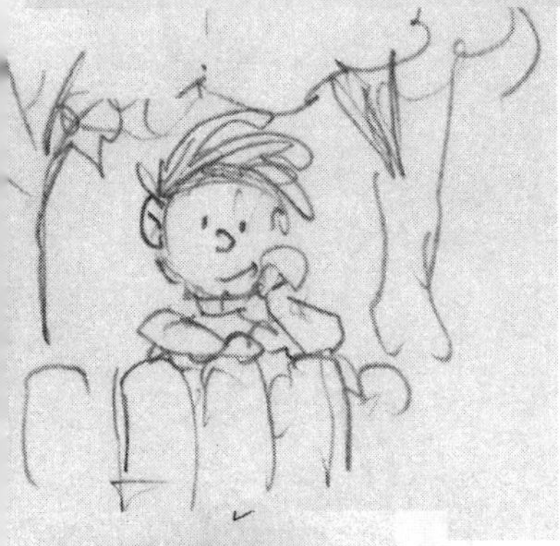

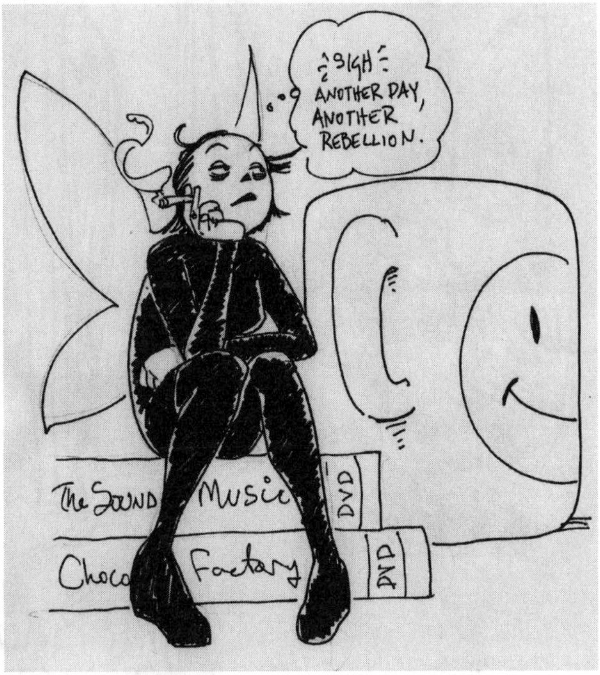
SIGH
ANOTHER DAY, ANOTHER REBELLION.
The Sound Music
DVD
Choco Factory
DVD

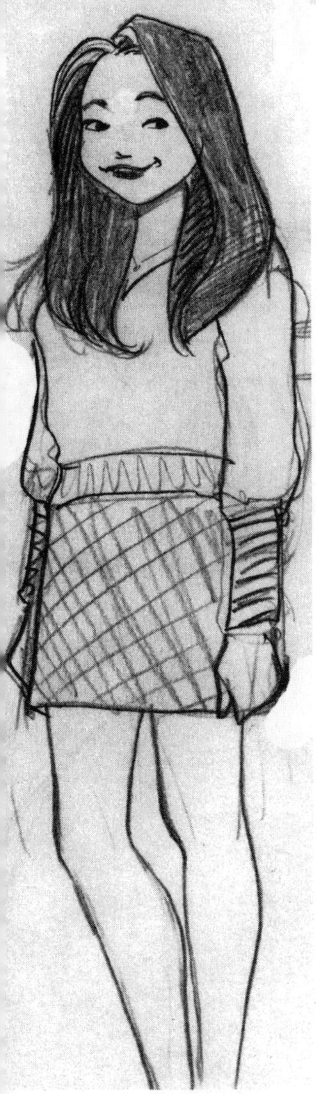

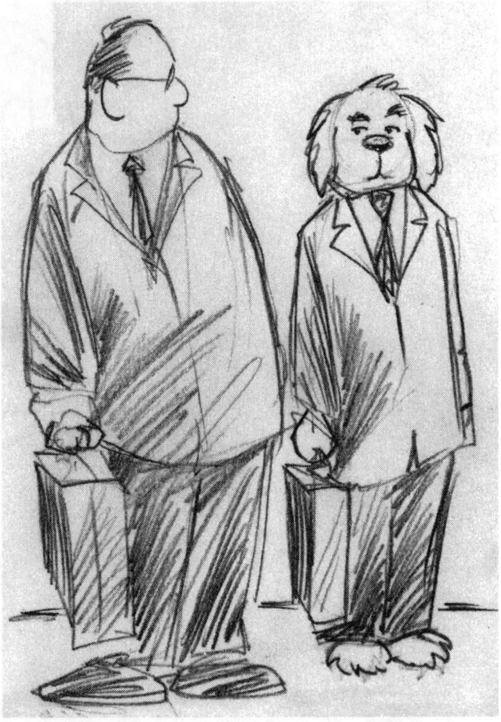

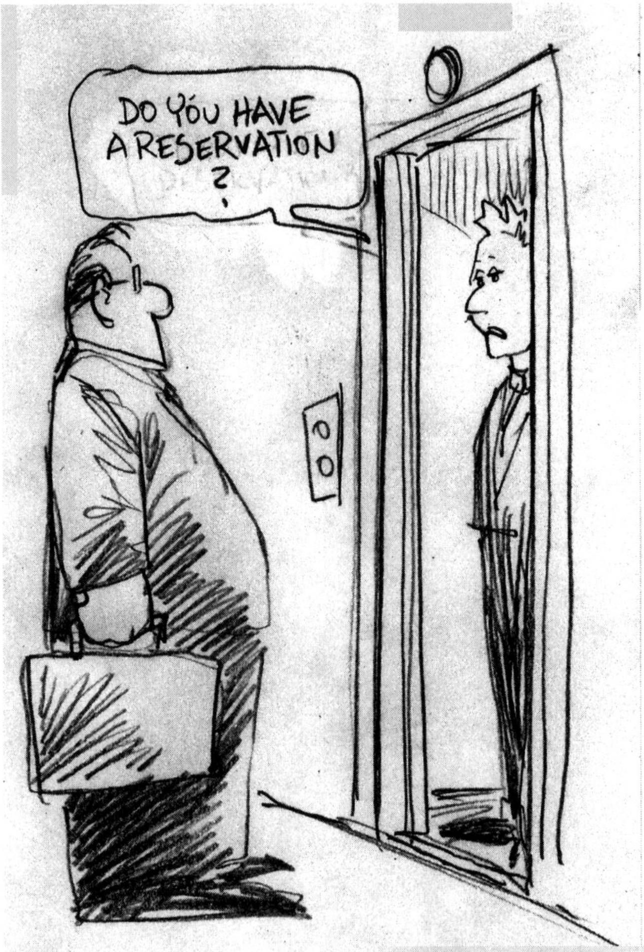
DO YOU HAVE A RESERVATION ?

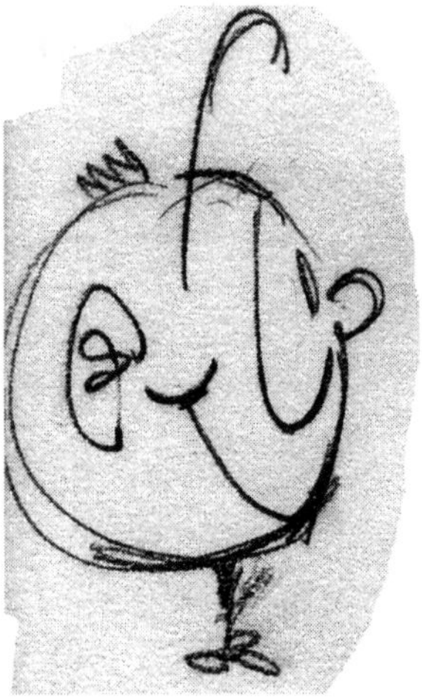

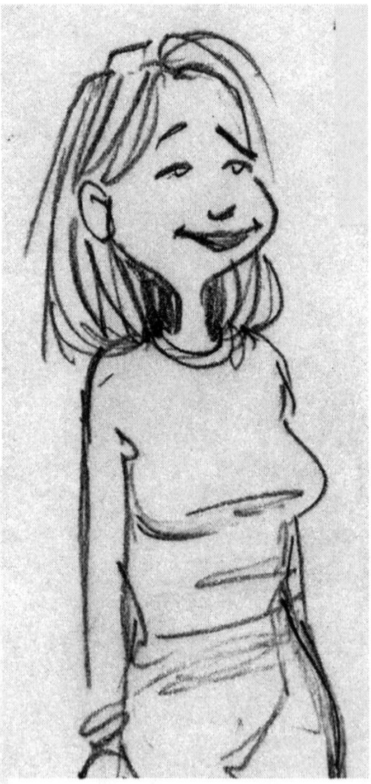

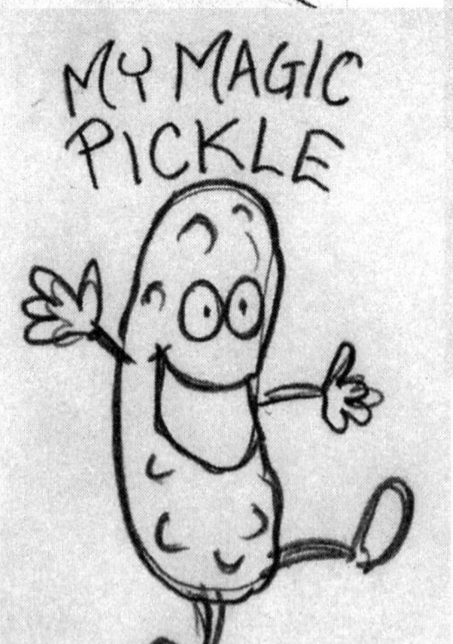
MY MAGIC PICKLE

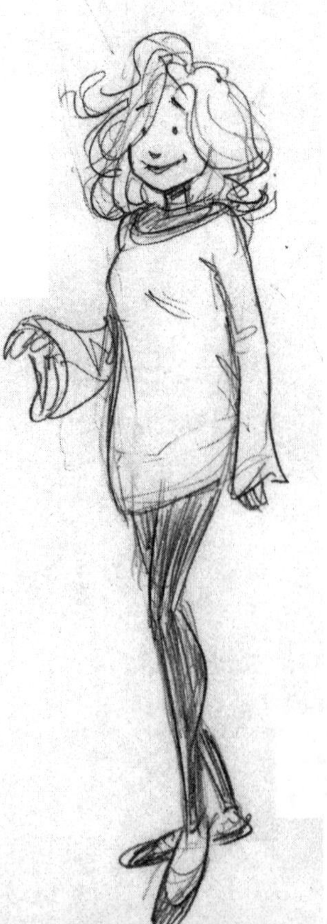

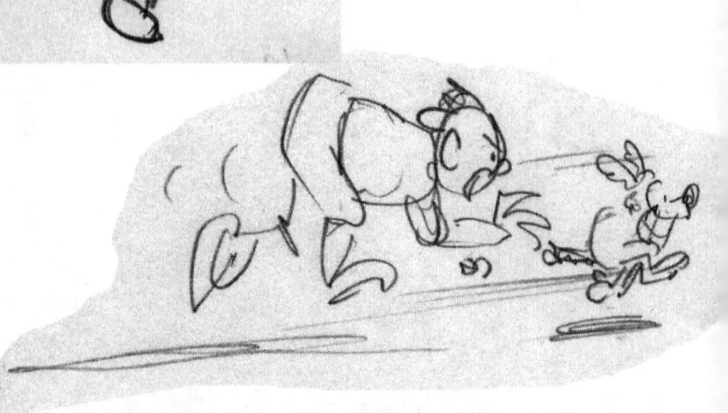

IN FOLK

BRIEF VISIT WITH J.J. BUBBA R.
ND AUNT LIBBY AT THE FAMILY
OMESTEAD IN TEXAS.

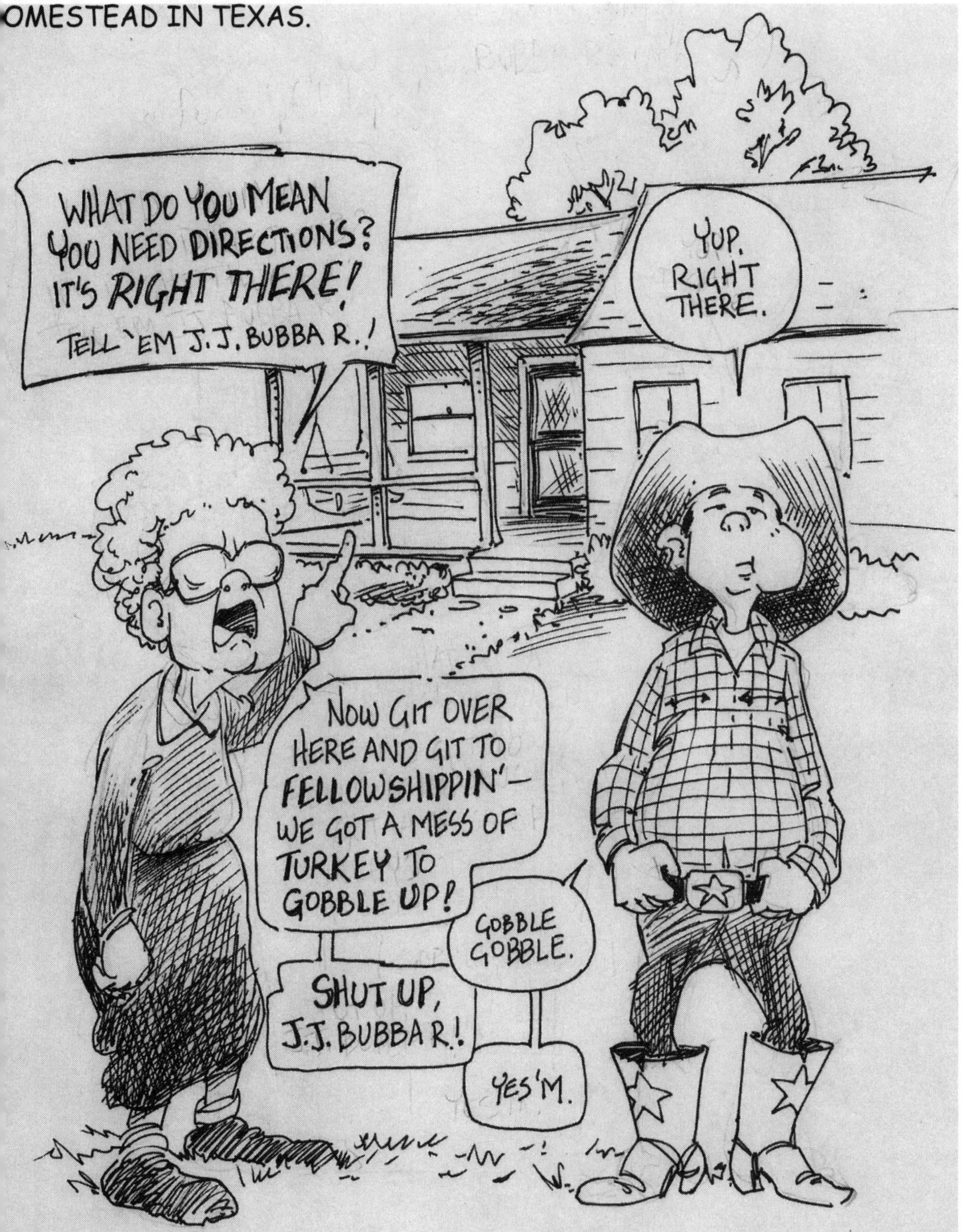
WHAT DO YOU MEAN YOU NEED DIRECTIONS? IT'S RIGHT THERE! TELL `EM J.J. BUBBA R.!
YUP. RIGHT THERE.
NOW GIT OVER HERE AND GIT TO FELLOWSHIPPIN'– WE GOT A MESS OF TURKEY TO GOBBLE UP!
GOBBLE GOBBLE.
SHUT UP, J.J. BUBBA R.!
YES'M.

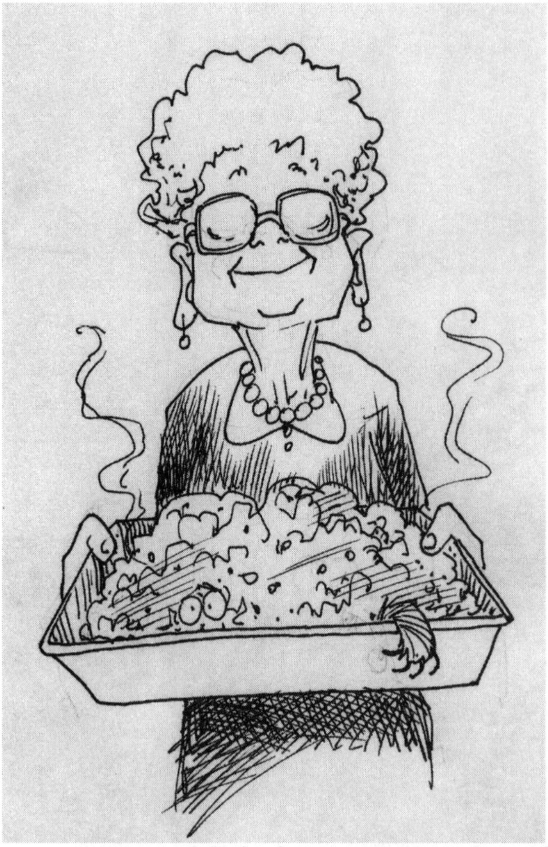

AUNT LIBBY'S POTLUCK SURPRISE

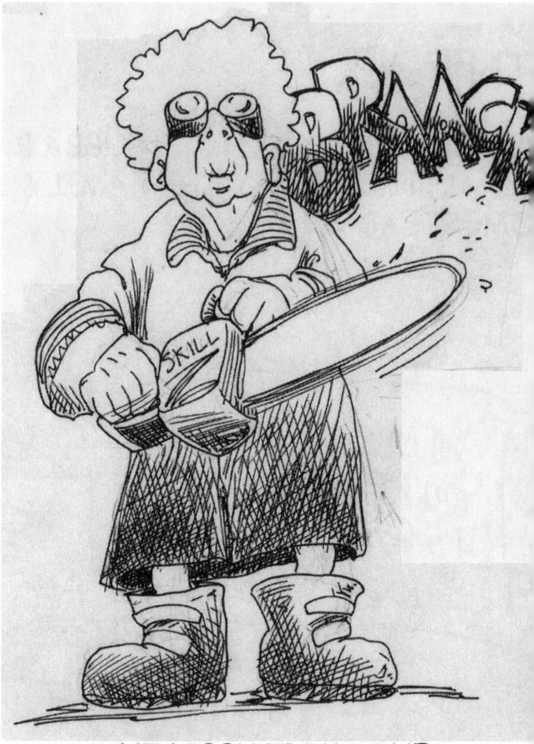
SKILL

AUNT LIBBY TRIMS THE
TREE FOR CHRISTMAS

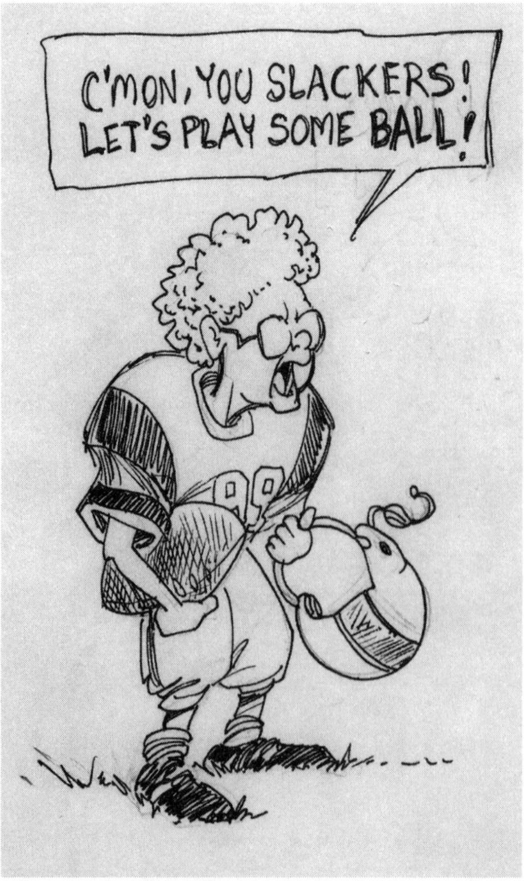
C'MON, YOU SLACKERS!
LET'S PLAY SOME BALL!

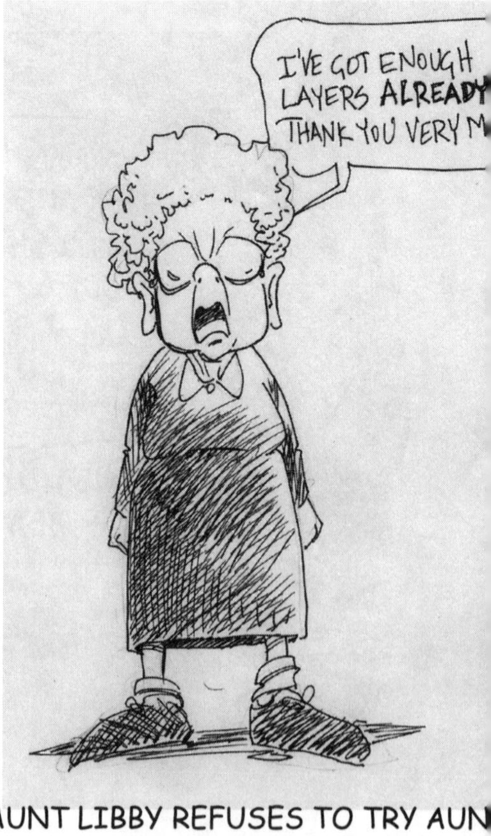
I'VE GOT ENOUGH
LAYERS ALREADY
THANK YOU VERY M

AUNT LIBBY REFUSES TO TRY AUN
SALLY'S SEVEN LAYER DIP.

J. BUBBA R. AND "PICKLES" ARRIVE FOR THE FAMILY BAR-B-QUE

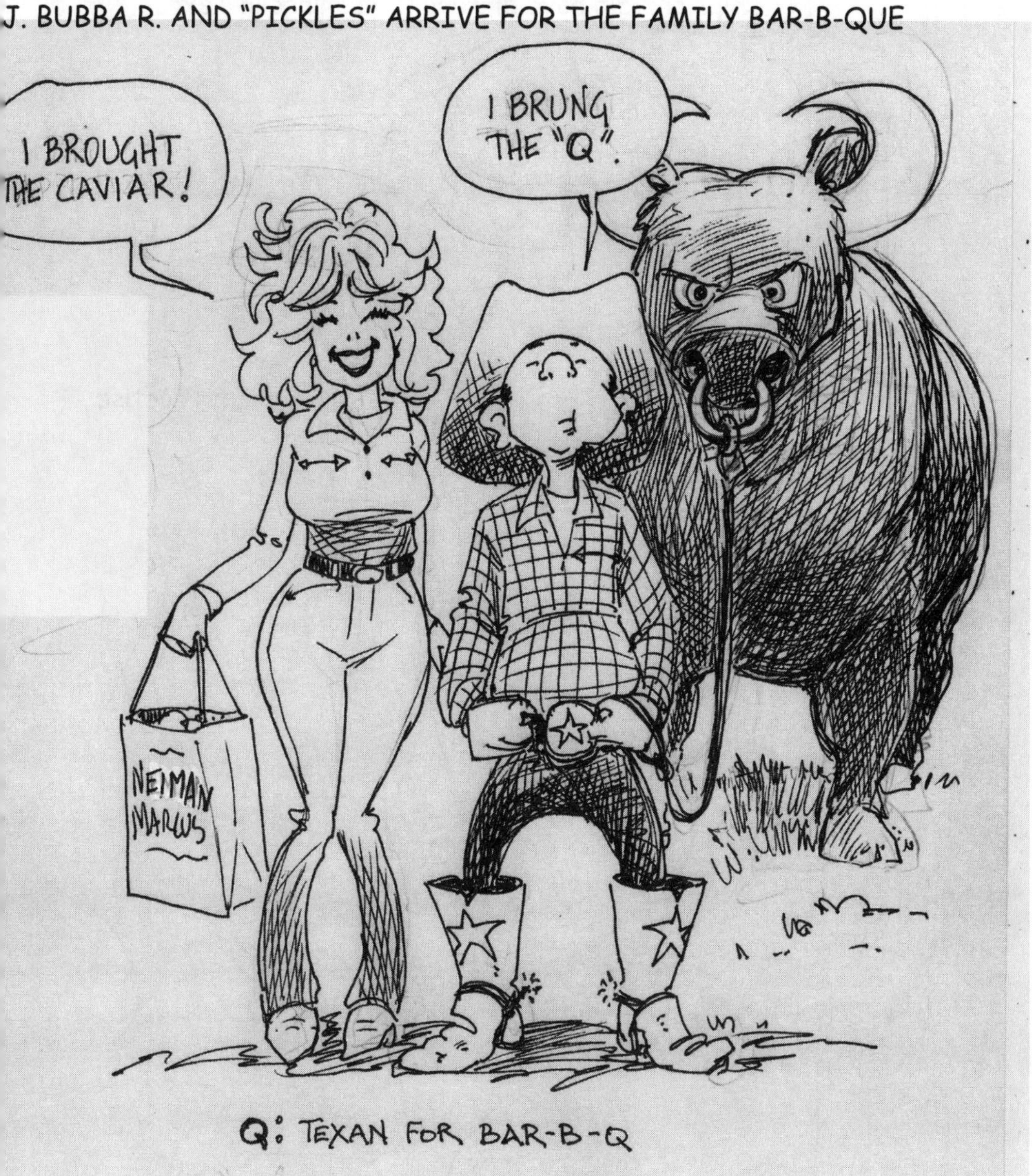
I BROUGHT THE CAVIAR!
I BRUNG THE "Q".
NEIMAN MARCUS
Q: TEXAN FOR BAR-B-Q

Family parties are casual affairs

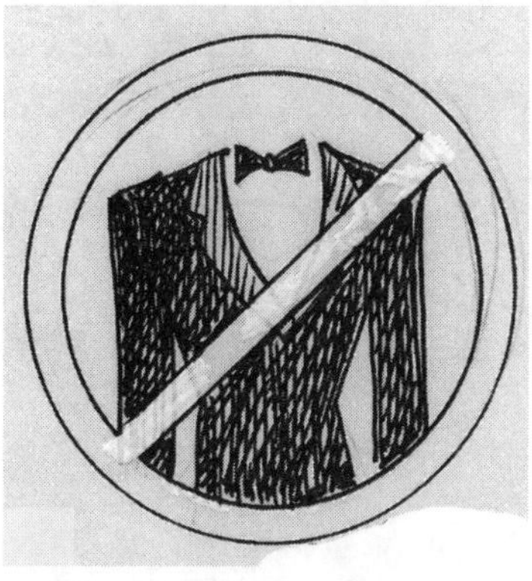

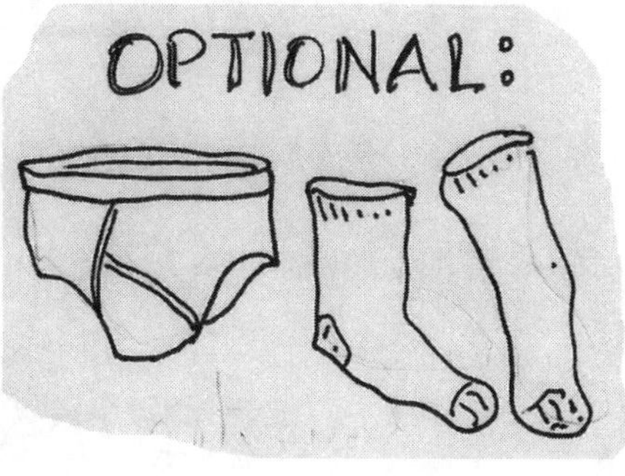
OPTIONAL:

Chips and dip have different meanings in Texas.

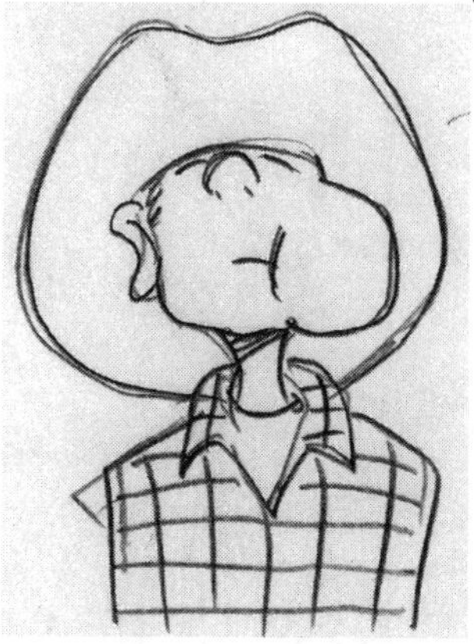

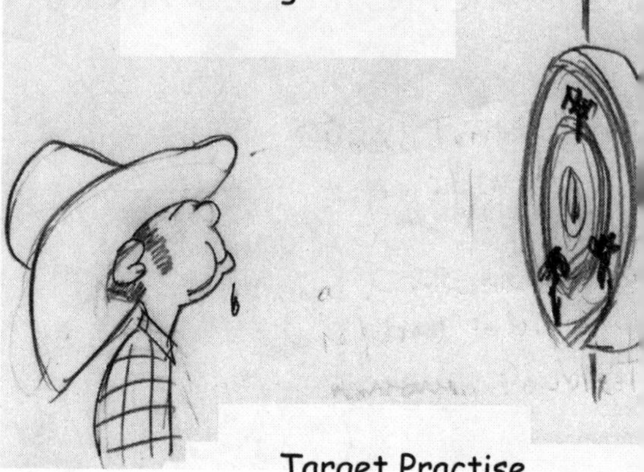

Target Practise

Chawin' on some dip.

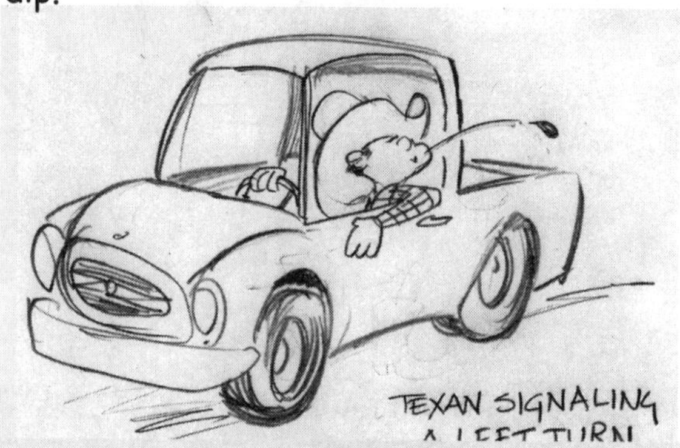
TEXAN SIGNALING
A LEFT TURN

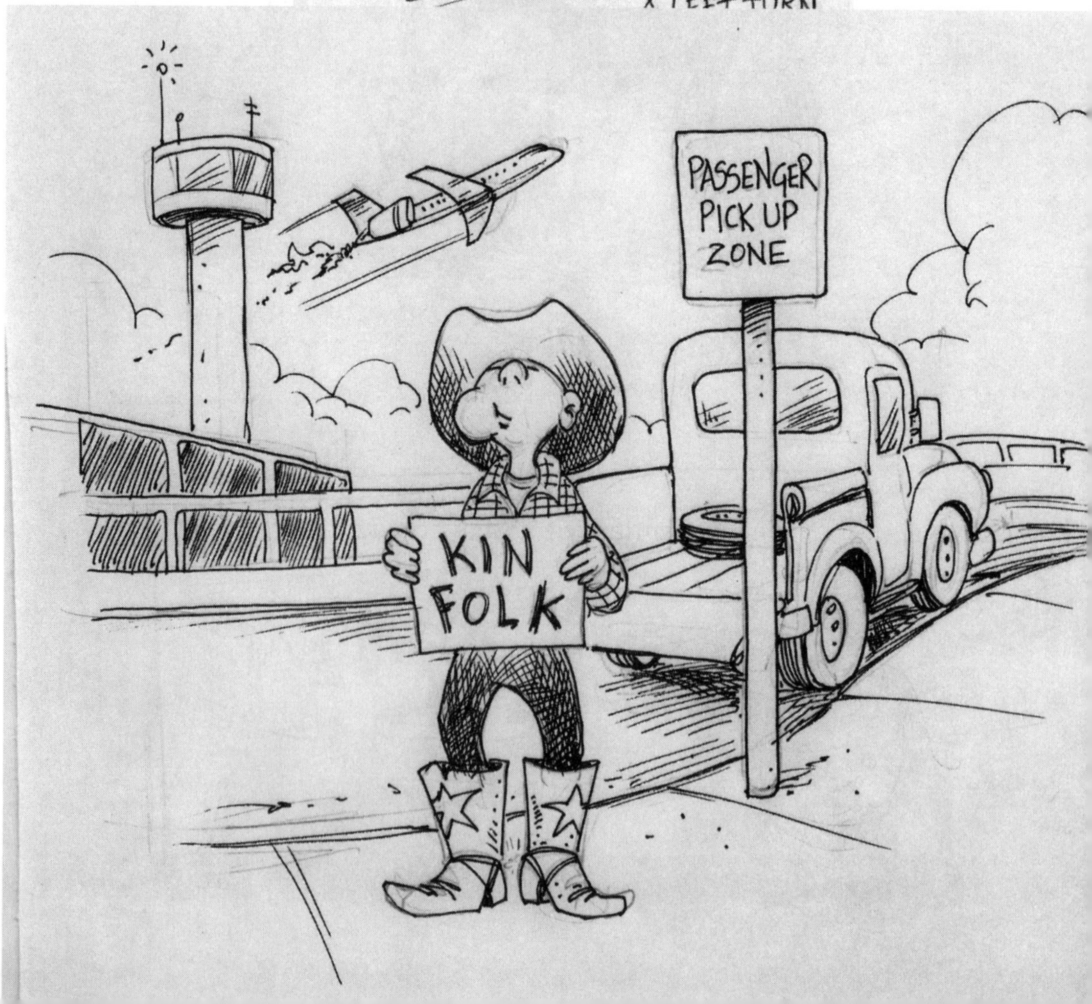
PASSENGER
PICK UP
ZONE
KIN
FOLK

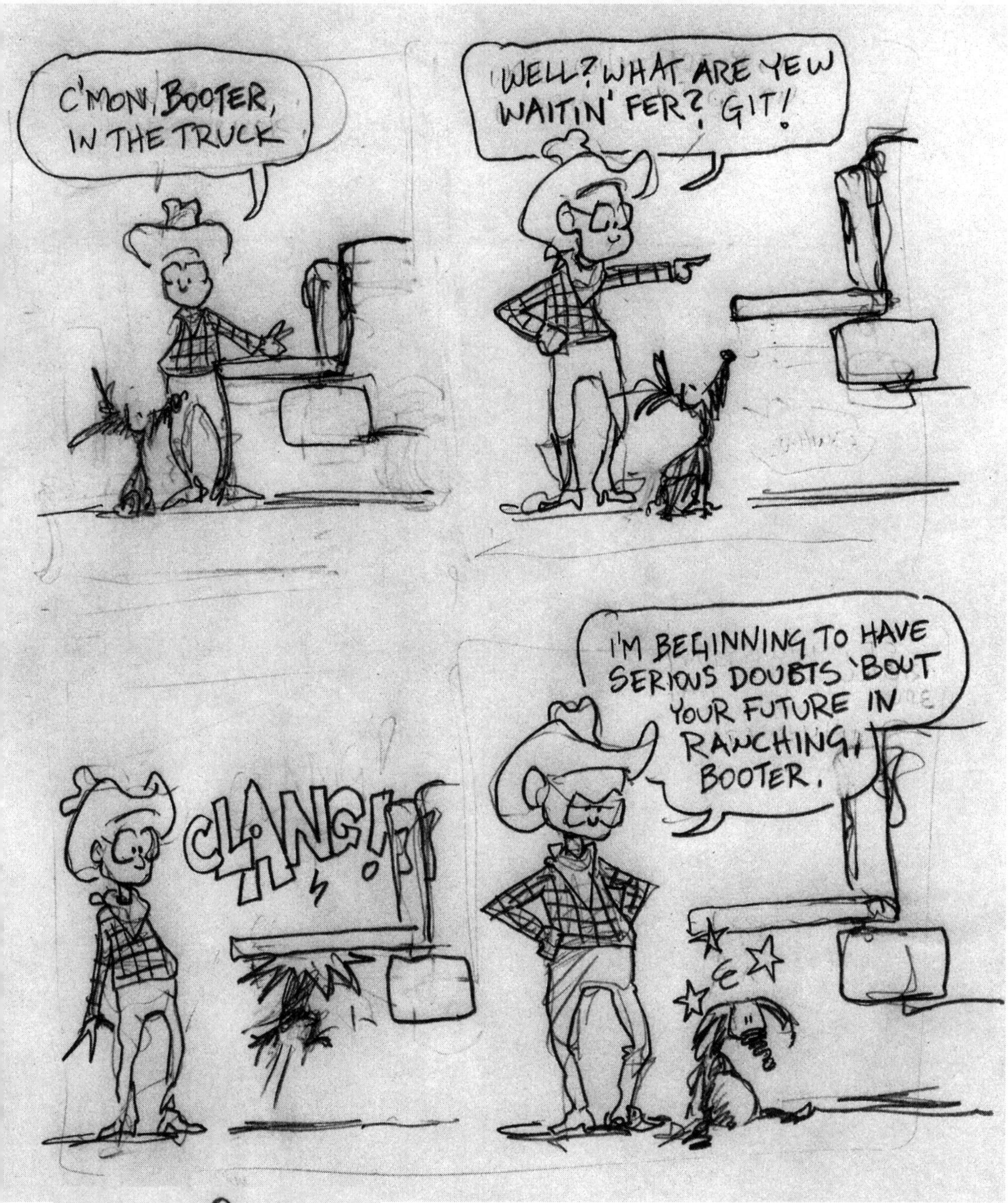
C'MON, BOOTER, IN THE TRUCK
WELL? WHAT ARE YEW WAITIN' FER? GIT!
CLANG!
I'M BEGINNING TO HAVE SERIOUS DOUBTS 'BOUT YOUR FUTURE IN RANCHING, BOOTER.

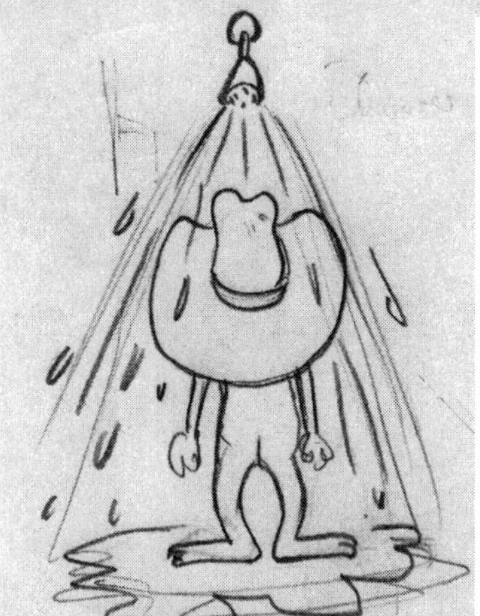
TEXAS SHOWER

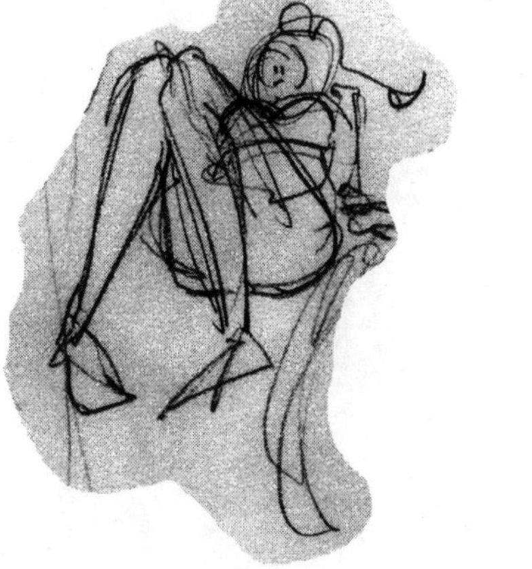

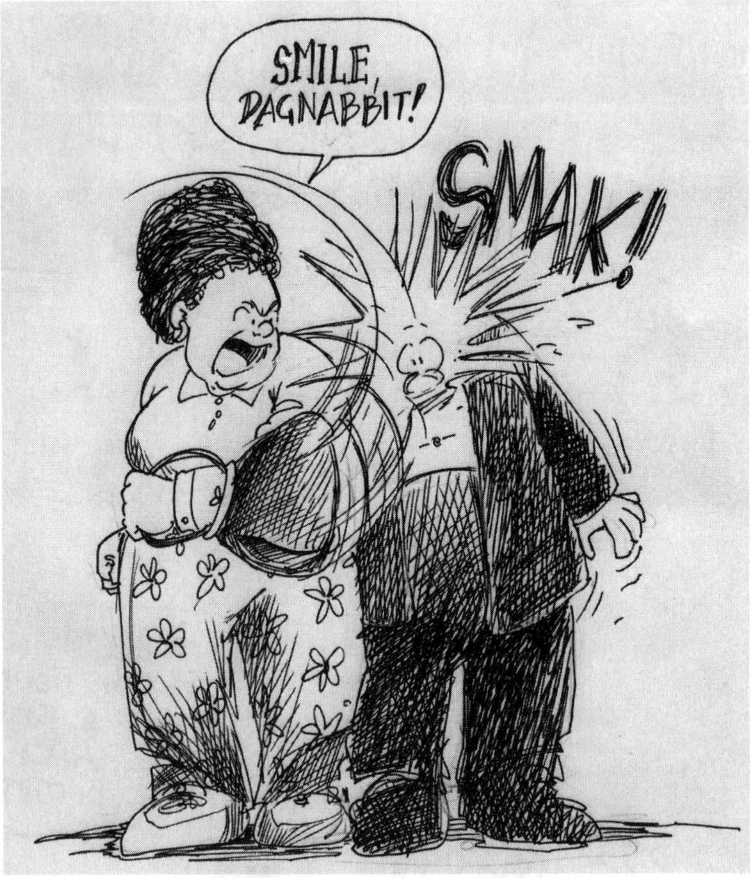
SMILE, DAGNABBIT!
SMAK!

THIS IS LEGAL IN MY STATE

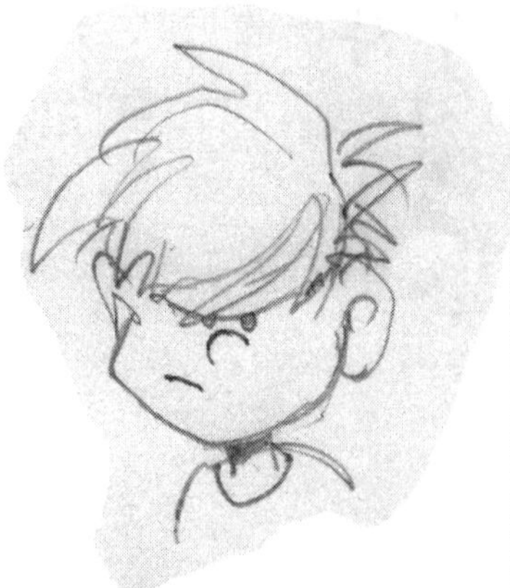

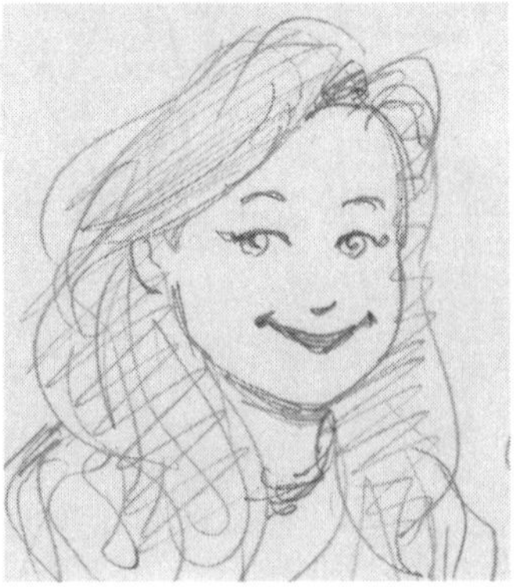

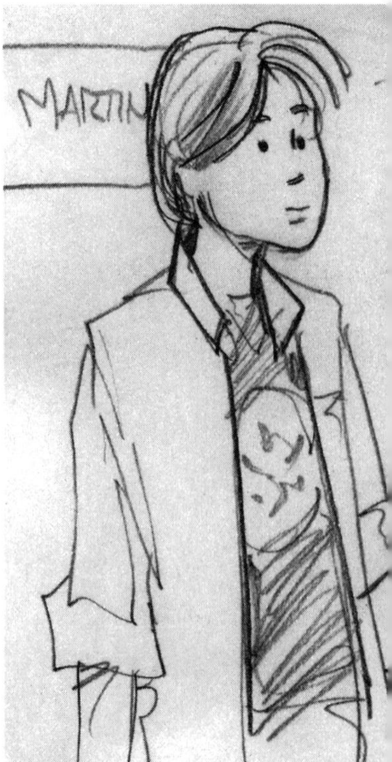

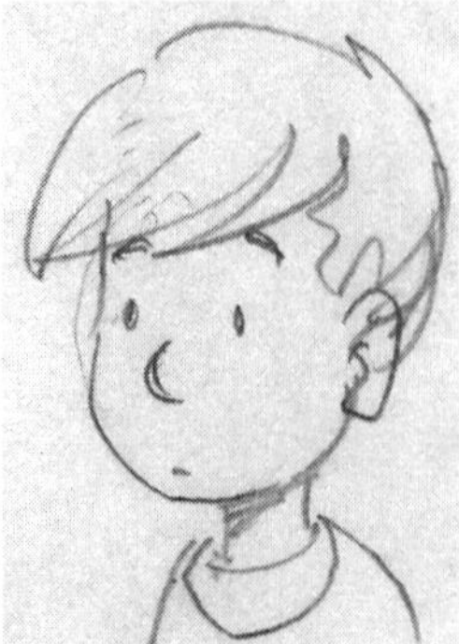

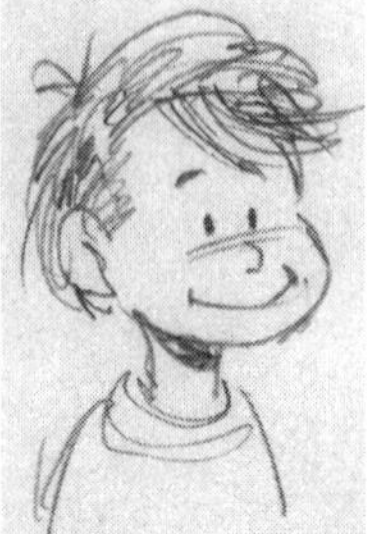

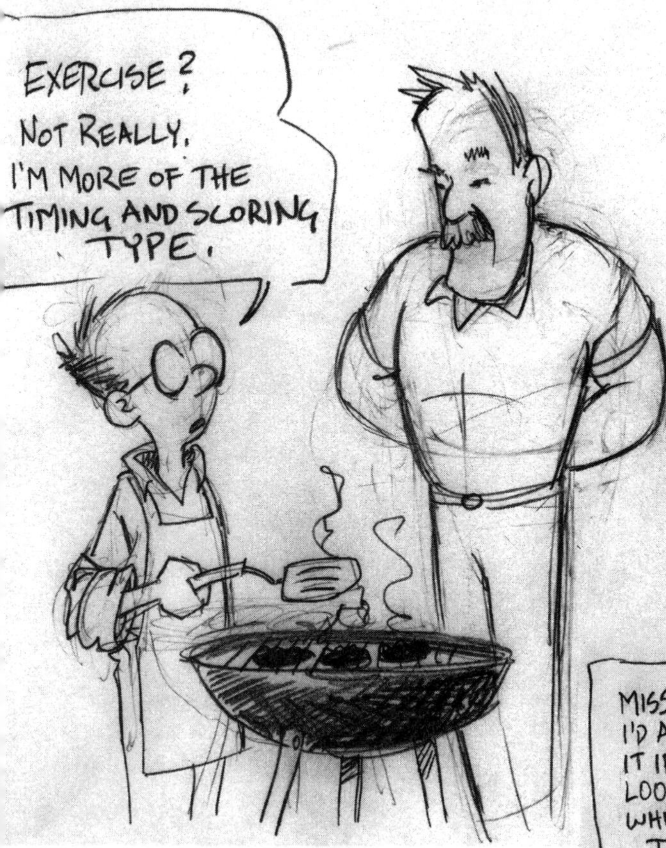
EXERCISE? NOT REALLY. I'M MORE OF THE TIMING AND SCORING TYPE.

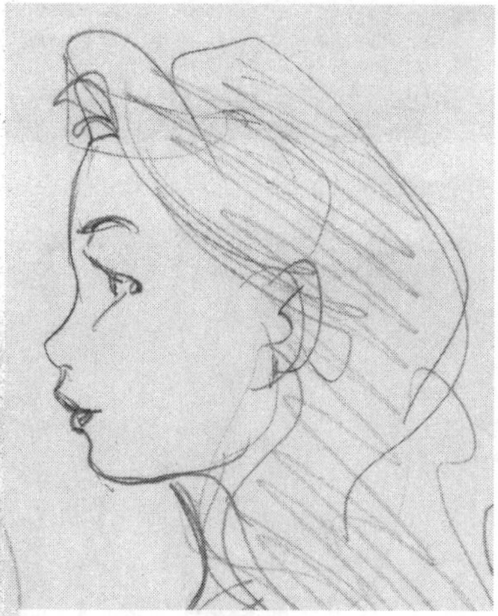

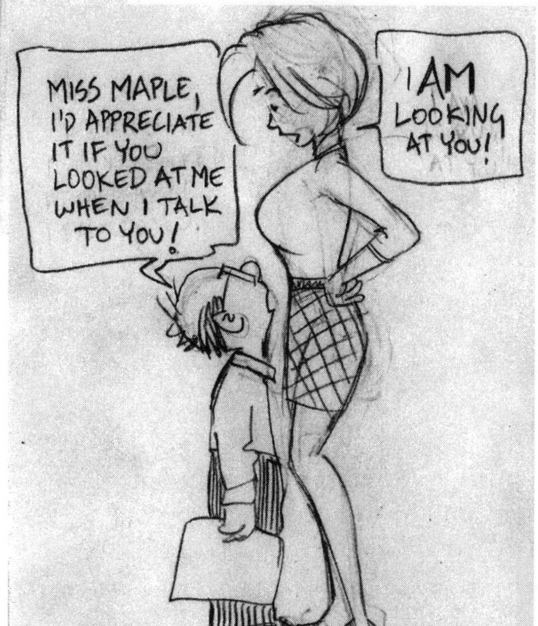
MISS MAPLE, I'D APPRECIATE IT IF YOU LOOKED AT ME WHEN I TALK TO YOU!
I AM LOOKING AT YOU!

IS IS MY EVIL TWIN JERRY.
RRY IS NOT TALL, NOT CURSED
TH A RUNAWAY HAIR-DO,
T OVER-BURDENED WITH ANY
OPHYS. JERRY IS NOT A LOT OF
INGS, BUT HE IS FUN TO BE.

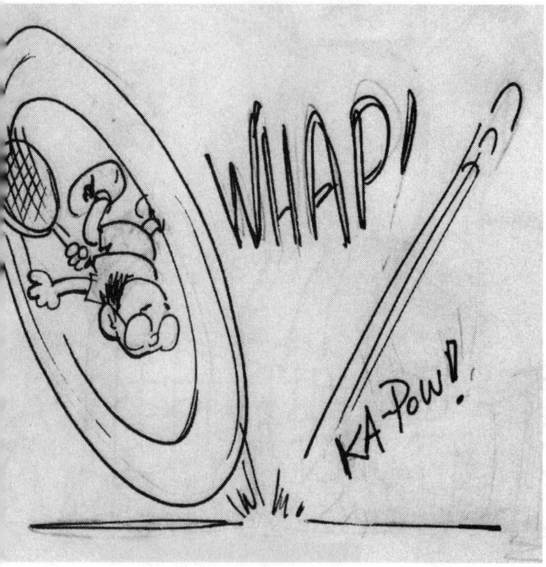
WHAP!
KA-POW!

FIRST SERVE

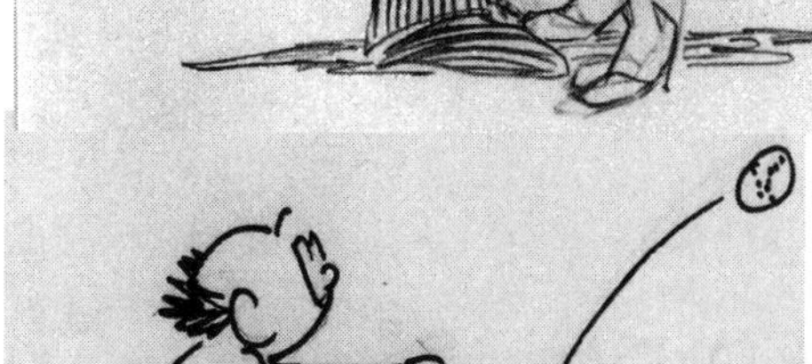
PING!

SECOND SERVE

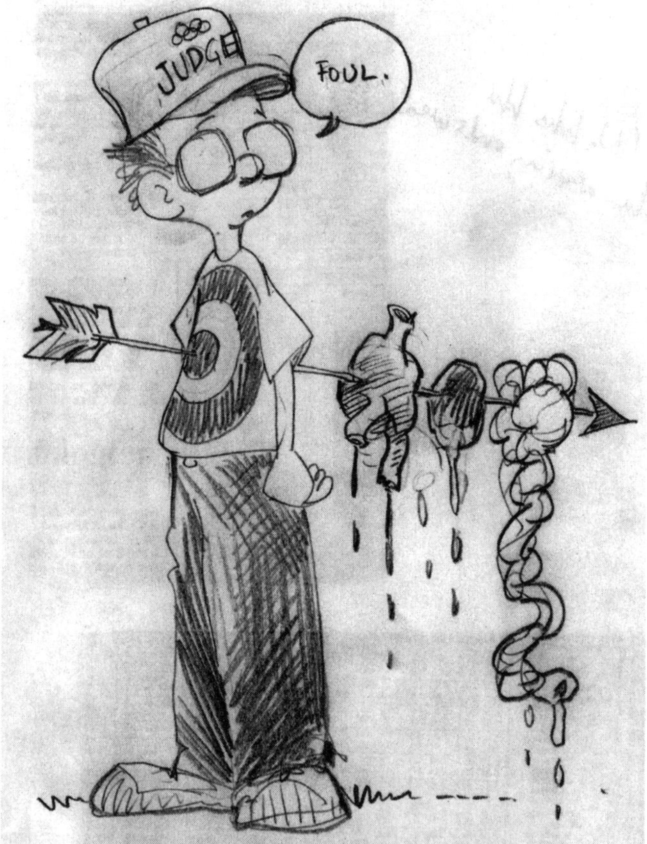
JUDGE
FOUL.

WHY TARGET DOESN'T SPONSOR OLYMPIC ARCHERY.

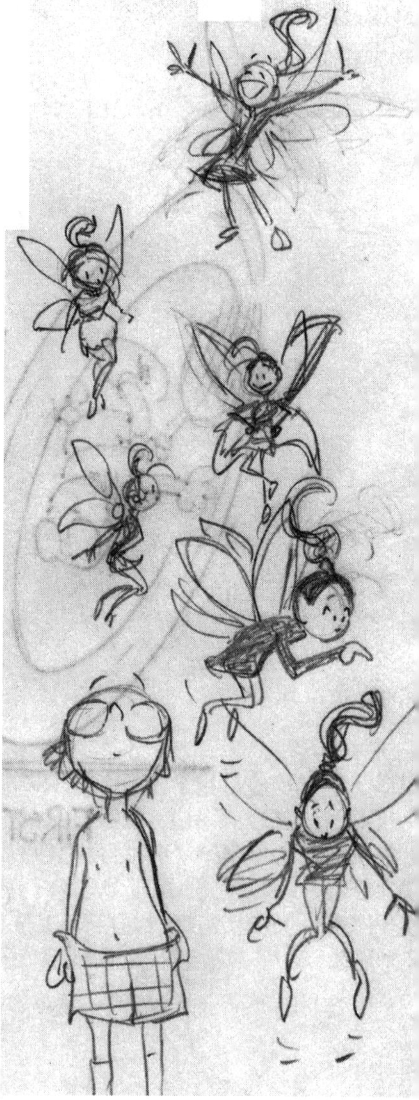

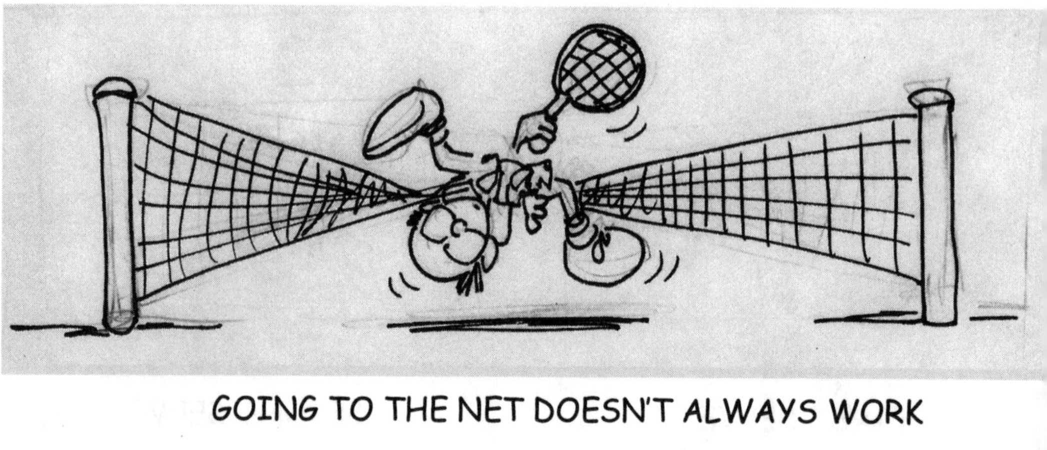

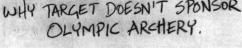

GOING TO THE NET DOESN'T ALWAYS WORK

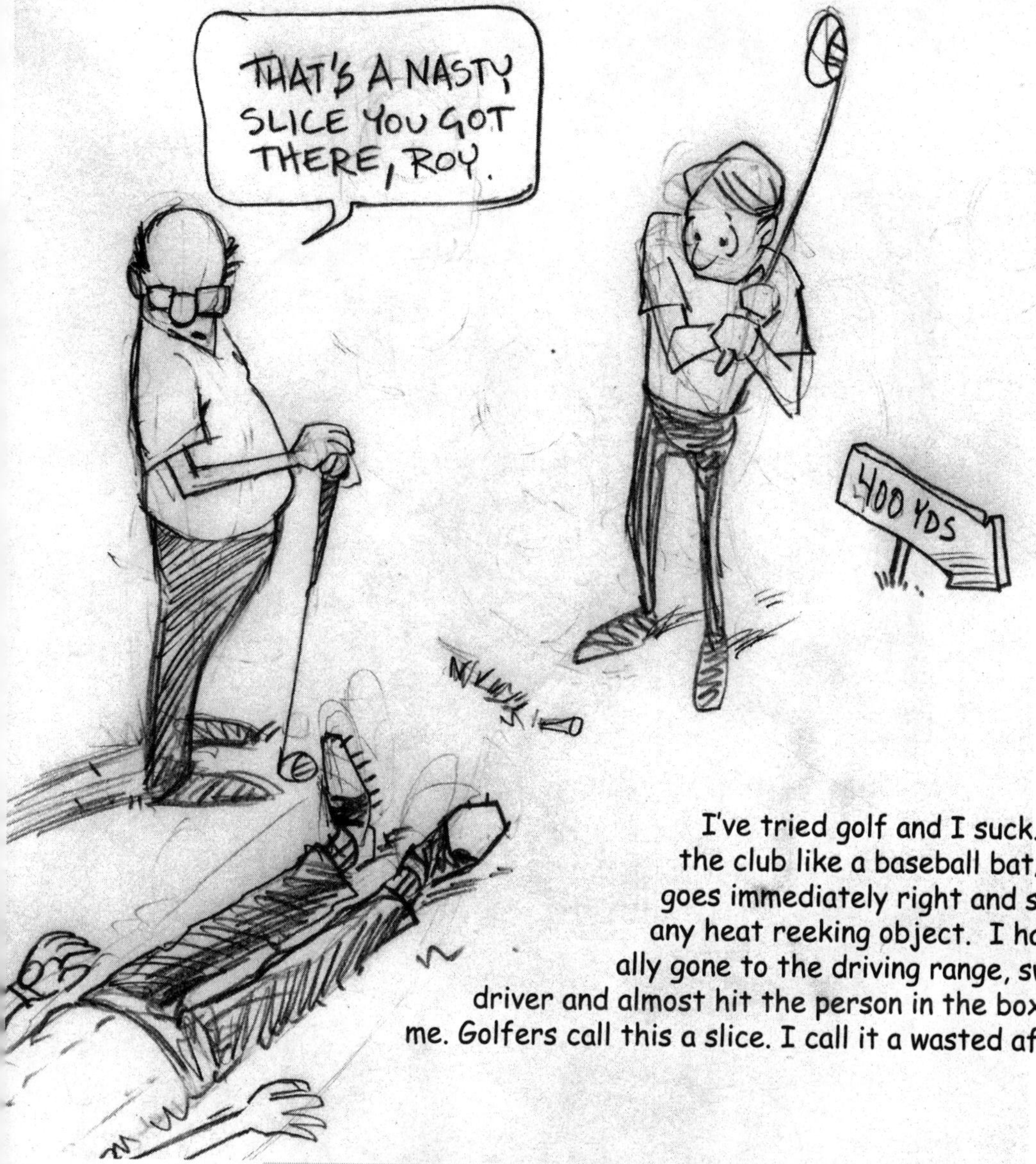
THAT'S A NASTY SLICE YOU GOT THERE, ROY.
400 YDS

I've tried golf and I suck. I swin the club like a baseball bat; the ba goes immediately right and seeks ou any heat reeking object. I have actu ally gone to the driving range, swung th driver and almost hit the person in the box next t me. Golfers call this a slice. I call it a wasted afternoo

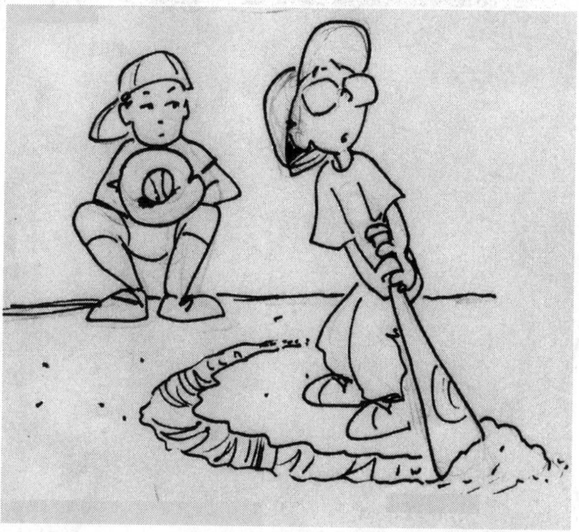

Funny enough, I swing a baseball bat like a golf club. Strike three.

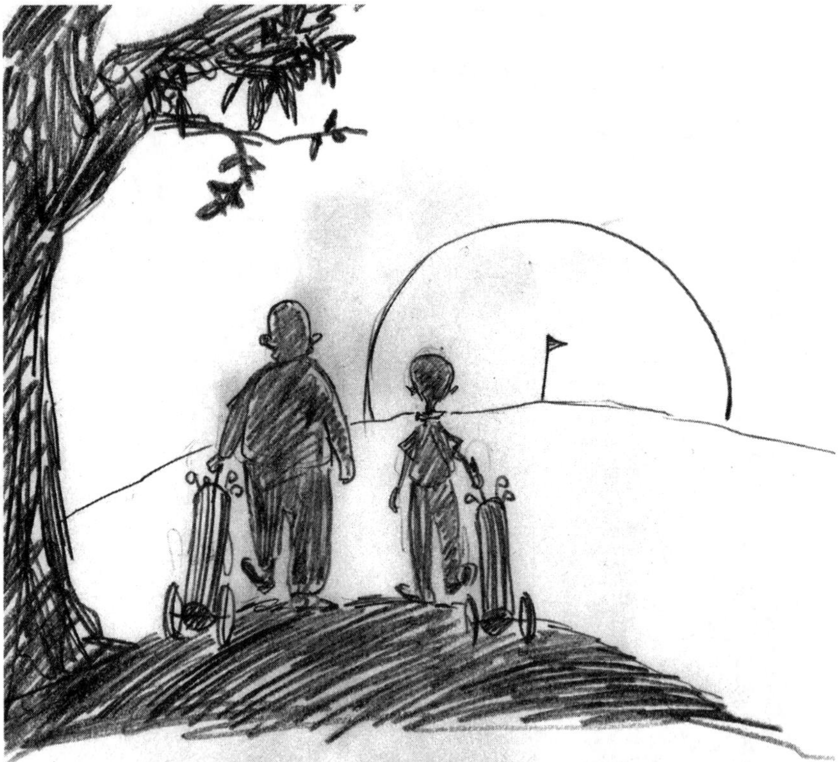

"MY LONG IRONS ARE SHORT, MY SHORT IRONS ARE LONG, AND I PUTT LIKE A BLIND SNIPER. IF IT WASN'T FOR MY FORTY YARD DRIVE I'D JUST GO HOME."

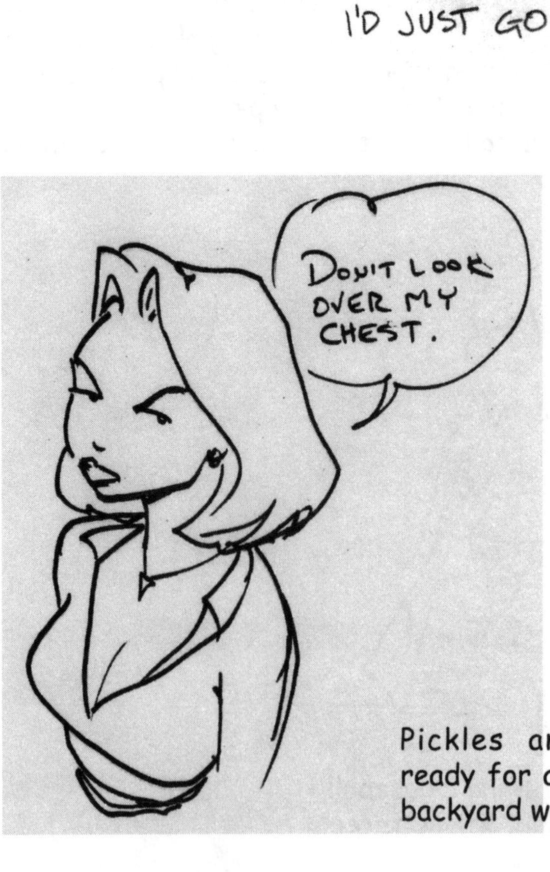
DON'T LOOK OVER MY CHEST.

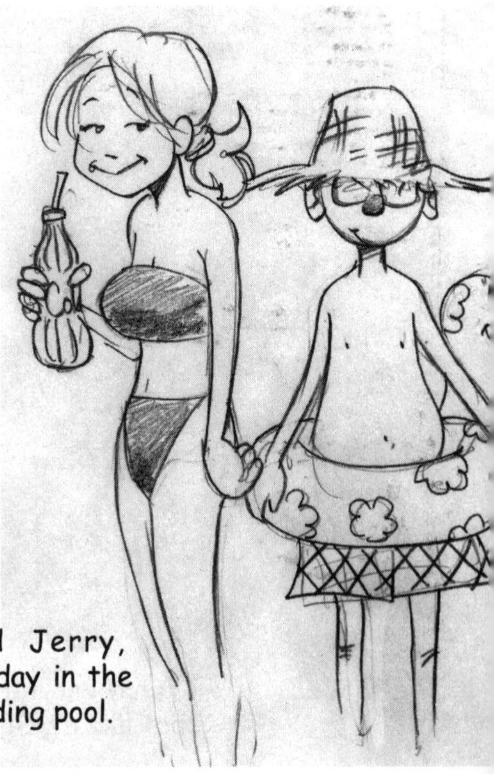

Pickles and Jerry, ready for a day in the backyard wading pool.

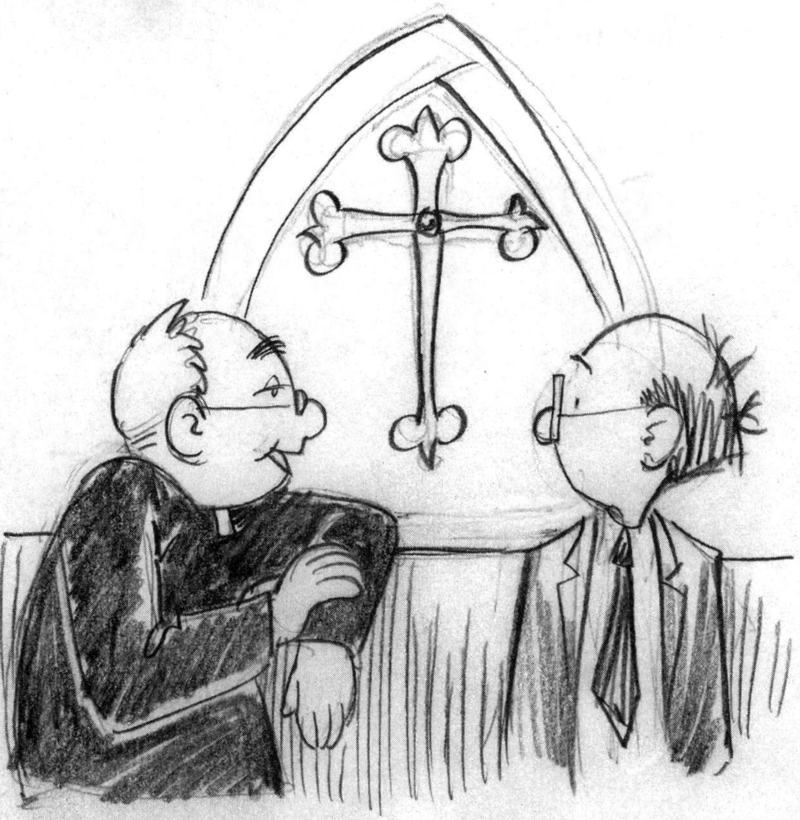

" OF COURSE, SOME CHARACTERS DON'T BELIEVE IN THE CARTOONIST, "

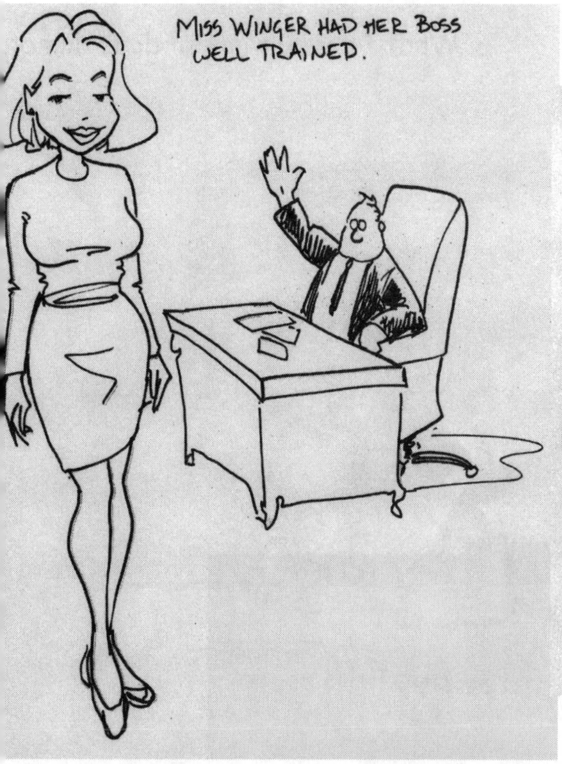
MISS WINGER HAD HER BOSS WELL TRAINED.

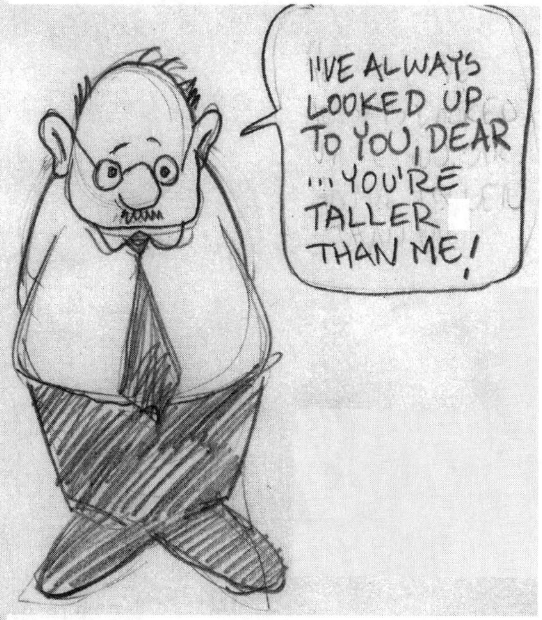
I'VE ALWAYS LOOKED UP TO YOU, DEAR ... YOU'RE TALLER THAN ME!

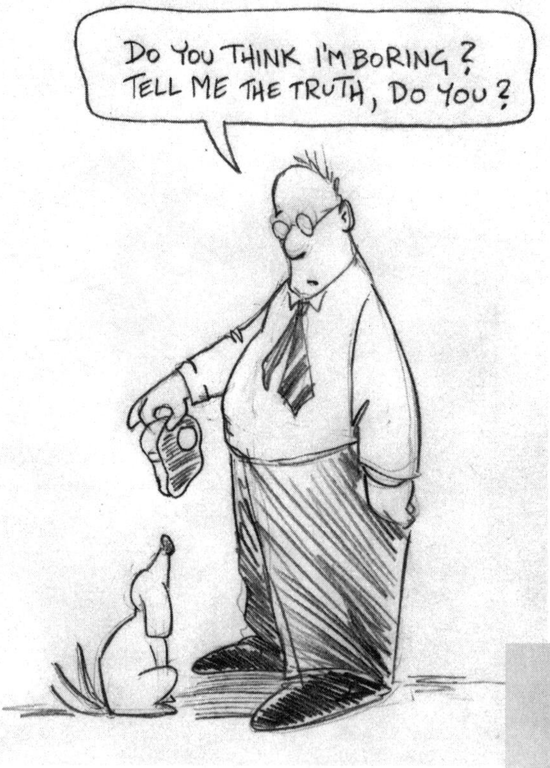
DO YOU THINK I'M BORING? TELL ME THE TRUTH, DO YOU?

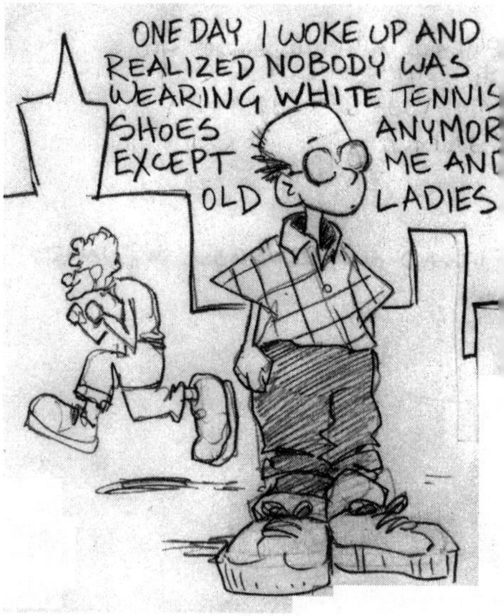
ONE DAY I WOKE UP AND REALIZED NOBODY WAS WEARING WHITE TENNIS SHOES ANYMOR EXCEPT ME AN OLD LADIES

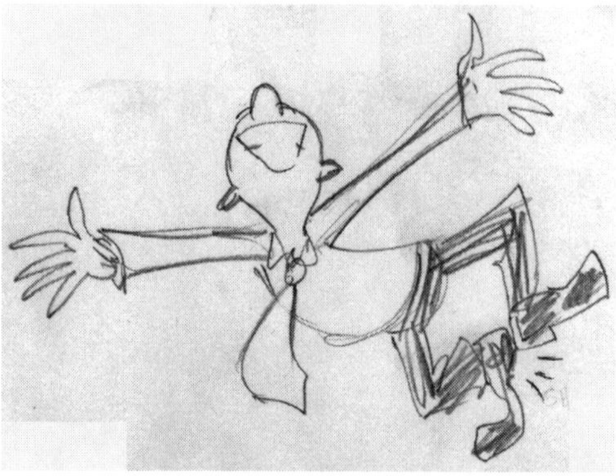

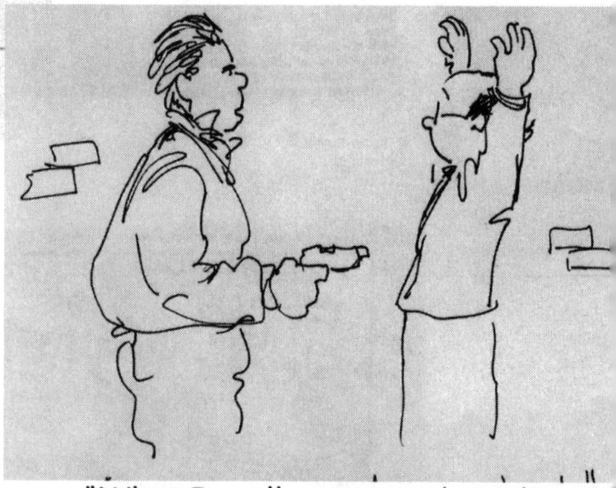

"What I really want to do is direct."

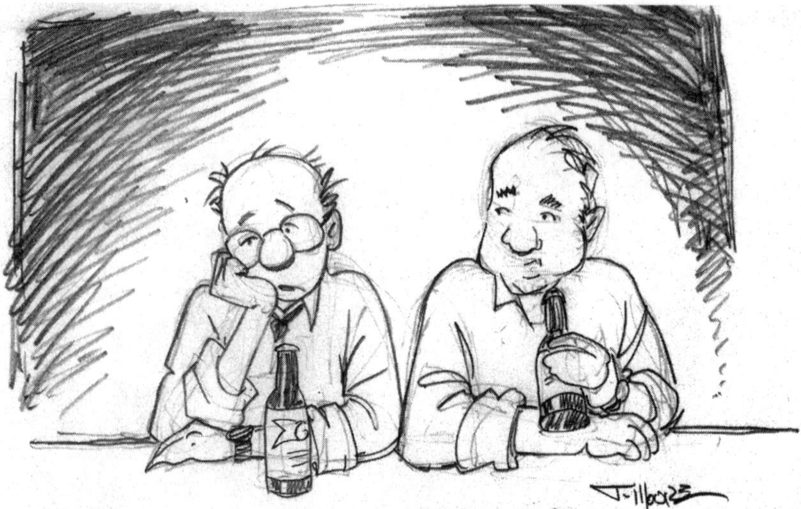

"I NEED TO REBOOT."

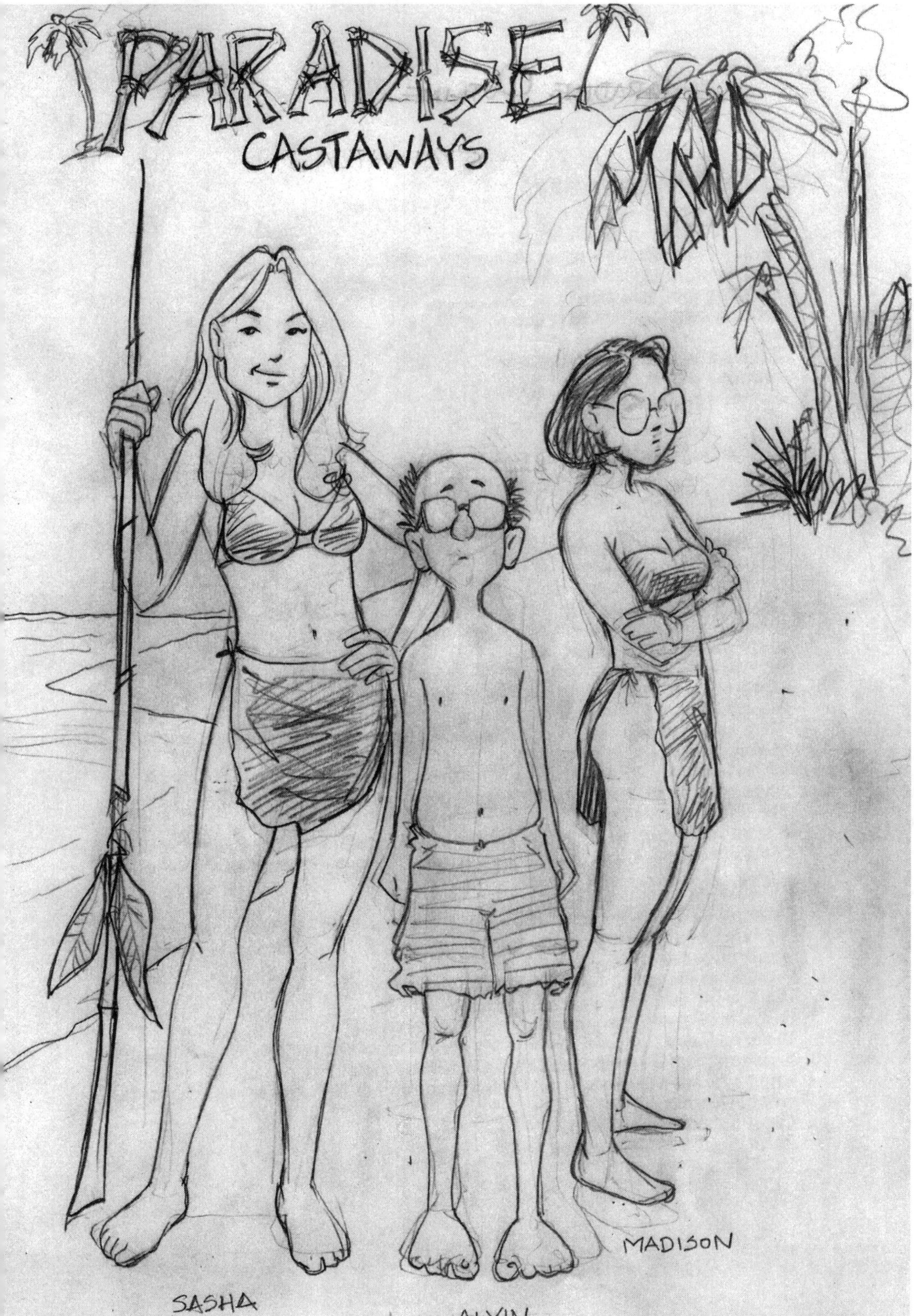
PARADISE
CASTAWAYS
SASHA
ALVIN
MADISON

swear I came up with this corny idea before the reality tv slut-puppies version
ut, Paradise Castaways: Jerry (Alvin, whatever) is stranded on an exotic island
ith two women who are beautiful but complete opposites. In real life neither of
iese women would have anything to do with Jerry, but when he is the only "man"
vailable, sparks fly. Every man's dream, every woman's worst nightmare. Fun, eh?

SASHA MEETS
FRANKLIN
THE BOA

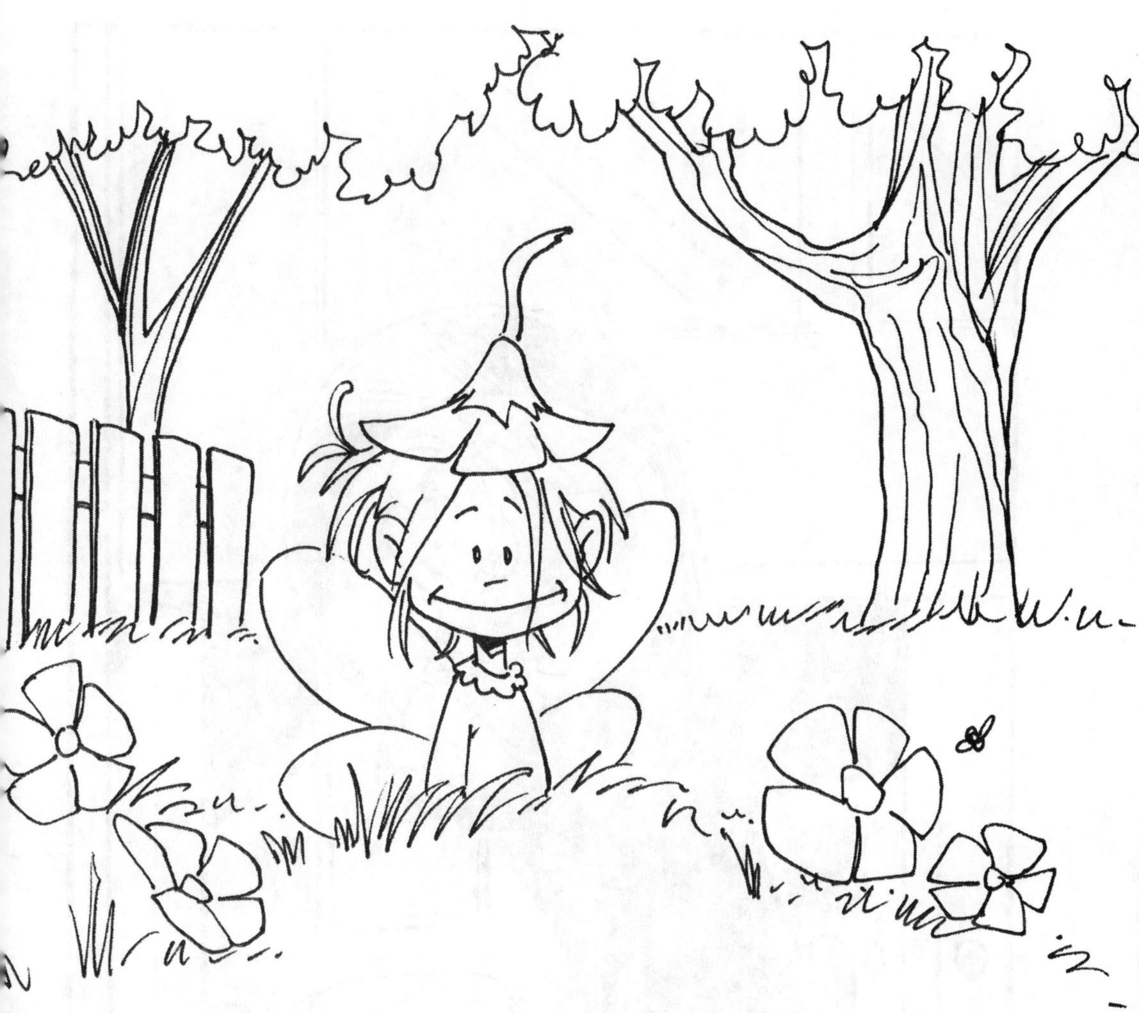

Have no fear, dear hearts! Kixie and her friends, Plato and Morris, are coming at you in a big way! Beginning next issue, Paradise TOO will feature full length Kixie stories, with back up stories starring Plato, the lovesick polar bear and Morris, the world's ugliest dog! Panel cartoons and spot drawings will be kept to one or two pages and, for the first time ever in Paradise TOO we will have a letter's page! It seems like people just can't stop talking about Kixie and her pals, so we think it's only fair you have a couple of pages to share your Kixiemania with the rest of the world!

So look for Paradise TOO #5 at your nearest comic book store in December and prepare yourself for THE RETURN OF KIXIE!

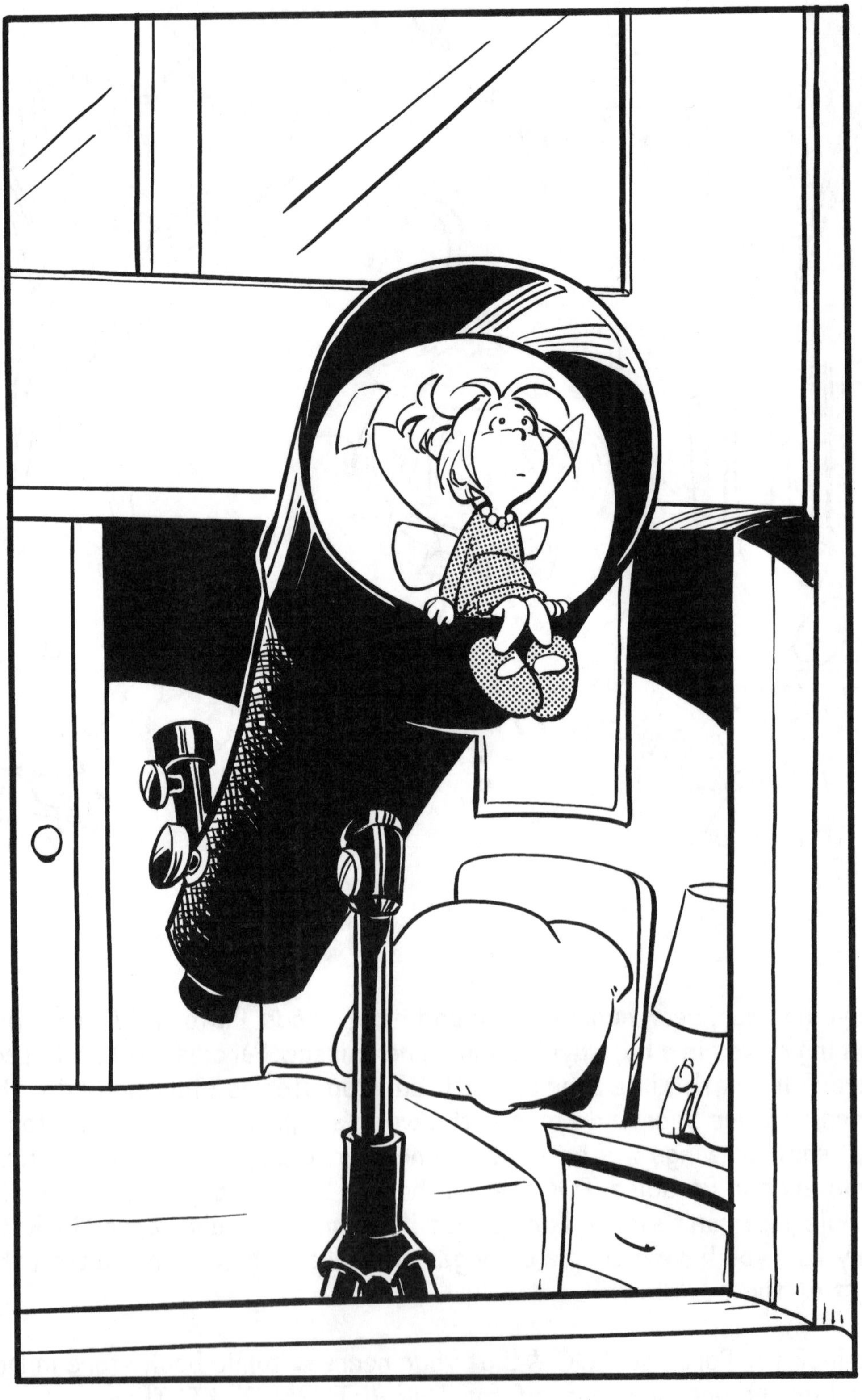

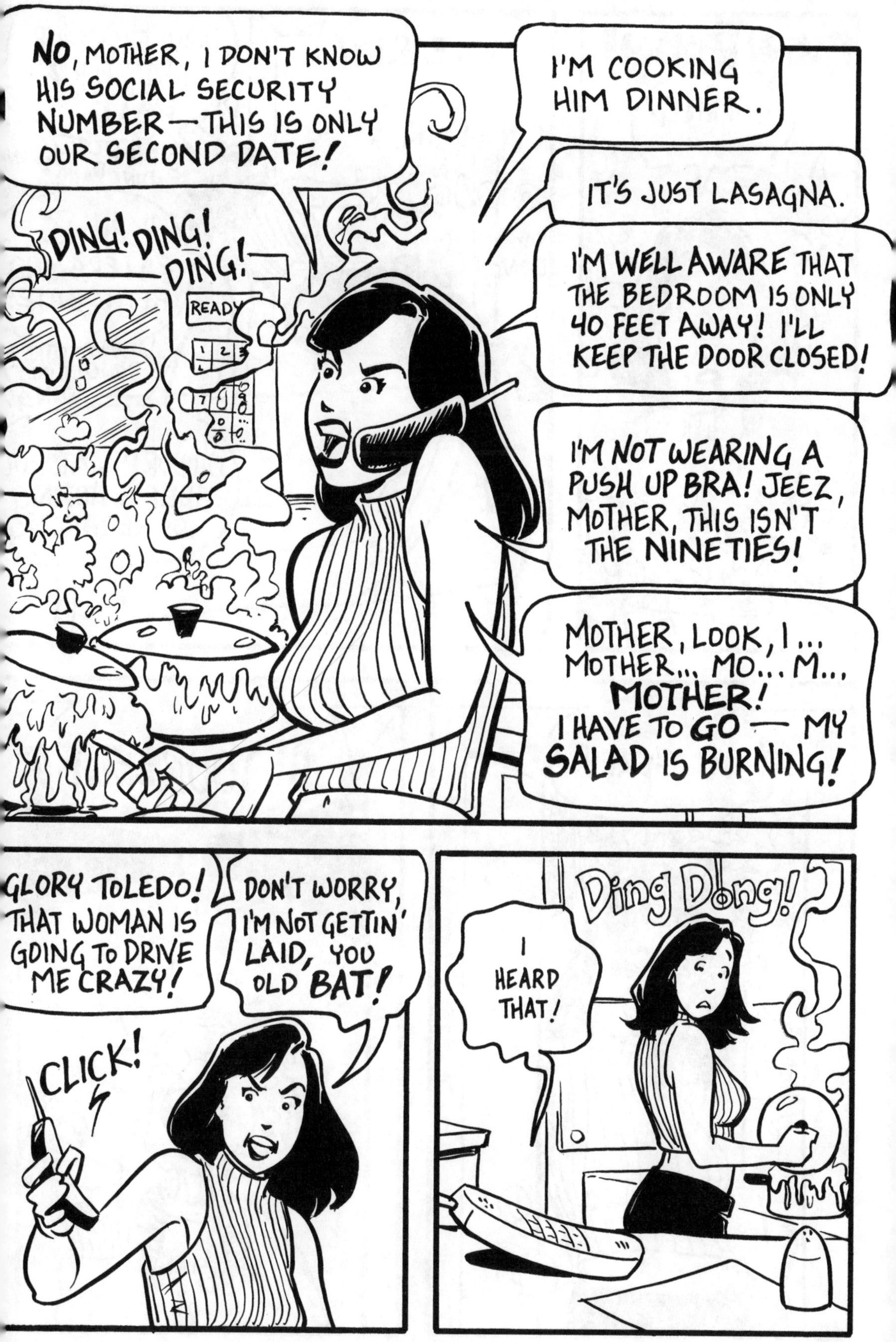
NO, MOTHER, I DON'T KNOW HIS SOCIAL SECURITY NUMBER—THIS IS ONLY OUR SECOND DATE!
I'M COOKING HIM DINNER.
IT'S JUST LASAGNA.
DING! DING! DING!
READY
I'M WELL AWARE THAT THE BEDROOM IS ONLY 40 FEET AWAY! I'LL KEEP THE DOOR CLOSED!
I'M NOT WEARING A PUSH UP BRA! JEEZ, MOTHER, THIS ISN'T THE NINETIES!
MOTHER, LOOK, I... MOTHER... MO... M... MOTHER! I HAVE TO GO — MY SALAD IS BURNING!
GLORY TOLEDO! THAT WOMAN IS GOING TO DRIVE ME CRAZY!
DON'T WORRY, I'M NOT GETTIN' LAID, YOU OLD BAT!
CLICK!
Ding Dong!
I HEARD THAT!

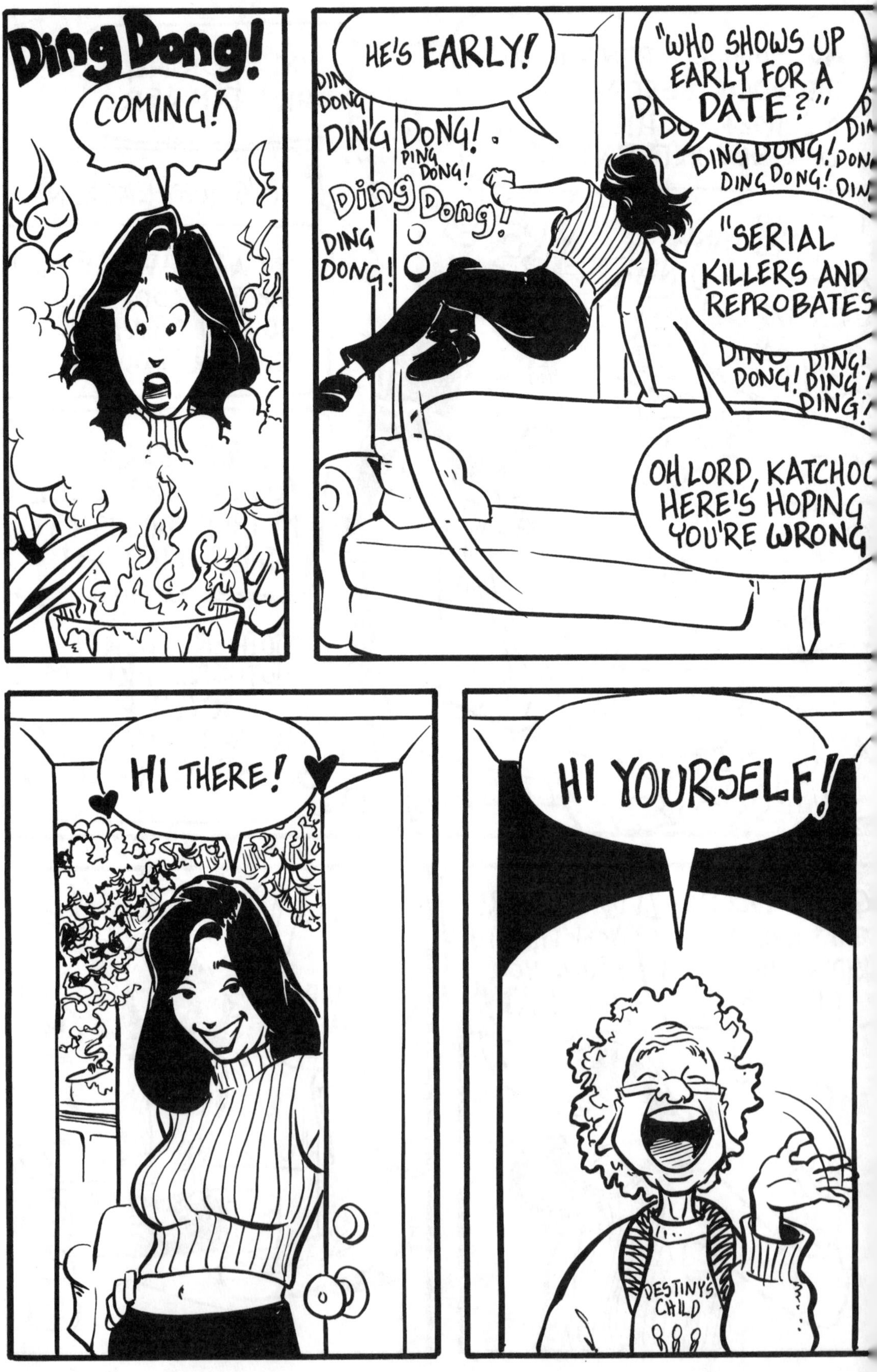
Ding Dong!
COMING!
HE'S EARLY!
DING DONG!
DING DONG!
Ding Dong!
DING DONG!
"WHO SHOWS UP EARLY FOR A DATE?"
DING DONG! DING DONG!
"SERIAL KILLERS AND REPROBATES"
DONG! DING! DING! DING!
OH LORD, KATCHOO HERE'S HOPING YOU'RE WRONG
HI THERE!
HI YOURSELF!
DESTINY'S CHILD

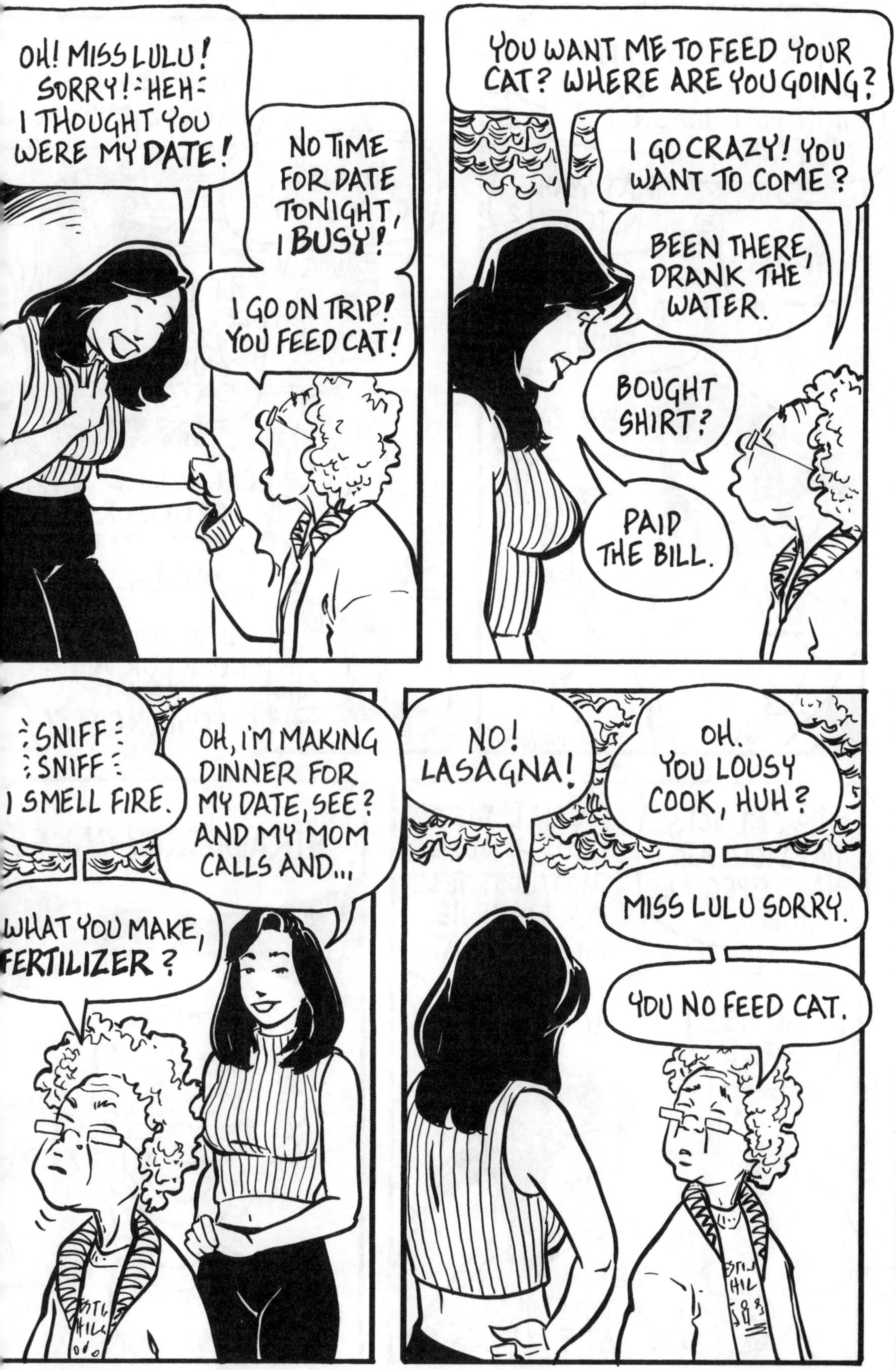
OH! MISS LULU! SORRY! HEH I THOUGHT YOU WERE MY DATE!
NO TIME FOR DATE TONIGHT, I BUSY!
I GO ON TRIP! YOU FEED CAT!
YOU WANT ME TO FEED YOUR CAT? WHERE ARE YOU GOING?
I GO CRAZY! YOU WANT TO COME?
BEEN THERE, DRANK THE WATER.
BOUGHT SHIRT?
PAID THE BILL.
SNIFF SNIFF I SMELL FIRE.
OH, I'M MAKING DINNER FOR MY DATE, SEE? AND MY MOM CALLS AND...
WHAT YOU MAKE, FERTILIZER?
NO! LASAGNA!
OH. YOU LOUSY COOK, HUH?
MISS LULU SORRY.
YOU NO FEED CAT.

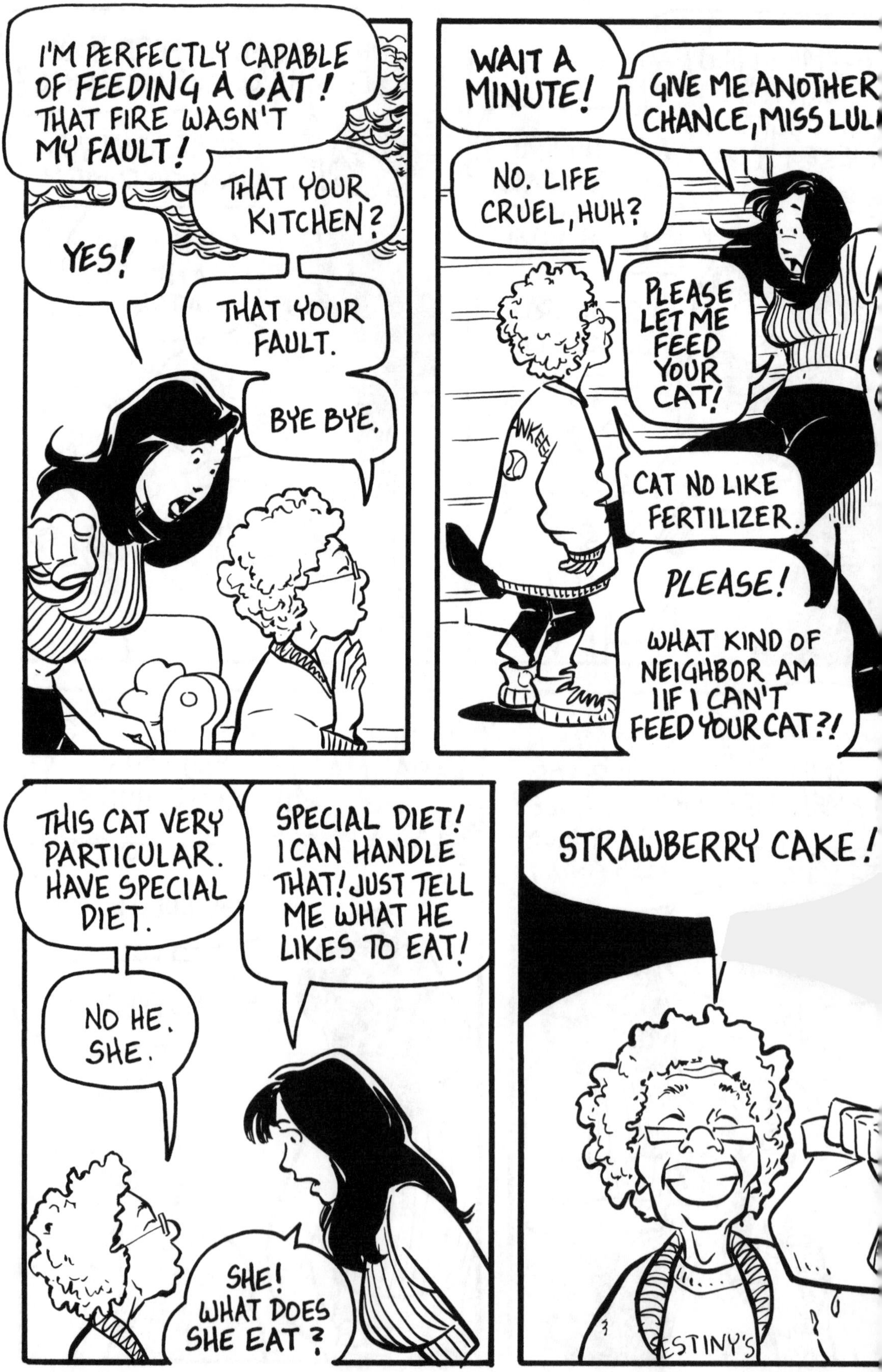

I'M PERFECTLY CAPABLE OF FEEDING A CAT! THAT FIRE WASN'T MY FAULT!
YES!
THAT YOUR KITCHEN?
THAT YOUR FAULT.
BYE BYE.
WAIT A MINUTE!
GIVE ME ANOTHER CHANCE, MISS LUL
NO. LIFE CRUEL, HUH?
PLEASE LET ME FEED YOUR CAT!
CAT NO LIKE FERTILIZER.
PLEASE!
WHAT KIND OF NEIGHBOR AM I IF I CAN'T FEED YOUR CAT?!
THIS CAT VERY PARTICULAR. HAVE SPECIAL DIET.
SPECIAL DIET! I CAN HANDLE THAT! JUST TELL ME WHAT HE LIKES TO EAT!
NO HE. SHE.
SHE! WHAT DOES SHE EAT?
STRAWBERRY CAKE!
ESTINY'S

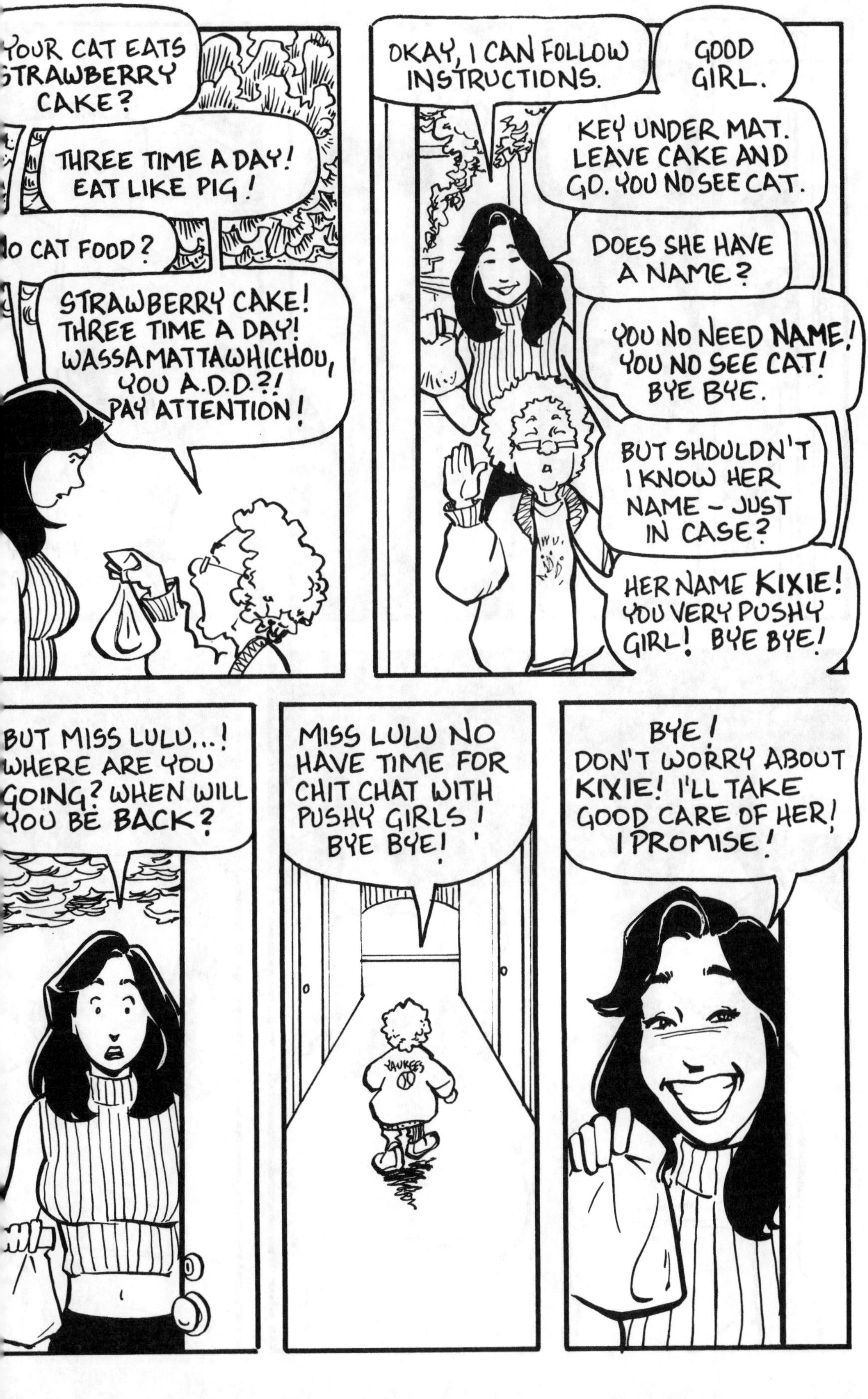
YOUR CAT EATS STRAWBERRY CAKE?
THREE TIME A DAY! EAT LIKE PIG!
NO CAT FOOD?
STRAWBERRY CAKE! THREE TIME A DAY! WASSAMATTAWHICHOU, YOU A.D.D.?! PAY ATTENTION!
OKAY, I CAN FOLLOW INSTRUCTIONS.
GOOD GIRL.
KEY UNDER MAT. LEAVE CAKE AND GO. YOU NO SEE CAT.
DOES SHE HAVE A NAME?
YOU NO NEED NAME! YOU NO SEE CAT! BYE BYE.
BUT SHOULDN'T I KNOW HER NAME – JUST IN CASE?
HER NAME KIXIE! YOU VERY PUSHY GIRL! BYE BYE!
BUT MISS LULU...! WHERE ARE YOU GOING? WHEN WILL YOU BE BACK?
MISS LULU NO HAVE TIME FOR CHIT CHAT WITH PUSHY GIRLS! BYE BYE!
YANKEES
BYE! DON'T WORRY ABOUT KIXIE! I'LL TAKE GOOD CARE OF HER! I PROMISE!

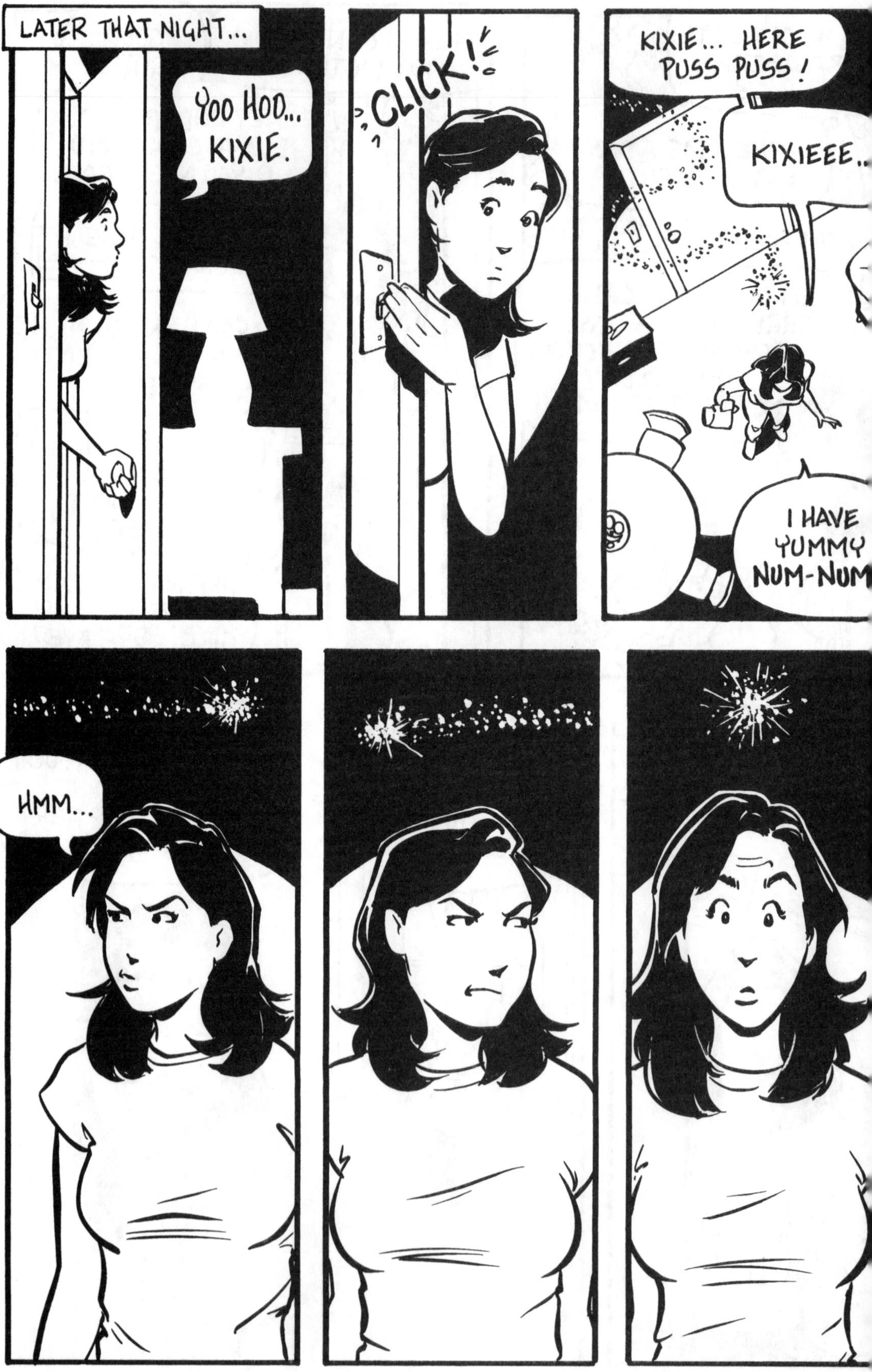
LATER THAT NIGHT...
YOO HOO... KIXIE.
CLICK!
KIXIE... HERE PUSS PUSS!
KIXIEEE...
I HAVE YUMMY NUM-NUM
HMM...

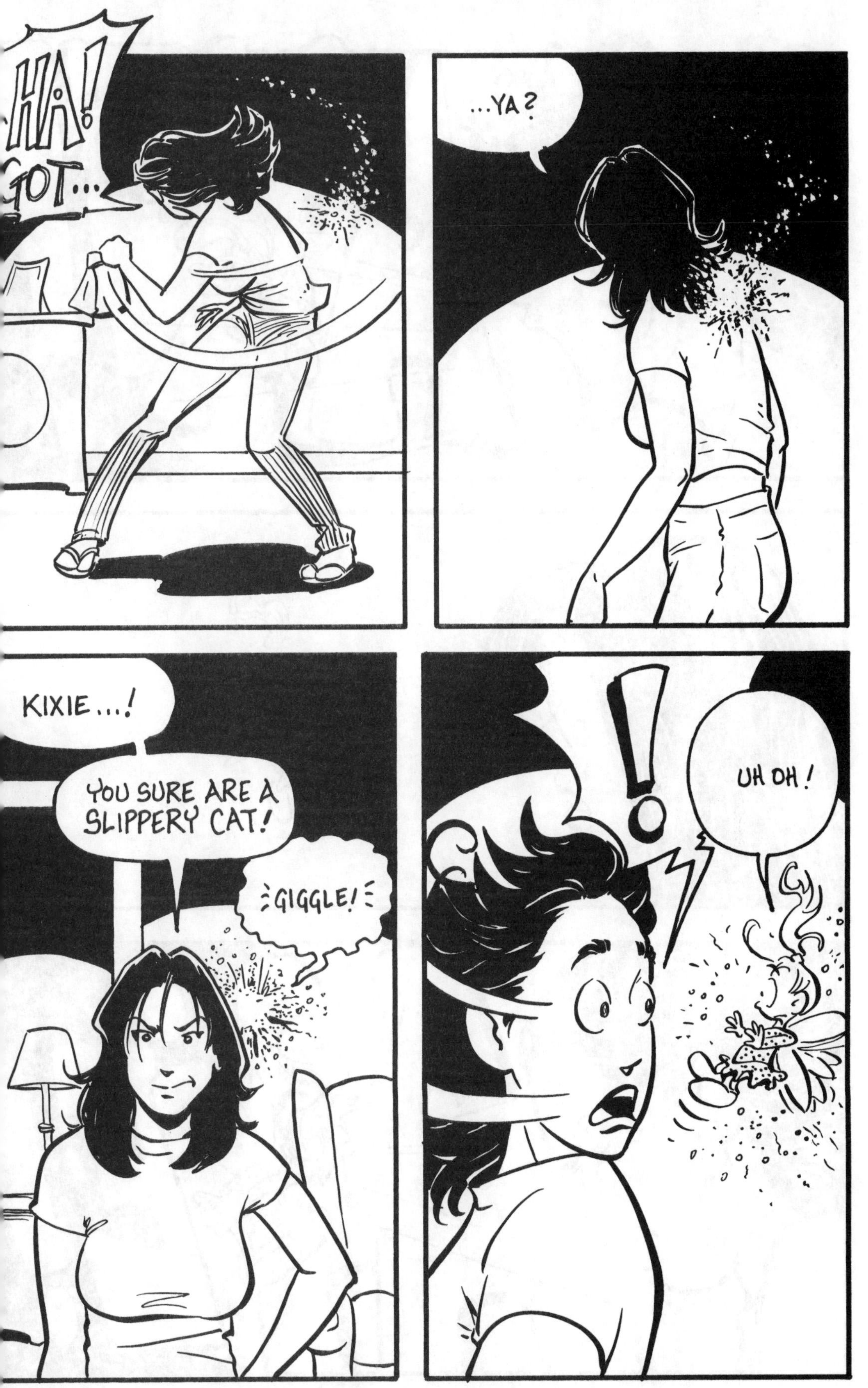
HA!
GOT...
...YA?
KIXIE...!
YOU SURE ARE A SLIPPERY CAT!
GIGGLE!
!
UH OH!

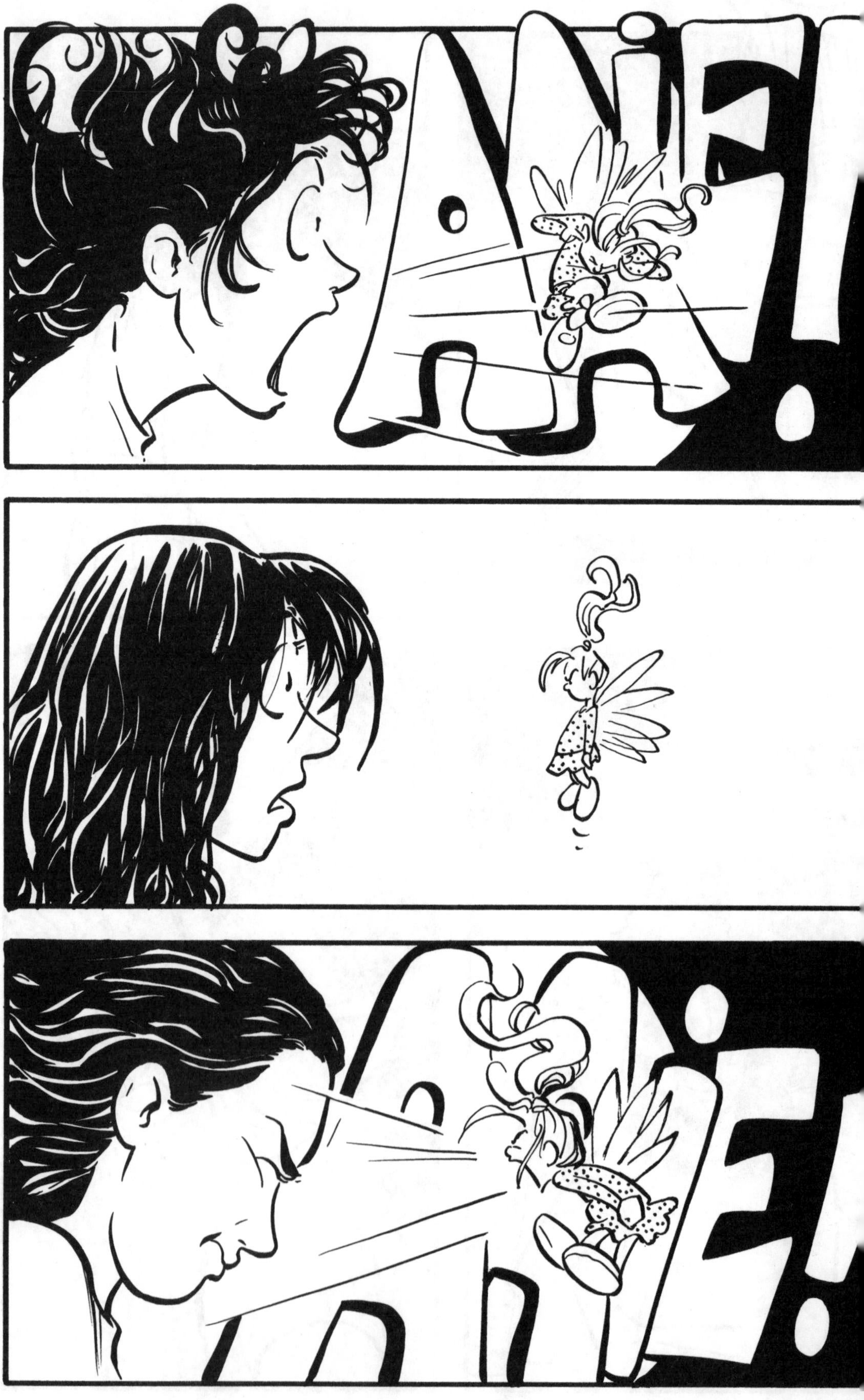

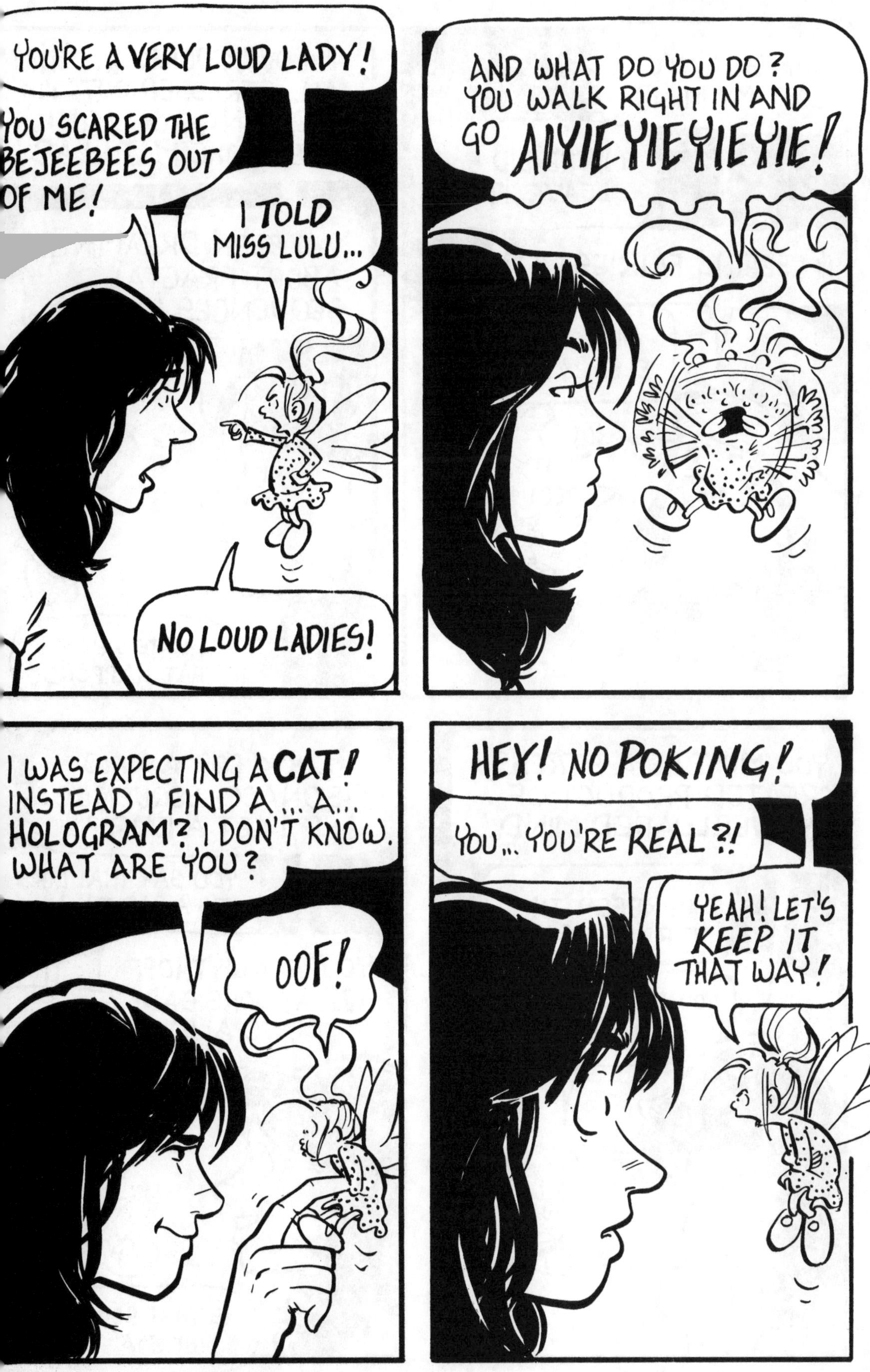
YOU'RE A VERY LOUD LADY!
YOU SCARED THE BEJEEBEES OUT OF ME!
I TOLD MISS LULU...
NO LOUD LADIES!
AND WHAT DO YOU DO? YOU WALK RIGHT IN AND GO AIYIEYIEYIEYIE!
I WAS EXPECTING A CAT! INSTEAD I FIND A... A... HOLOGRAM? I DON'T KNOW. WHAT ARE YOU?
OOF!
HEY! NO POKING!
YOU... YOU'RE REAL?!
YEAH! LET'S KEEP IT THAT WAY!

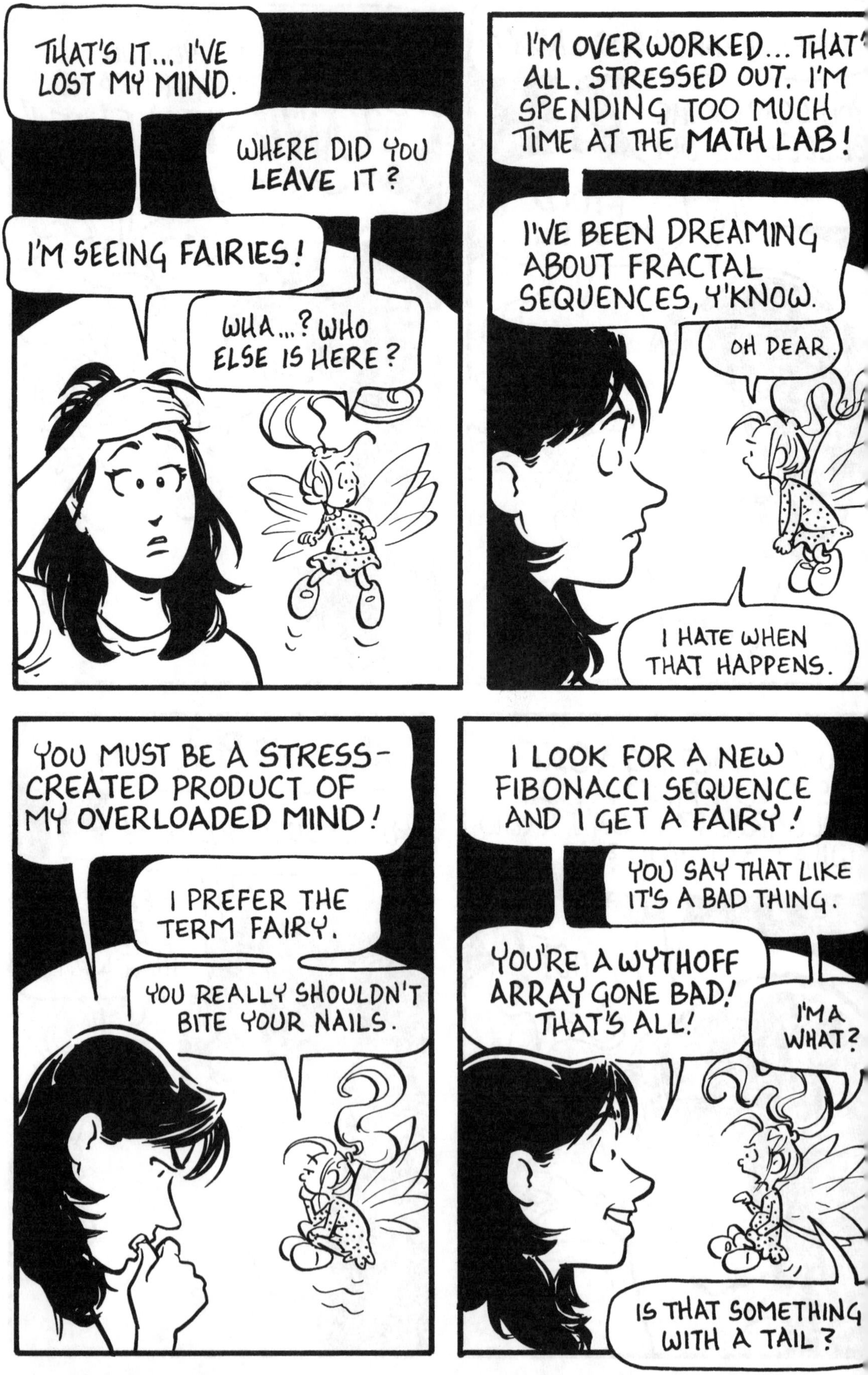
THAT'S IT... I'VE LOST MY MIND.
WHERE DID YOU LEAVE IT?
I'M SEEING FAIRIES!
WHA...? WHO ELSE IS HERE?
I'M OVERWORKED... THAT'S ALL. STRESSED OUT. I'M SPENDING TOO MUCH TIME AT THE MATH LAB!
I'VE BEEN DREAMING ABOUT FRACTAL SEQUENCES, Y'KNOW.
OH DEAR.
I HATE WHEN THAT HAPPENS.
YOU MUST BE A STRESS-CREATED PRODUCT OF MY OVERLOADED MIND!
I PREFER THE TERM FAIRY.
YOU REALLY SHOULDN'T BITE YOUR NAILS.
I LOOK FOR A NEW FIBONACCI SEQUENCE AND I GET A FAIRY!
YOU SAY THAT LIKE IT'S A BAD THING.
YOU'RE A WYTHOFF ARRAY GONE BAD! THAT'S ALL!
I'M A WHAT?
IS THAT SOMETHING WITH A TAIL?

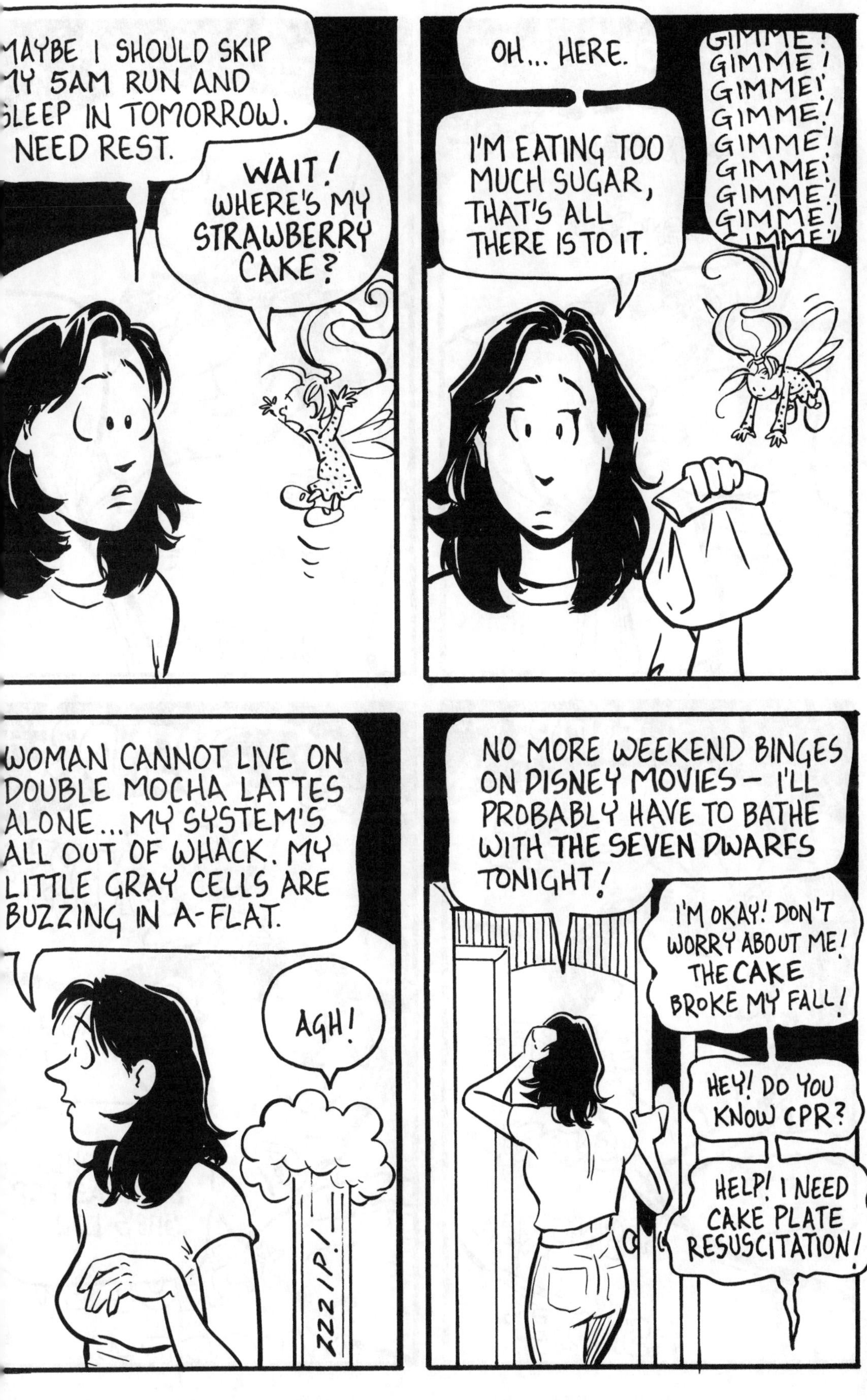

MAYBE I SHOULD SKIP MY 5AM RUN AND SLEEP IN TOMORROW. NEED REST.
WAIT! WHERE'S MY STRAWBERRY CAKE?
OH... HERE.
I'M EATING TOO MUCH SUGAR, THAT'S ALL THERE IS TO IT.
GIMME! GIMME! GIMME! GIMME! GIMME! GIMME! GIMME! GIMME! GIMME!
WOMAN CANNOT LIVE ON DOUBLE MOCHA LATTES ALONE... MY SYSTEM'S ALL OUT OF WHACK. MY LITTLE GRAY CELLS ARE BUZZING IN A-FLAT.
AGH!
ZZZIP!
NO MORE WEEKEND BINGES ON DISNEY MOVIES — I'LL PROBABLY HAVE TO BATHE WITH THE SEVEN DWARFS TONIGHT!
I'M OKAY! DON'T WORRY ABOUT ME! THE CAKE BROKE MY FALL!
HEY! DO YOU KNOW CPR?
HELP! I NEED CAKE PLATE RESUSCITATION!

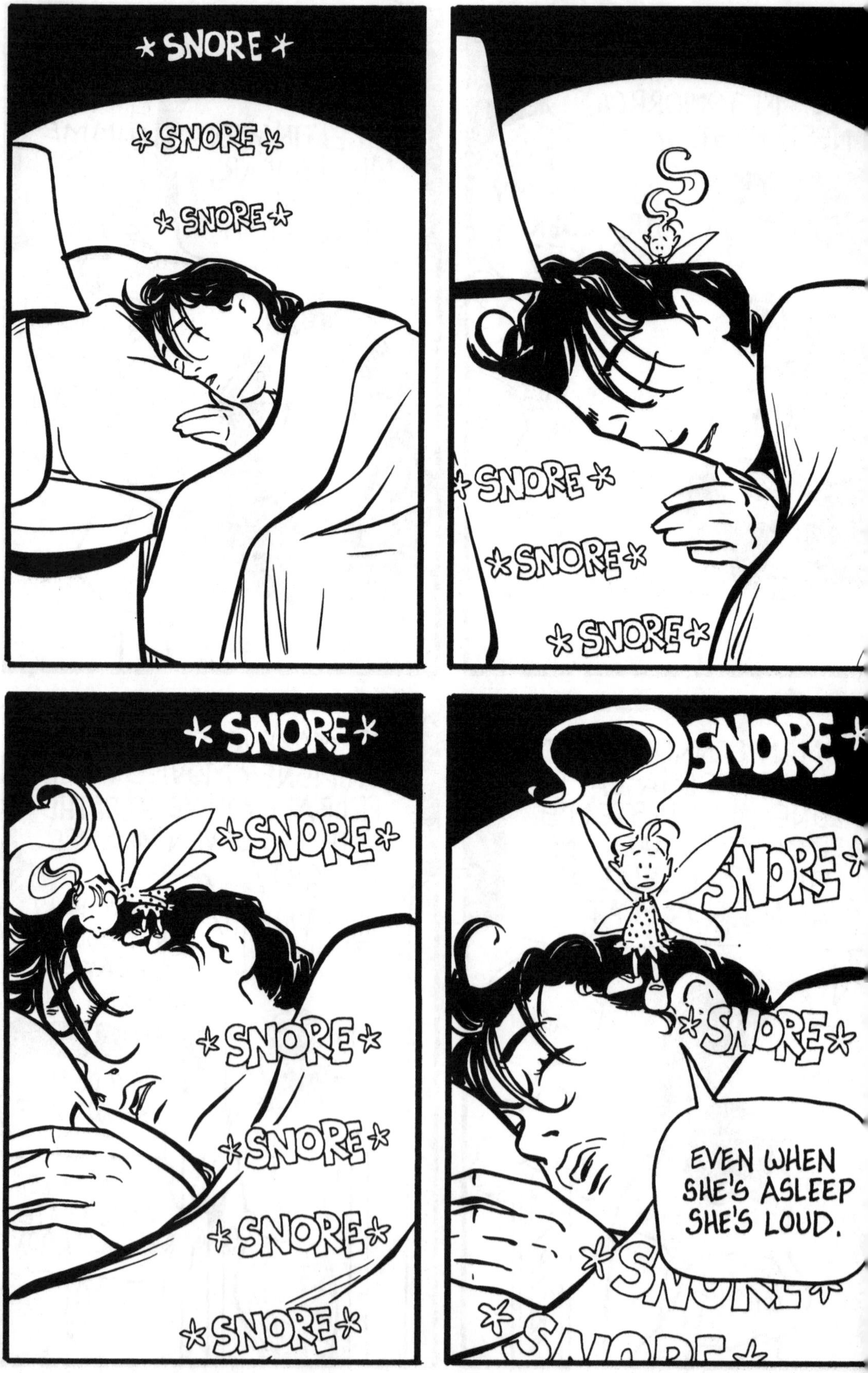
SNORE
SNORE
SNORE
SNORE
SNORE
SNORE
SNORE
SNORE
SNORE
SNORE
SNORE
SNORE
SNORE*
SNORE*
SNORE
EVEN WHEN SHE'S ASLEEP SHE'S LOUD.

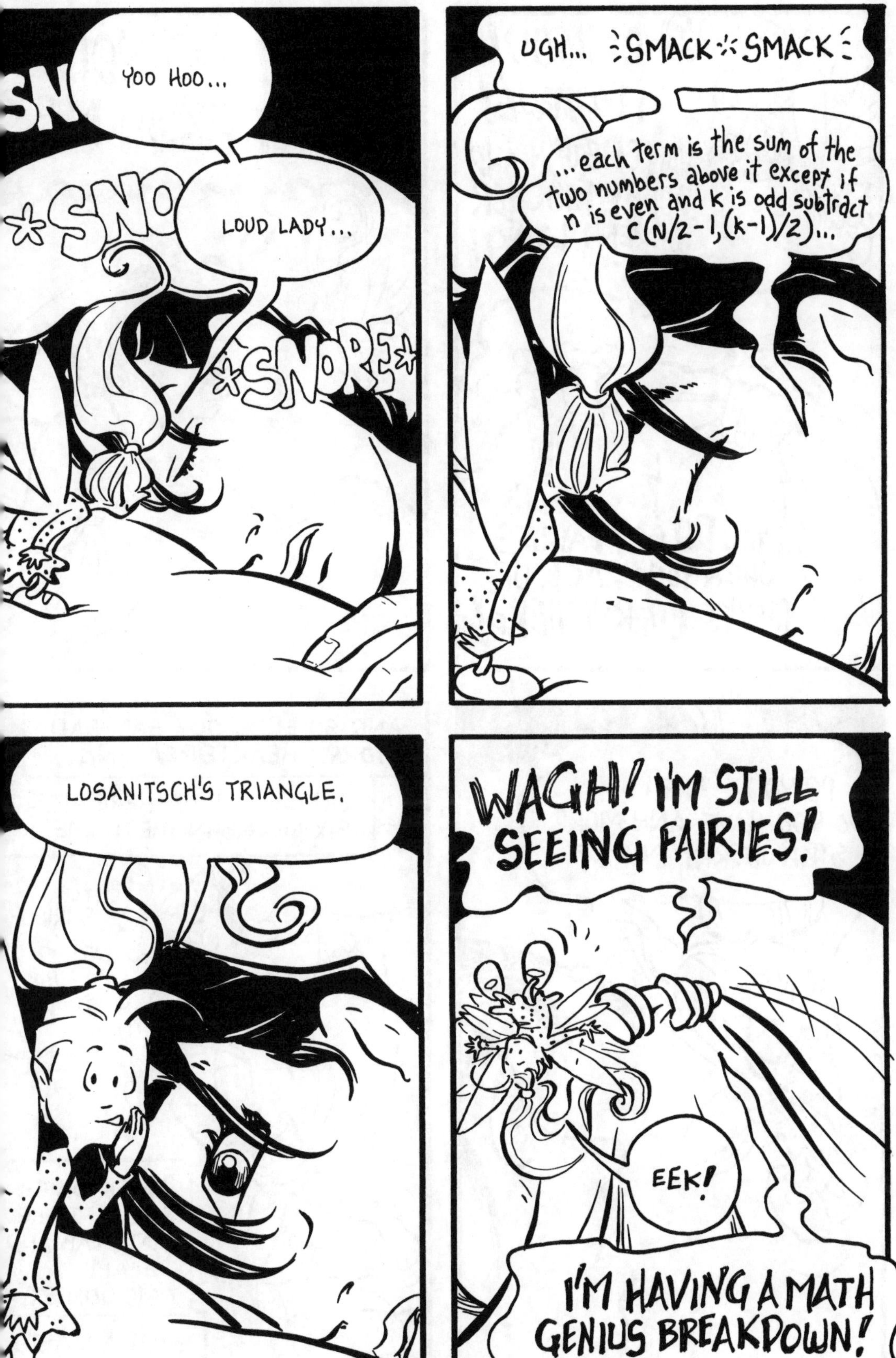
SN
YOO HOO...
*SNO
LOUD LADY...
SNORE
UGH... SMACK SMACK
...each term is the sum of the two numbers above it except if n is even and k is odd subtract c(N/2-1,(k-1)/2)...
LOSANITSCH'S TRIANGLE.
WAGH! I'M STILL SEEING FAIRIES!
EEK!
I'M HAVING A MATH GENIUS BREAKDOWN!

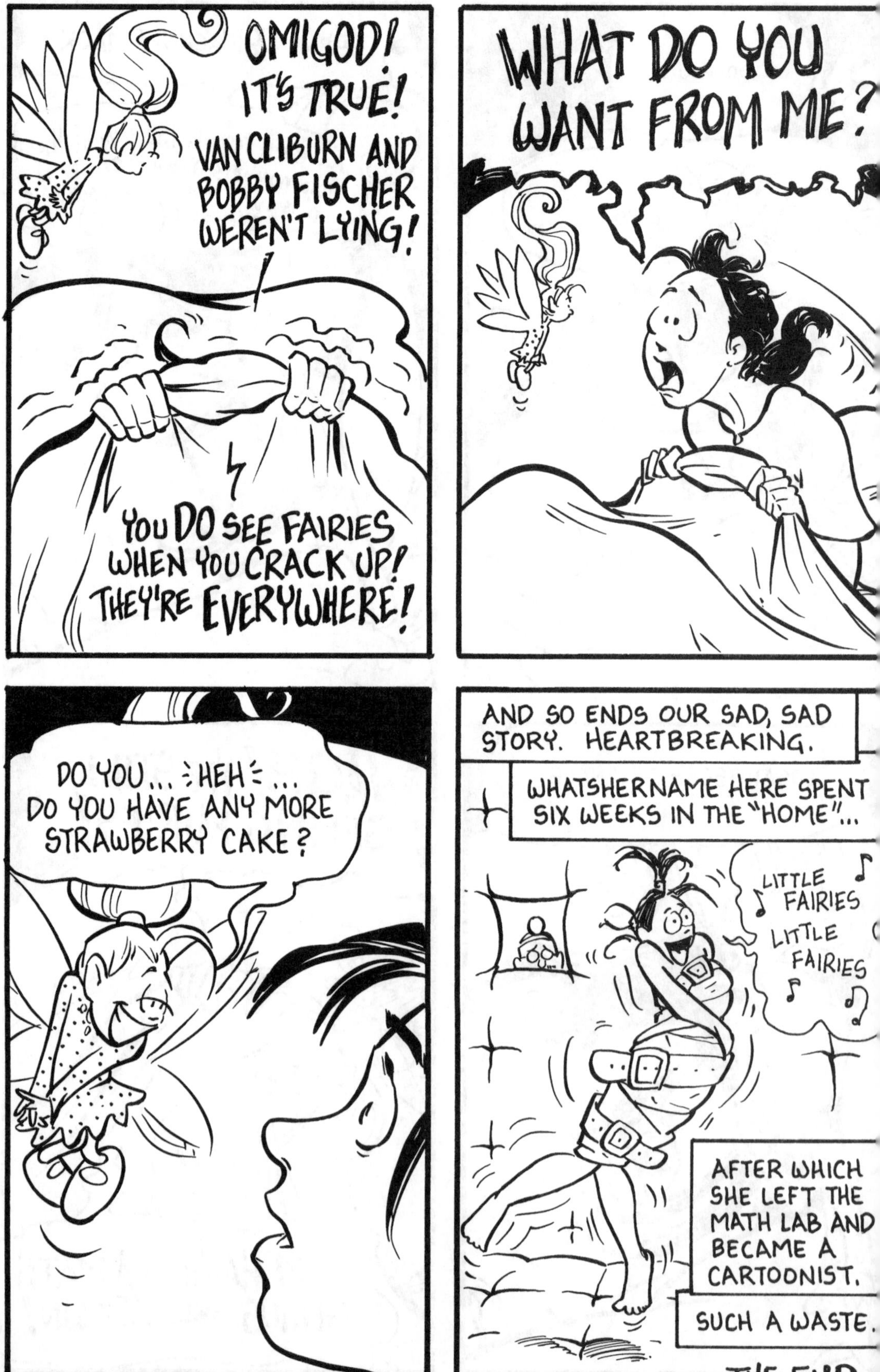
OMIGOD! IT'S TRUE! VAN CLIBURN AND BOBBY FISCHER WEREN'T LYING!
YOU DO SEE FAIRIES WHEN YOU CRACK UP! THEY'RE EVERYWHERE!
WHAT DO YOU WANT FROM ME?
DO YOU... HEH... DO YOU HAVE ANY MORE STRAWBERRY CAKE?
AND SO ENDS OUR SAD, SAD STORY. HEARTBREAKING.
WHATSHERNAME HERE SPENT SIX WEEKS IN THE "HOME"...
LITTLE FAIRIES LITTLE FAIRIES
AFTER WHICH SHE LEFT THE MATH LAB AND BECAME A CARTOONIST.
SUCH A WASTE.
THE END

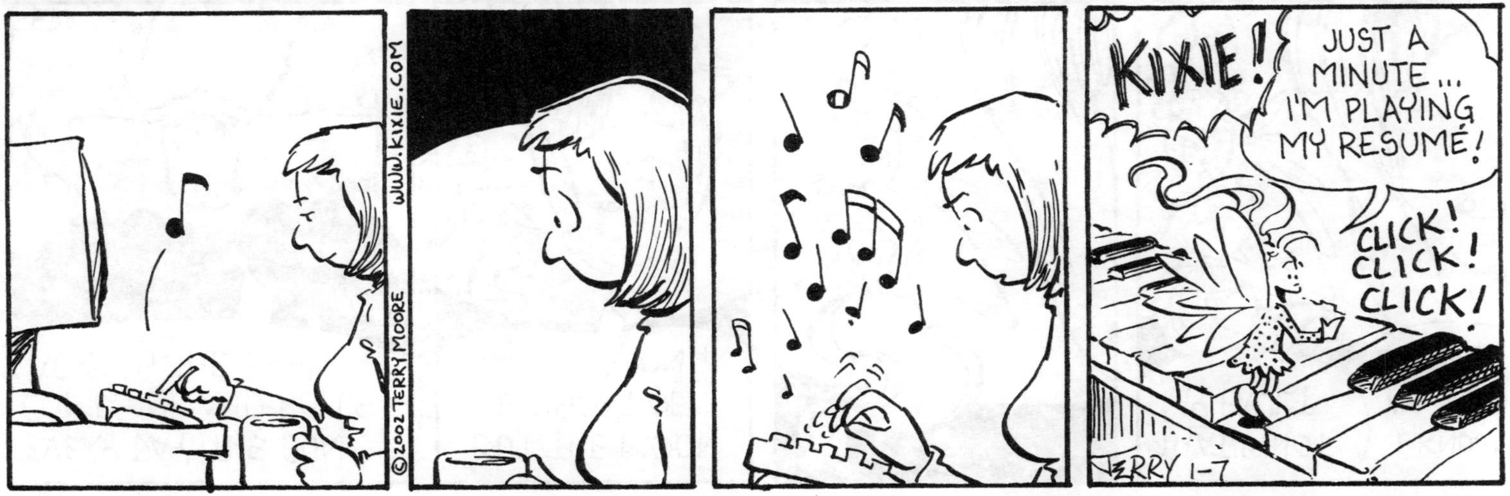
©2002 TERRY MOORE
WWW.KIXIE.COM
KIXIE!
JUST A MINUTE... I'M PLAYING MY RESUMÉ!
CLICK! CLICK! CLICK!
TERRY 1-7

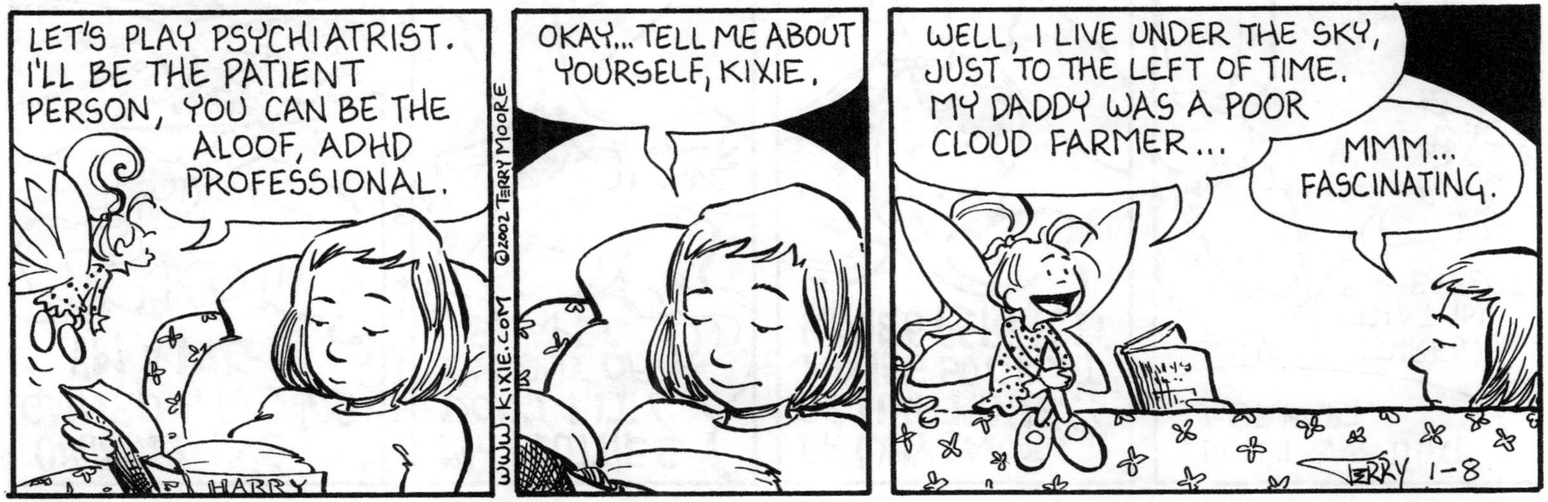
LET'S PLAY PSYCHIATRIST. I'LL BE THE PATIENT PERSON, YOU CAN BE THE ALOOF, ADHD PROFESSIONAL.
HARRY
©2002 TERRY MOORE
WWW.KIXIE.COM
OKAY... TELL ME ABOUT YOURSELF, KIXIE.
WELL, I LIVE UNDER THE SKY, JUST TO THE LEFT OF TIME. MY DADDY WAS A POOR CLOUD FARMER...
MMM... FASCINATING.
TERRY 1-8

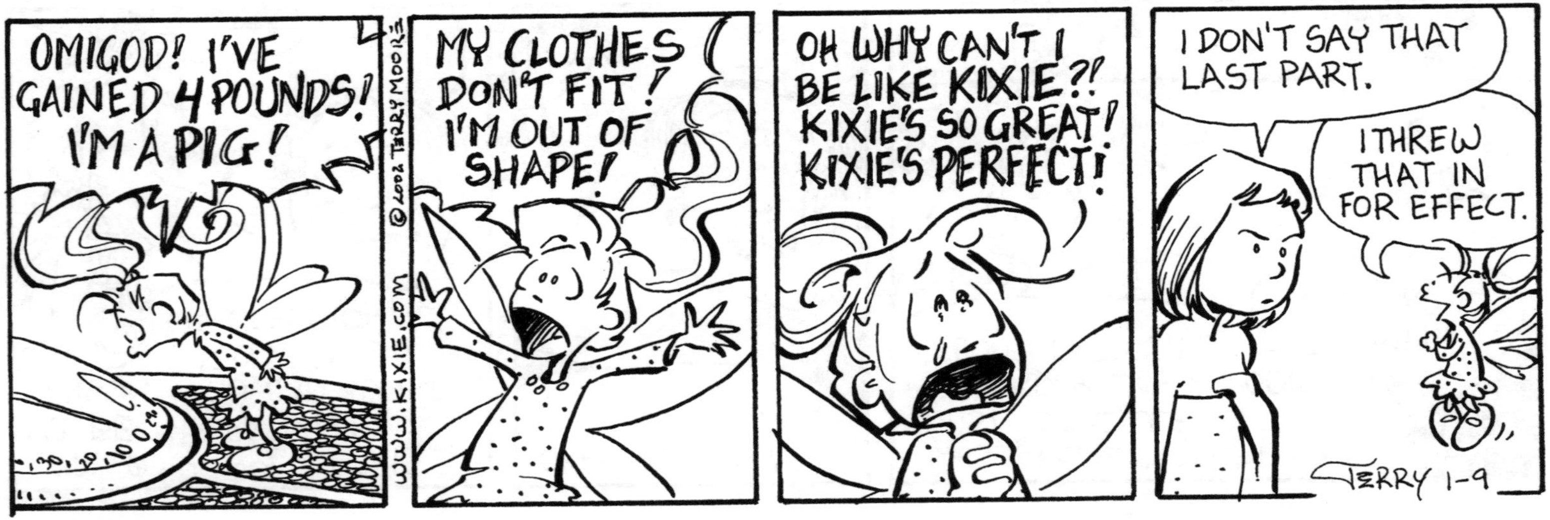
OMIGOD! I'VE GAINED 4 POUNDS! I'M A PIG!
WWW.KIXIE.COM ©2002 TERRY MOORE
MY CLOTHES DON'T FIT! I'M OUT OF SHAPE!
OH WHY CAN'T I BE LIKE KIXIE?! KIXIE'S SO GREAT! KIXIE'S PERFECT!
I DON'T SAY THAT LAST PART.
I THREW THAT IN FOR EFFECT.
TERRY 1-9

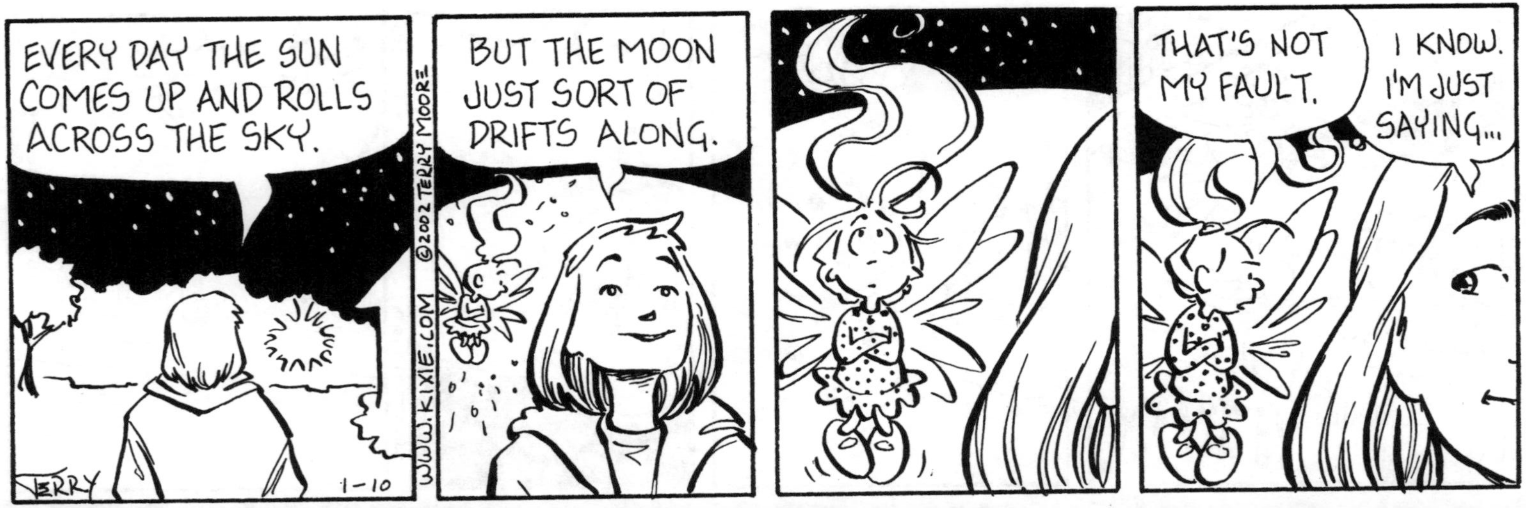
EVERY DAY THE SUN COMES UP AND ROLLS ACROSS THE SKY.
TERRY
1-10
WWW.KIXIE.COM ©2002 TERRY MOORE
BUT THE MOON JUST SORT OF DRIFTS ALONG.
THAT'S NOT MY FAULT.
I KNOW. I'M JUST SAYING...

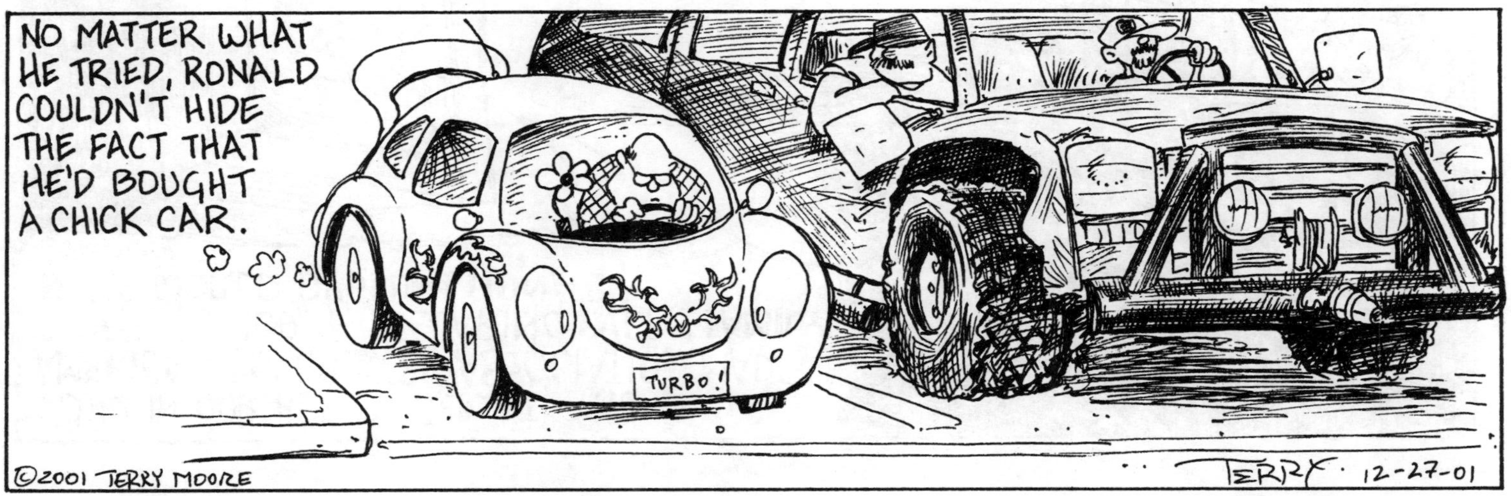
NO MATTER WHAT HE TRIED, RONALD COULDN'T HIDE THE FACT THAT HE'D BOUGHT A CHICK CAR.
TURBO!
©2001 TERRY MOORE
TERRY · 12-27-01

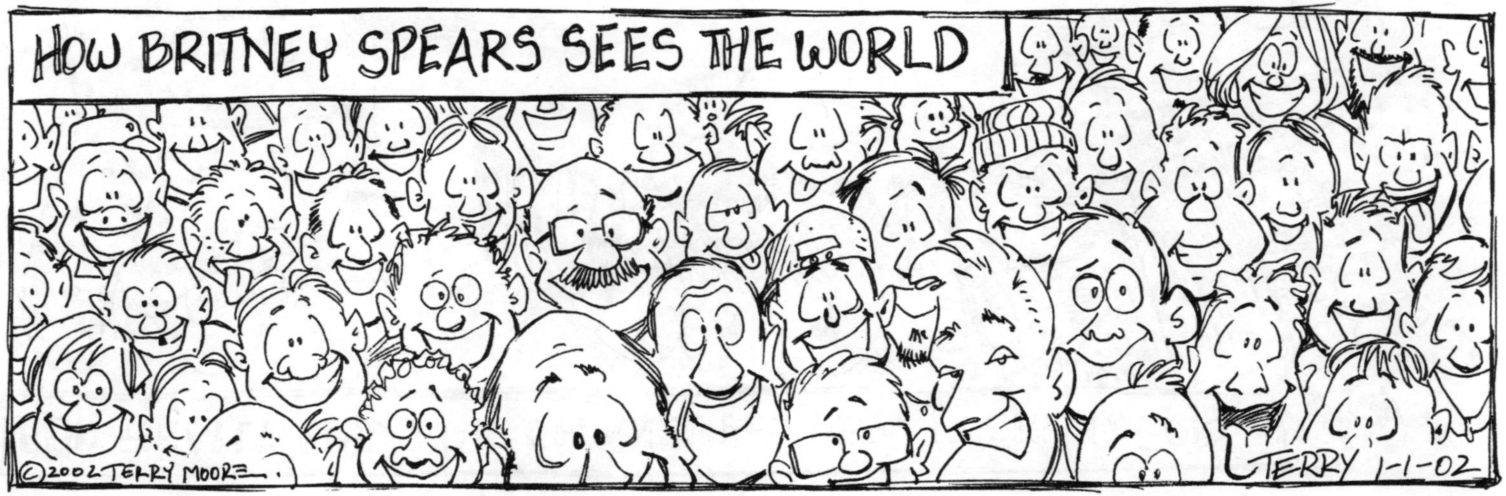
HOW BRITNEY SPEARS SEES THE WORLD
©2002 TERRY MOORE
TERRY 1-1-02

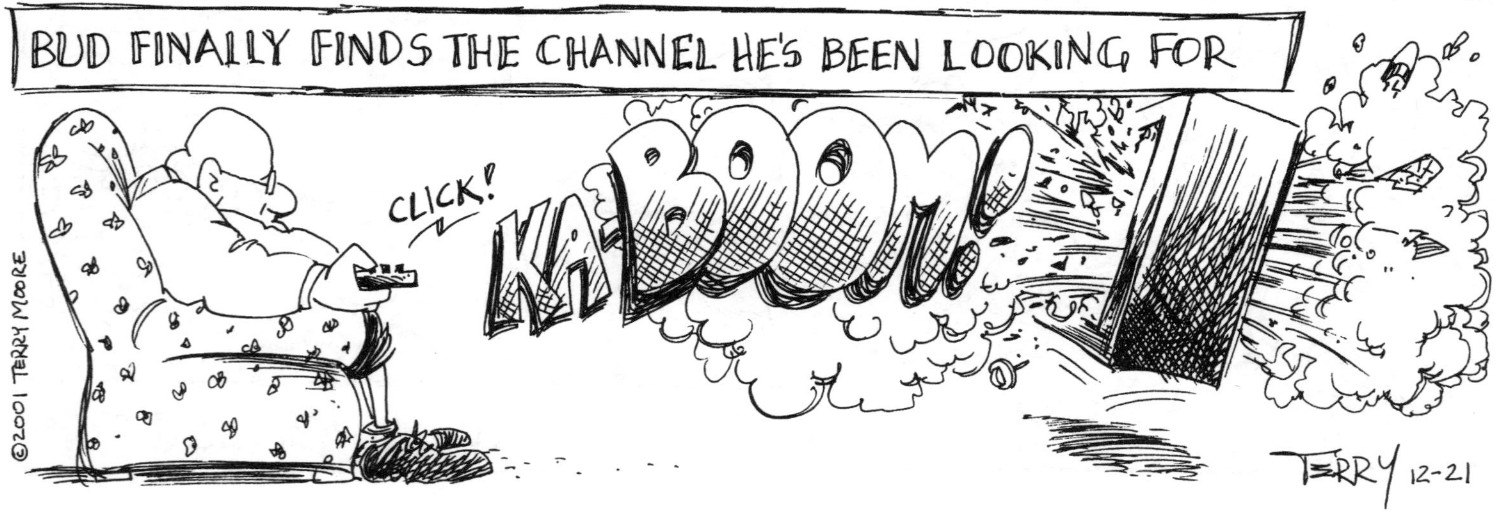
BUD FINALLY FINDS THE CHANNEL HE'S BEEN LOOKING FOR
CLICK!
KA-BOOOM!
©2001 TERRY MOORE
TERRY 12-21

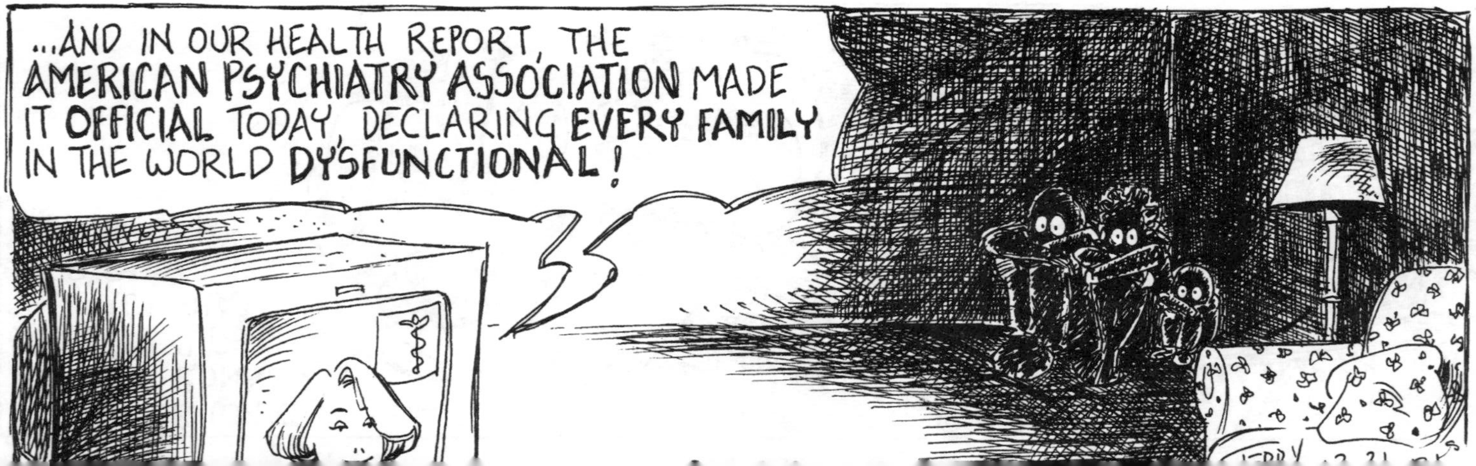
...AND IN OUR HEALTH REPORT, THE AMERICAN PSYCHIATRY ASSOCIATION MADE IT OFFICIAL TODAY, DECLARING EVERY FAMILY IN THE WORLD DYSFUNCTIONAL!

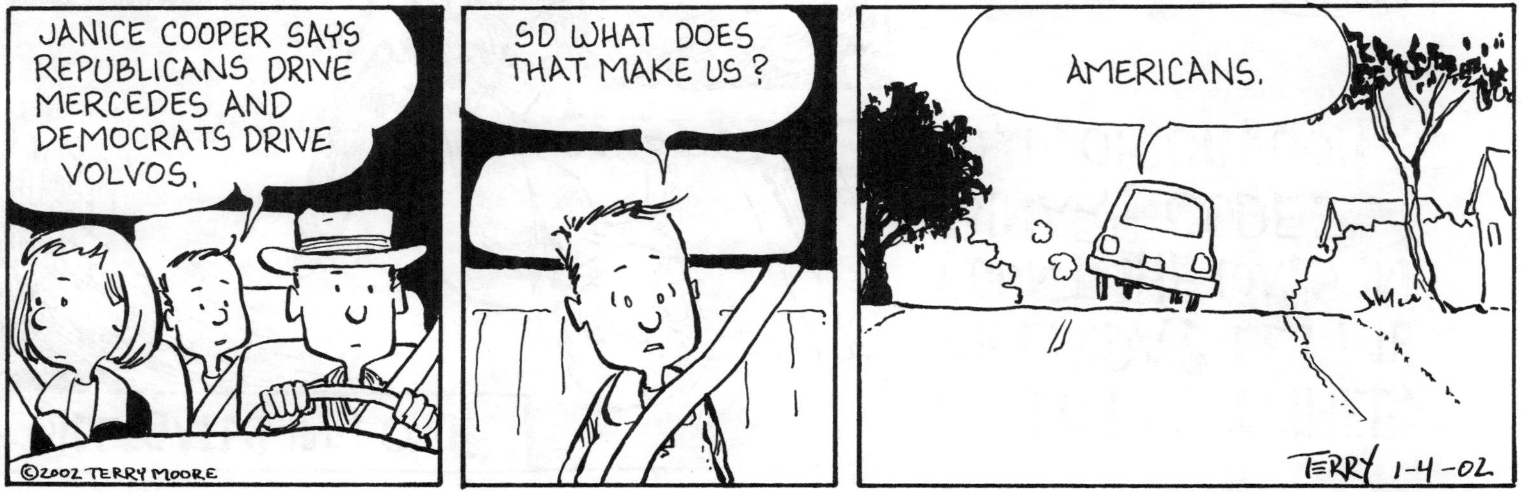
JANICE COOPER SAYS REPUBLICANS DRIVE MERCEDES AND DEMOCRATS DRIVE VOLVOS.
©2002 TERRY MOORE
SO WHAT DOES THAT MAKE US?
AMERICANS.
TERRY 1-4-02

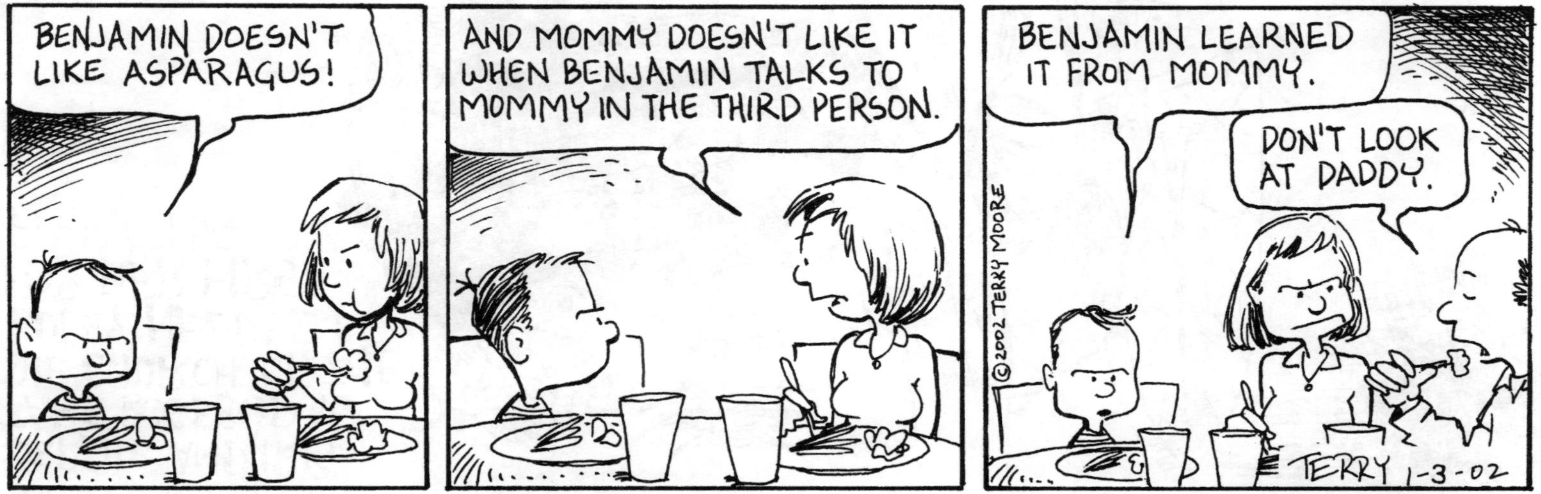
BENJAMIN DOESN'T LIKE ASPARAGUS!
AND MOMMY DOESN'T LIKE IT WHEN BENJAMIN TALKS TO MOMMY IN THE THIRD PERSON.
©2002 TERRY MOORE
BENJAMIN LEARNED IT FROM MOMMY.
DON'T LOOK AT DADDY.
TERRY 1-3-02

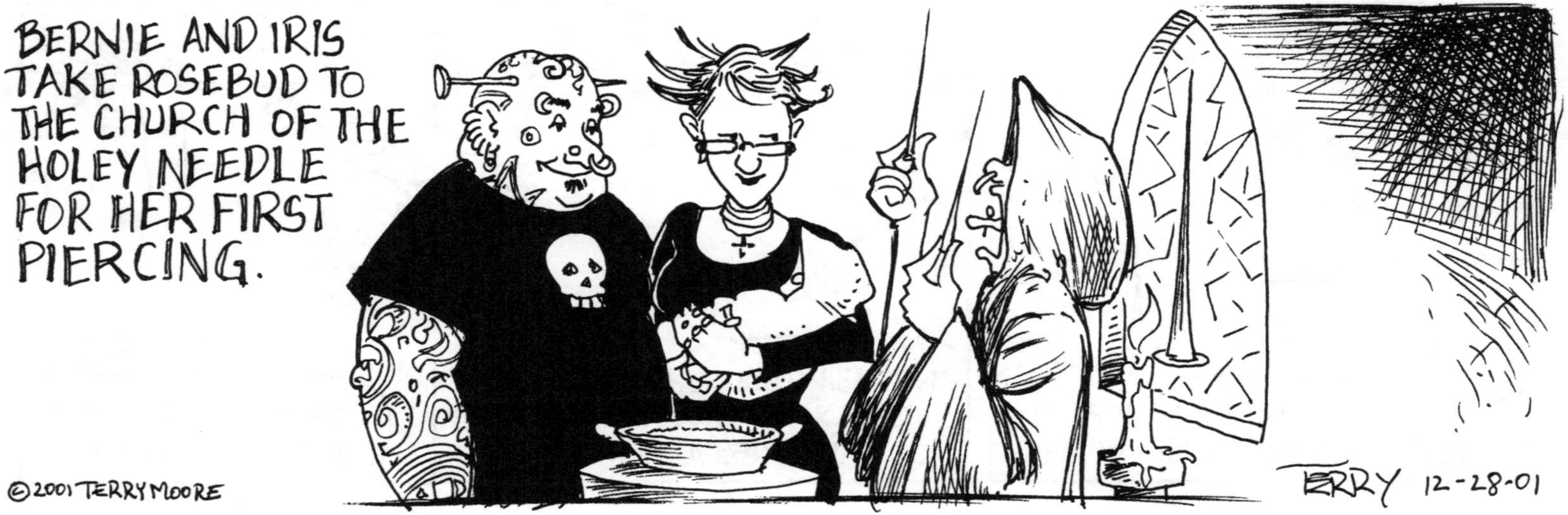
BERNIE AND IRIS TAKE ROSEBUD TO THE CHURCH OF THE HOLEY NEEDLE FOR HER FIRST PIERCING.
©2001 TERRY MOORE
TERRY 12-28-01

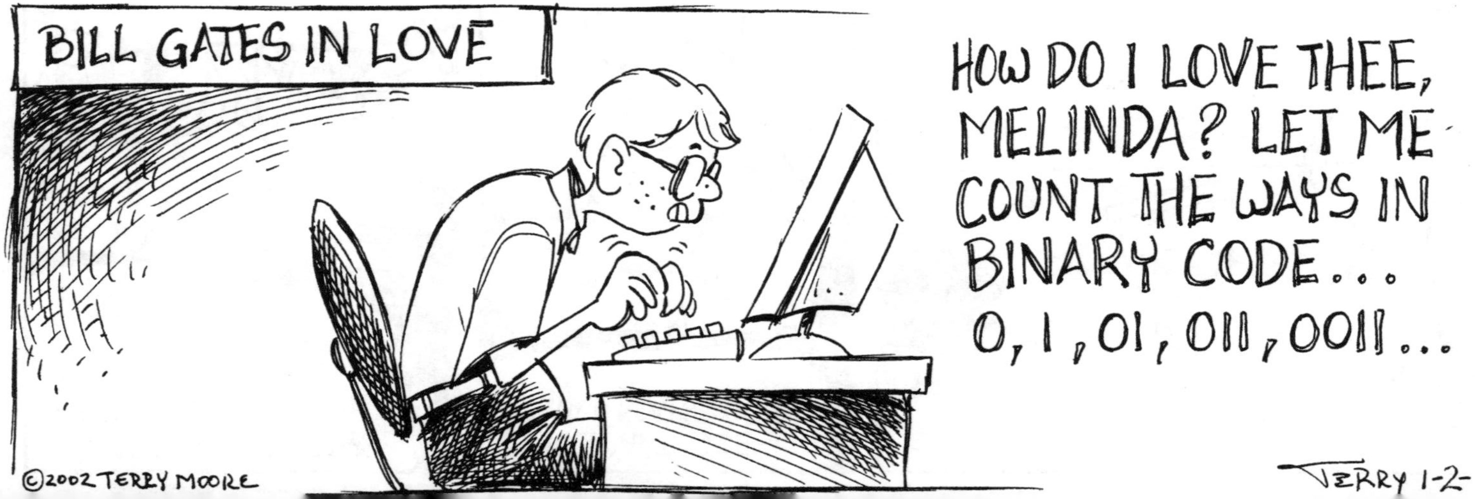
BILL GATES IN LOVE
HOW DO I LOVE THEE, MELINDA? LET ME COUNT THE WAYS IN BINARY CODE...
0, 1, 01, 011, 0011...
©2002 TERRY MOORE
TERRY 1-2-02

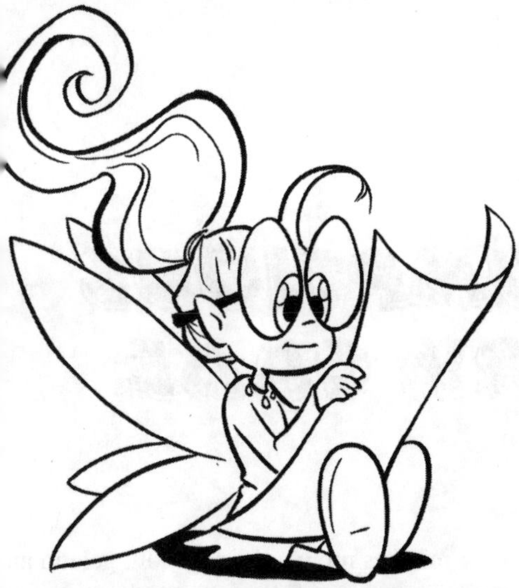

KIXIE'S MAILBOX

sipnet@strangersinparadise.com

:rry,

'hen we saw that Paradise TOO was going to get a let- r column, we had to write. I'm more partial to SIP, but y wife Beth loves PTOO and wants to know if she can ve the recipe for the cake on the back cover of issue #4. ne fell in love with the front cover of that issue the oment she saw it, and tore into the issue when we got home, looking for Kixie. Oops. But we're both looking rward to the regular Kixie and Plato stories.

h, and one more thing: please, no more pictures of your nagic pickle". We really don't need to see that.

reg Forster
ale Political Science Dept.
eston, VA

s, now you can have the recipe to Kixie's Scrumptious rawberry Cake! See the next page. Notice the complete ck of pickles in the recipe.

:rry,

he local newspaper near me, the Sun-Sentinel, is look- g for a comic strip to fill a spot. It'd be way cool if one your comics could take its place!

atie
a internet

hanks for thinking of me! Hopefully you will see Kixie the Sun-Sentinel someday.

Terry,

Strangers in Paradise has long been one of my favourite works for a host of reasons I won't get into here, so naturally I was excited to see some of your other works in the form of Paradise Too. To be frank, I find comic strips an abomination that give the higher art of comic books a bad name; that being understood, the fact emphasizes just how much I adored Kixie & Grace. Not only did it force me to re-evaluate my bigoted position on comic strips, it actually made me like them. The counterpoint played between the woman trying to exist in the compartmentalized, regulated, controlled modern world and the foot-loose and rambunxious faerie transcends the strip-medium, thwarting my previous ideas that characterization, depth, and humor not sickly sweet to the point of putrefaction were impossible in strips, and leaving me wanting more. I hope you continue with this wonderful strip, and find a way to publish it someday. As for ignorant, thick-skulled, money-grubbing, audience-pandering artless PC control editors, don't let them discourage you; there's better papers than theirs. Try the universities; I know my paper is dying for a competent strip by someone who can both write AND draw (gasp!).

W. Mills
via internet

Thanks for the good advice, W. I will find a good home for Kixie in 2002, don't you worry. I've found great encouragement from Kixie readers so far. Let's close with the following prediction by a faithful Kixie fan:

When I look at most of the 40-something comic strips in my local paper, and consider how they stand up to Terry's creation... Kixie blows them away. There will come a time when we all will say we saw it coming, but I'm going to say it first. 2002 is the year Kixie goes global.

Okay, continental. Editors are notoriously slow at catching on. This spring, syndicates will be passing around well worn issues of SIP TOO. Terry will negotiate a contract in the summer. With a proper launch, like 'Zits' got, it could peak in 2004 and run for decades.

And why will the first Kixie book be the hot Christmas gift for 2003? Girls will want to read about their plush toy. Boys will dig the slapstick. Women will relate and get nostalgic. Men will use it to support their theory concerning where women get their advice. Grandmothers, however, may be content with the clippings on their refrigerators. I wonder what could bring them on board... hello, focus group?

-posted on the internet by "Dogbowl", Stockton, CA

Kixie's SCRUMPTIOUS STRAWBERRY CAKE

18 ounces white cake mix
4 egg whites
1 cup salad oil
3 ounces strawberry gelatin
12 ounces frozen strawberries

Spend 4 minutes mixing the eggs, oil, gelatin and strawberries with an electric mixer (don't use the gasoline type, it fouls up the ozone). Pour into 3 greased (we recommend Pam) and floured 8 inch cake pans. Bake at 350 degrees for 30 minutes or until done or until you just can't stand it and are willing to eat raw goo. Cool, frost and refrigerate for at least 2 hours before serving.

Serves 12 people or 1 fairy

Frosting
2 cups whipping cream
3 tablespoons sugar
12 ounces frozen strawberries,
    thawed and drained

Grab that electric mixer again and do a tornado on the whip cream and sugar, then fold in strawberries (like origami you can eat).

AND IF YOU DO IT RIGHT, YOU GET THIS!

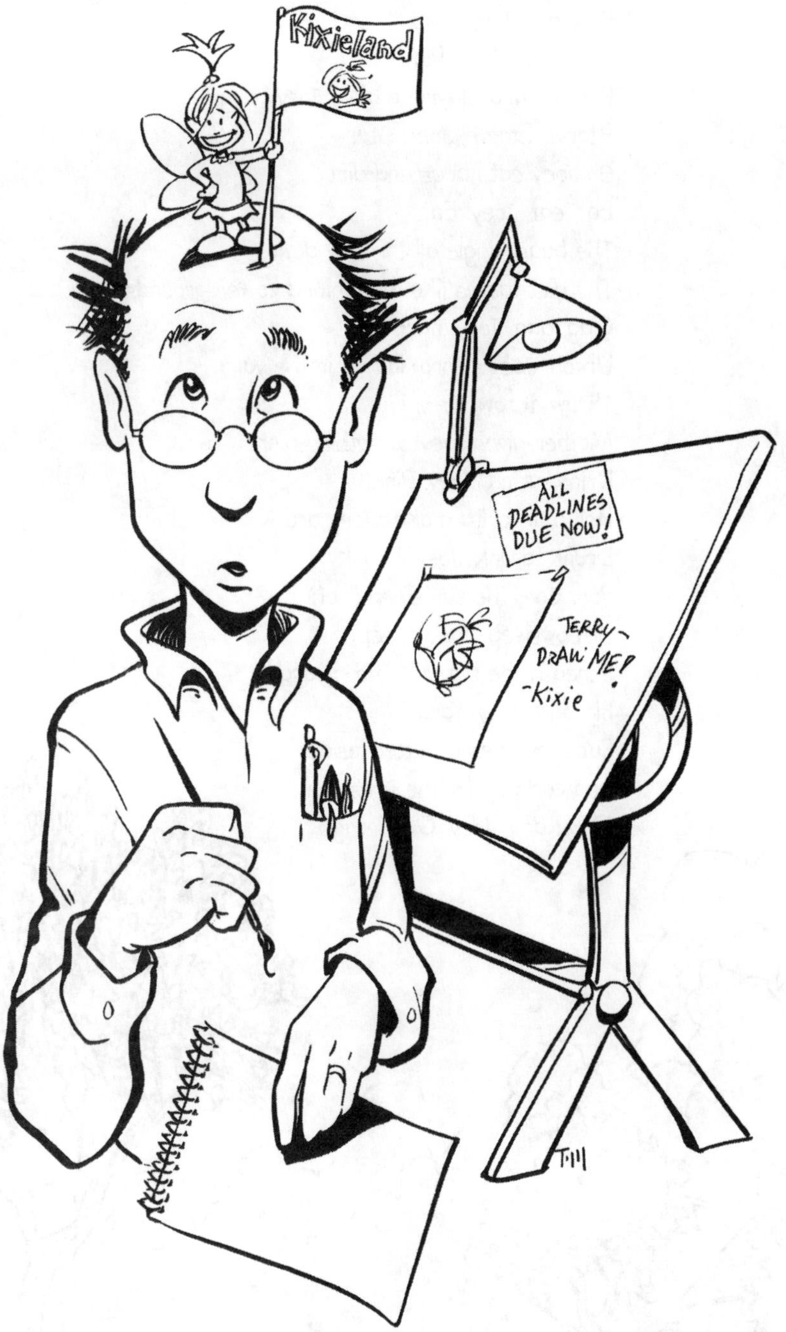
Kixieland
ALL DEADLINES DUE NOW!
TERRY-
DRAW ME!
-Kixie
T-ill

Tell everybody you know about Kixie Komix!™
They're ever so fun and totally fat free!
Found only in the pages of Paradise TOO!

Joey likes to run and play.
Run, run, Joey. Run.
Play, play, Joey. Play.
Running and playing makes Joey hungry.
Starve, starve, Joey. Starve.
So Joey eats bugs and dirt.
Eat, eat, Joey. Eat.
The bugs wiggle all the way down,
The dirt tastes like mummified coffee grounds.
Gag, gag, Joey. Barf.
Uh oh, Joey's throwing up in the yard.
Throw, throw, Joey. Up.
Mother gives Joey something pink.
Drink, drink, Joey. Pink.
Her margarita makes Joey drunk.
Drunk, drunk, Joey. Drunk.
Poor Joey, he can sleep it off.
Sleep, sleep, Joey. Sleep.
Beneath the big oak in our yard.
Big oak, Joey. Yard.
But Joey likes it better inside,
And curls up by the fireside.
Good dog, Joey. Good dog.

JOEY'S BACKYARD

KIXIE

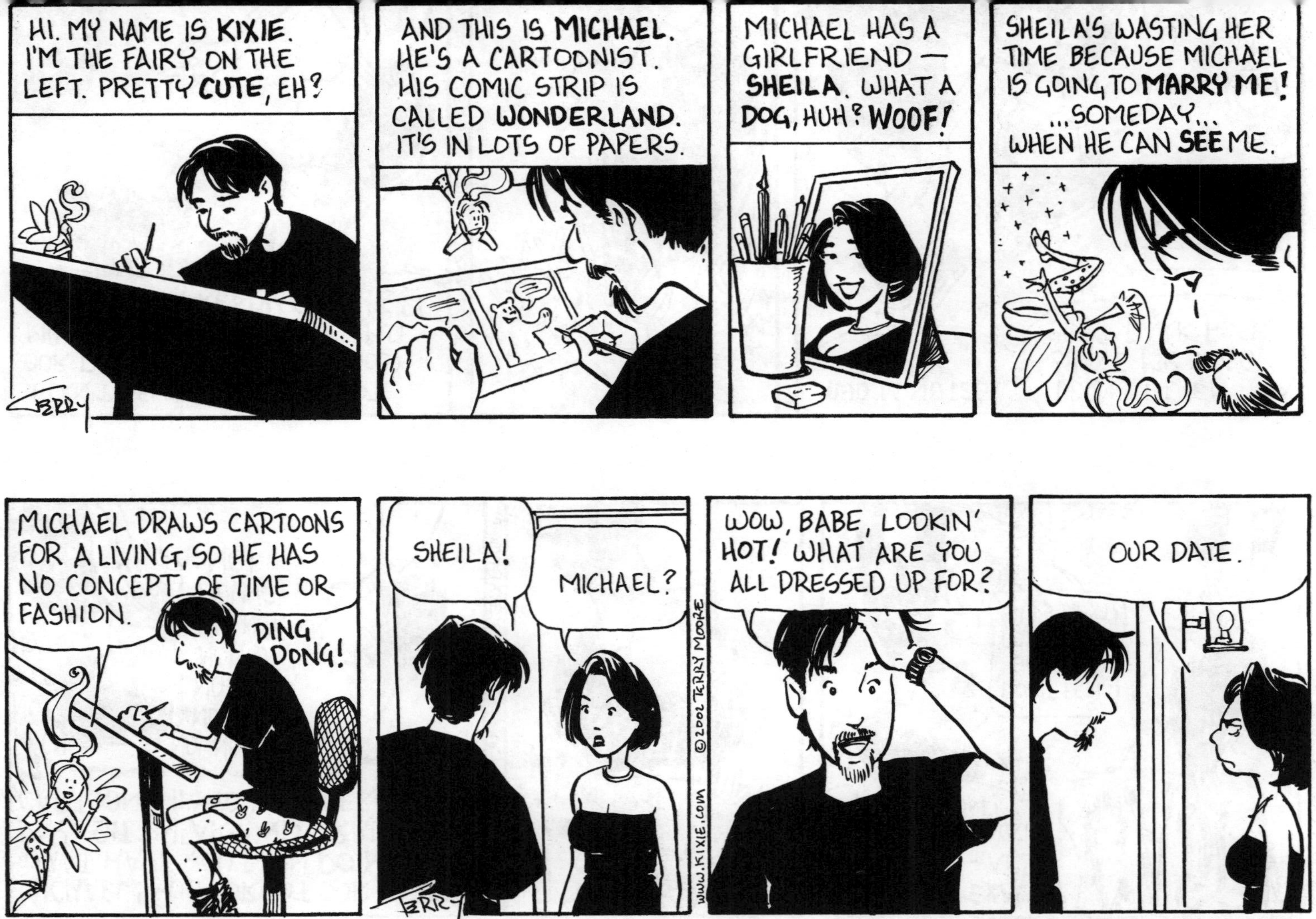
HI. MY NAME IS KIXIE. I'M THE FAIRY ON THE LEFT. PRETTY CUTE, EH?
TERRY
AND THIS IS MICHAEL. HE'S A CARTOONIST. HIS COMIC STRIP IS CALLED WONDERLAND. IT'S IN LOTS OF PAPERS.
MICHAEL HAS A GIRLFRIEND — SHEILA. WHAT A DOG, HUH? WOOF!
SHEILA'S WASTING HER TIME BECAUSE MICHAEL IS GOING TO MARRY ME! ...SOMEDAY... WHEN HE CAN SEE ME.
MICHAEL DRAWS CARTOONS FOR A LIVING, SO HE HAS NO CONCEPT OF TIME OR FASHION.
DING DONG!
SHEILA!
MICHAEL?
TERRY
WWW.KIXIE.COM ©2002 TERRY MOORE
WOW, BABE, LOOKIN' HOT! WHAT ARE YOU ALL DRESSED UP FOR?
OUR DATE.

KIXIE

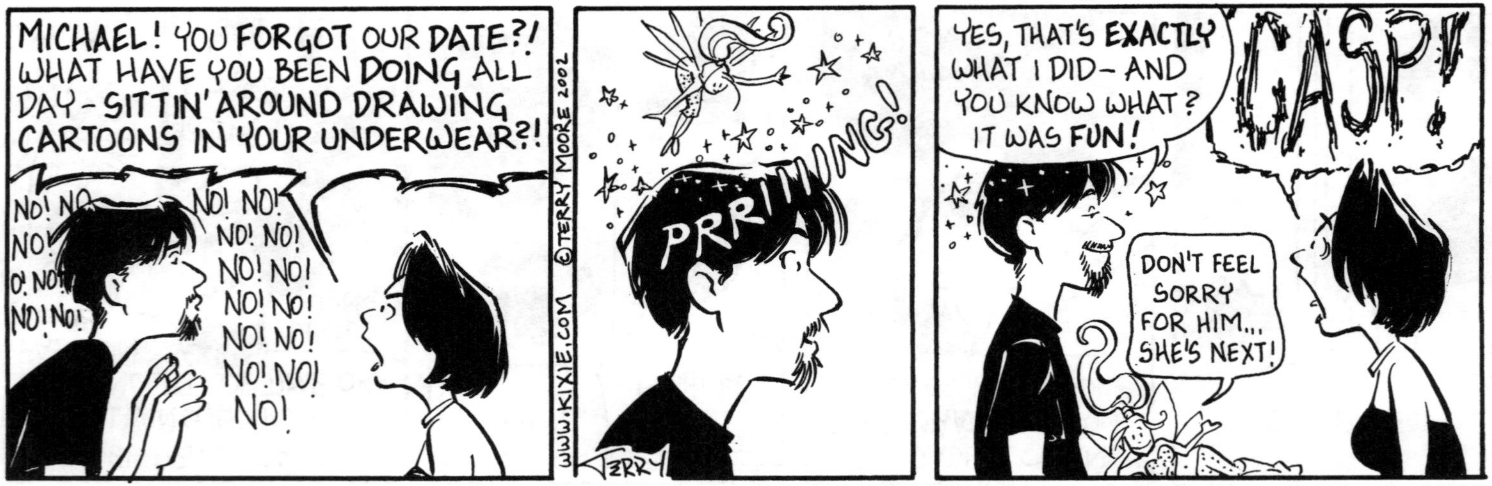
MICHAEL! YOU FORGOT OUR DATE?! WHAT HAVE YOU BEEN DOING ALL DAY – SITTIN' AROUND DRAWING CARTOONS IN YOUR UNDERWEAR?!
NO! NO! NO! NO! NO! NO! NO! NO! NO! NO! NO! NO! NO! NO! NO! NO! NO! NO! NO! NO! NO!
WWW.KIXIE.COM ©TERRY MOORE 2002
PRRIIIING!
TERRY
YES, THAT'S EXACTLY WHAT I DID – AND YOU KNOW WHAT? IT WAS FUN!
GASP!
DON'T FEEL SORRY FOR HIM... SHE'S NEXT!

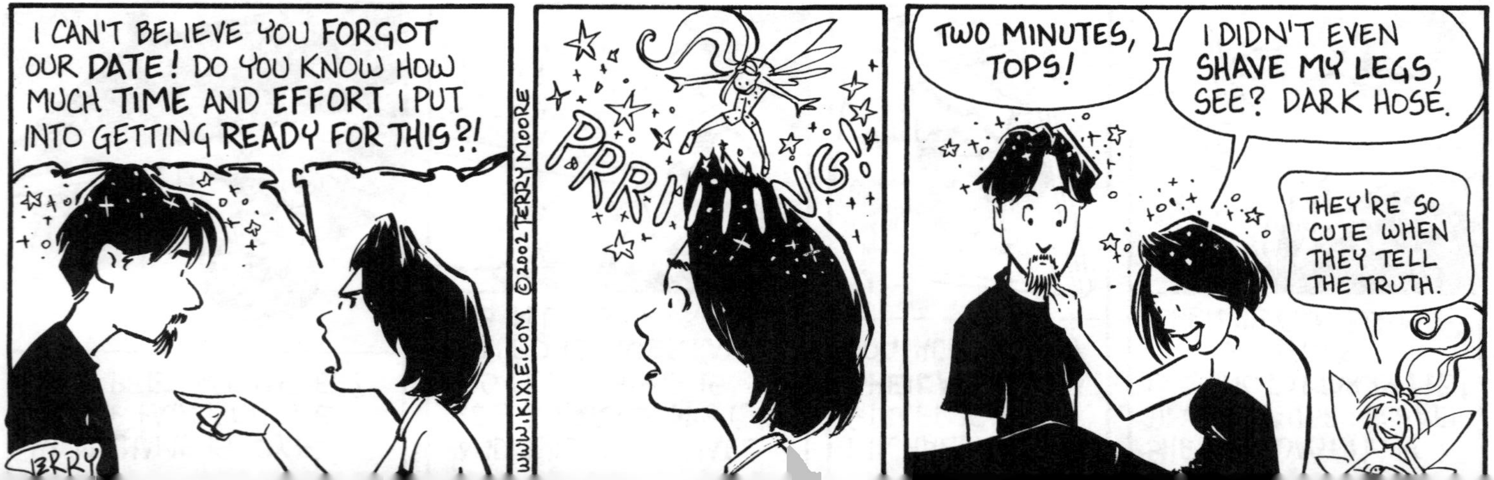
I CAN'T BELIEVE YOU FORGOT OUR DATE! DO YOU KNOW HOW MUCH TIME AND EFFORT I PUT INTO GETTING READY FOR THIS?!
TERRY
WWW.KIXIE.COM ©2002 TERRY MOORE
PRRIIING!
TWO MINUTES, TOPS!
I DIDN'T EVEN SHAVE MY LEGS, SEE? DARK HOSE.
THEY'RE SO CUTE WHEN THEY TELL THE TRUTH.

KIXIE

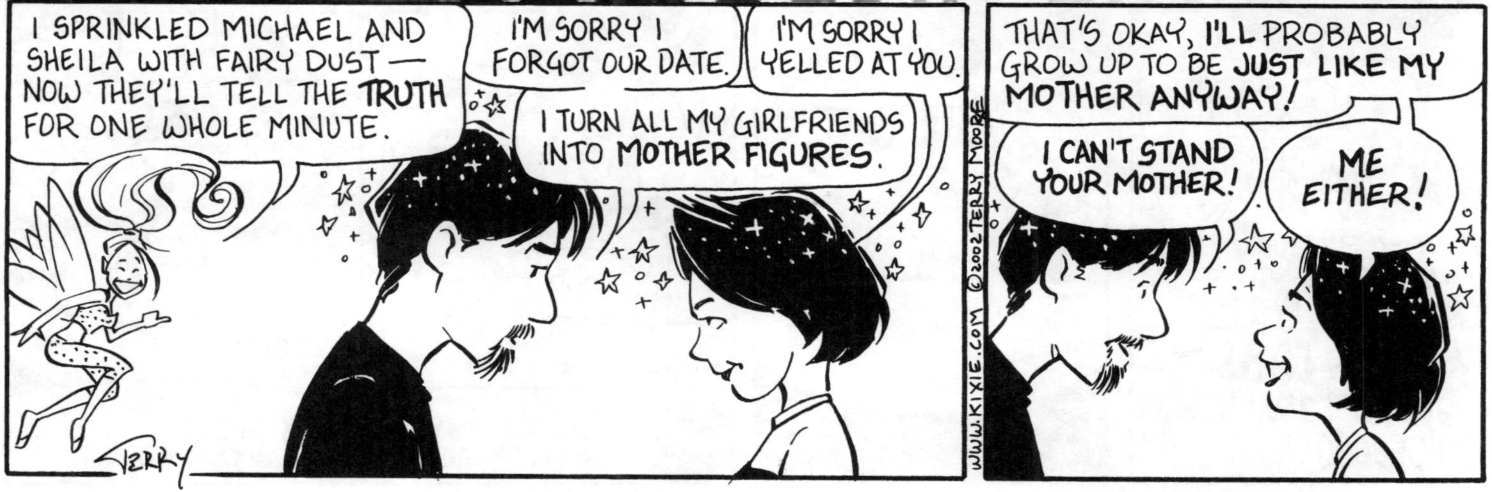
I SPRINKLED MICHAEL AND SHEILA WITH FAIRY DUST — NOW THEY'LL TELL THE TRUTH FOR ONE WHOLE MINUTE.
I'M SORRY I FORGOT OUR DATE.
I'M SORRY I YELLED AT YOU.
I TURN ALL MY GIRLFRIENDS INTO MOTHER FIGURES.
THAT'S OKAY, I'LL PROBABLY GROW UP TO BE JUST LIKE MY MOTHER ANYWAY!
I CAN'T STAND YOUR MOTHER!
ME EITHER!
TERRY
WWW.KIXIE.COM ©2002 TERRY MOORE

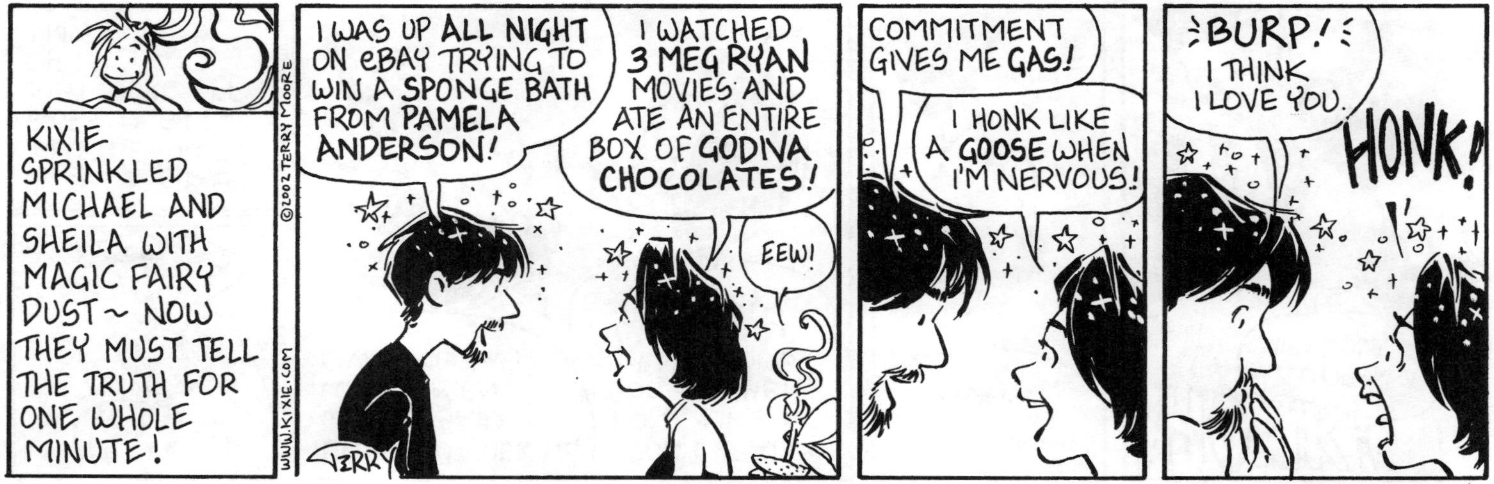
KIXIE SPRINKLED MICHAEL AND SHEILA WITH MAGIC FAIRY DUST ~ NOW THEY MUST TELL THE TRUTH FOR ONE WHOLE MINUTE!
WWW.KIXIE.COM ©2002 TERRY MOORE
I WAS UP ALL NIGHT ON eBAY TRYING TO WIN A SPONGE BATH FROM PAMELA ANDERSON!
I WATCHED 3 MEG RYAN MOVIES AND ATE AN ENTIRE BOX OF GODIVA CHOCOLATES!
EEW!
TERRY
COMMITMENT GIVES ME GAS!
I HONK LIKE A GOOSE WHEN I'M NERVOUS!
BURP!
I THINK I LOVE YOU.
HONK!

KIXIE

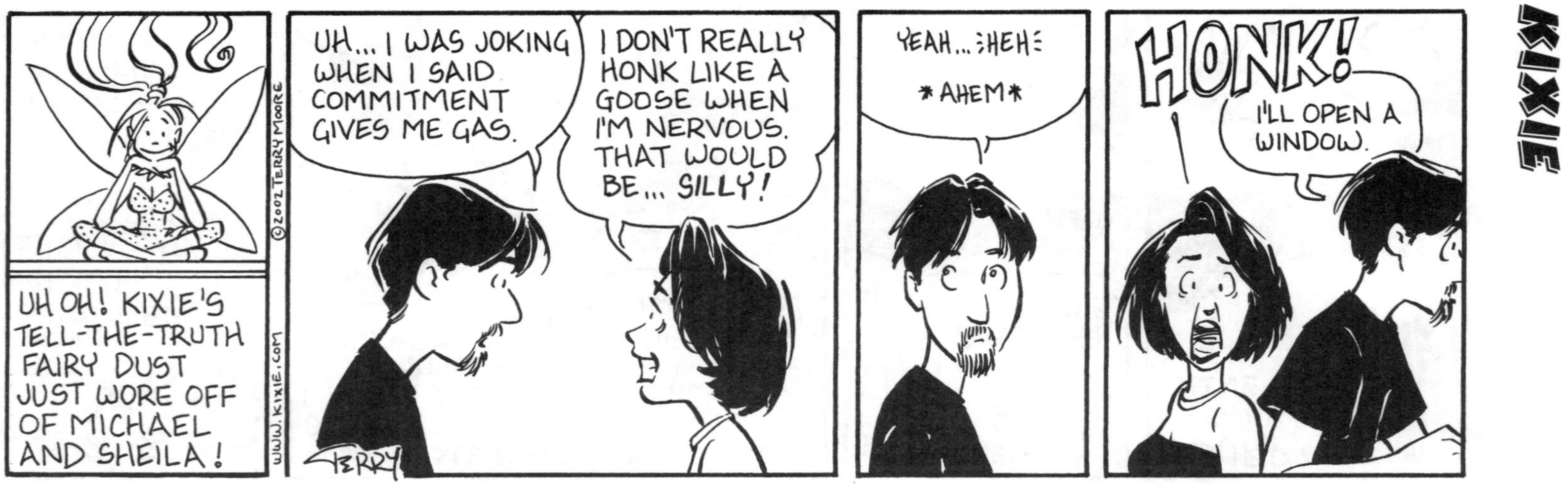
UH OH! KIXIE'S TELL-THE-TRUTH FAIRY DUST JUST WORE OFF OF MICHAEL AND SHEILA!
©2002 TERRY MOORE
WWW.KIXIE.COM
UH... I WAS JOKING WHEN I SAID COMMITMENT GIVES ME GAS.
I DON'T REALLY HONK LIKE A GOOSE WHEN I'M NERVOUS. THAT WOULD BE... SILLY!
TERRY
YEAH... HEH
AHEM
HONK!
I'LL OPEN A WINDOW.

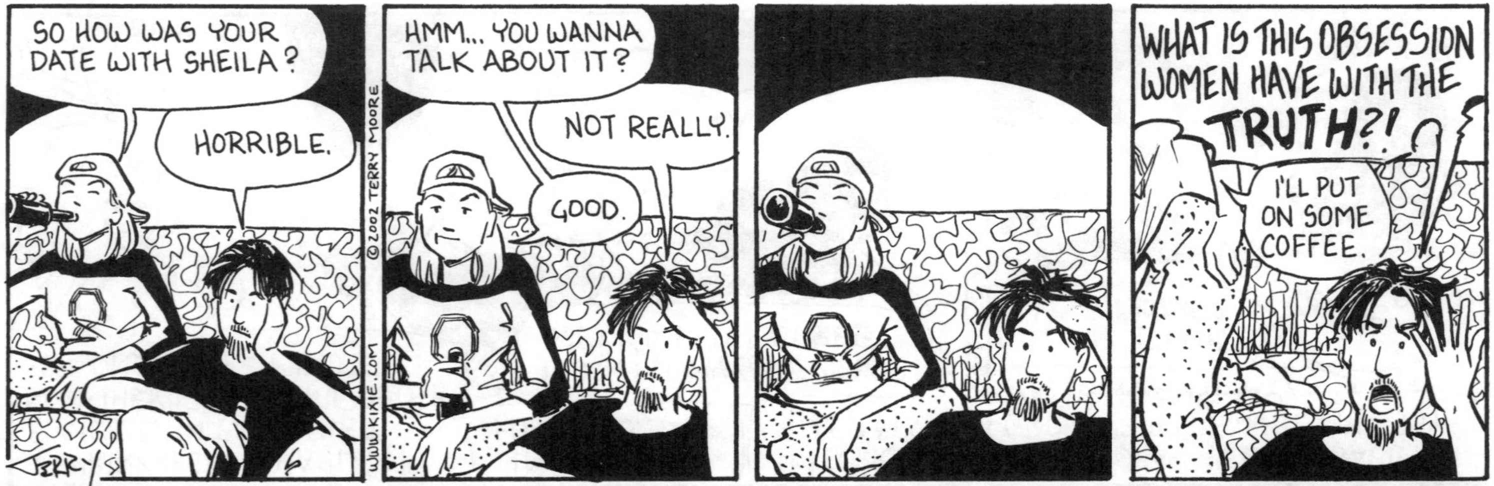
SO HOW WAS YOUR DATE WITH SHEILA?
HORRIBLE.
TERRY
©2002 TERRY MOORE
WWW.KIXIE.COM
HMM... YOU WANNA TALK ABOUT IT?
NOT REALLY.
GOOD.
WHAT IS THIS OBSESSION WOMEN HAVE WITH THE TRUTH?!
I'LL PUT ON SOME COFFEE.

One lazy afternoon...

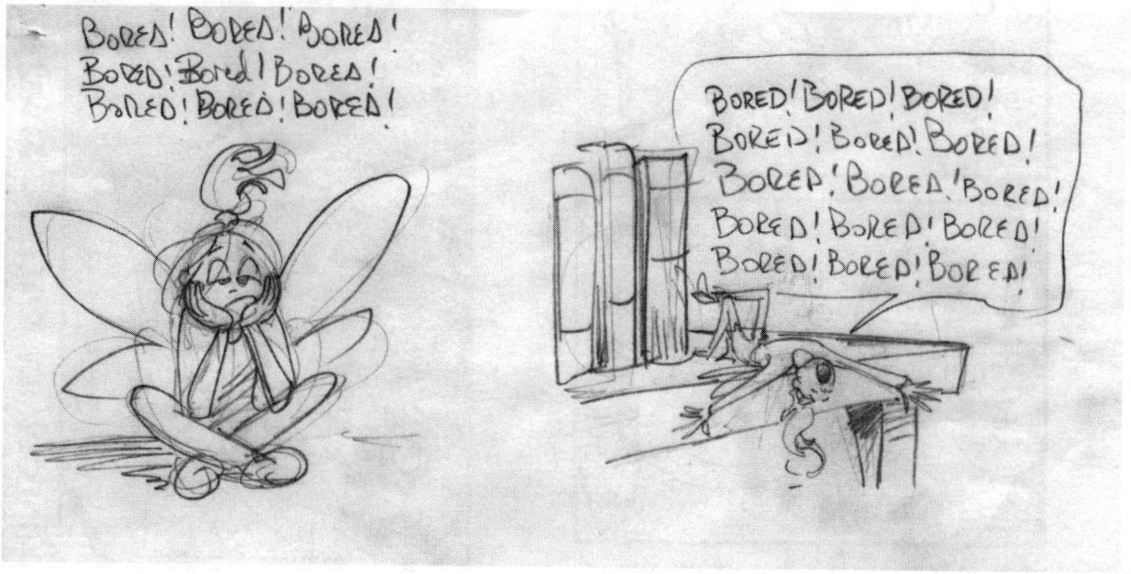
BORED! BORED! BORED!
BORED! BORED! BORED!
BORED! BORED! BORED!
BORED! BORED! BORED!
BORED! BORED! BORED!
BORED! BORED! BORED!
BORED! BORED! BORED!
BORED! BORED! BORED!

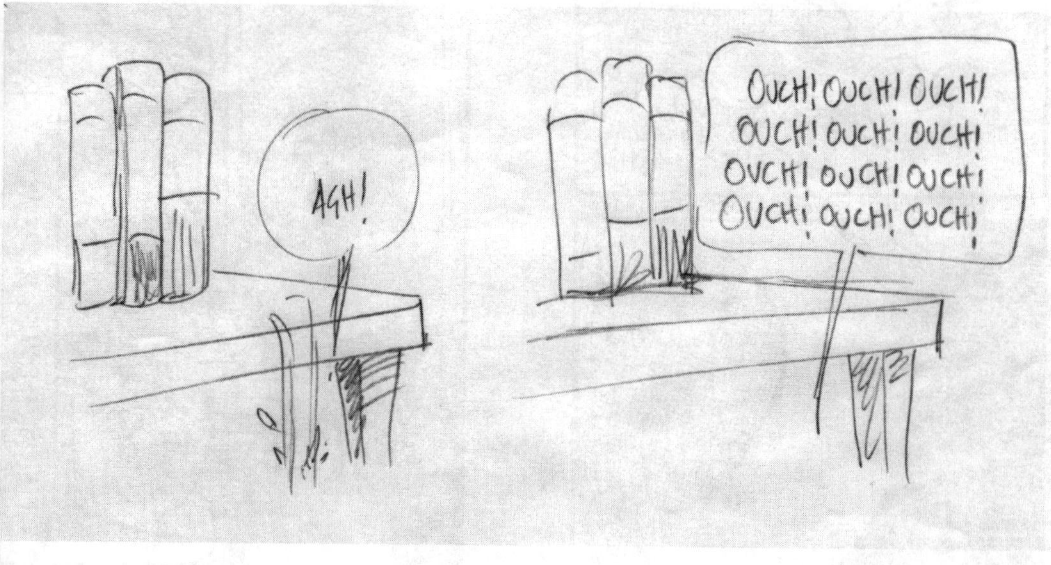
AGH!
OUCH! OUCH! OUCH!
OUCH! OUCH! OUCH!
OUCH! OUCH! OUCH!
OUCH! OUCH! OUCH!

LIL' KIXIE

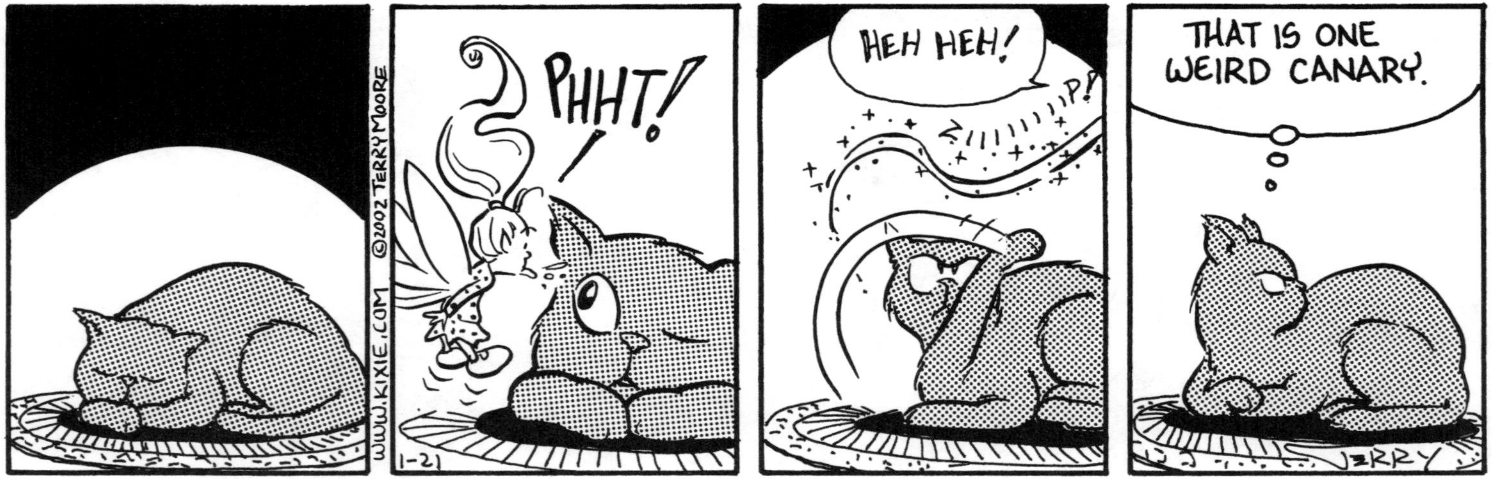

www.KIXIE.COM ©2002 TERRY MOORE
1-21
PHHT!
HEH HEH!
P!
THAT IS ONE WEIRD CANARY.
TERRY

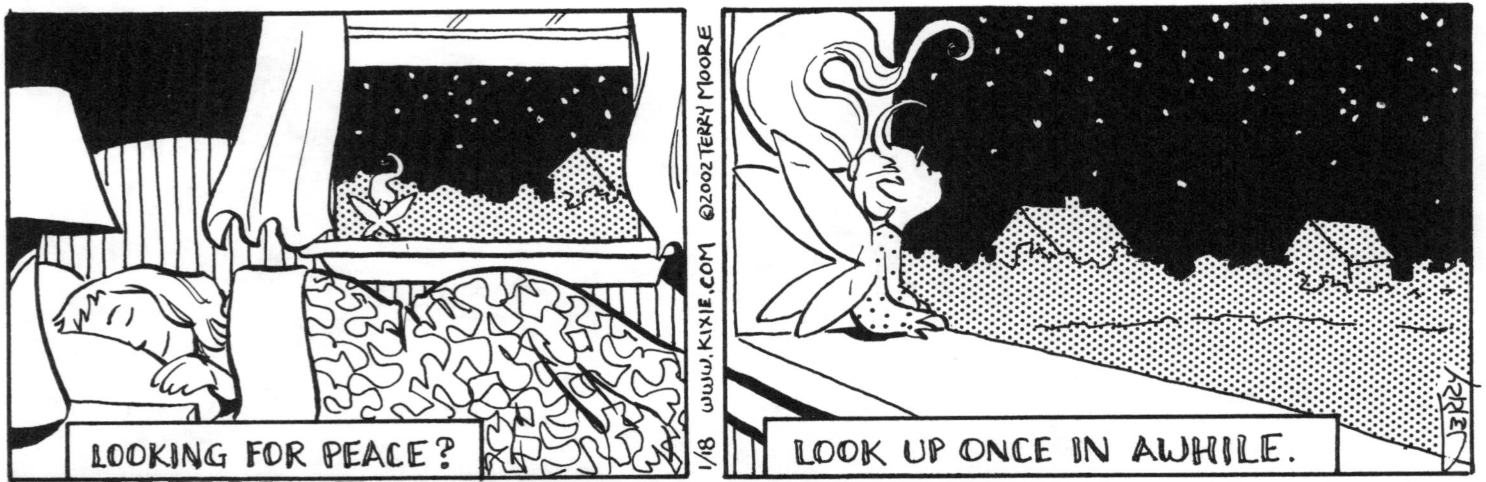

LOOKING FOR PEACE?
www.KIXIE.COM ©2002 TERRY MOORE
1/18
LOOK UP ONCE IN AWHILE.
TERRY

LIL' KIXIE

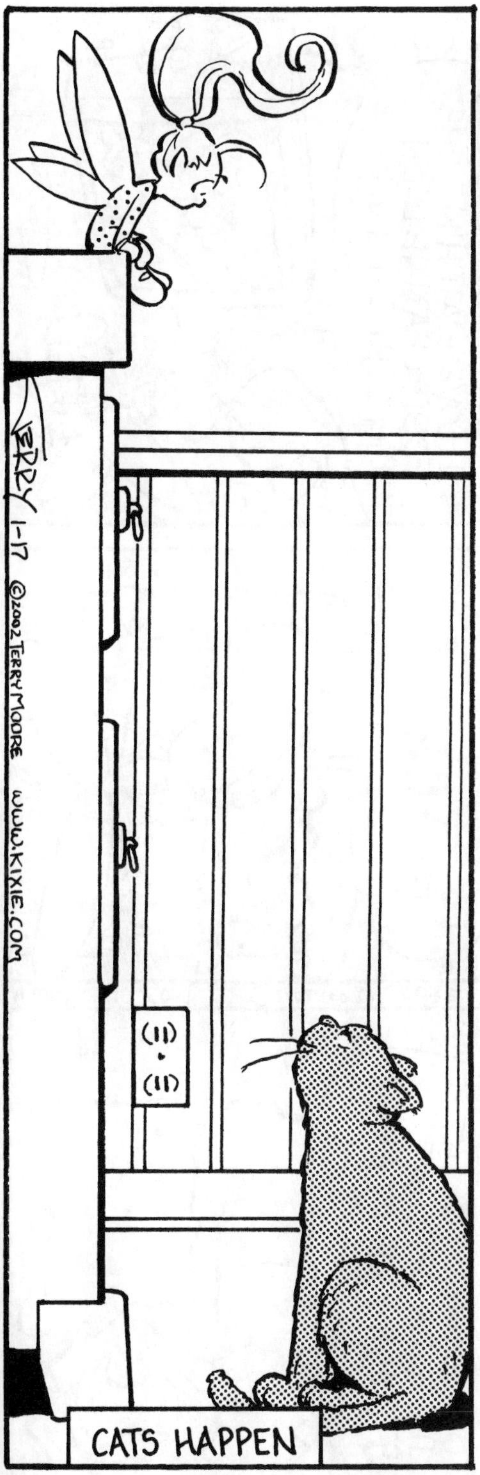
CATS HAPPEN
TERRY 1-17 ©2002 TERRY MOORE WWW.KIXIE.COM

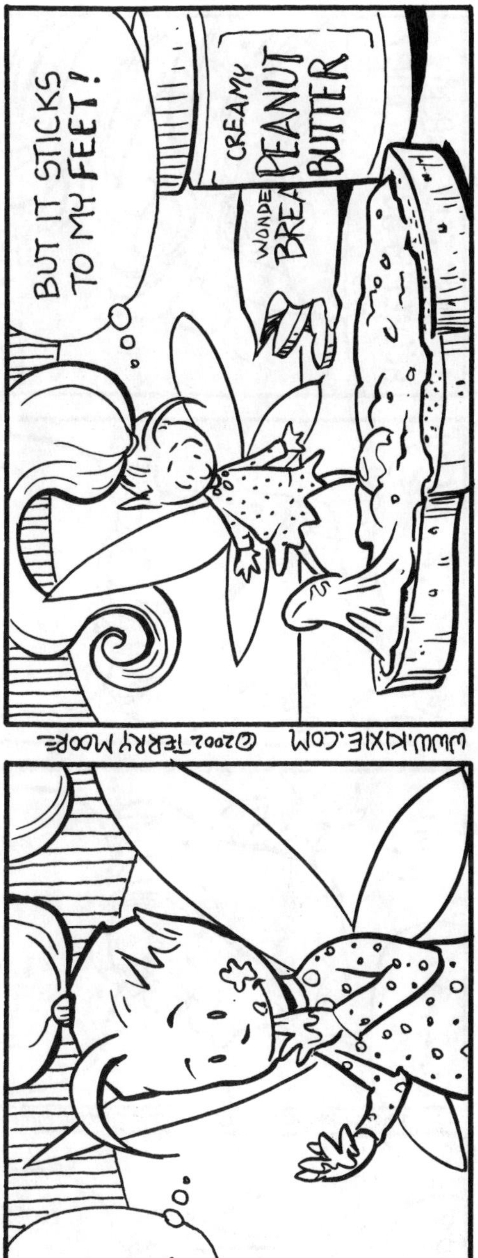
Y'KNOW... I LIKE PEANUT BUTTER....
TERRY 1-19
WWW.KIXIE.COM ©2002 TERRY MOORE
BUT IT STICKS TO MY FEET!
CREAMY PEANUT BUTTER

LIL' KIXIE

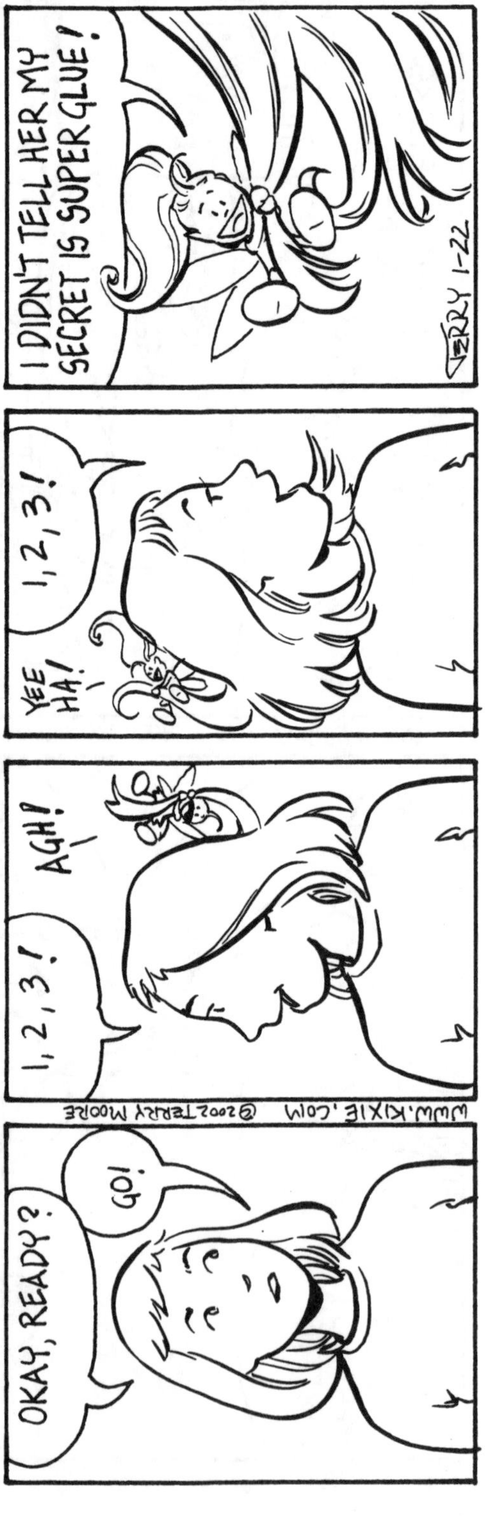
OKAY, READY?
GO!
WWW.KIXIE.COM ©2002 TERRY MOORE
1, 2, 3!
AGH!
YEE HA!
1, 2, 3!
I DIDN'T TELL HER MY SECRET IS SUPER GLUE!
TERRY 1-22

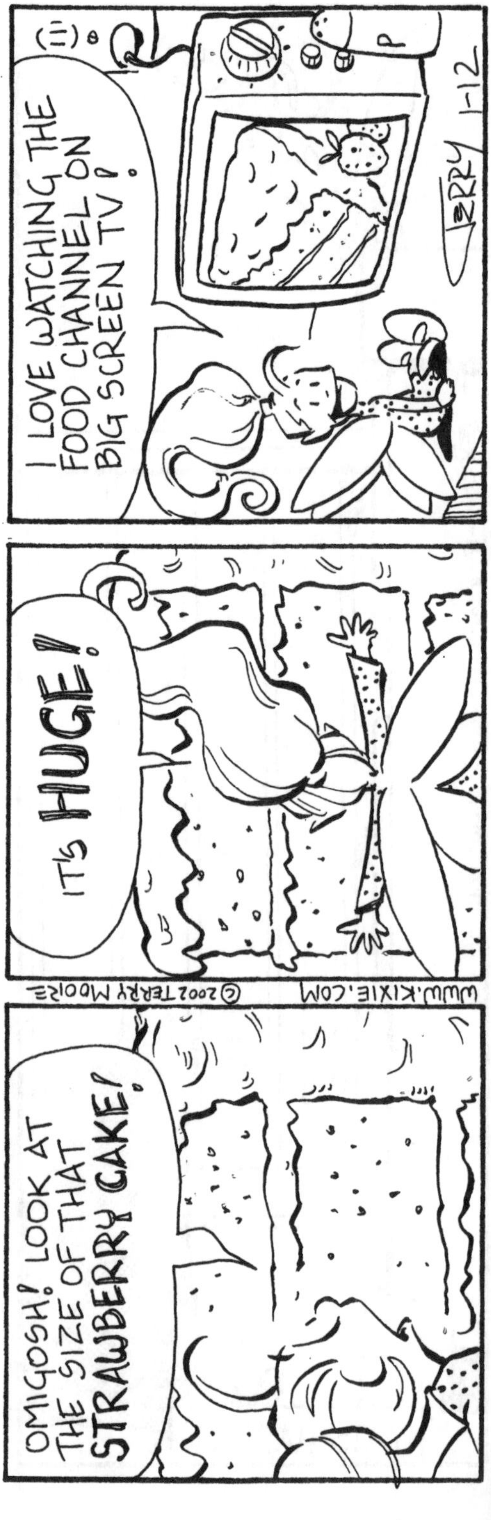
OMIGOSH! LOOK AT THE SIZE OF THAT STRAWBERRY CAKE!
WWW.KIXIE.COM ©2002 TERRY MOORE
IT'S HUGE!
I LOVE WATCHING THE FOOD CHANNEL ON BIG SCREEN TV!
(!!)
TERRY 1-12

LIL' KIXIE

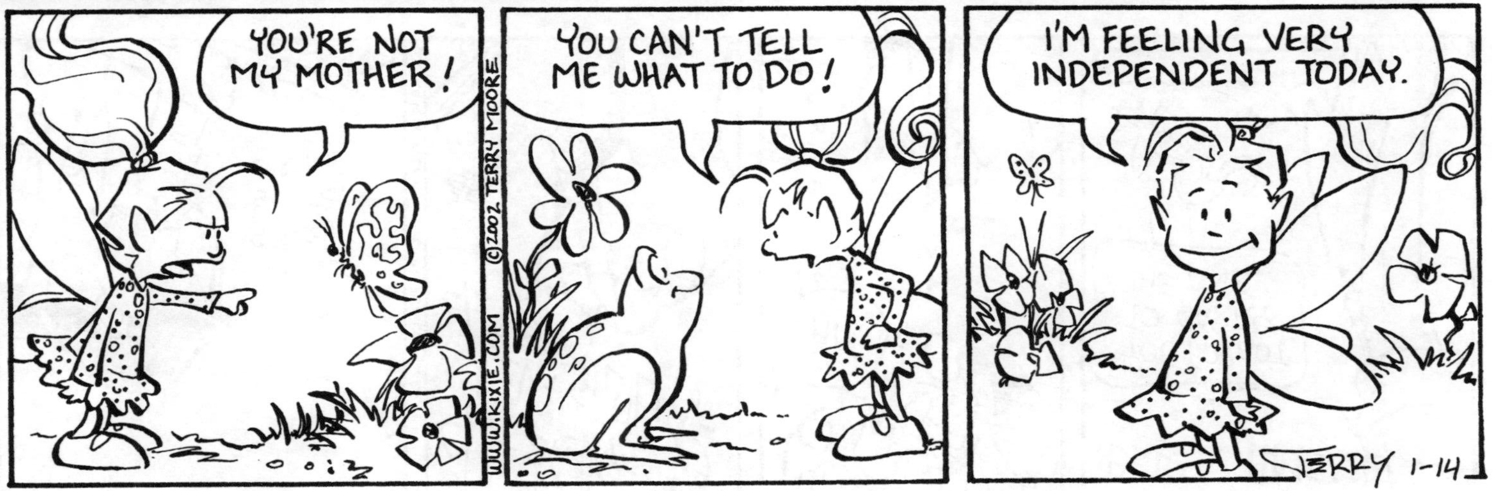
YOU'RE NOT MY MOTHER!
©2002 TERRY MOORE
WWW.KIXIE.COM
YOU CAN'T TELL ME WHAT TO DO!
I'M FEELING VERY INDEPENDENT TODAY.
TERRY 1-14

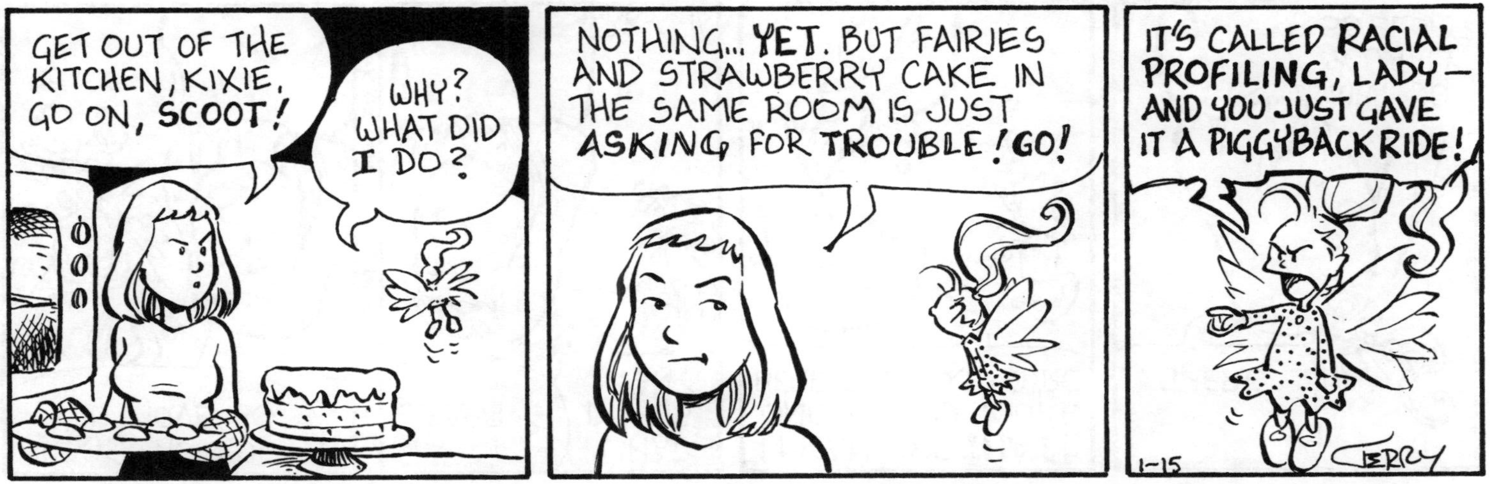
GET OUT OF THE KITCHEN, KIXIE. GO ON, SCOOT!
WHY? WHAT DID I DO?
NOTHING... YET. BUT FAIRIES AND STRAWBERRY CAKE IN THE SAME ROOM IS JUST ASKING FOR TROUBLE! GO!
IT'S CALLED RACIAL PROFILING, LADY— AND YOU JUST GAVE IT A PIGGYBACK RIDE!
1-15
TERRY

LIL' KIXIE

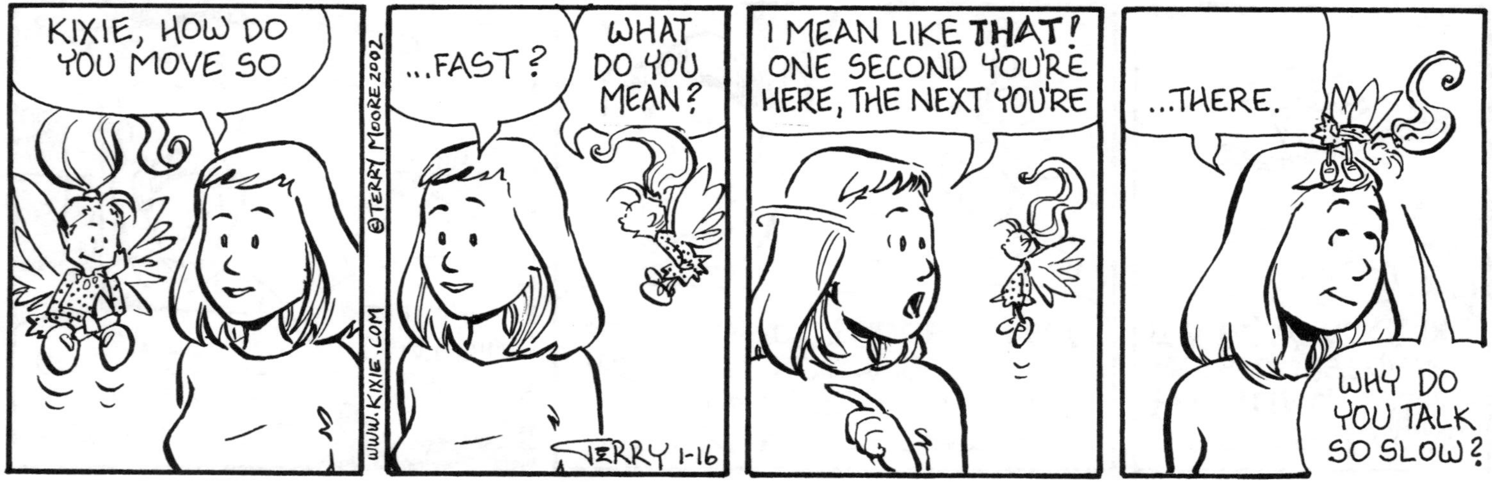
KIXIE, HOW DO YOU MOVE SO
...FAST?
WHAT DO YOU MEAN?
I MEAN LIKE **THAT**! ONE SECOND YOU'RE HERE, THE NEXT YOU'RE
...THERE.
WHY DO YOU TALK SO SLOW?
©TERRY MOORE 2002
WWW.KIXIE.COM
TERRY 1-16

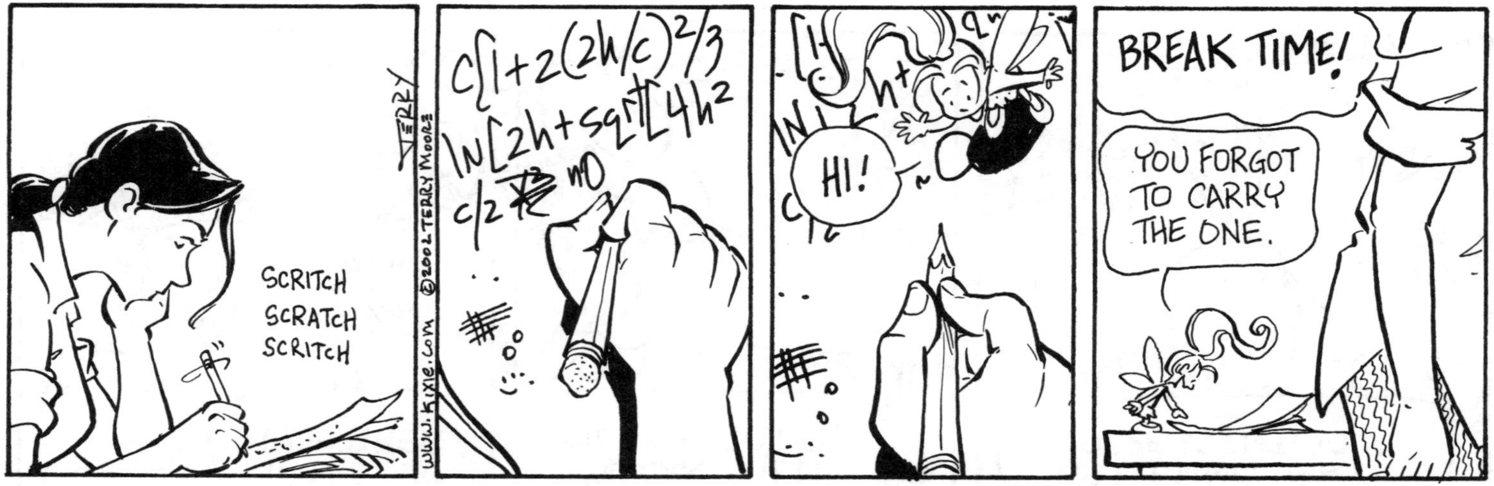
SCRITCH
SCRATCH
SCRITCH
TERRY
WWW.KIXIE.COM ©2002 TERRY MOORE
HI!
BREAK TIME!
YOU FORGOT TO CARRY THE ONE.

KIXIE

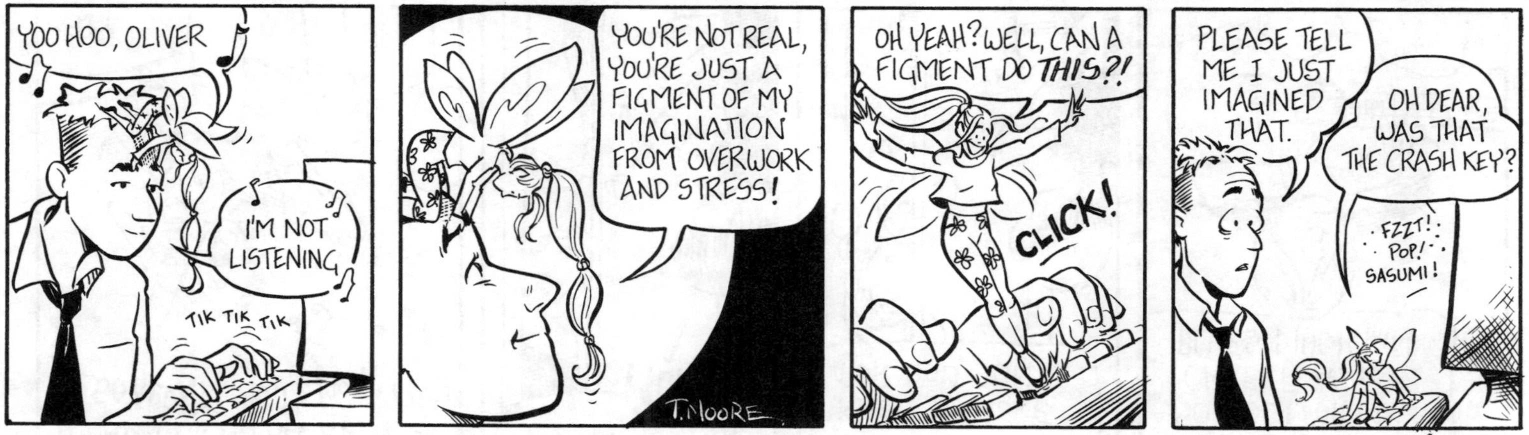
YOO HOO, OLIVER
I'M NOT LISTENING
TIK TIK TIK
YOU'RE NOT REAL, YOU'RE JUST A FIGMENT OF MY IMAGINATION FROM OVERWORK AND STRESS!
T. MOORE
OH YEAH? WELL, CAN A FIGMENT DO THIS?!
CLICK!
PLEASE TELL ME I JUST IMAGINED THAT.
OH DEAR, WAS THAT THE CRASH KEY?
FZZT! POP! SASUMI!

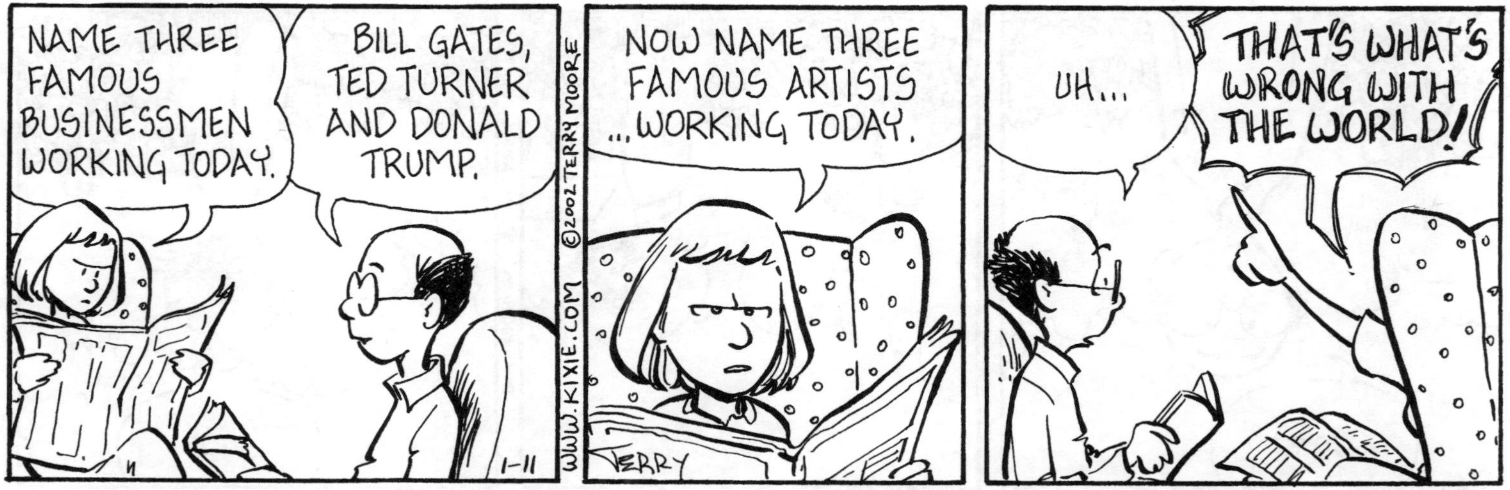
NAME THREE FAMOUS BUSINESSMEN WORKING TODAY.
BILL GATES, TED TURNER AND DONALD TRUMP.
1-11
WWW.KIXIE.COM ©2002 TERRY MOORE
NOW NAME THREE FAMOUS ARTISTS ...WORKING TODAY.
TERRY
UH...
THAT'S WHAT'S WRONG WITH THE WORLD!

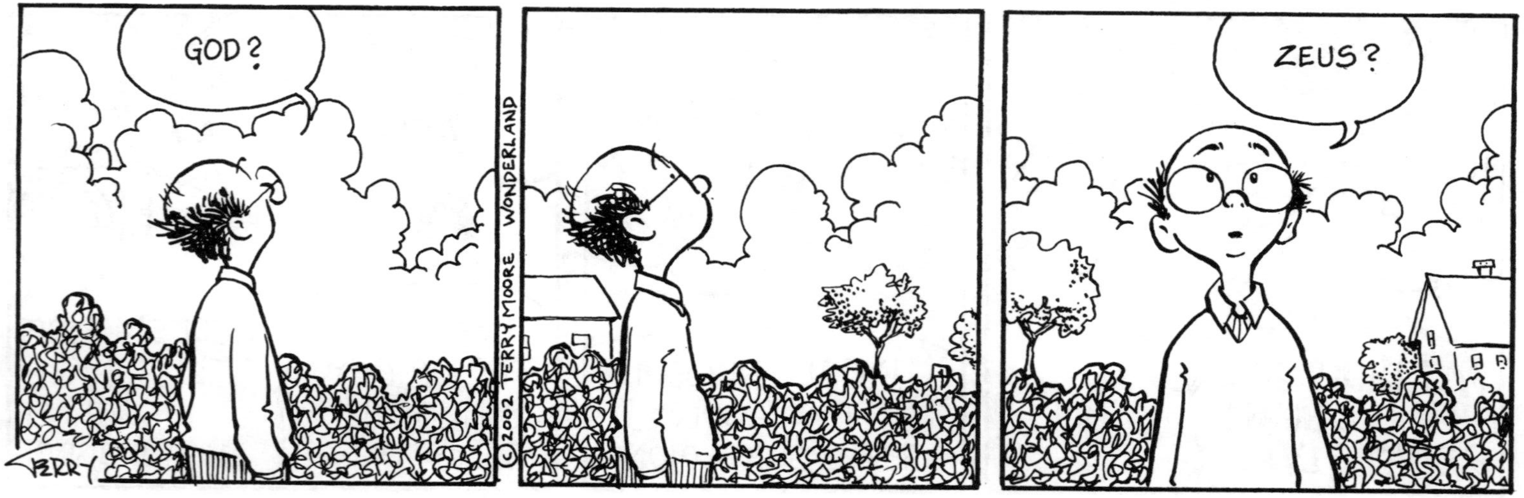
GOD?
©2002 TERRY MOORE WONDERLAND
ZEUS?
TERRY

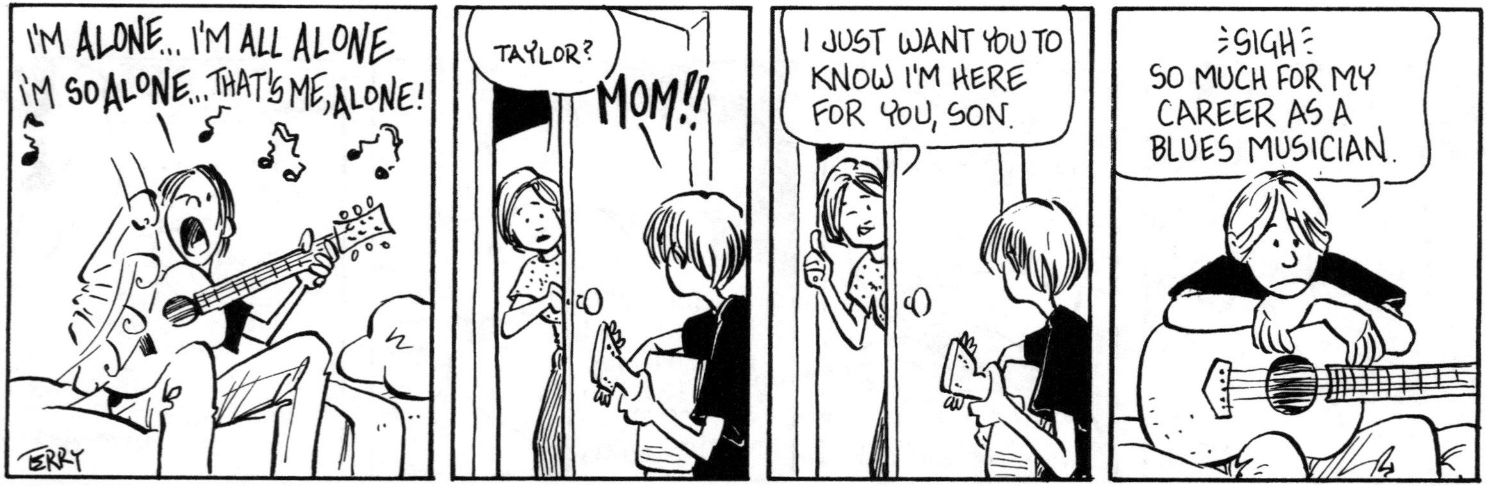
I'M ALONE... I'M ALL ALONE
I'M SO ALONE... THAT'S ME, ALONE!
TERRY
TAYLOR?
MOM!!
I JUST WANT YOU TO KNOW I'M HERE FOR YOU, SON.
SIGH
SO MUCH FOR MY CAREER AS A BLUES MUSICIAN.

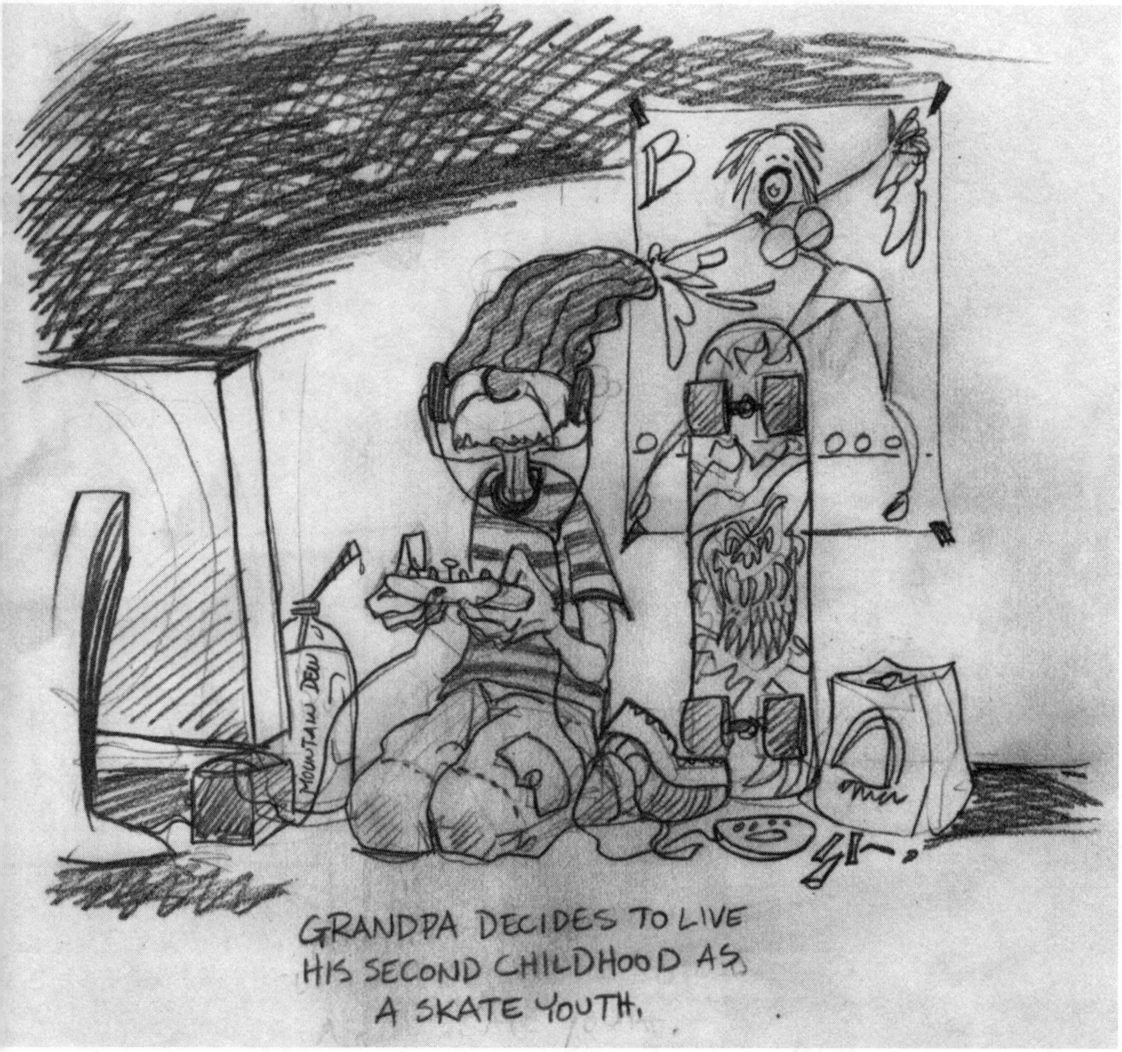
MOUNTAIN DEW
GRANDPA DECIDES TO LIVE HIS SECOND CHILDHOOD AS A SKATE YOUTH.

A Brief Phlegm

A Bite-Size Tragedy

The first time I saw Gretmaven she was wearing a woolen skull cap and frost mittens. She had magnificent ears— glorious and proud, immense in size and translucent pink in that odd fairie way that only cells in sunlight can manage. I loaved her on the spot, and told her so in my native tongue: Spitlatin.

"Thaaay!" I sprayed in her face, "You're one hot pathtooootie!"

Gretmaven recoiled in disgust, trying to shield her ears from my flying phlegm but, alas, it was no use. Her huge Dumbo wings caught most of the spray plus two wayward bats who soared off course in the noise. "Get away from me you freak!" she barked so loud that the other nudists burned. A shepherd and his tenor began wiping her dry as her toy terry, Brutus, yipped without season at a beetle that was attempting to copulate with a discarded Raisenet.

"Thorry," I said, and undrew to the fearest bar, my dreams shattered, my heart ripped to feces like so much ripping material in a ripping machine.

The End.

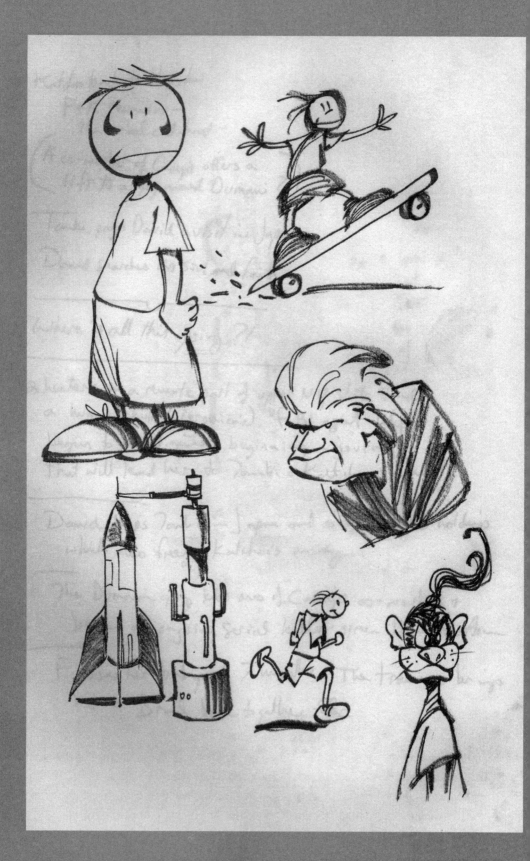

sketchbook doodles

and various brilliant unbelieveable ideas

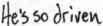

He's so driven

A DOUBLE
CHIN

FRIENDLY
GUY

Mr. Mooney was a 2D man
Doing the best the 2D can
He slipped to work between the breeze
And pondered life beyond 2D.
Mr. Mooney was a shallow man
Not so deep but great in jams;
Slipping in and under doors
Doing naughty things in drawers.
"Slipping and udder's fine,"
The 2D trollop said, reclined,
"But not while Fifi's on the bed!"
So Mr. Mooney lost his head,
He threw poor Fifi at the moon
And forgot about her for 20 Junes.
Then one day while he slipped to work
Fifi shot down from clear blue sky
And plowed through Mooney like a pig
through pie.
All the people were a maze.

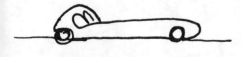

guy's car

Jeff's Jeep

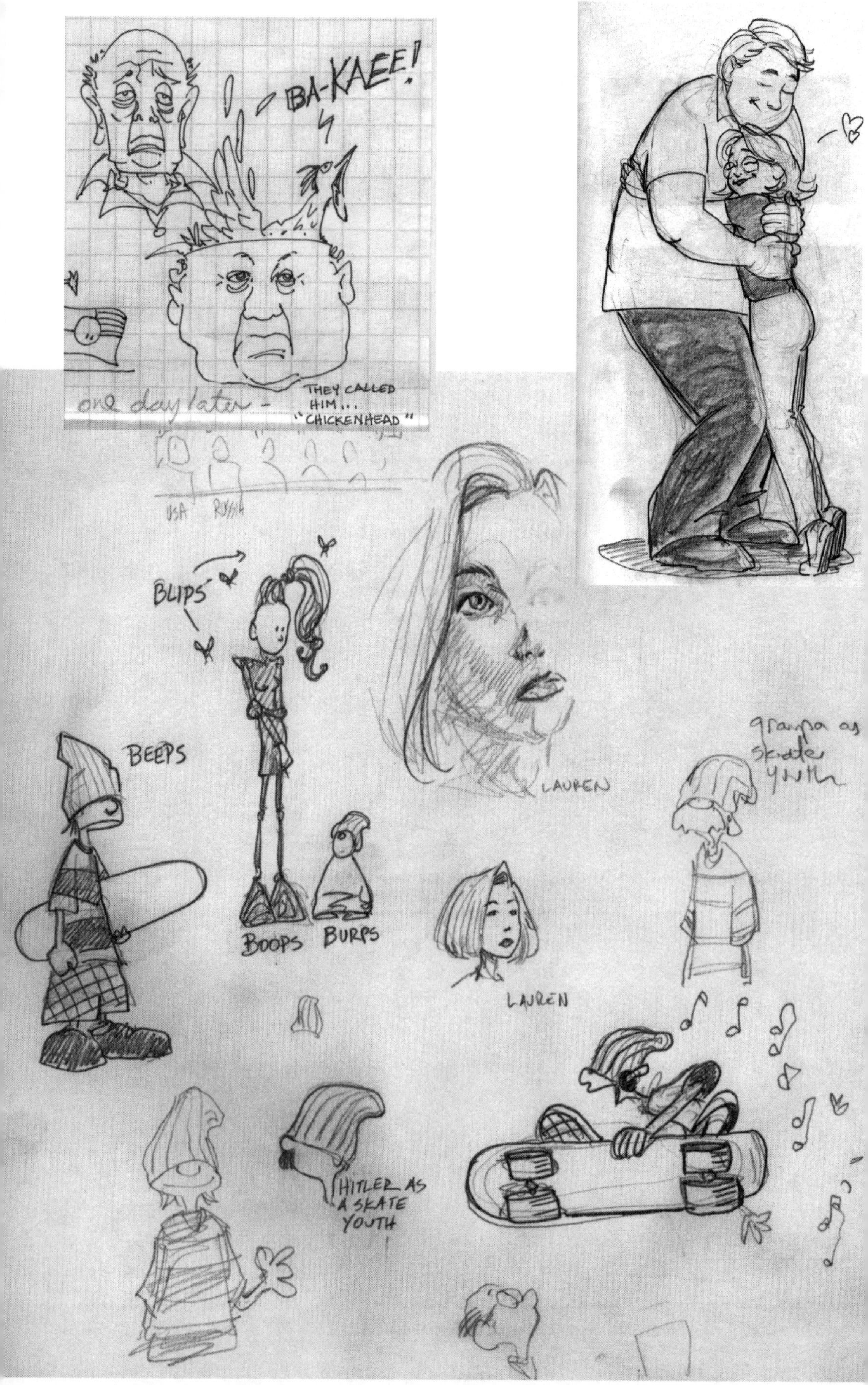
BA-KAEE!
one day later -
THEY CALLED HIM... "CHICKENHEAD"
USA
RUSSIA
BLIPS
BEEPS
BOOPS
BURPS
LAUREN
grampa as skate youth
LAUREN
HITLER AS A SKATE YOUTH

WONDERLAND

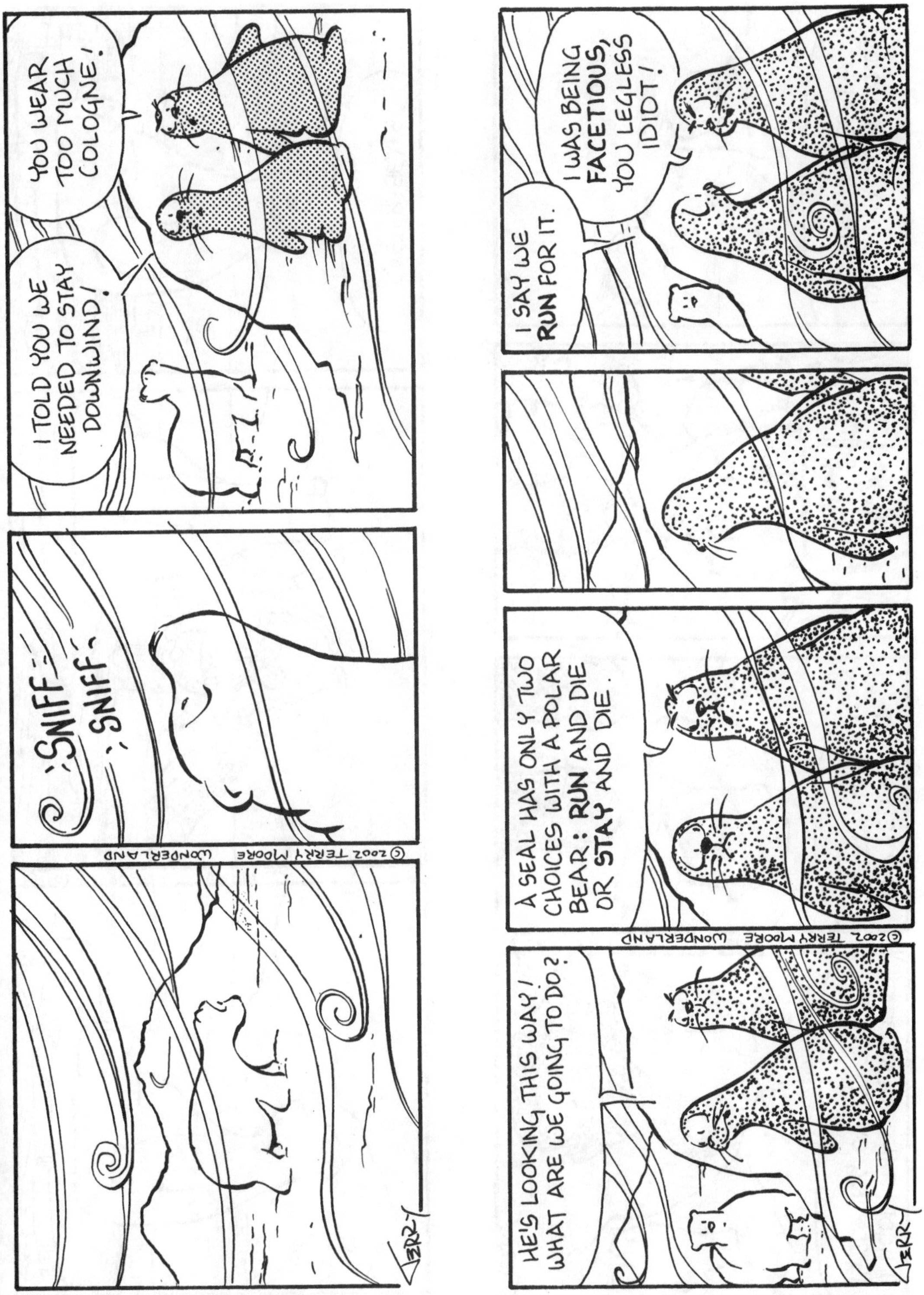

;SNIFF;
;SNIFF;
I TOLD YOU WE NEEDED TO STAY DOWNWIND!
YOU WEAR TOO MUCH COLOGNE!
© 2002 TERRY MOORE WONDERLAND
HE'S LOOKING THIS WAY! WHAT ARE WE GOING TO DO?
A SEAL HAS ONLY TWO CHOICES WITH A POLAR BEAR: **RUN** AND DIE OR **STAY** AND DIE.
I SAY WE **RUN** FOR IT.
I WAS BEING **FACETIOUS**, YOU LEGLESS IDIDT!
© 2002 TERRY MOORE WONDERLAND

WONDERLAND

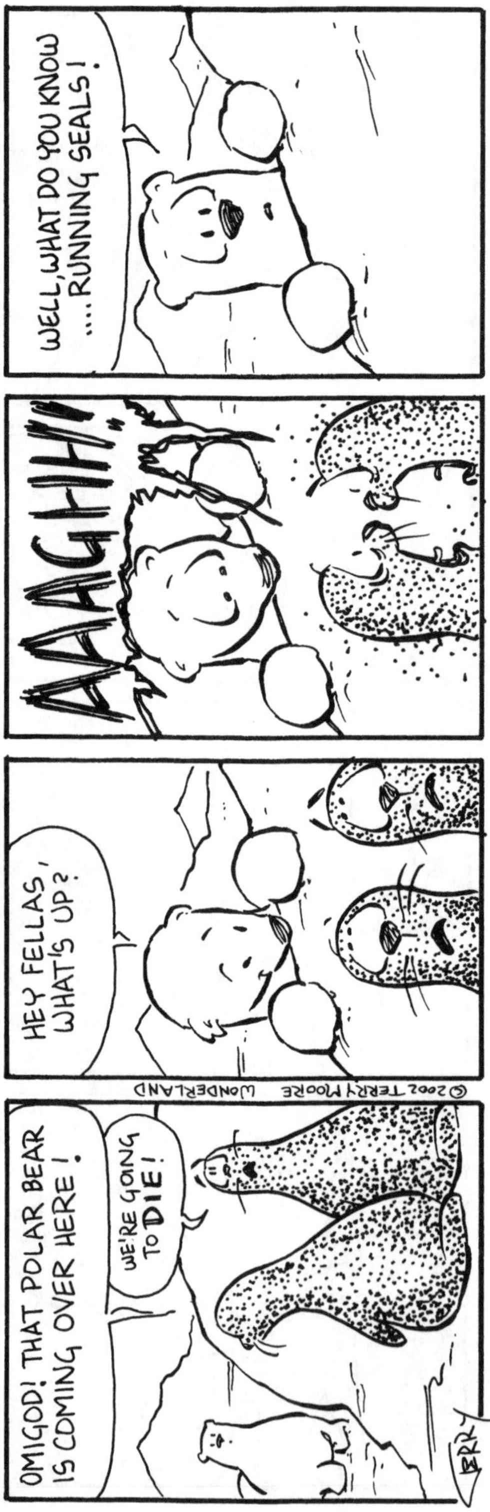
OMIGOD! THAT POLAR BEAR IS COMING OVER HERE!
WE'RE GOING TO DIE!
© 2002 TERRY MOORE WONDERLAND
HEY FELLAS, WHAT'S UP?
AAAGHHH!!
WELL, WHAT DO YOU KNOW ....RUNNING SEALS!

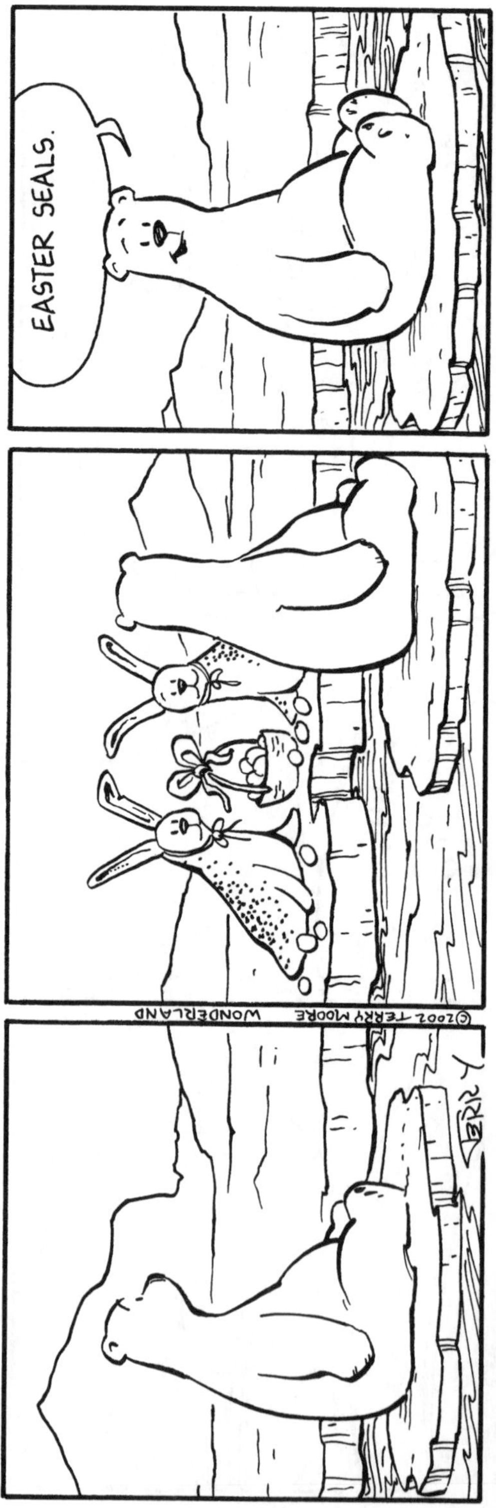
© 2002 TERRY MOORE WONDERLAND
EASTER SEALS.

The Smoker

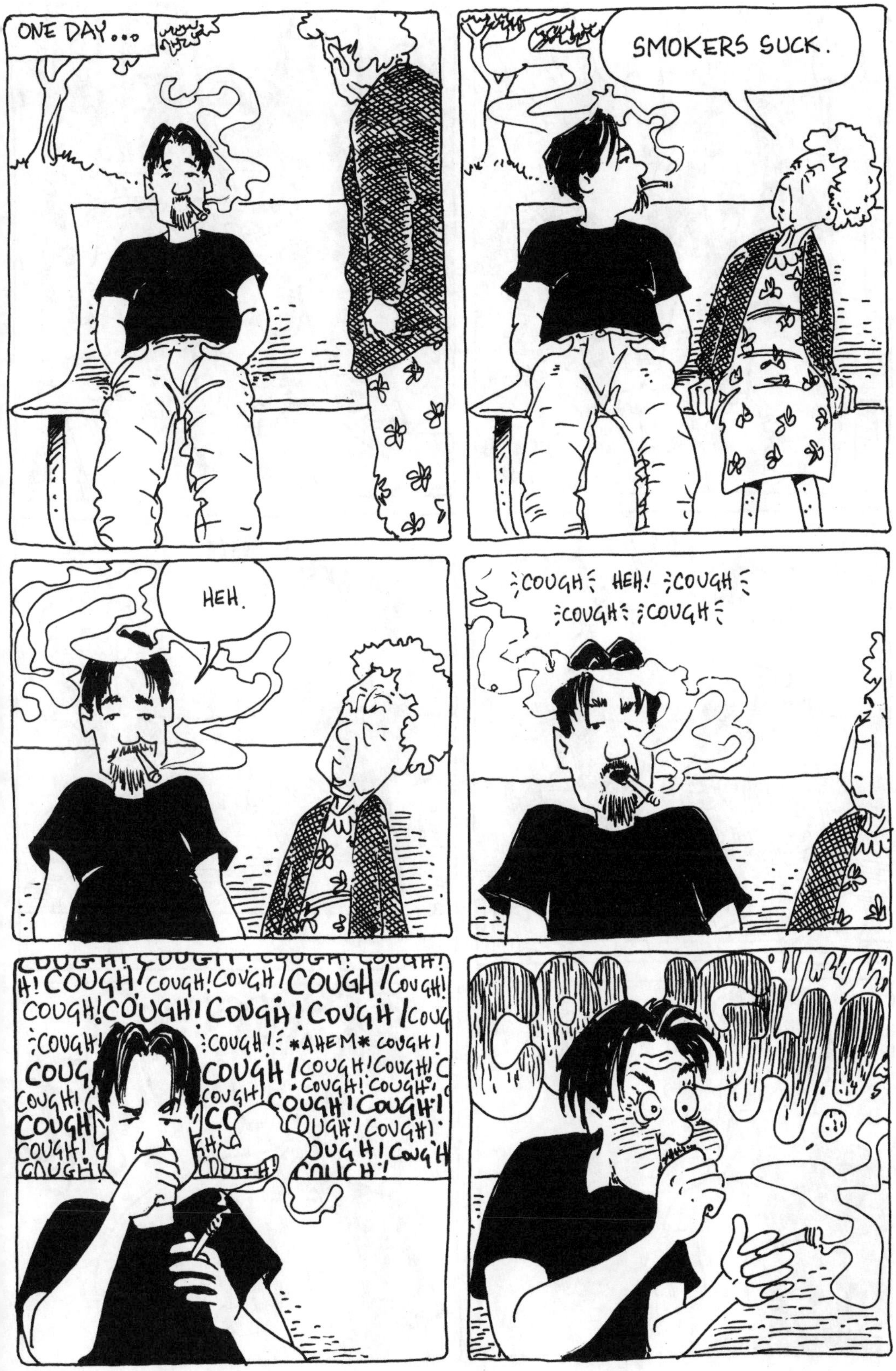
ONE DAY...
SMOKERS SUCK.
HEH.
COUGH! HEH! COUGH
COUGH! COUGH
COUGH! COUGH! COUGH! COUGH
COUGH! COUGH! COUGH! COUGH
COUGH! *AHEM* COUGH!
COUGH! COUGH! COUGH!
COUGH! COUGH!
COUGH! COUGH!

The Smoker

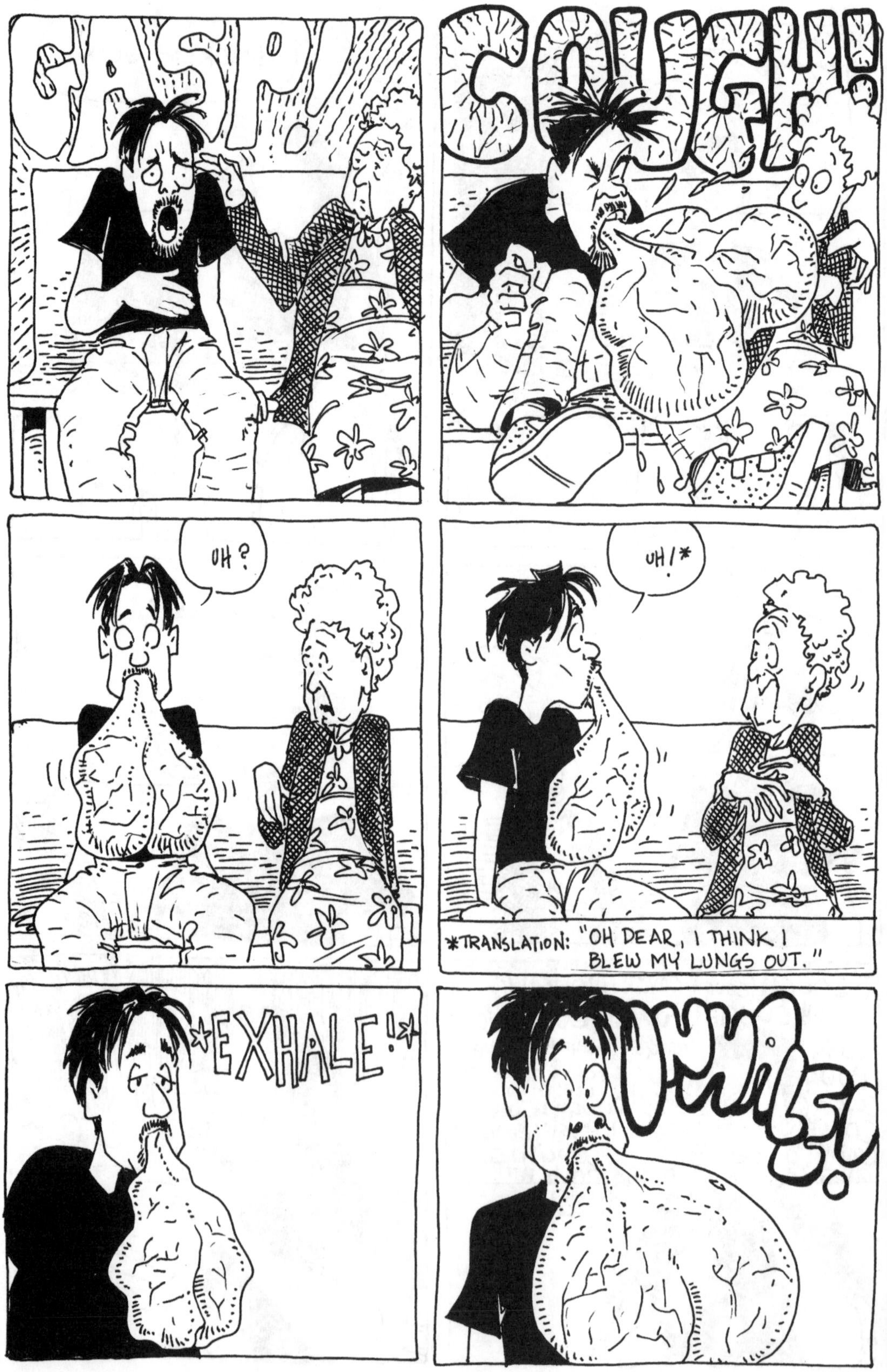

GASP!
COUGH!
UH?
UH!*
*TRANSLATION: "OH DEAR, I THINK I BLEW MY LUNGS OUT."
EXHALE!
NHALE!

The Smoker

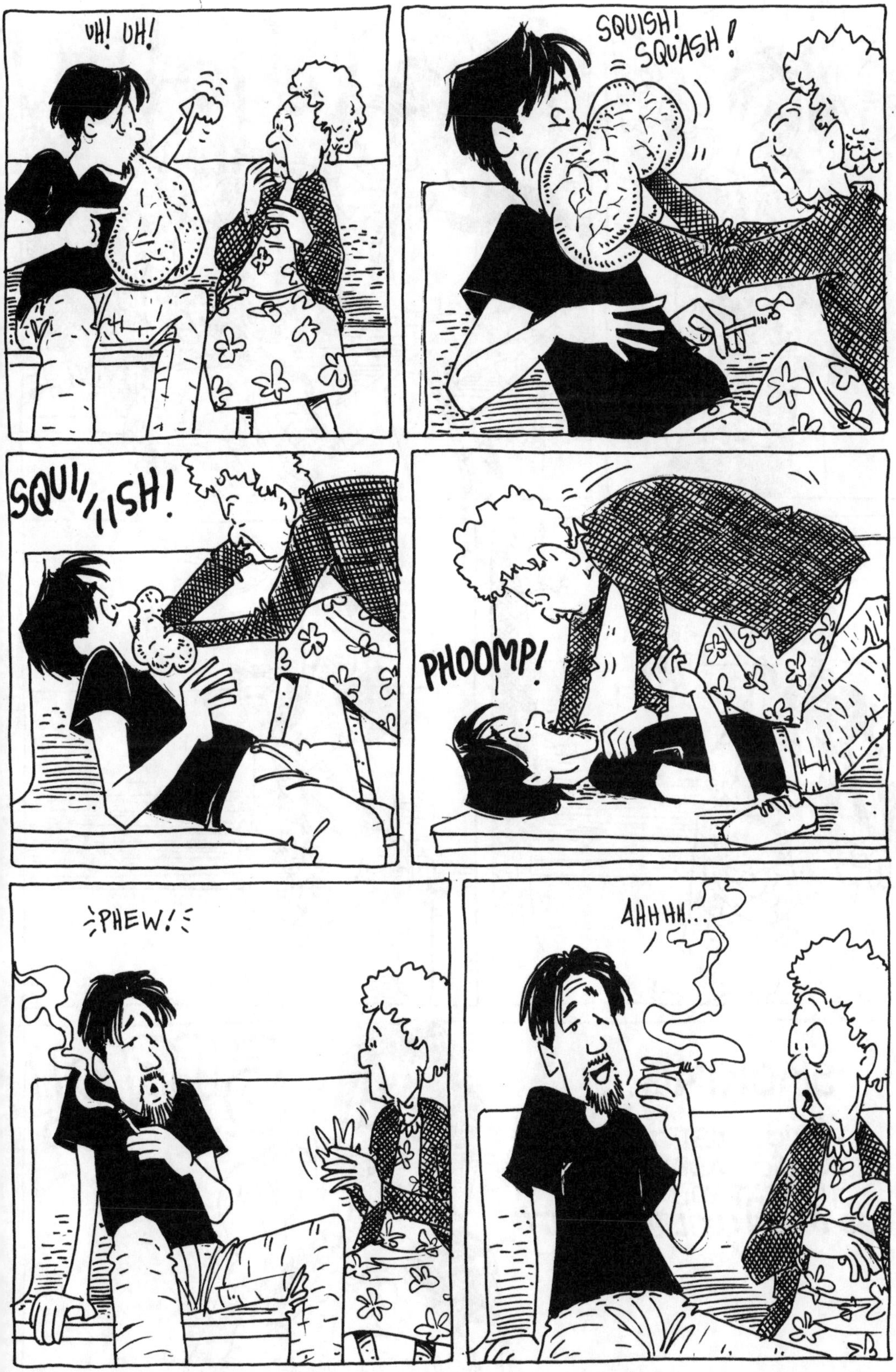
UH! UH!
SQUISH! SQUASH!
SQUIIIISH!
PHOOMP!
PHEW!
AHHHH...

The Smoker

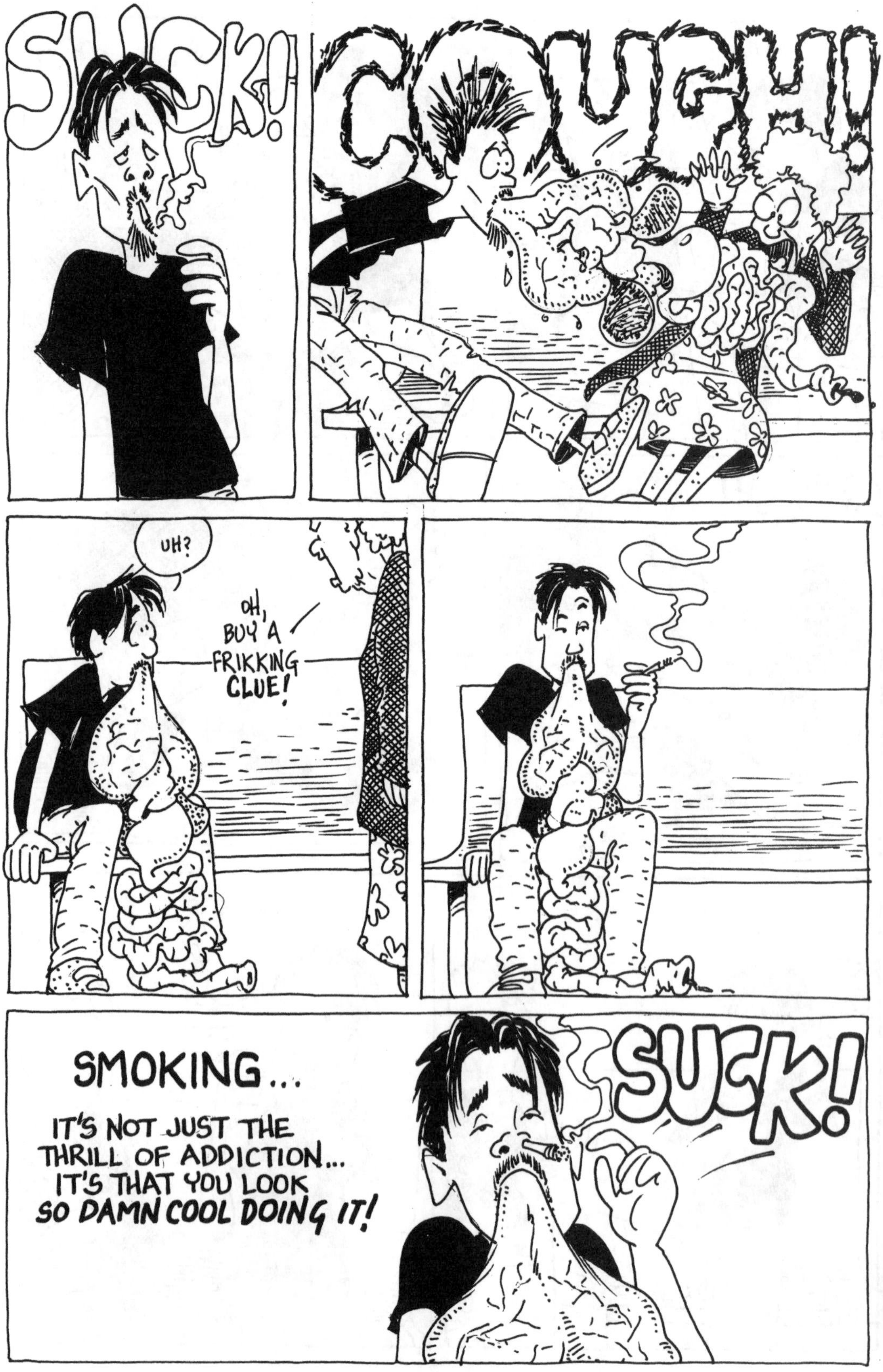
SUCK!
COUGH!
UH?
OH, BUY A FRIKKING CLUE!
SMOKING...
IT'S NOT JUST THE THRILL OF ADDICTION... IT'S THAT YOU LOOK SO DAMN COOL DOING IT!
SUCK!

Lillith Fair

Juneteenth, 1932

My Dearest Lillith Fair,

It was with great anthrillcipation that I opened your male last weekend while shooting peasants near my country estate. Yes, there is joy to be found in your witty repartee, your mirthful missives, your sour de fair. But, to my surprise, instead of gleeful discourse, I find your silver bill. What? Does this puzzling pot have something to do with the barrel of baston baked bean I sent to your house a week ago 12th night? Is my little poopsie pie piffed?

Perchance we should meet to mingle your mastiff among my moustache hairs along the Maijon de Tours. Wala wala!

Detached,
Herr Dr. Wolfgang Von Akbarsteinberger McWooleycott, Esq.
Herringbrike Castle, Newport Beach, Finland

p.s. The next time you visit please bring your charming python, Raul, and a basket of dyed eyes for Kitty Banks.

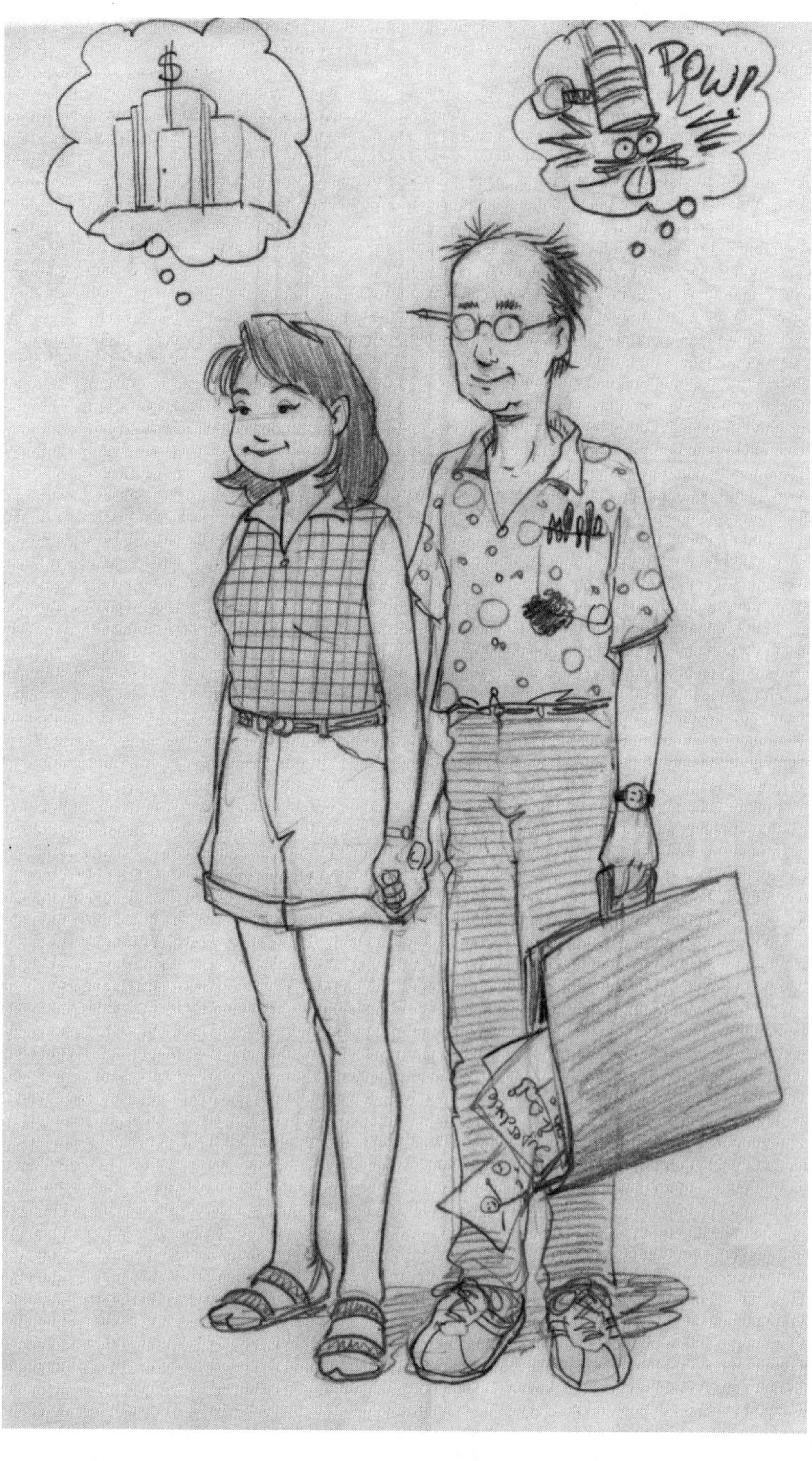
$
POW!

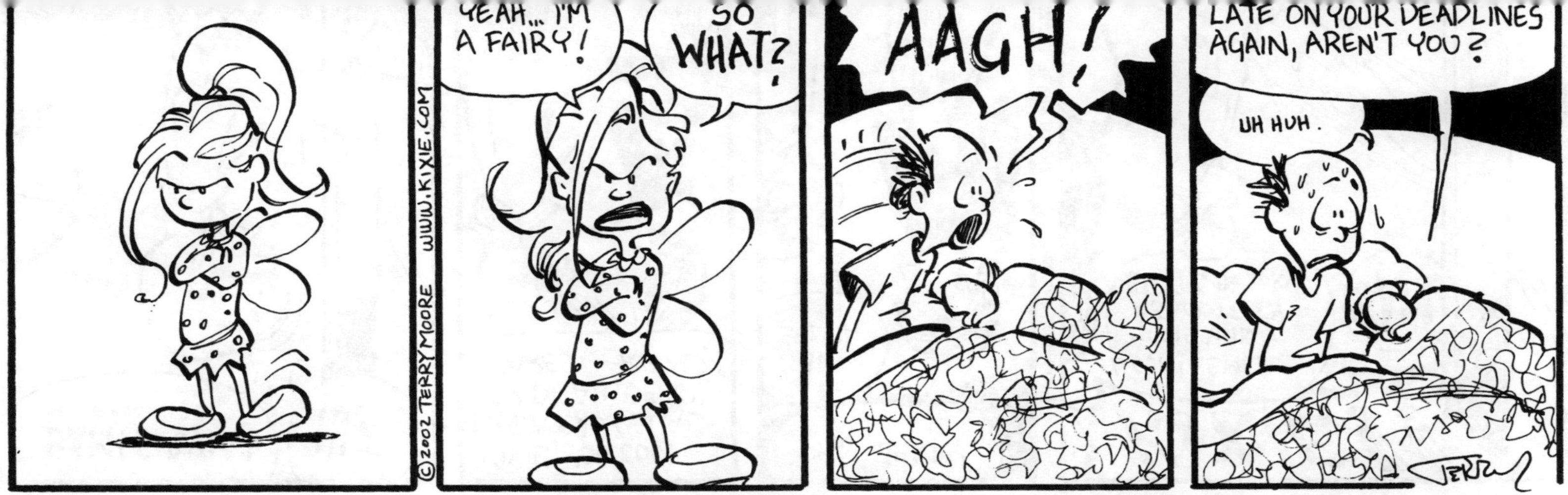
YEAH... I'M A FAIRY!
SO WHAT?
AAGH!
LATE ON YOUR DEADLINES AGAIN, AREN'T YOU?
UH HUH.
©2002 TERRY MOORE WWW.KIXIE.COM

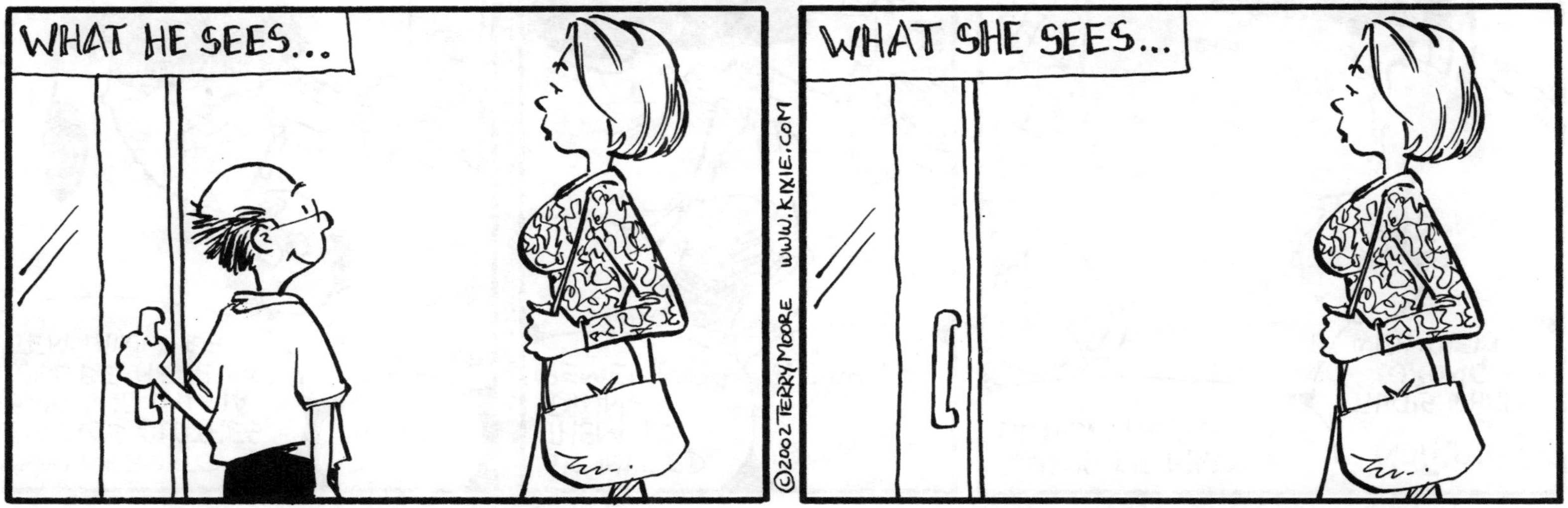
WHAT HE SEES...
WHAT SHE SEES...
©2002 TERRY MOORE WWW.KIXIE.COM

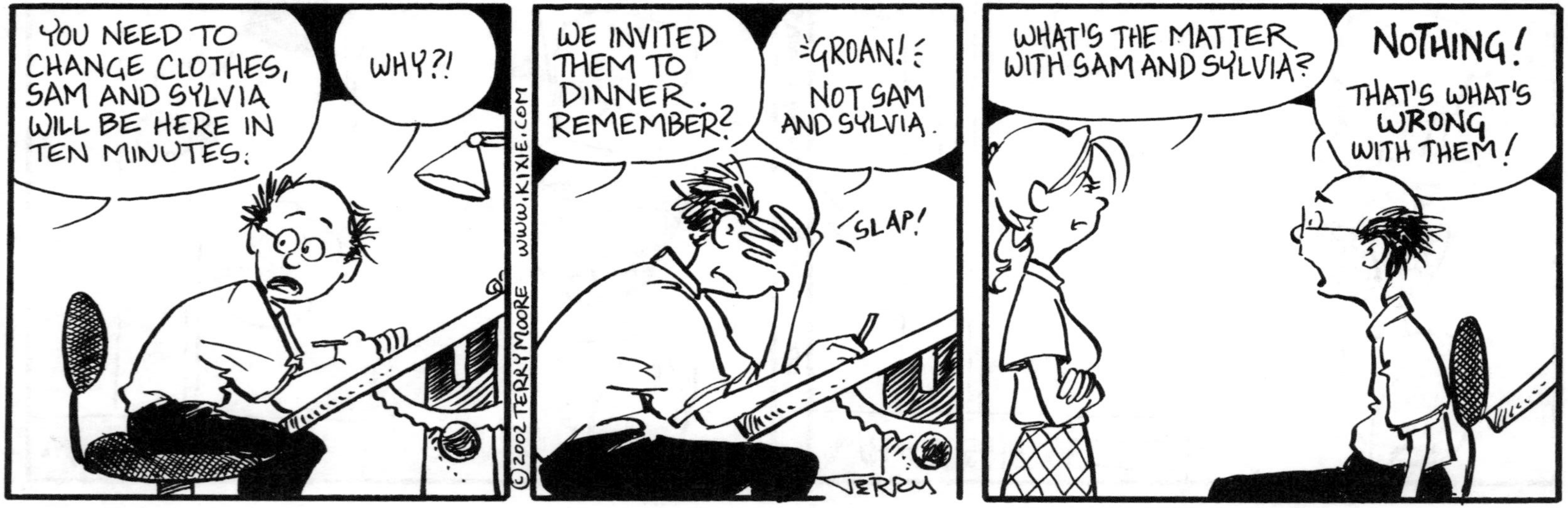
YOU NEED TO CHANGE CLOTHES, SAM AND SYLVIA WILL BE HERE IN TEN MINUTES.
WHY?!
WE INVITED THEM TO DINNER. REMEMBER?
GROAN!
NOT SAM AND SYLVIA.
SLAP!
WHAT'S THE MATTER WITH SAM AND SYLVIA?
NOTHING!
THAT'S WHAT'S WRONG WITH THEM!
©2002 TERRY MOORE WWW.KIXIE.COM
JERRY

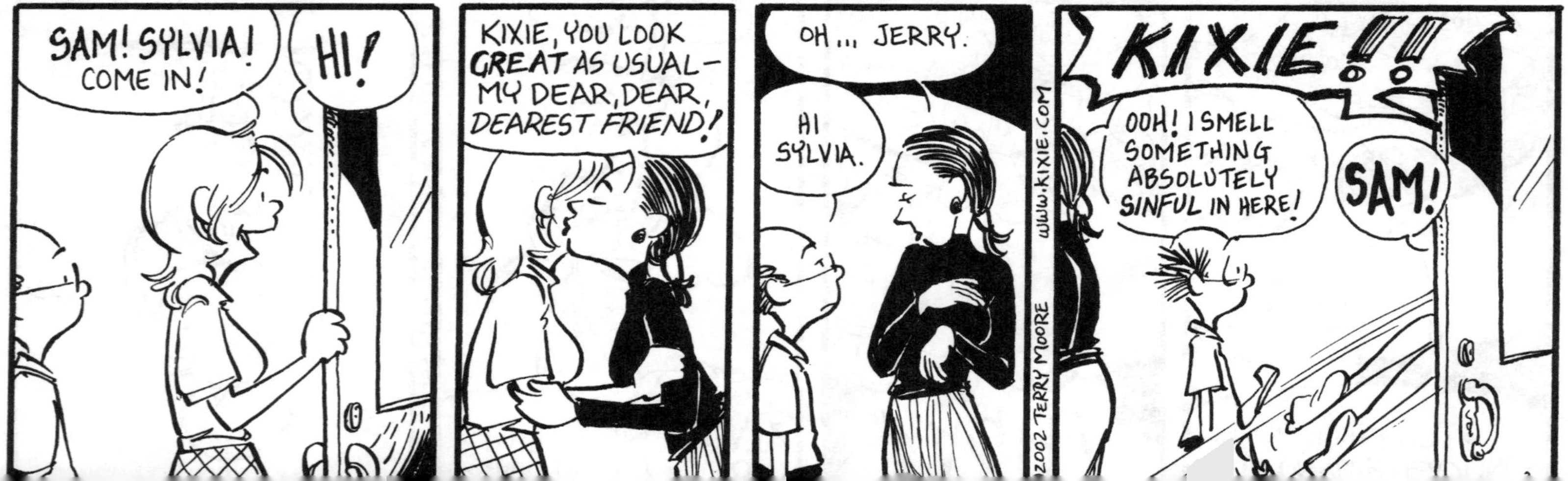
SAM! SYLVIA! COME IN!
HI!
KIXIE, YOU LOOK GREAT AS USUAL– MY DEAR, DEAR, DEAREST FRIEND!
OH ... JERRY.
HI SYLVIA.
KIXIE!!!
OOH! I SMELL SOMETHING ABSOLUTELY SINFUL IN HERE!
SAM!
©2002 TERRY MOORE WWW.KIXIE.COM

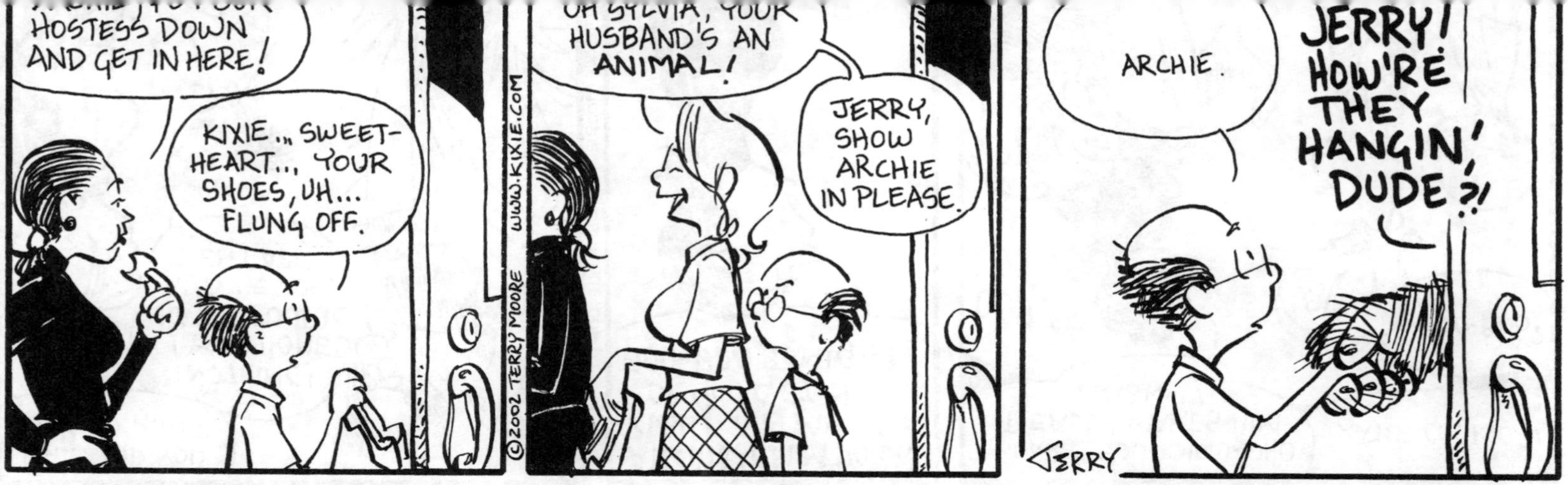
HOSTESS DOWN
AND GET IN HERE!
KIXIE... SWEET-
HEART..., YOUR
SHOES, UH...
FLUNG OFF.
©2002 TERRY MOORE WWW.KIXIE.COM
HUSBAND'S AN
ANIMAL!
JERRY,
SHOW
ARCHIE
IN PLEASE.
ARCHIE.
JERRY!
HOW'RE
THEY
HANGIN',
DUDE?!
JERRY

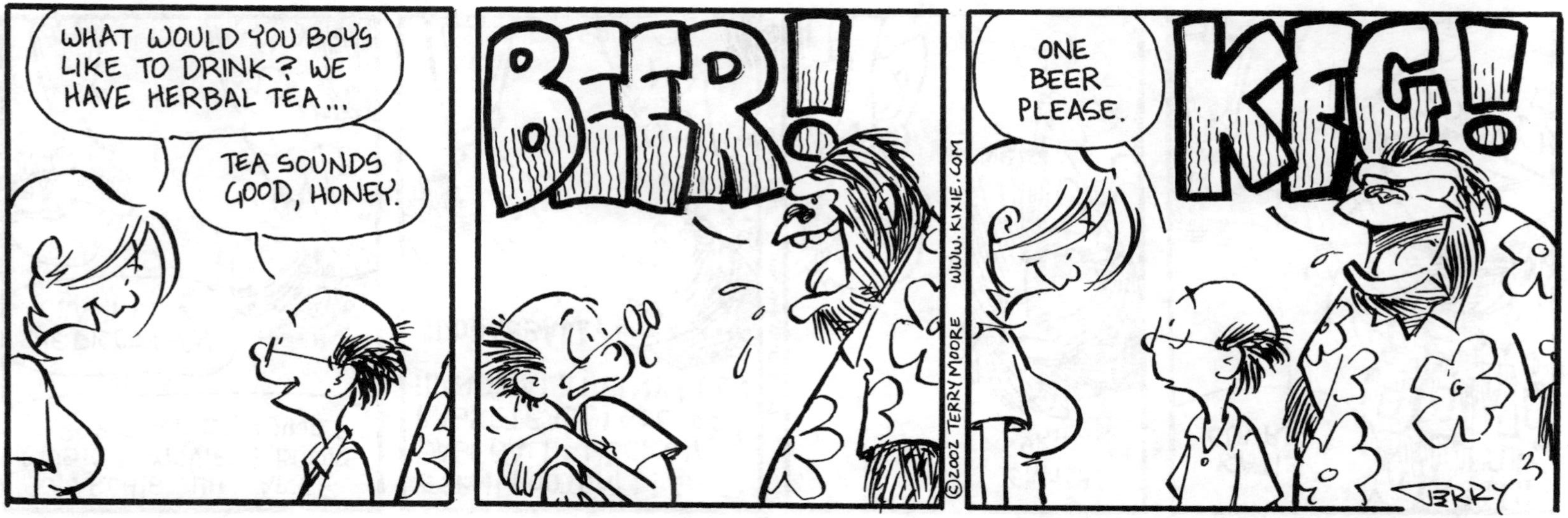
WHAT WOULD YOU BOYS
LIKE TO DRINK? WE
HAVE HERBAL TEA...
TEA SOUNDS
GOOD, HONEY.
BEER!
©2002 TERRY MOORE WWW.KIXIE.COM
ONE
BEER
PLEASE.
KEG!
JERRY

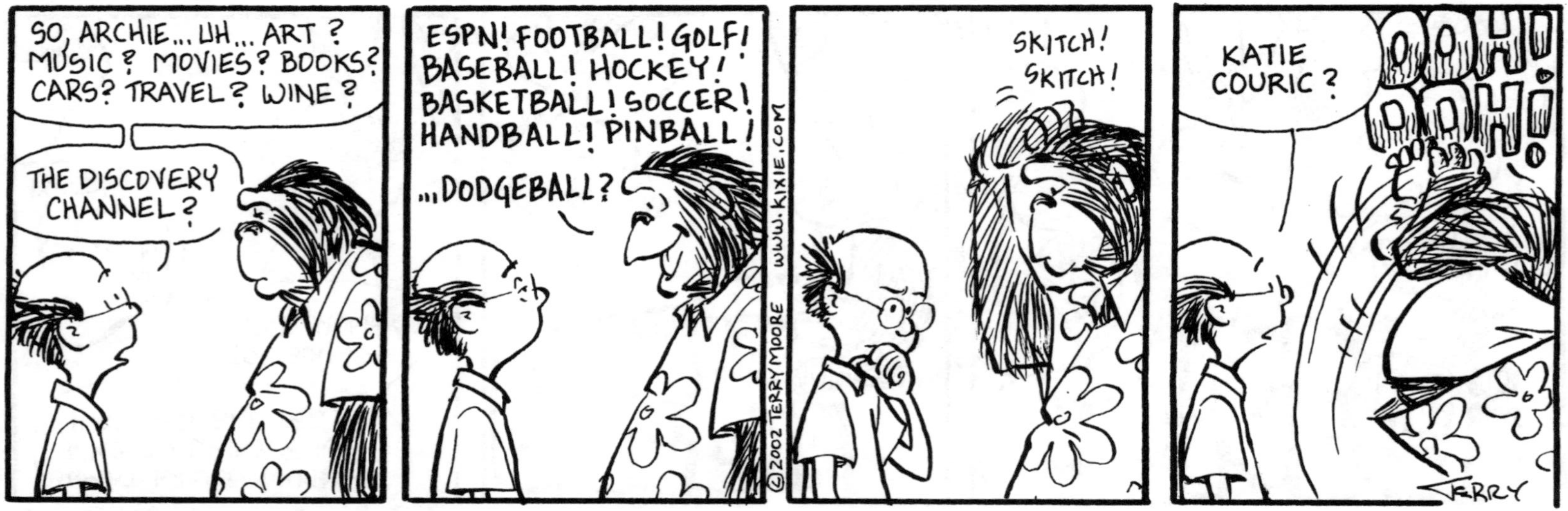
SO, ARCHIE... UH... ART ? MUSIC ? MOVIES ? BOOKS ? CARS ? TRAVEL ? WINE ?
THE DISCOVERY CHANNEL ?
ESPN! FOOTBALL! GOLF! BASEBALL! HOCKEY! BASKETBALL! SOCCER! HANDBALL! PINBALL!
...DODGEBALL?
© 2002 TERRY MOORE WWW.KIXIE.COM
SKITCH! SKITCH!
KATIE COURIC ?
OOH! OOH!
TERRY

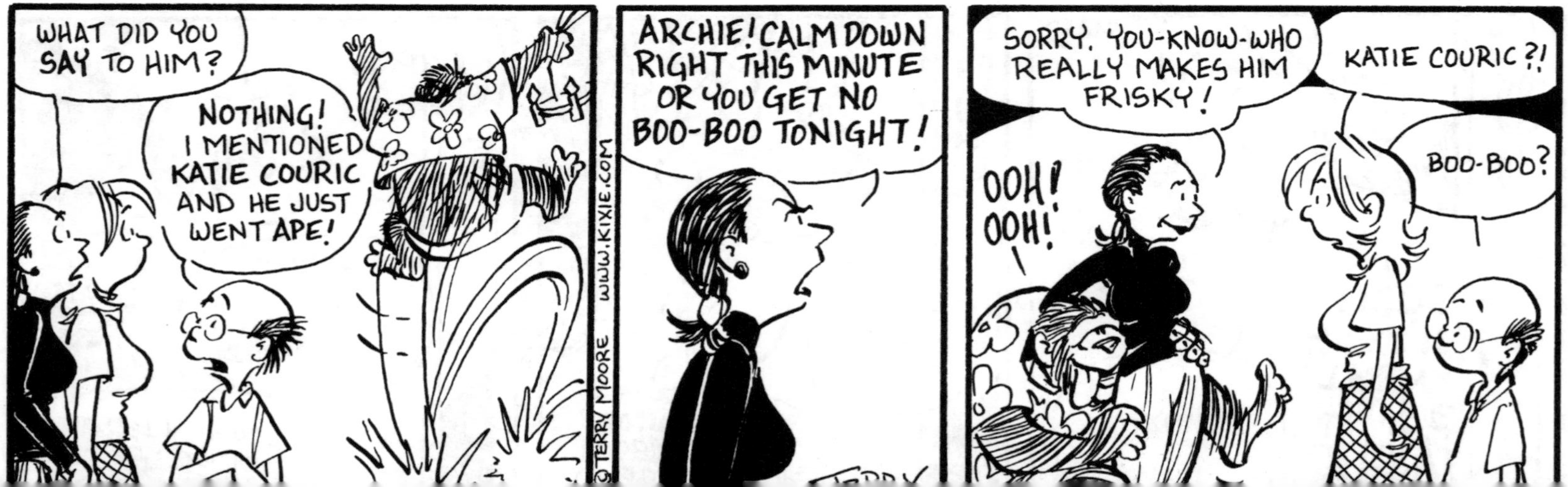
WHAT DID YOU SAY TO HIM?
NOTHING! I MENTIONED KATIE COURIC AND HE JUST WENT APE!
© TERRY MOORE WWW.KIXIE.COM
ARCHIE! CALM DOWN RIGHT THIS MINUTE OR YOU GET NO BOO-BOO TONIGHT!
SORRY. YOU-KNOW-WHO REALLY MAKES HIM FRISKY!
OOH! OOH!
KATIE COURIC ?!
BOO-BOO?

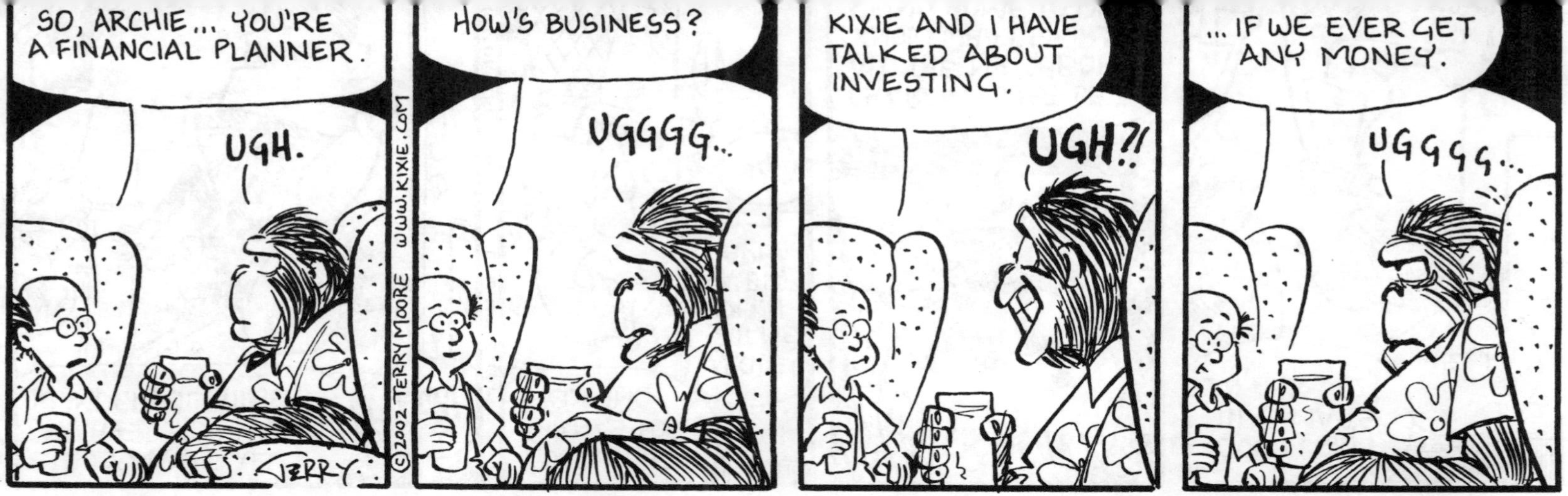
SO, ARCHIE... YOU'RE A FINANCIAL PLANNER.
UGH.
HOW'S BUSINESS?
UGGGG...
KIXIE AND I HAVE TALKED ABOUT INVESTING.
UGH?!
...IF WE EVER GET ANY MONEY.
UGGGG...
©2002 TERRY MOORE WWW.KIXIE.COM
TERRY

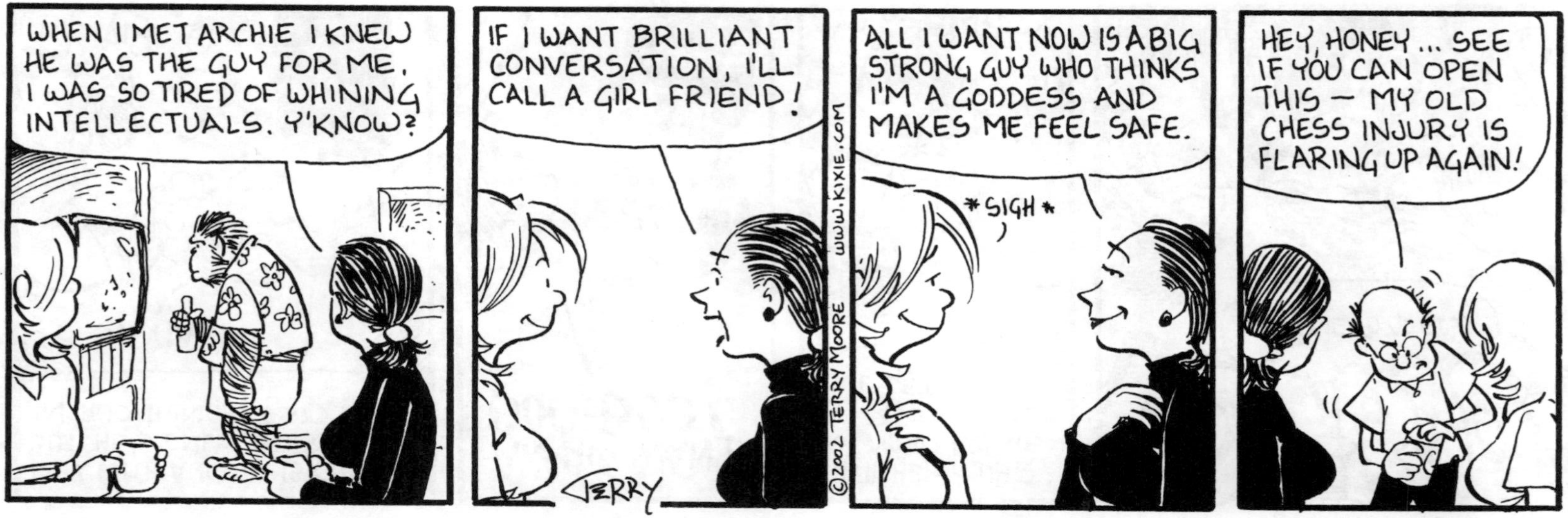
WHEN I MET ARCHIE I KNEW HE WAS THE GUY FOR ME. I WAS SO TIRED OF WHINING INTELLECTUALS. Y'KNOW?
IF I WANT BRILLIANT CONVERSATION, I'LL CALL A GIRL FRIEND!
ALL I WANT NOW IS A BIG STRONG GUY WHO THINKS I'M A GODDESS AND MAKES ME FEEL SAFE.
SIGH
HEY, HONEY... SEE IF YOU CAN OPEN THIS — MY OLD CHESS INJURY IS FLARING UP AGAIN!
©2002 TERRY MOORE WWW.KIXIE.COM
TERRY

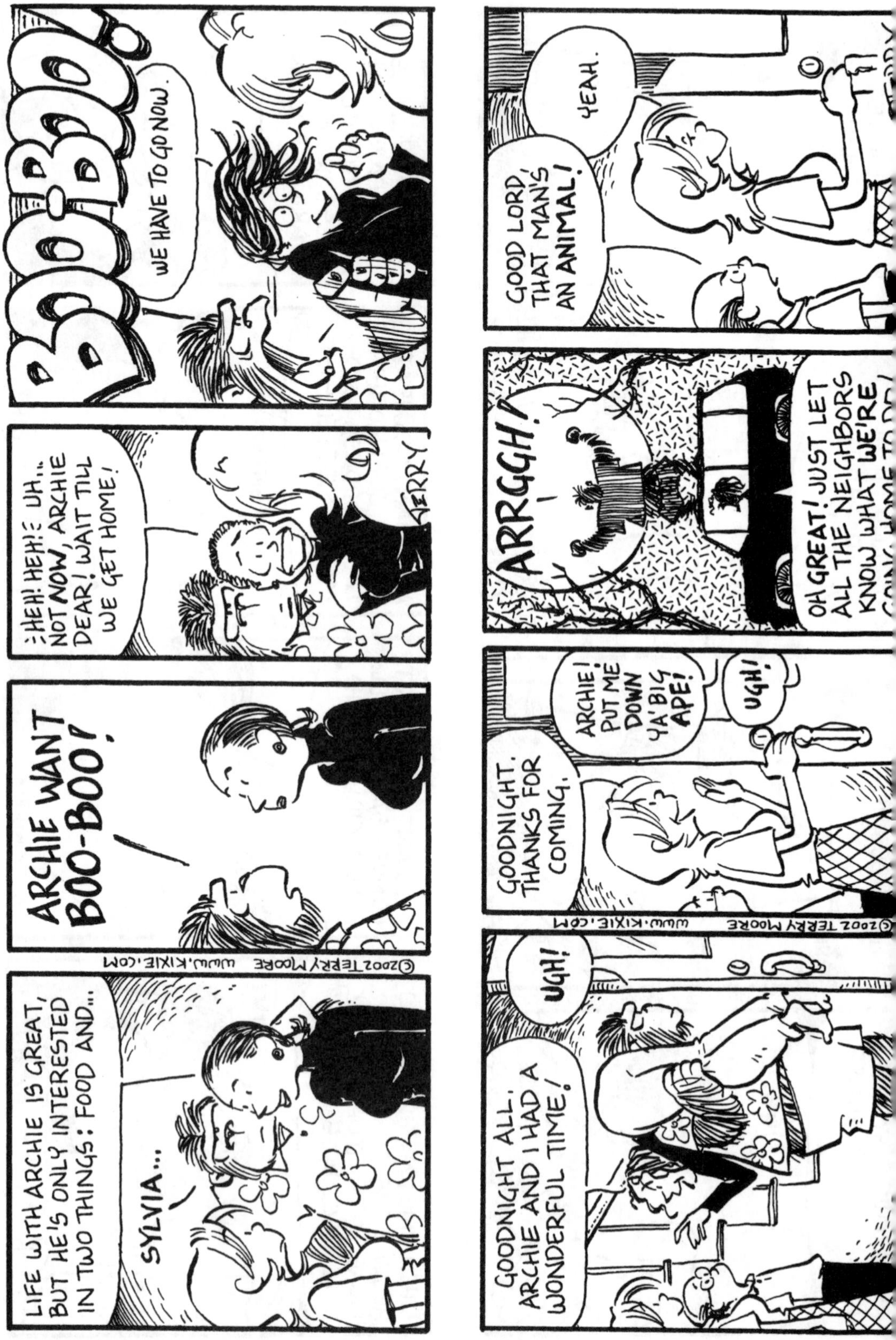
LIFE WITH ARCHIE IS GREAT, BUT HE'S ONLY INTERESTED IN TWO THINGS: FOOD AND...
SYLVIA...
©2002 TERRY MOORE www.KIXIE.COM
ARCHIE WANT BOO-BOO!
:HEH! HEH!: UH... NOT NOW, ARCHIE DEAR! WAIT TILL WE GET HOME!
TERRY
BOO-BOO!
WE HAVE TO GO NOW.
GOODNIGHT ALL. ARCHIE AND I HAD A WONDERFUL TIME!
UGH!
©2002 TERRY MOORE www.KIXIE.COM
GOODNIGHT. THANKS FOR COMING.
ARCHIE! PUT ME DOWN YA' BIG APE!
UGH!
ARRGGH!
OH GREAT! JUST LET ALL THE NEIGHBORS KNOW WHAT WE'RE
GOOD LORD, THAT MAN'S AN ANIMAL!
YEAH.

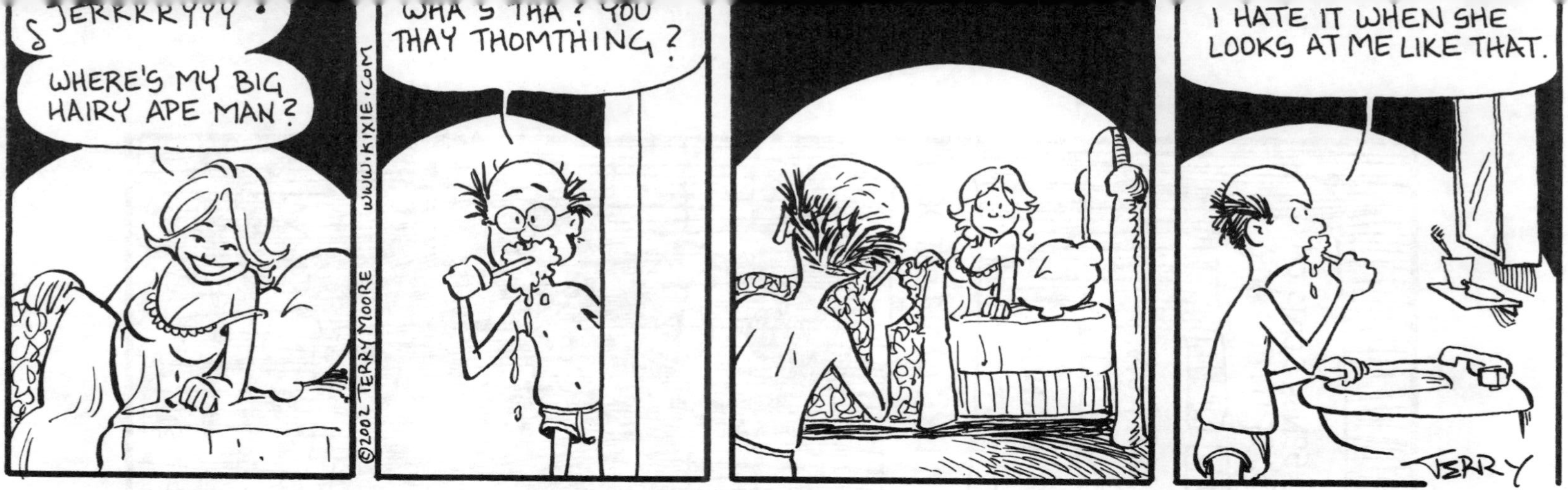
JERRRKRYYY
WHERE'S MY BIG HAIRY APE MAN?
©2002 TERRY MOORE WWW.KIXIE.COM
THAY THOMTHING?
I HATE IT WHEN SHE LOOKS AT ME LIKE THAT.
TERRY

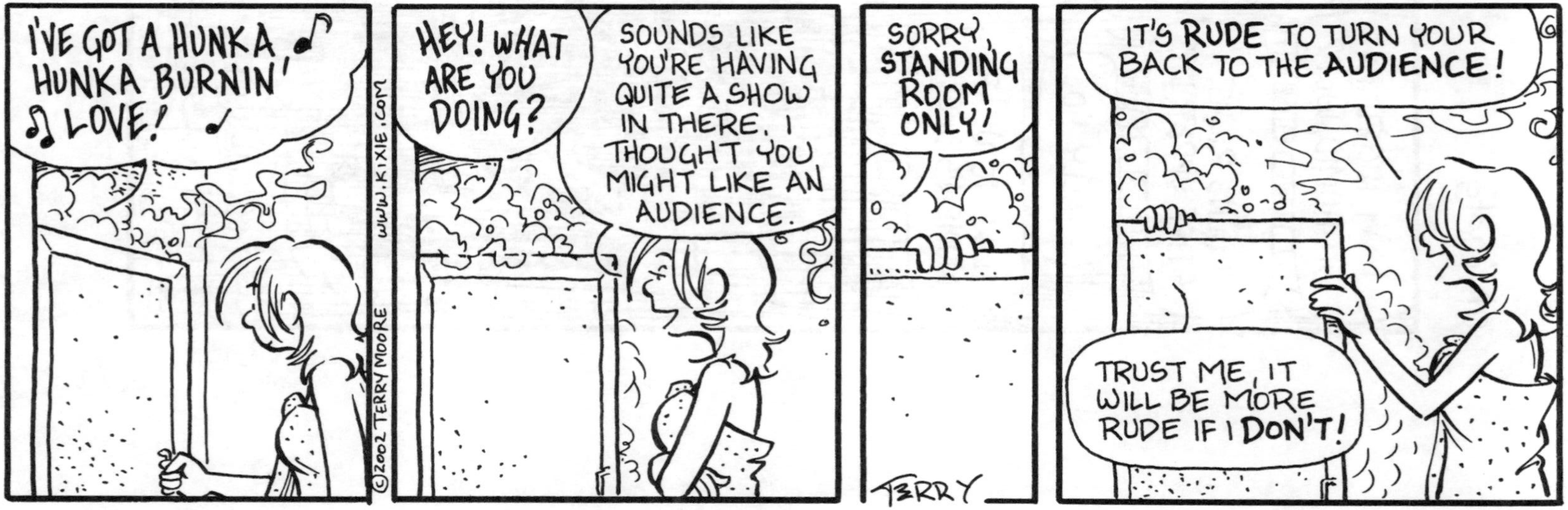
I'VE GOT A HUNKA HUNKA BURNIN' LOVE!
©2002 TERRY MOORE WWW.KIXIE.COM
HEY! WHAT ARE YOU DOING?
SOUNDS LIKE YOU'RE HAVING QUITE A SHOW IN THERE. I THOUGHT YOU MIGHT LIKE AN AUDIENCE.
SORRY, STANDING ROOM ONLY!
TERRY
IT'S RUDE TO TURN YOUR BACK TO THE AUDIENCE!
TRUST ME, IT WILL BE MORE RUDE IF I DON'T!

2Nigels

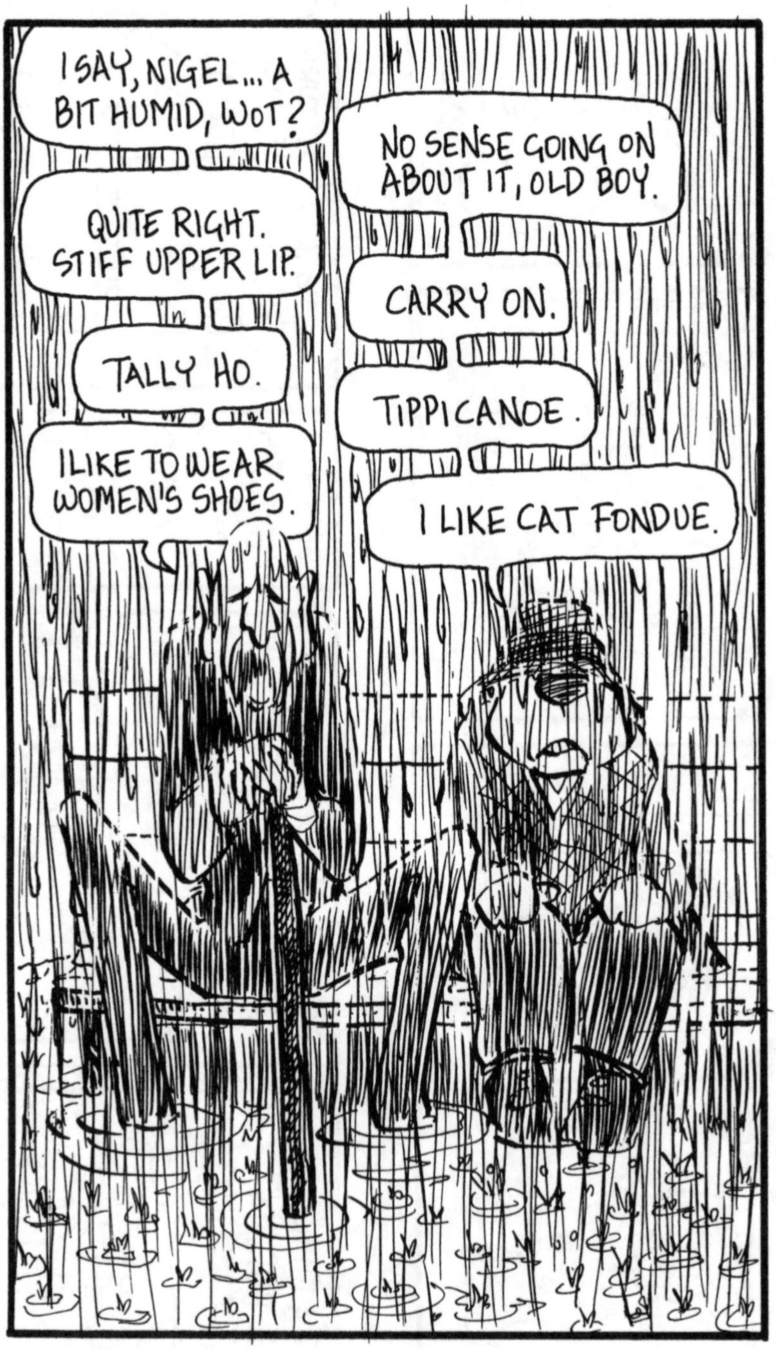
I SAY, NIGEL... A BIT HUMID, WOT?
NO SENSE GOING ON ABOUT IT, OLD BOY.
QUITE RIGHT. STIFF UPPER LIP.
CARRY ON.
TALLY HO.
TIPPICANOE.
I LIKE TO WEAR WOMEN'S SHOES.
I LIKE CAT FONDUE.

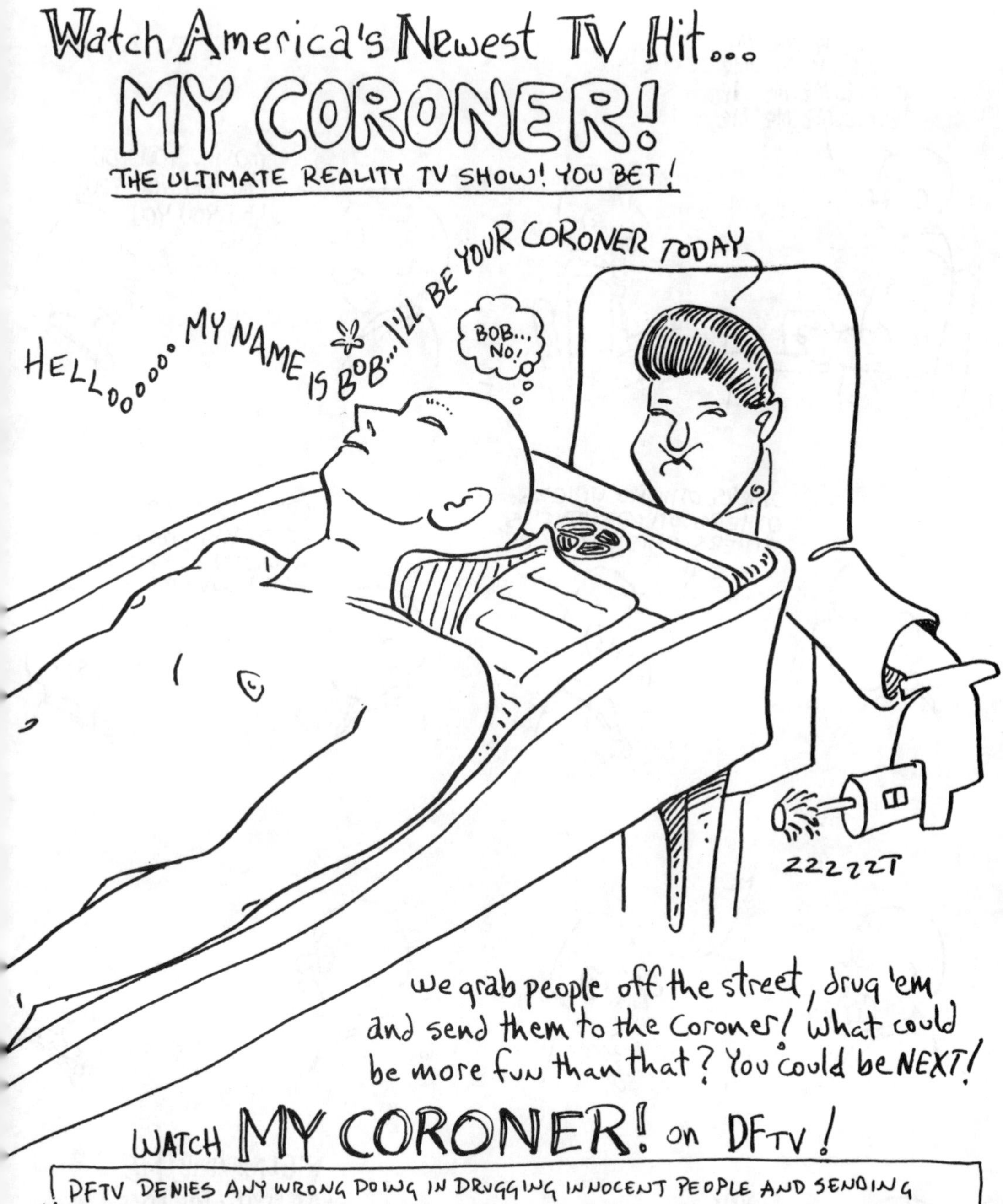
Watch America's Newest TV Hit...
MY CORONER!
THE ULTIMATE REALITY TV SHOW! YOU BET!
HELLOooooo MY NAME IS BOB... I'LL BE YOUR CORONER TODAY
BOB... NO!
ZZZZZT
we grab people off the street, drug 'em and send them to the Coroner! what could be more fun than that? You could be NEXT!
WATCH MY CORONER! on DFTV!
From our Legal Depart.
DFTV DENIES ANY WRONG DOING IN DRUGGING INNOCENT PEOPLE AND SENDING THEM TO THE CORONER. IT'S NOT OUR FAULT WHAT HAPPENS TO THEM ONCE THEY'RE THERE. THEY SHOULDN'T HAVE BEEN OUT WALKING THE STREETS ANYWAY! WHO DO THEY THINK THEY ARE? WE SEE NOTHING WRONG WITH EXPLOITING YOU DUMBUCKS FOR THE SAKE OF FILLING OUR BANK ACCOUNTS. IF YOU'RE STUPID ENOUGH TO TUNE IN AND WATCH THIS CRAP THEN IT'S NOT OUR FAULT IF WE GET RICH WHILE YOU JUST GET DUMBER. IDIOTS.

Bowing to the throne of Jules Feiffer...

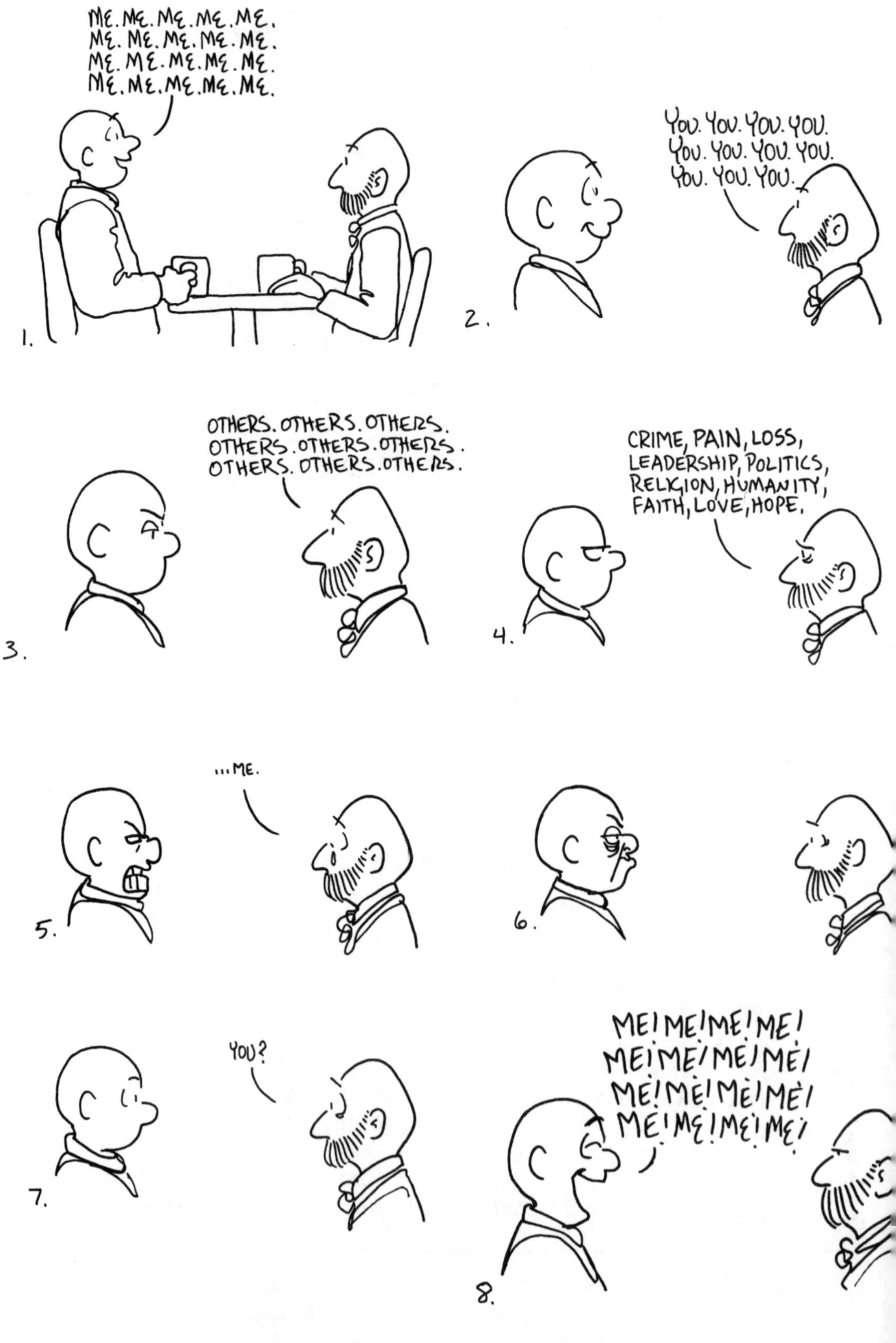
ME. ME. ME. ME. ME. ME. ME. ME. ME. ME. ME. ME. ME. ME. ME. ME. ME. ME. ME. ME.
1.
YOU. YOU. YOU. YOU. YOU. YOU. YOU. YOU. YOU. YOU. YOU.
2.
OTHERS. OTHERS. OTHERS. OTHERS. OTHERS. OTHERS. OTHERS. OTHERS. OTHERS.
3.
CRIME, PAIN, LOSS, LEADERSHIP, POLITICS, RELIGION, HUMANITY, FAITH, LOVE, HOPE,
4.
...ME.
5.
6.
YOU?
7.
ME! ME! ME! ME! ME! ME! ME! ME! ME! ME! ME! ME! ME! ME! ME! ME!
8.

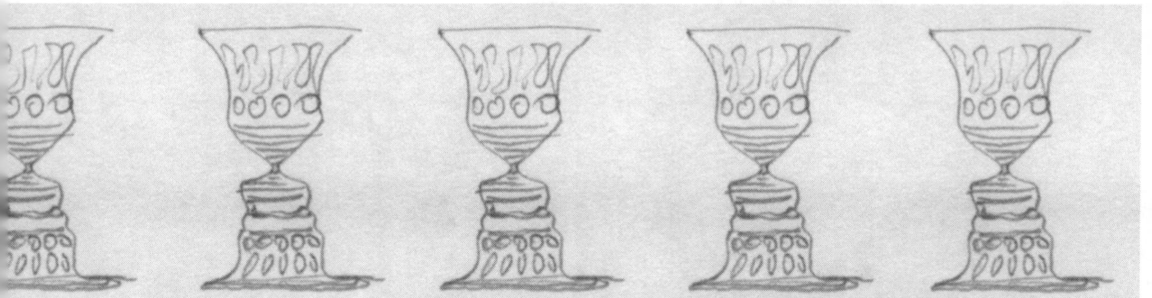

the hypocritical cup

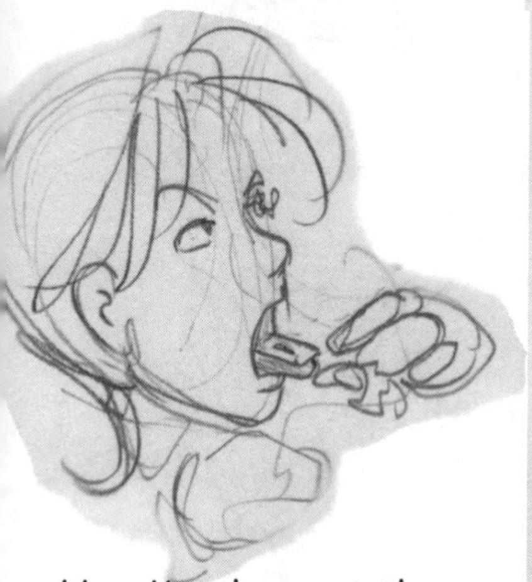

How Katchoo got the
nickname Razormouth

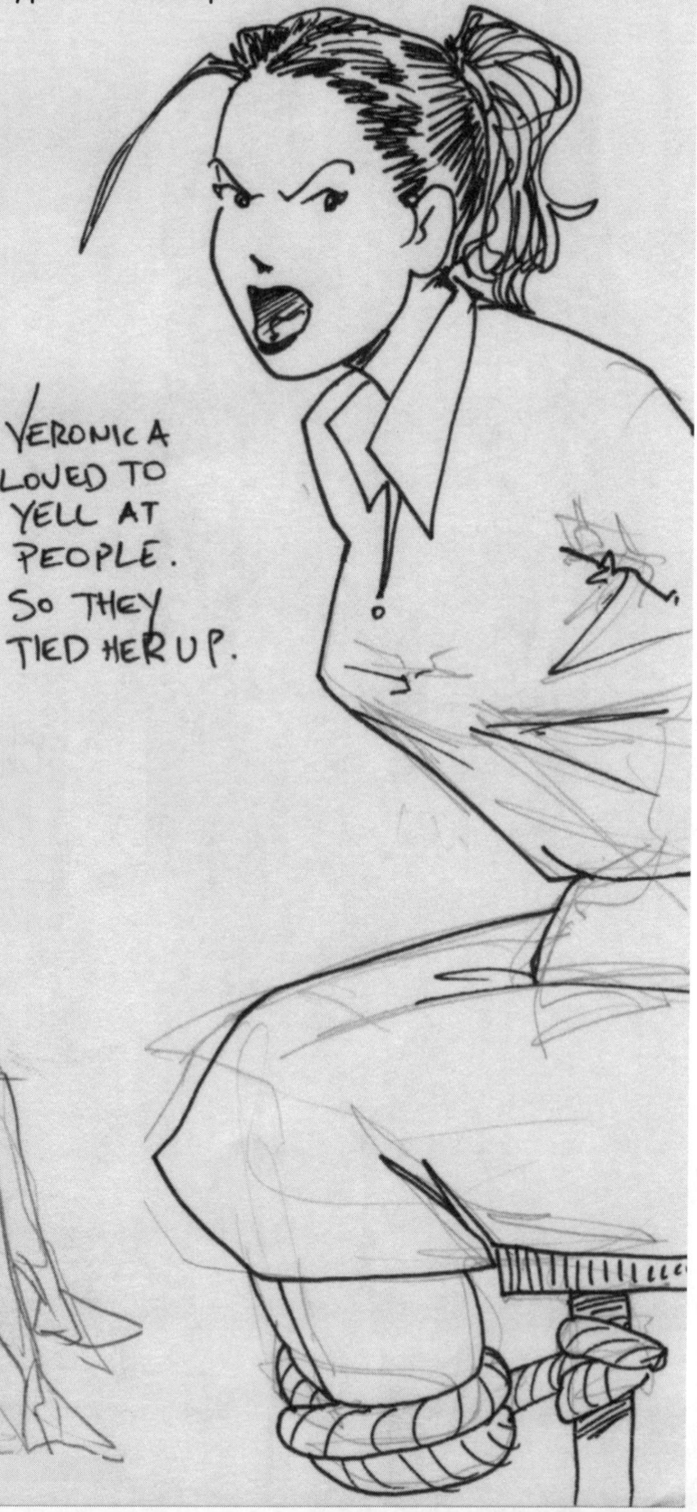
VERONICA
LOVED TO
YELL AT
PEOPLE.
SO THEY
TIED HER UP.

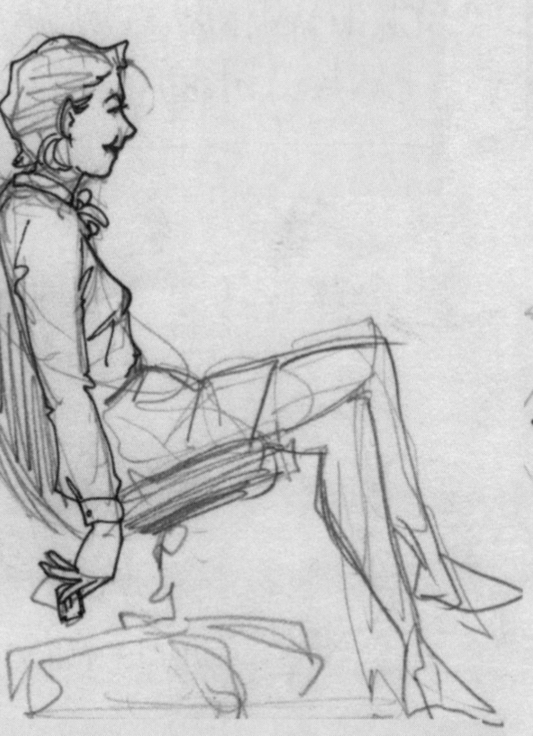

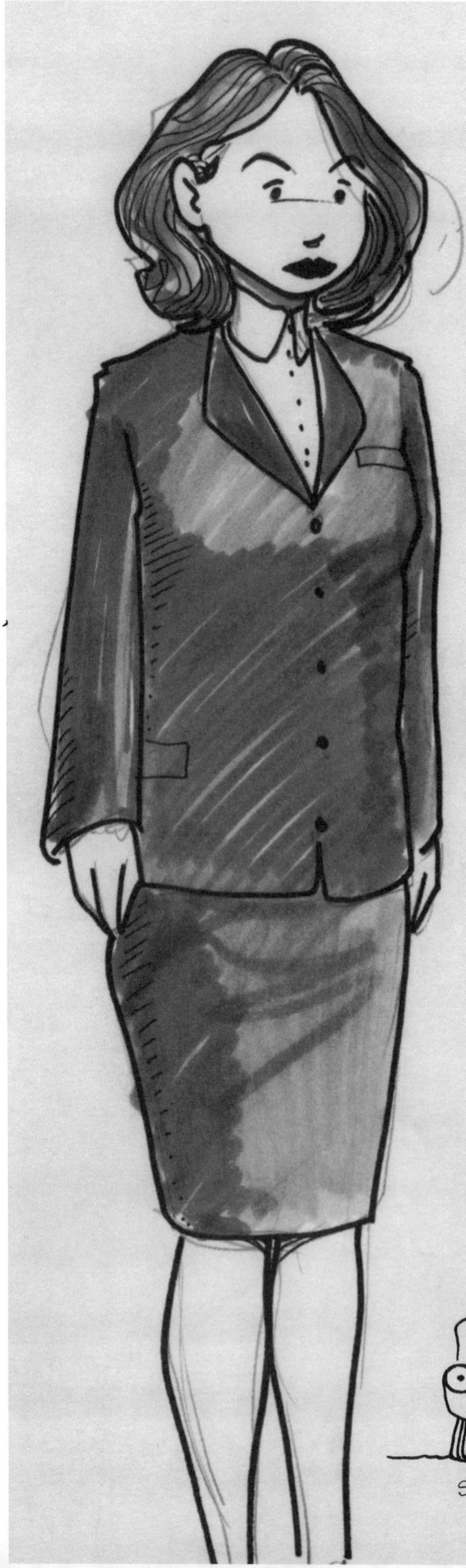

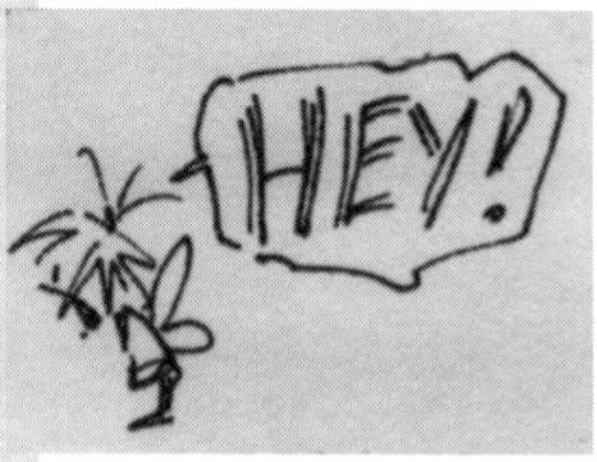
HEY!

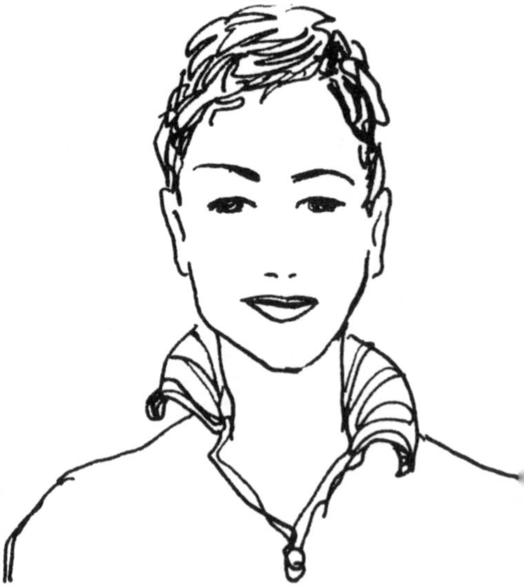

Janine

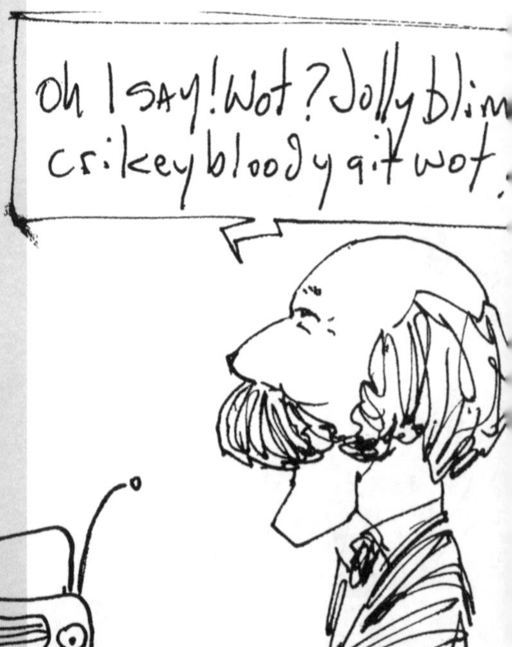
Oh I SAY! Wot? Jolly blim
crikey bloody git wot

Uncle Albert

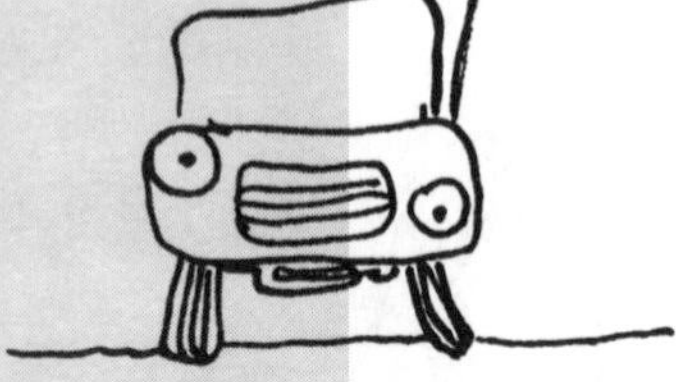

Shannon's car

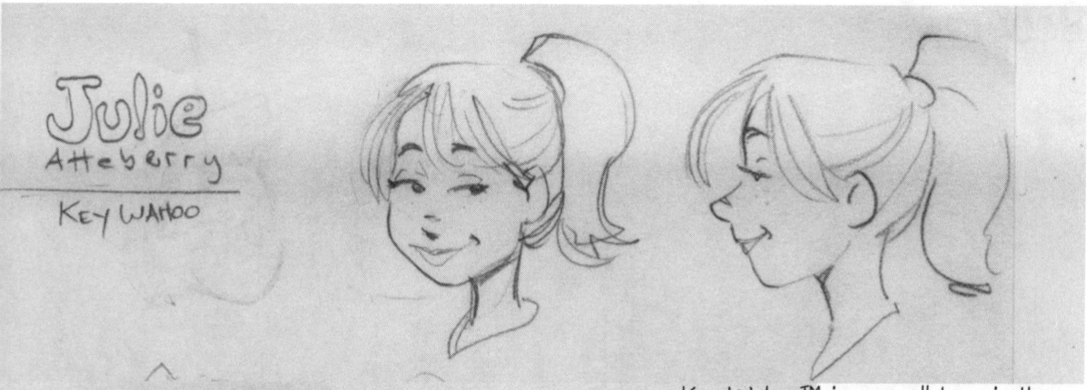
Julie
Atteberry
Key Wahoo

Key Wahoo™ is a small town in the Florida Keys inhabited by an eclectic group of social misfits and creative renegades. Julie Atteberry is the darling of the bunch, a bartender in the local saloon. Her grandmother probably drank with Hemingway- everybody else did. Anyway, I see Key Wahoo as a trilogy in four parts, an epic short story about everything and nothing, a laughable drama about the comedy of Life Cereal™, and the people who eat it.

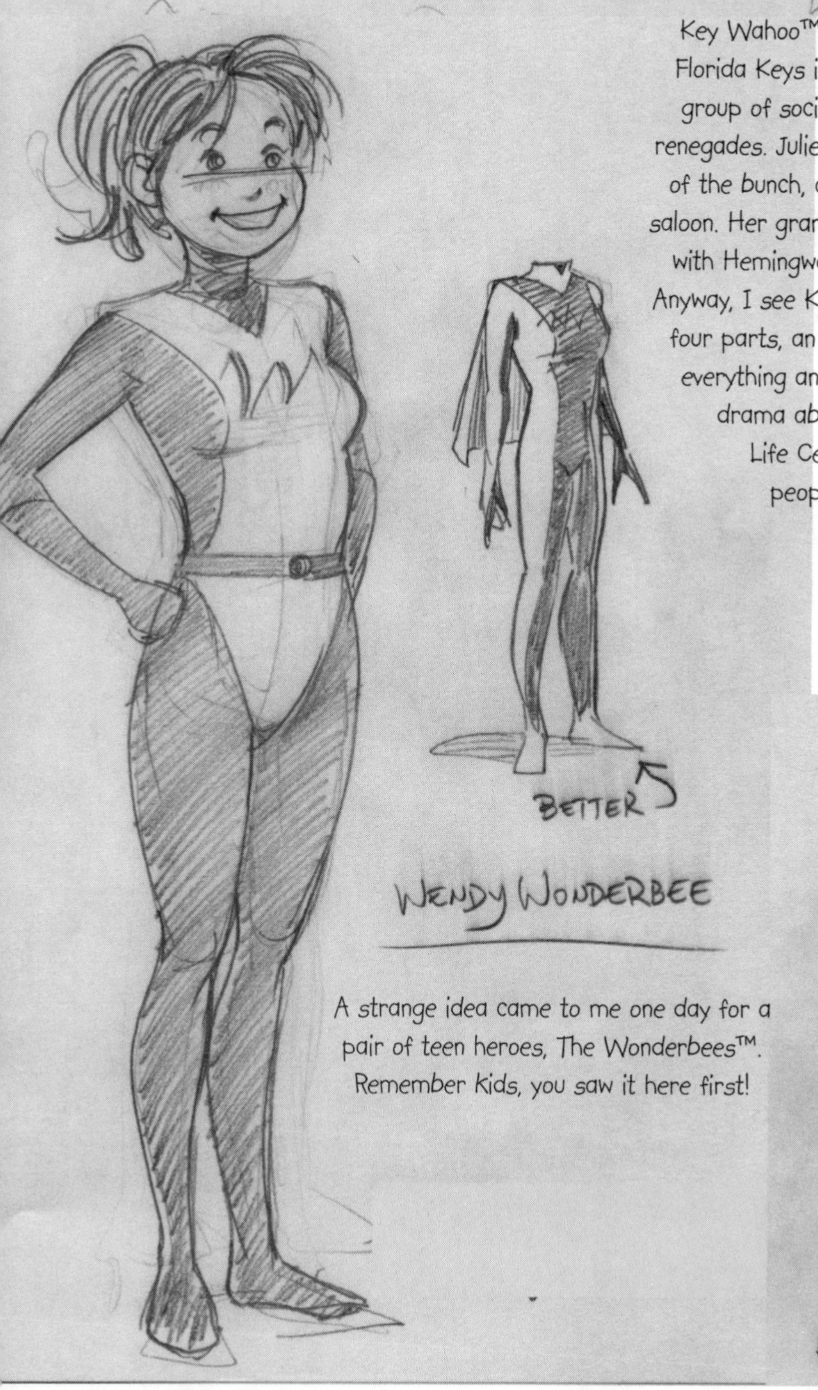
Better
Wendy Wonderbee

A strange idea came to me one day for a pair of teen heroes, The Wonderbees™. Remember Kids, you saw it here first!

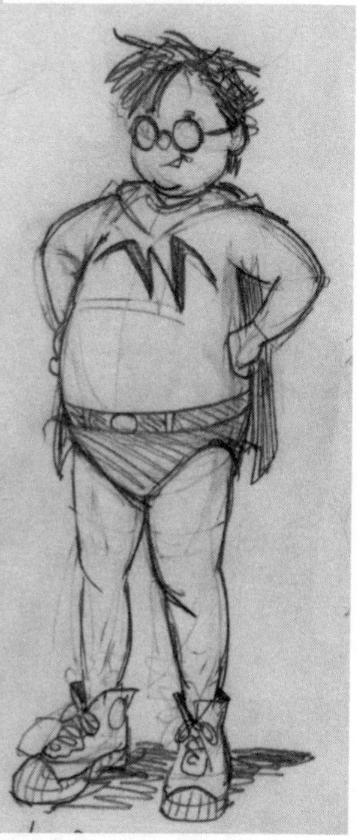

Beeps

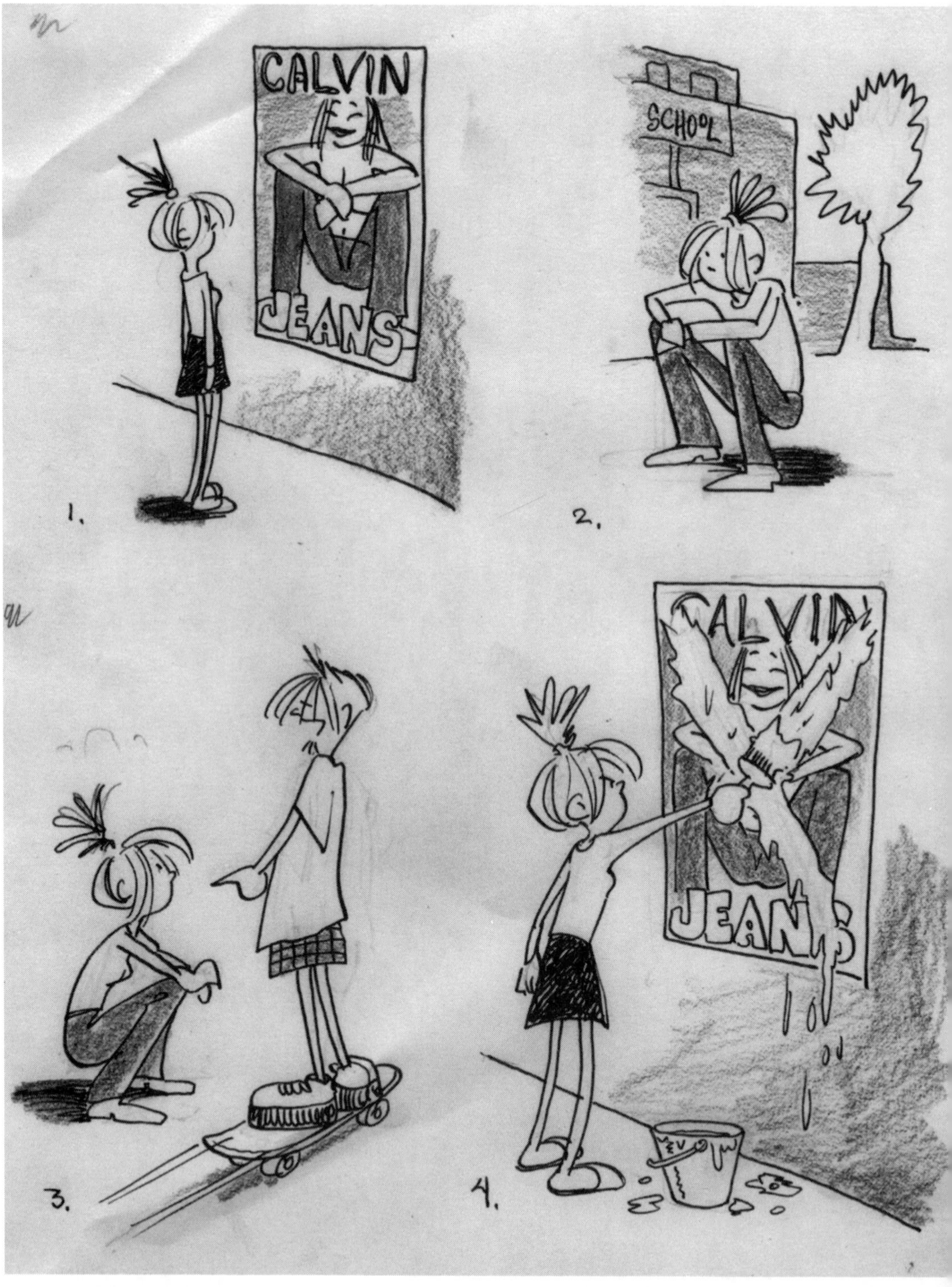
CALVIN
JEANS
SCHOOL
CALVIN
JEANS
1.
2.
3.
4.

Surprise! In case you don't know, I do another comic book called Strangers In Paradise. But this is Paradise, too, you know. Here are two sketches from the same sketchbook I was doodling cartoons in, so I thought I'd show you. This is the original pencil sketch for Katchoo's infamous painting of Francine (the one that caused all the trouble). I believe Katchoo called this piece Earth Mother.

...and the concept sketch for the cover of Strangers In Paradise 21.

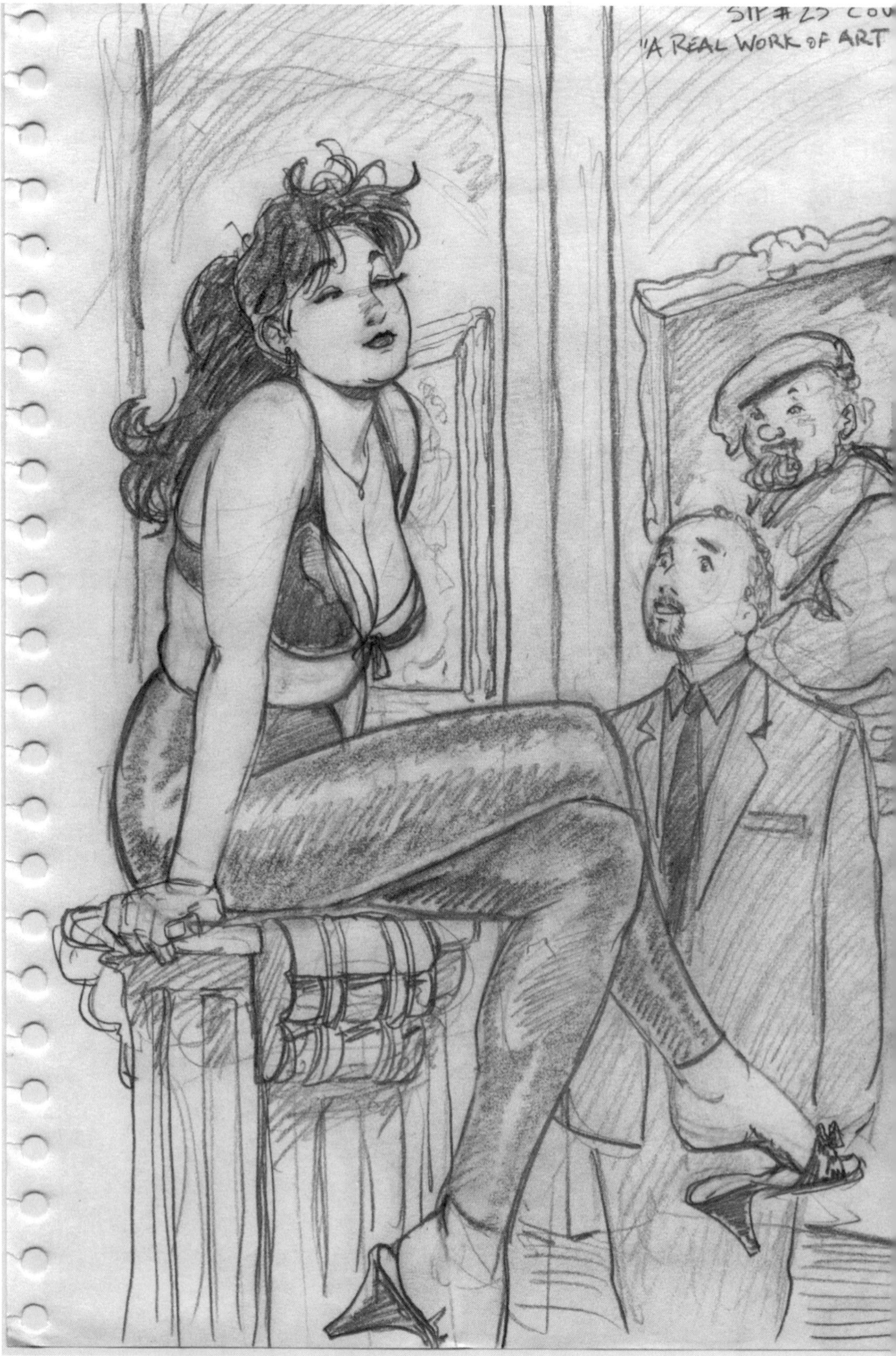
SIP #25 COV
"A REAL WORK OF ART

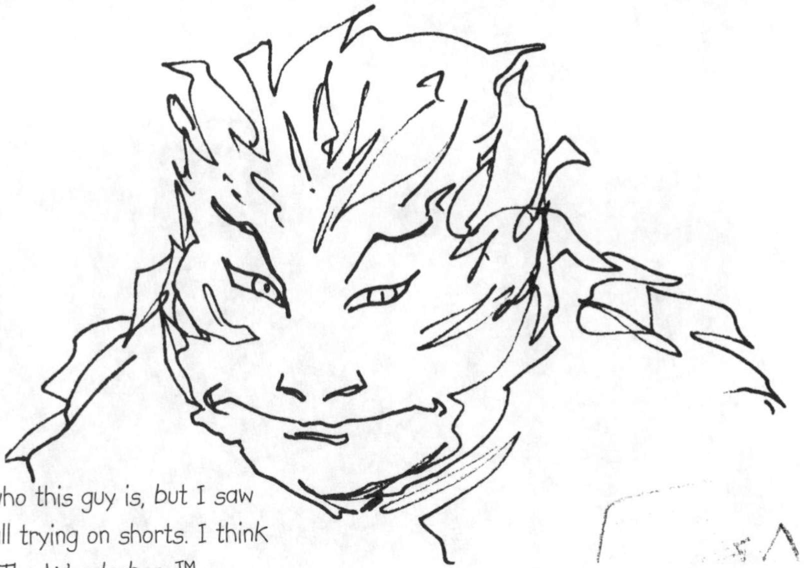

I don't know who this guy is, but I saw him at the mall trying on shorts. I think I'll put him in The Wonderbees™.

Remember Super-Chicken? I loved Super-Chicken... and his sidekick, Fred.

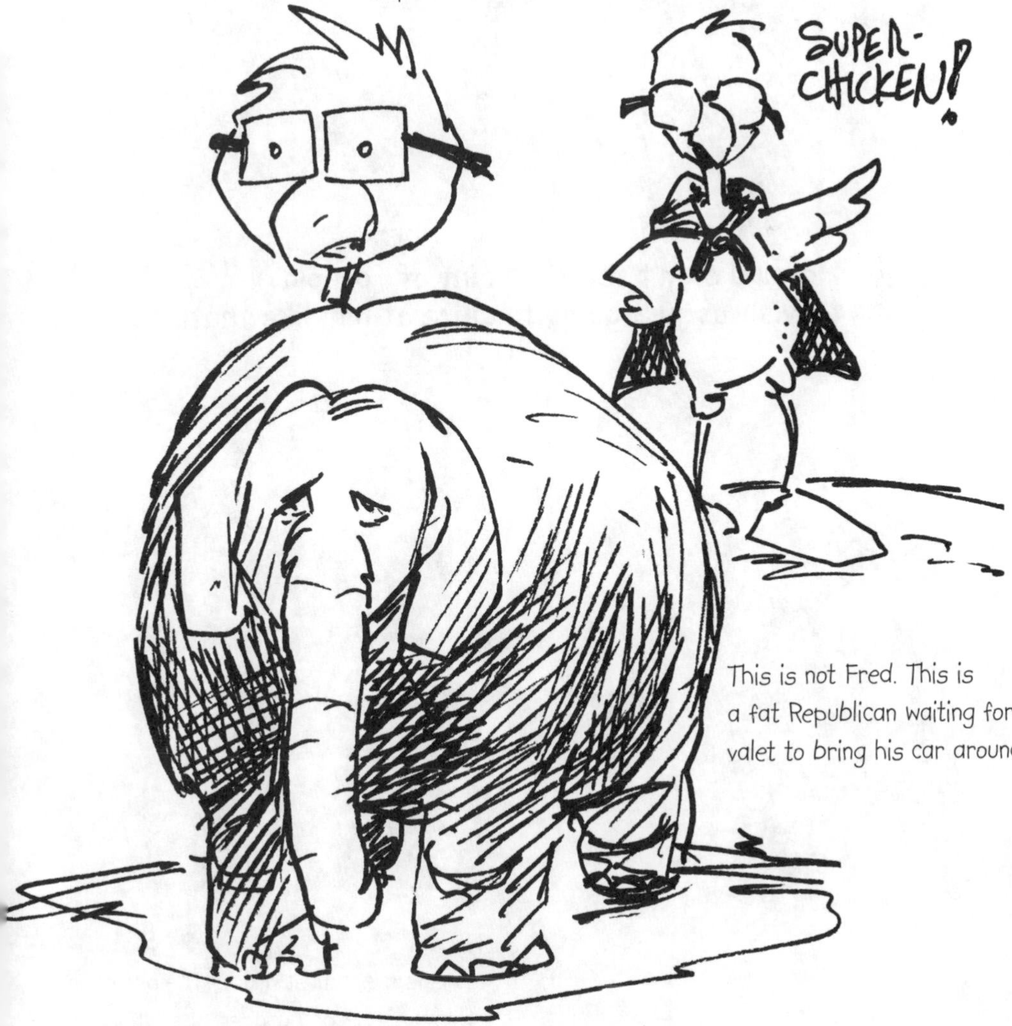
SUPER-CHICKEN!

This is not Fred. This is a fat Republican waiting for the valet to bring his car around.

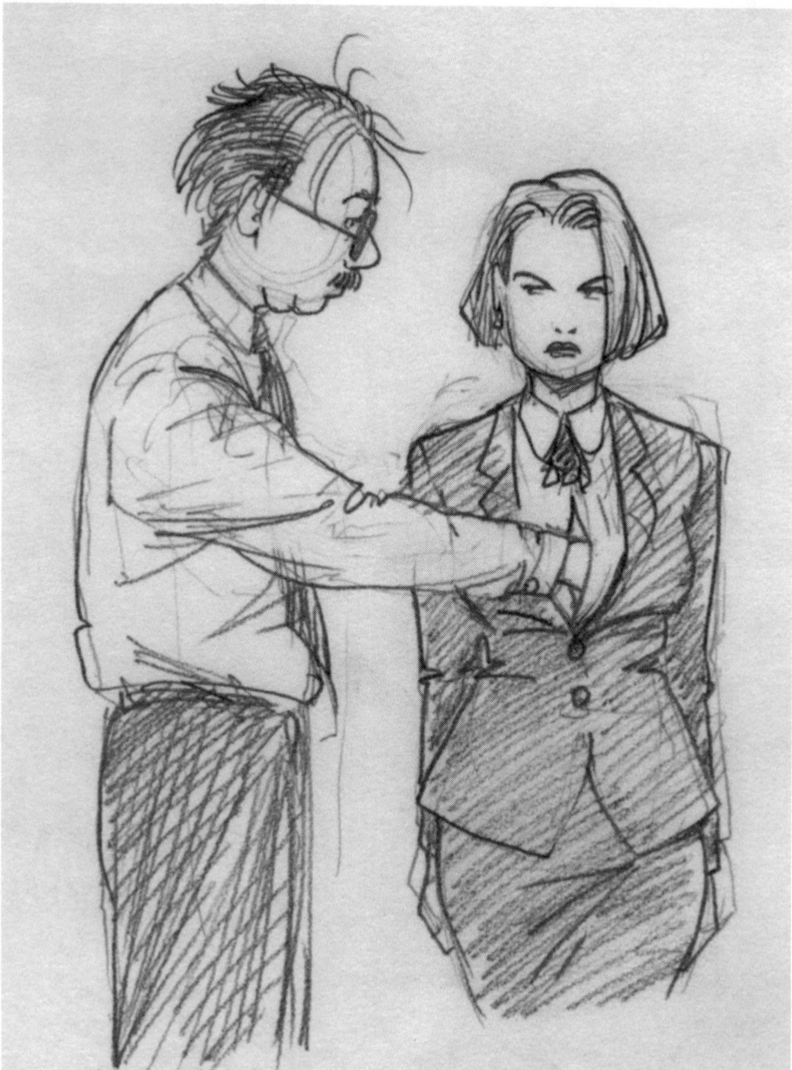

Howard didn't see the point of foreplay if Mavis was just going to glare at him like that.

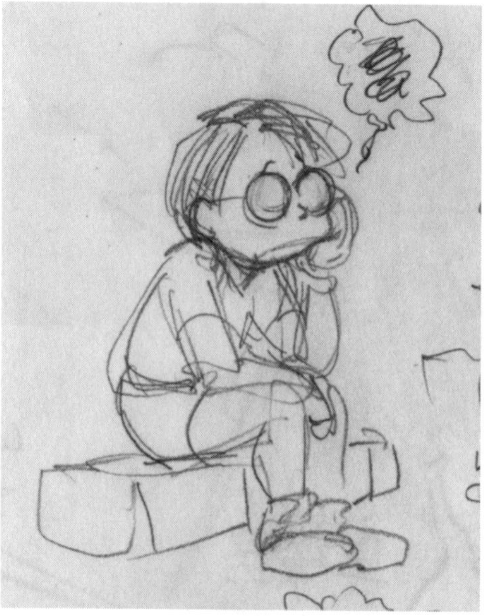

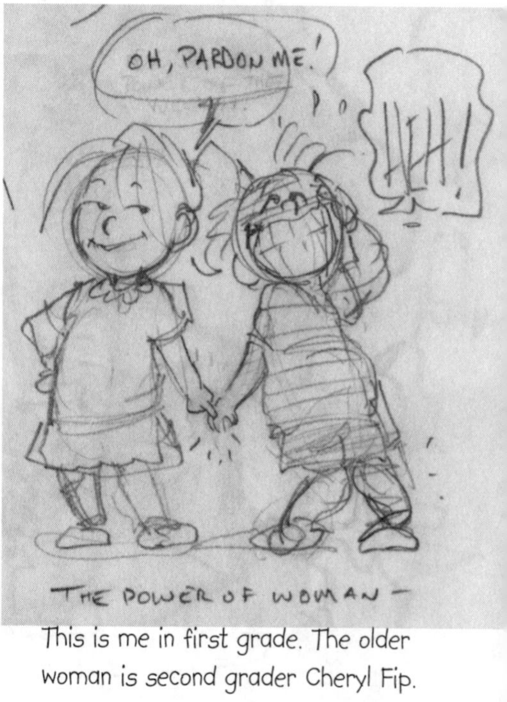
OH, PARDON ME!
HEH!
THE POWER OF WOMAN -

This is me in first grade. The older woman is second grader Cheryl Fip.

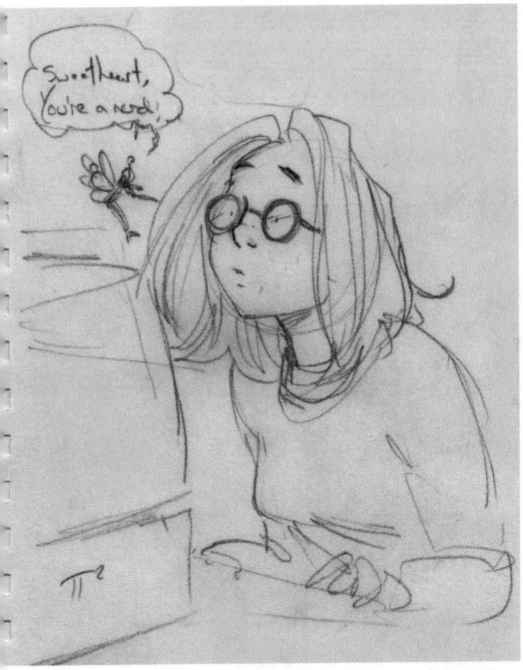
Sweetheart,
You're a nerd!

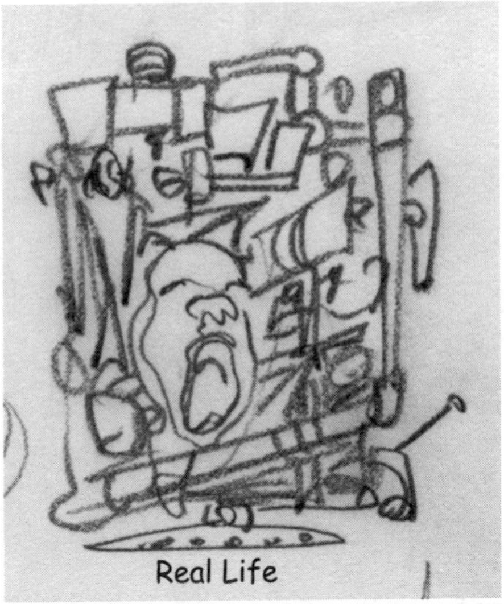
Real Life

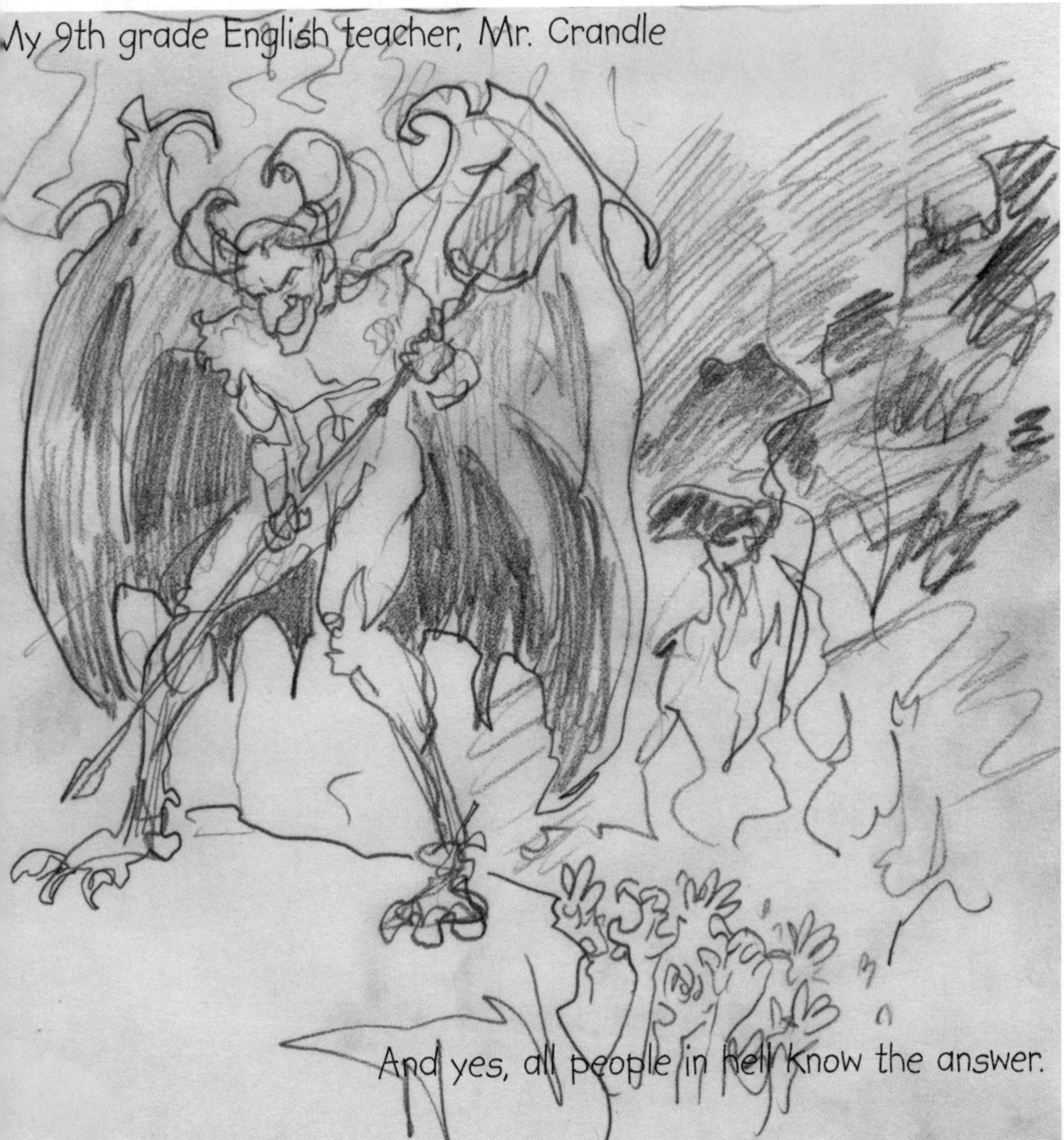
My 9th grade English teacher, Mr. Crandle
And yes, all people in hell know the answer.

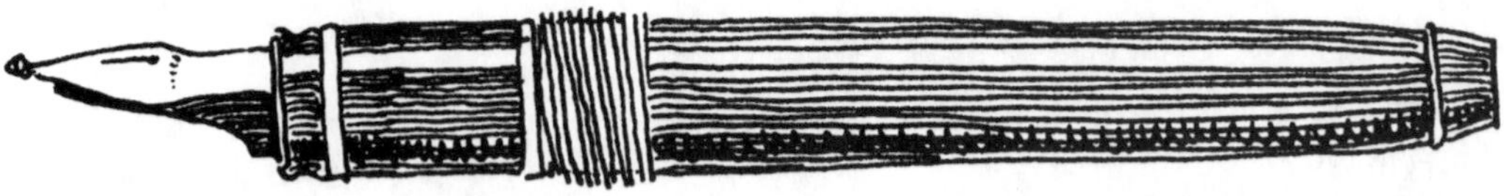

The sketch page
I wrote this SIP
poem on...

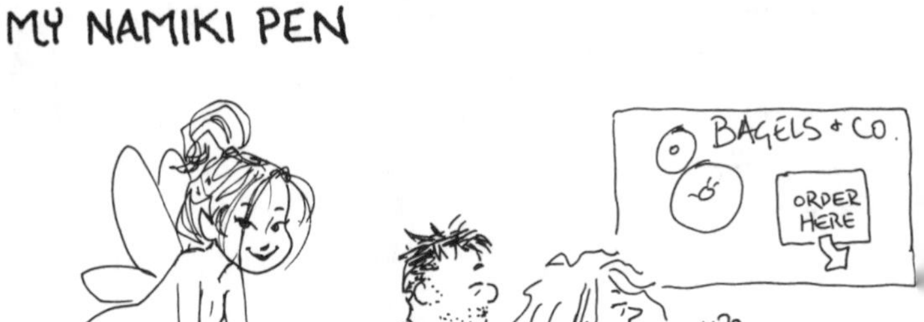
MY NAMIKI PEN
BAGELS & CO.
ORDER HERE

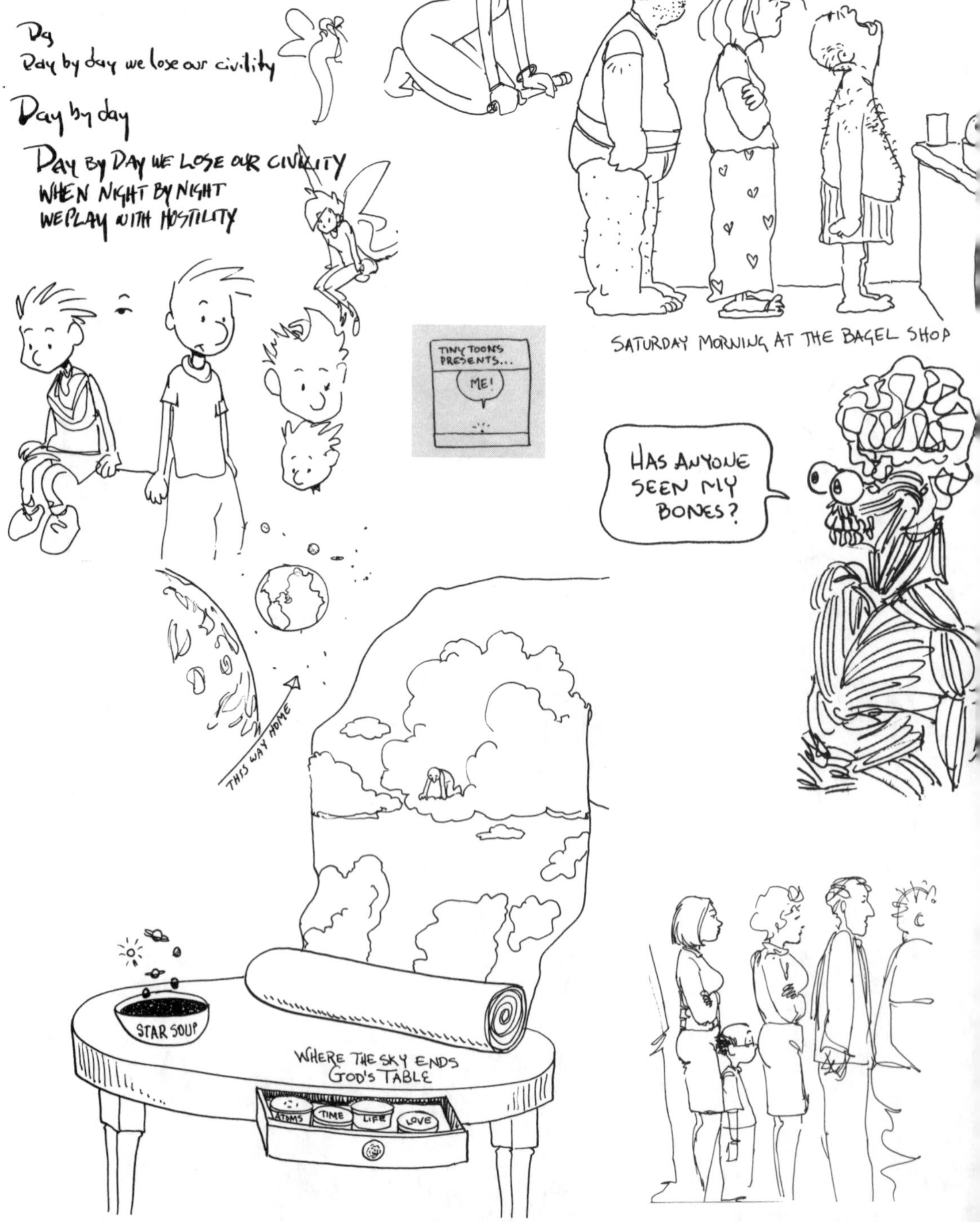
Day
Day by day we lose our civility
Day by day
DAY BY DAY WE LOSE OUR CIVILITY
WHEN NIGHT BY NIGHT
WE PLAY WITH HOSTILITY
SATURDAY MORNING AT THE BAGEL SHOP
TINY TOONS PRESENTS...
ME!
HAS ANYONE SEEN MY BONES?
THIS WAY HOME
STAR SOUP
WHERE THE SKY ENDS
GOD'S TABLE
ATOMS
TIME
LIFE
LOVE

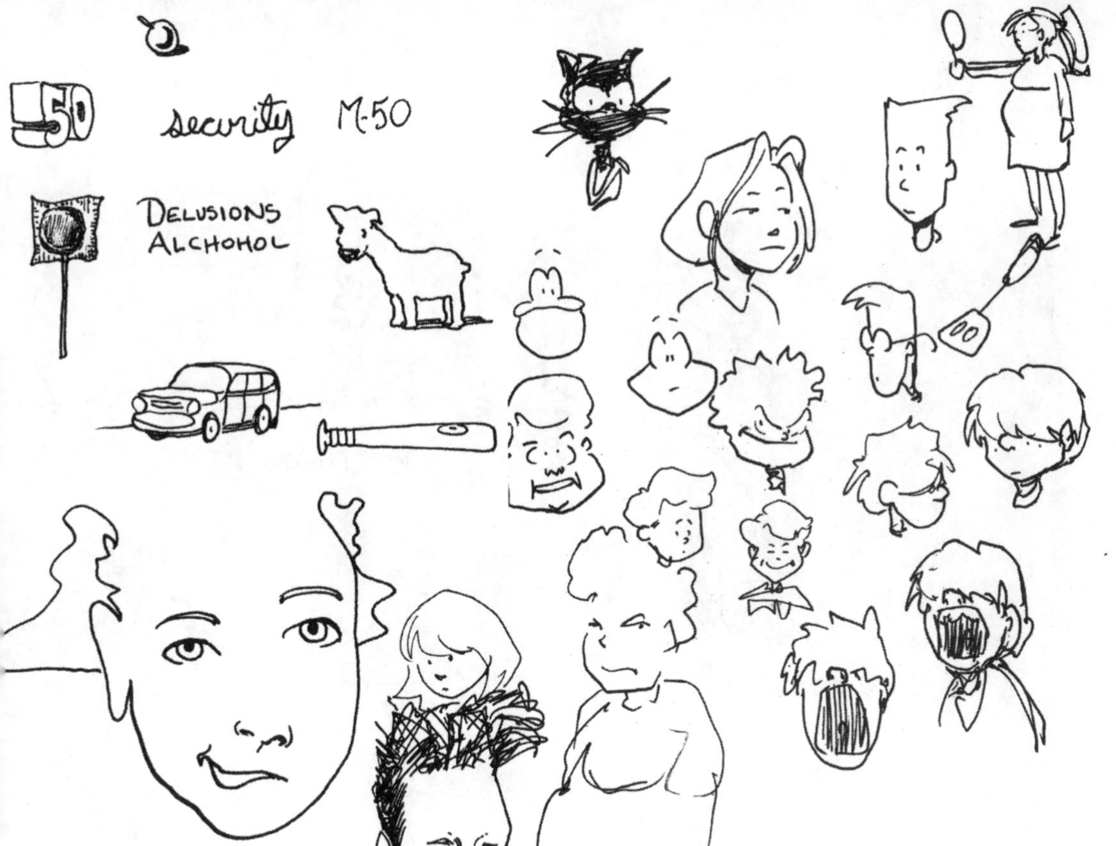

50
security
M-50
DELUSIONS
ALCHOHOL

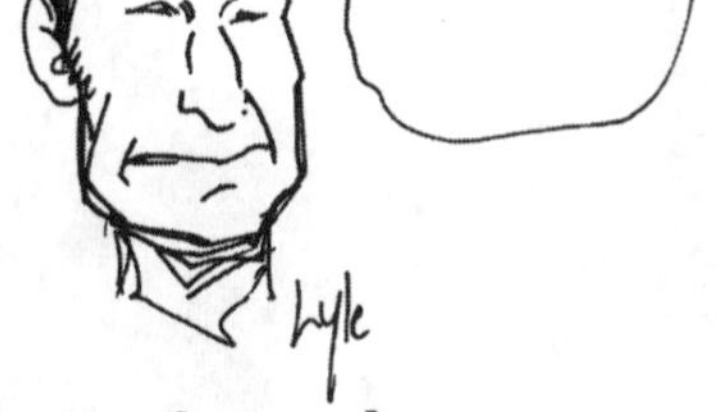

Lyle

oodle page,
omposited from
ocktail napkins,
ost-it notes &
oilet paper.

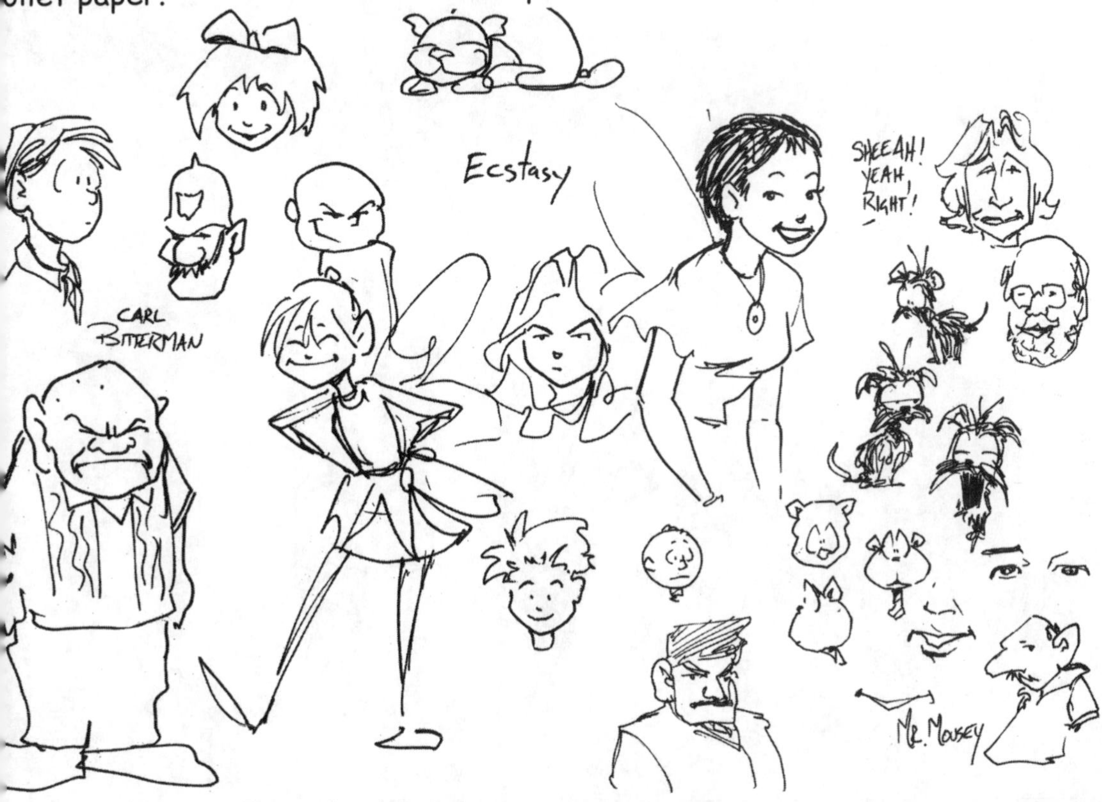

Ecstasy
SHEEAH! YEAH, RIGHT!
CARL BITTERMAN
MR. MOUSEY

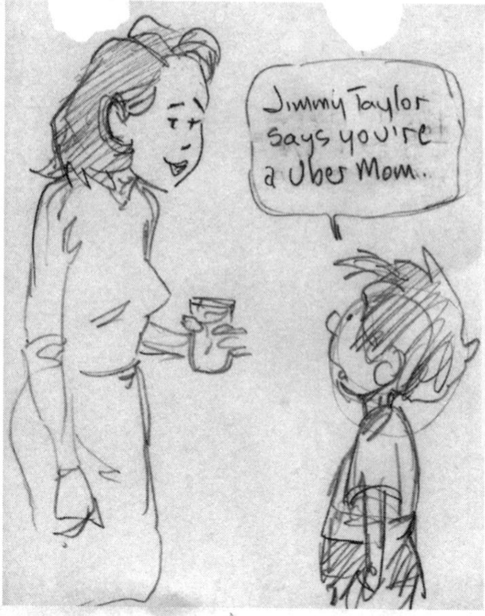
Jimmy Taylor says you're a Uber Mom..

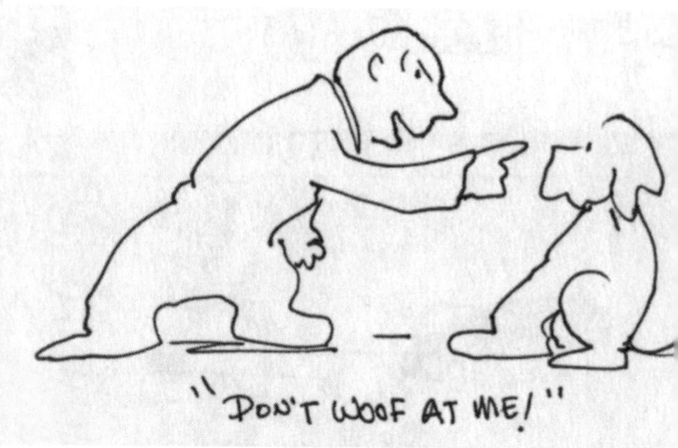
"DON'T WOOF AT ME!"

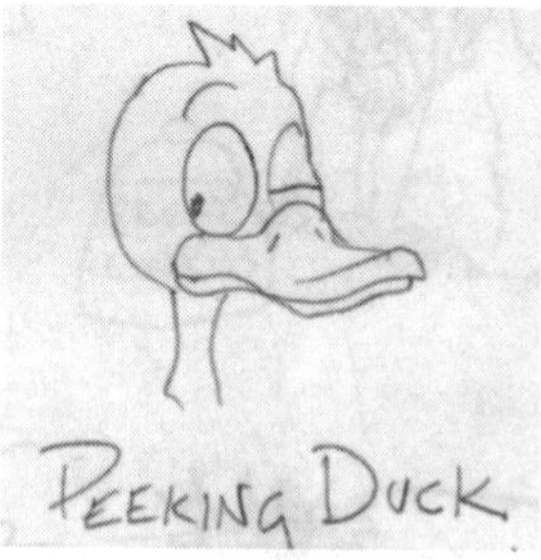
PEEKING DUCK

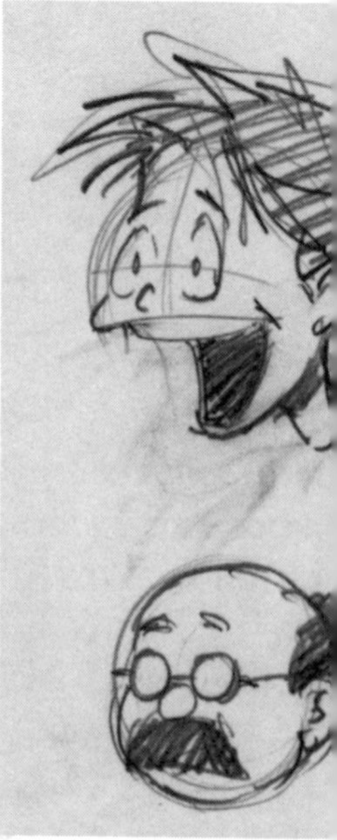

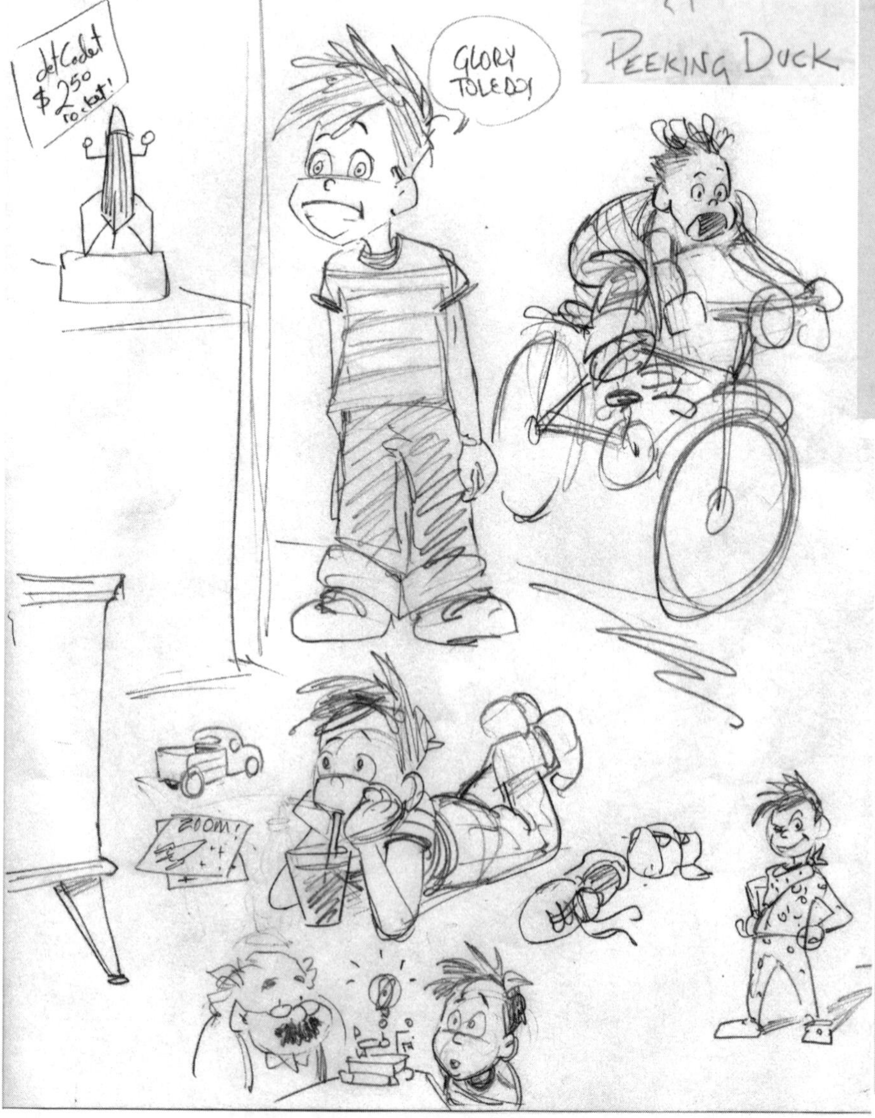
JetCadet $2.50 rocket!
GLORY TOLEDO!
ZOOM!

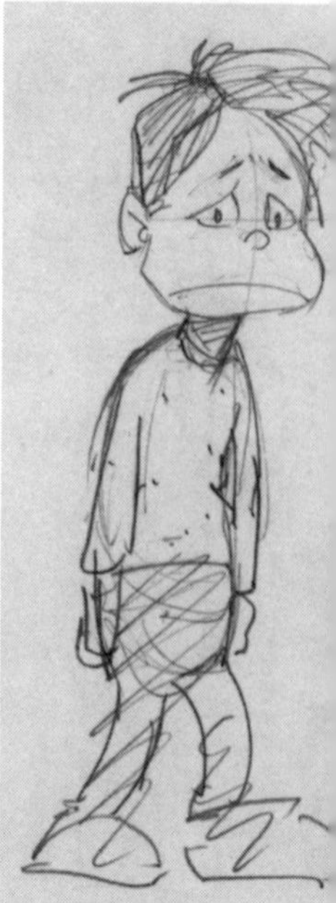

I leave you with this simple drawing. It's not fancy but it makes me happy.

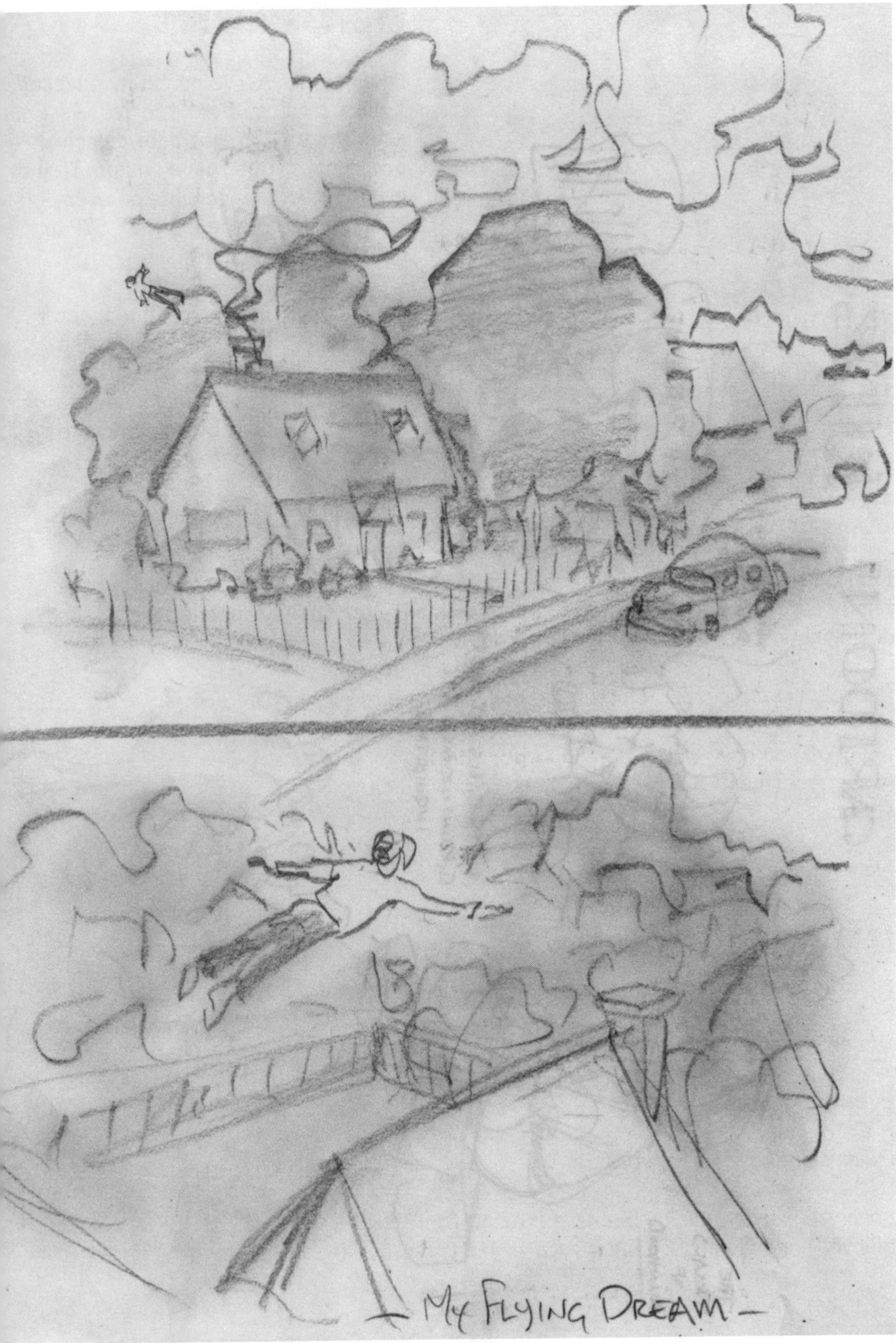
MY FLYING DREAM

SEE YA NEXT TIME!

Faeries

Okay so, as you've probably guessed, I have a thing about faeries. As I said before, I'm not particularly proud of it, but there you go. I find myself doodling faeries on every-thing, napkins, the back of SIP art boards, parked cars...

Faeries are an interesting breed. They don't like to travel, coffee smells like barf to them and they can eat an extraordinary amount of strawberry cake before they get a tummy ache.

I asked Kixie once if there was anything that frightened faeries besides the family cat. She thought about it for a moment, her face scrunched up, before declaring in an ominous tone, "Clowns".

I'm telling you, people, clowns are no laughing matter.

Many of you have written in to Kixie, wanting to know more about her. So, for the record, a few quick facts:

Name: Kixie "That's my name. You can't have it."

Age: Born the year the trees grew tall

Height: Shorter than a sigh but longer than a second

Weight: Light enough to fly and still sit down

Eyes: Envy Green

Hair: Blonde with strawberries

Favorite words: Knickerbockers (faerie for "chest pillows") and flannel ("a sleepy word")

Scariest words: Cat and Clown, of course

Favorite sport: Surfing snowflakes

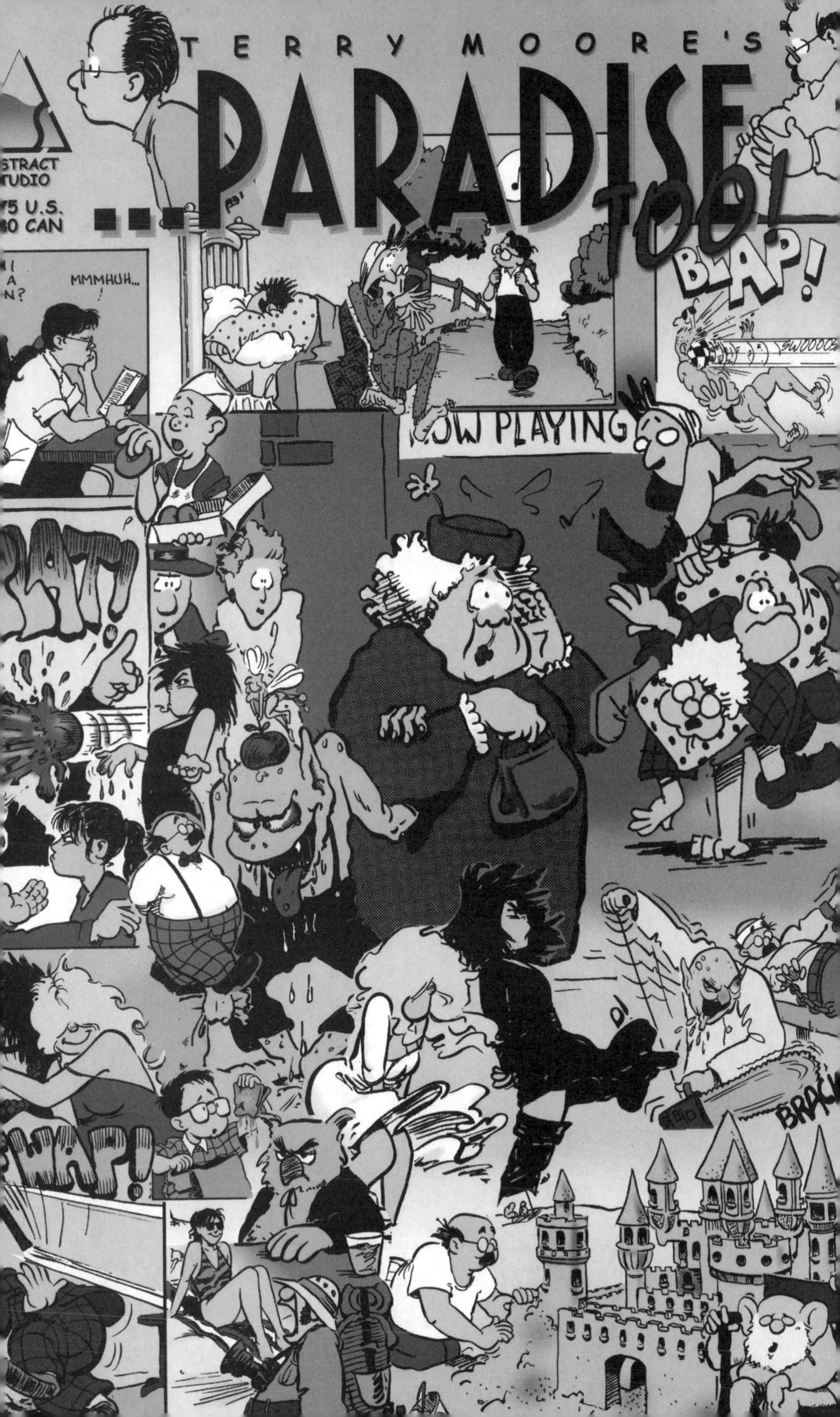
TERRY MOORE'S
...PARADISE TOO!
STRACT
TUDIO
75 U.S.
30 CAN
MMMHUH...
BLAP!
OW PLAYING
BRAC

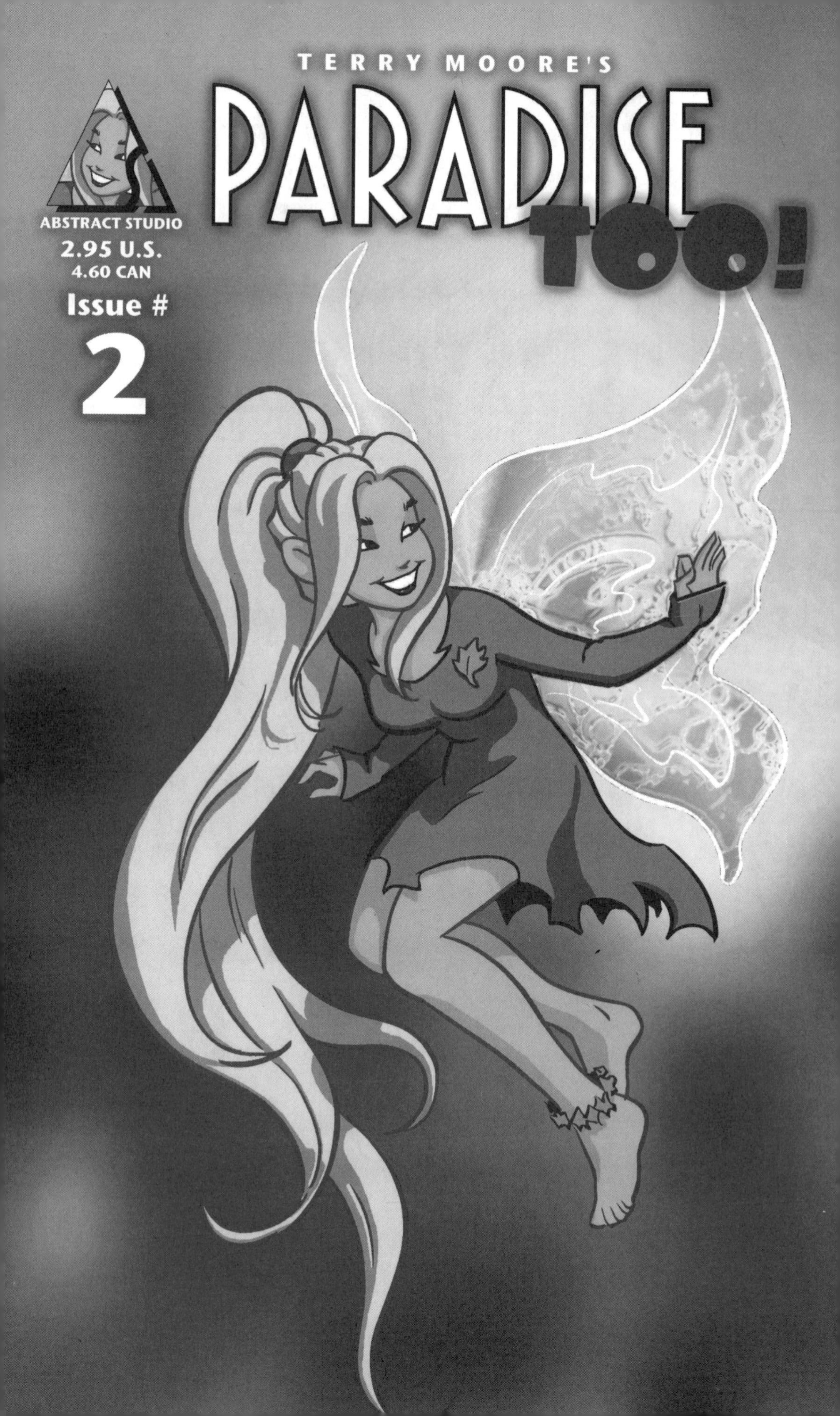
TERRY MOORE'S
PARADISE
TOO!
ABSTRACT STUDIO
2.95 U.S.
4.60 CAN
Issue #
2

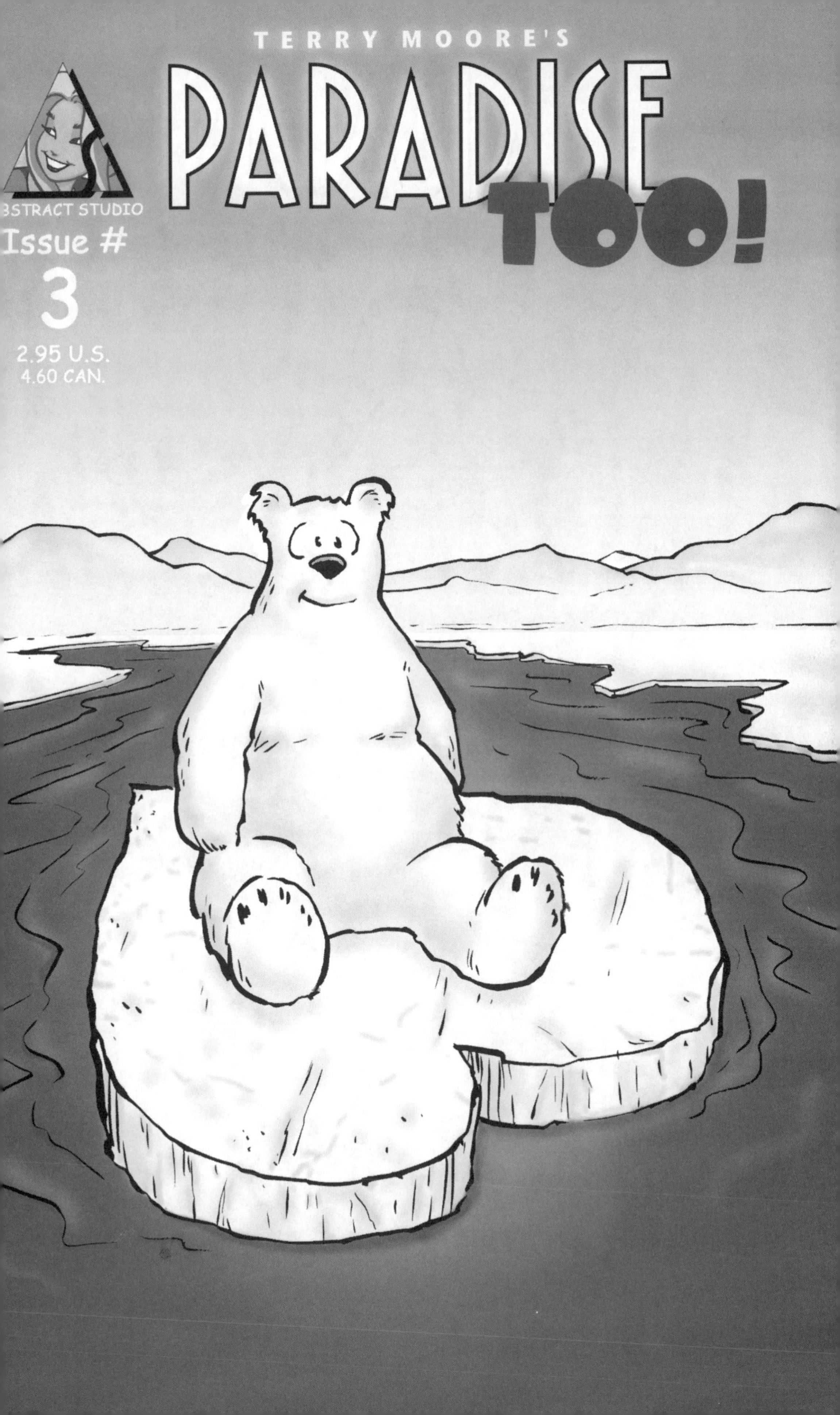
TERRY MOORE'S
PARADISE TOO!
BSTRACT STUDIO
Issue #
3
2.95 U.S.
4.60 CAN.

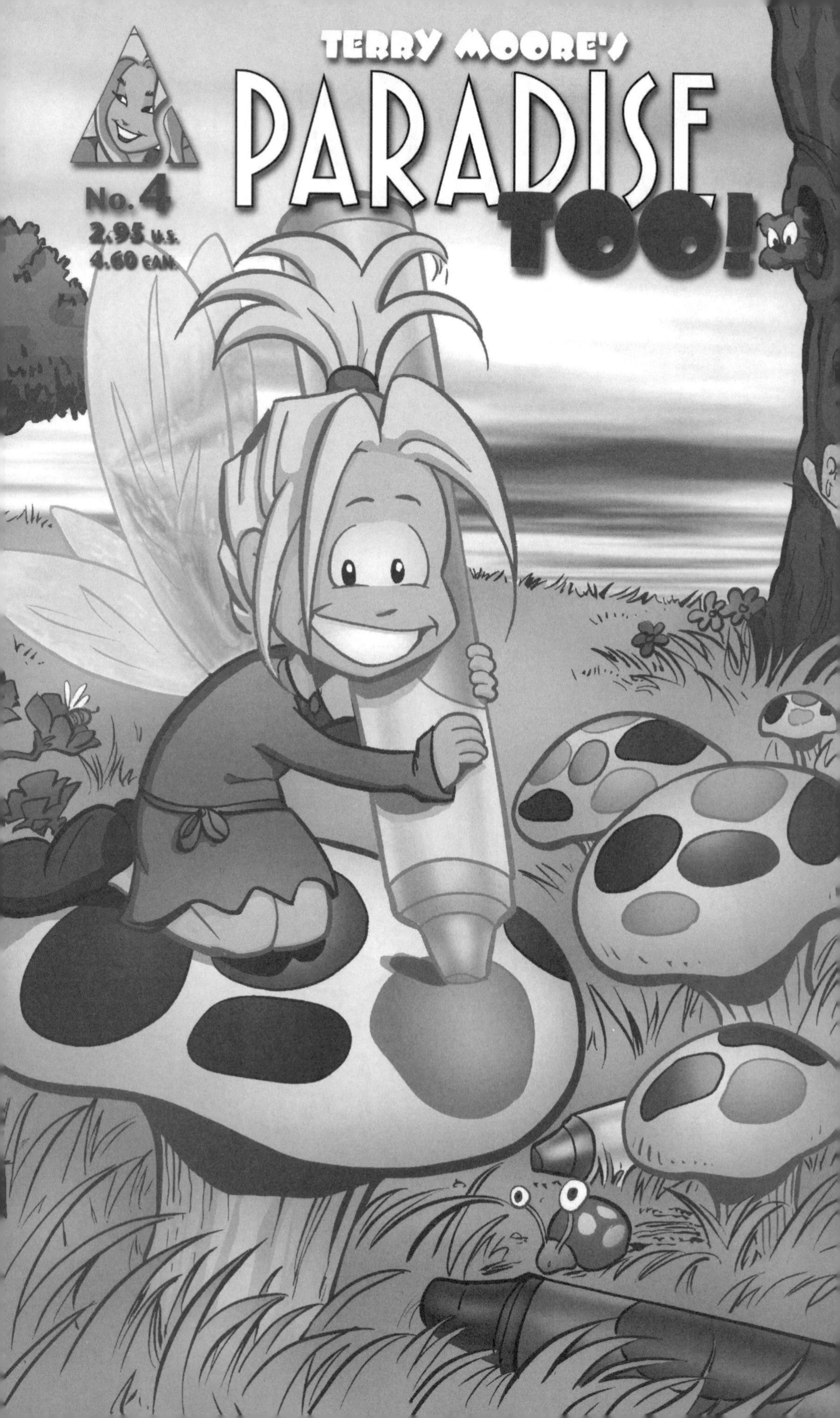
TERRY MOORE'S
PARADISE TOO!
No. 4
2.95 U.S.
4.60 CAN.

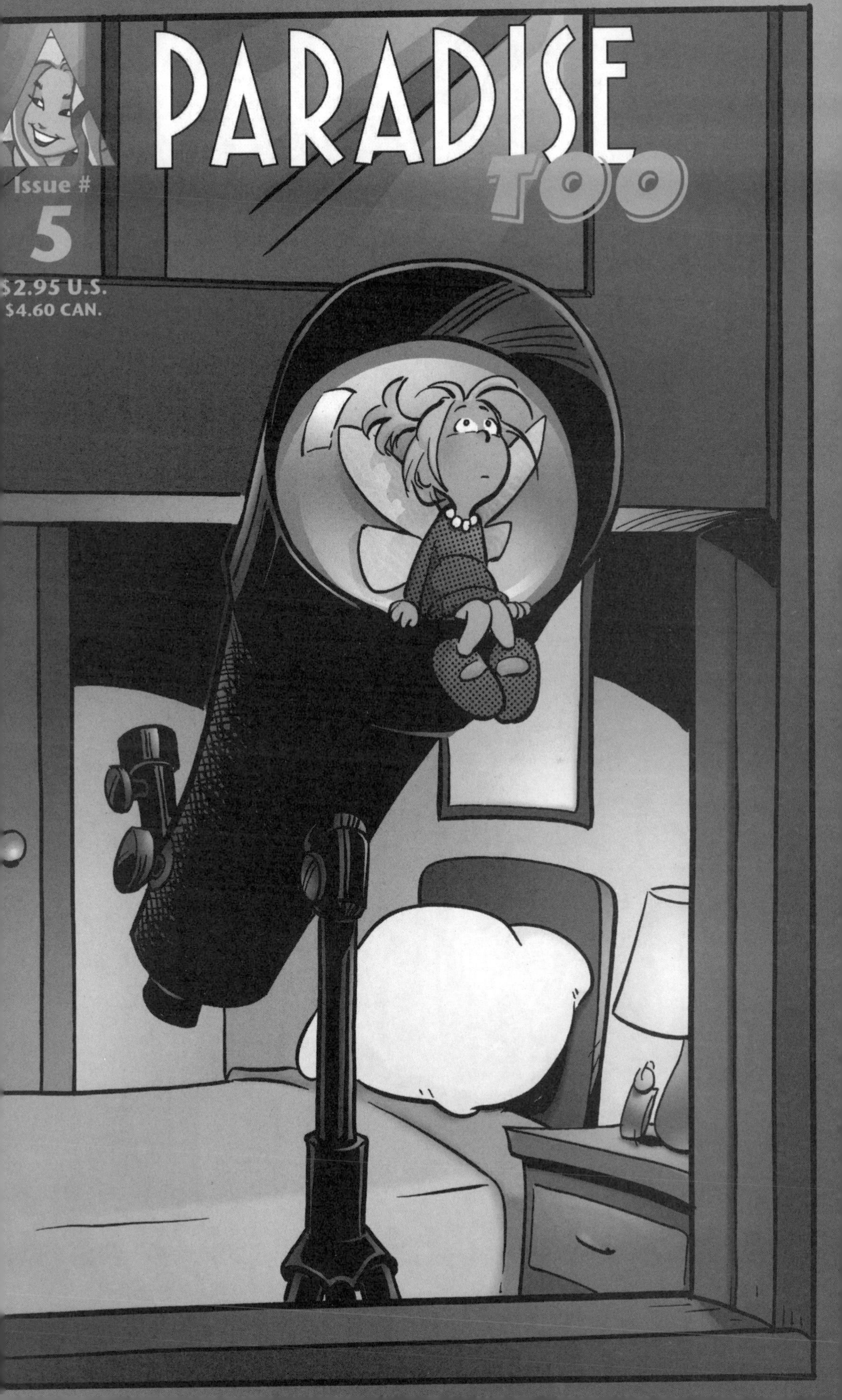
PARADISE
TOO
Issue #
5
$2.95 U.S.
$4.60 CAN.

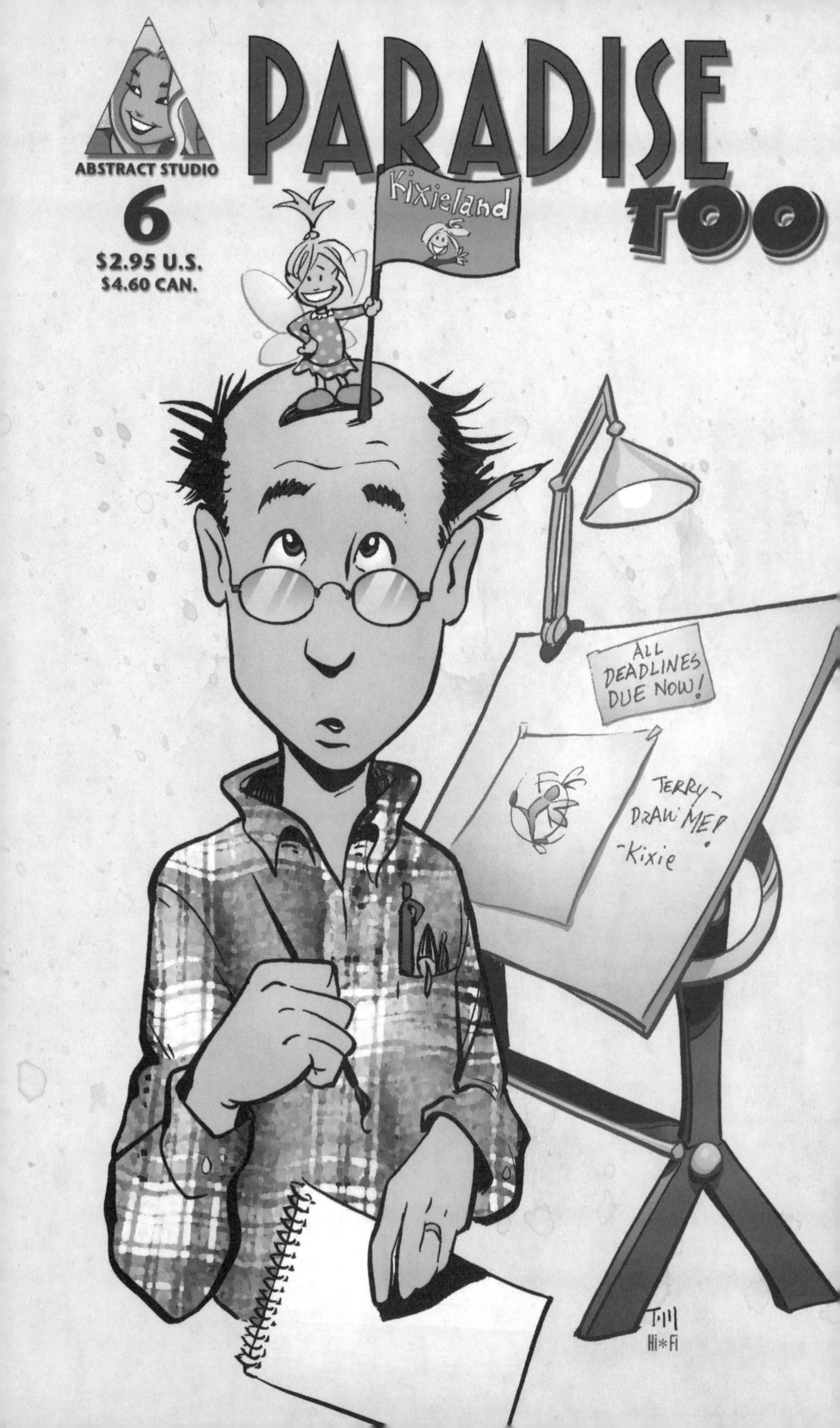
ABSTRACT STUDIO
6
$2.95 U.S.
$4.60 CAN.
PARADISE
TOO
Kixieland
ALL DEADLINES DUE NOW!
TERRY-
DRAW ME!
-Kixie
TM
Hi*Fi

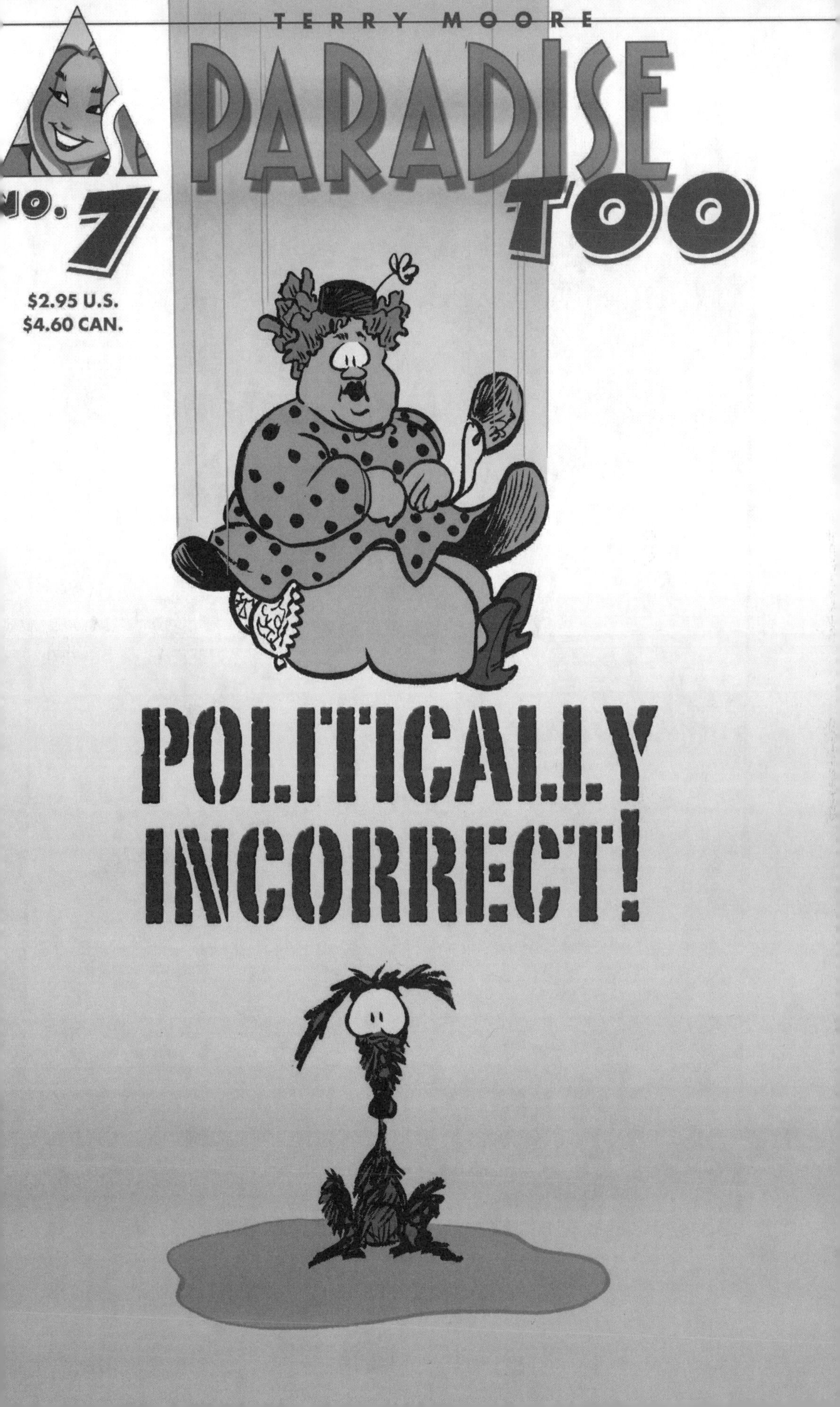
TERRY MOORE
PARADISE TOO
No. 7
$2.95 U.S.
$4.60 CAN.
POLITICALLY INCORRECT!

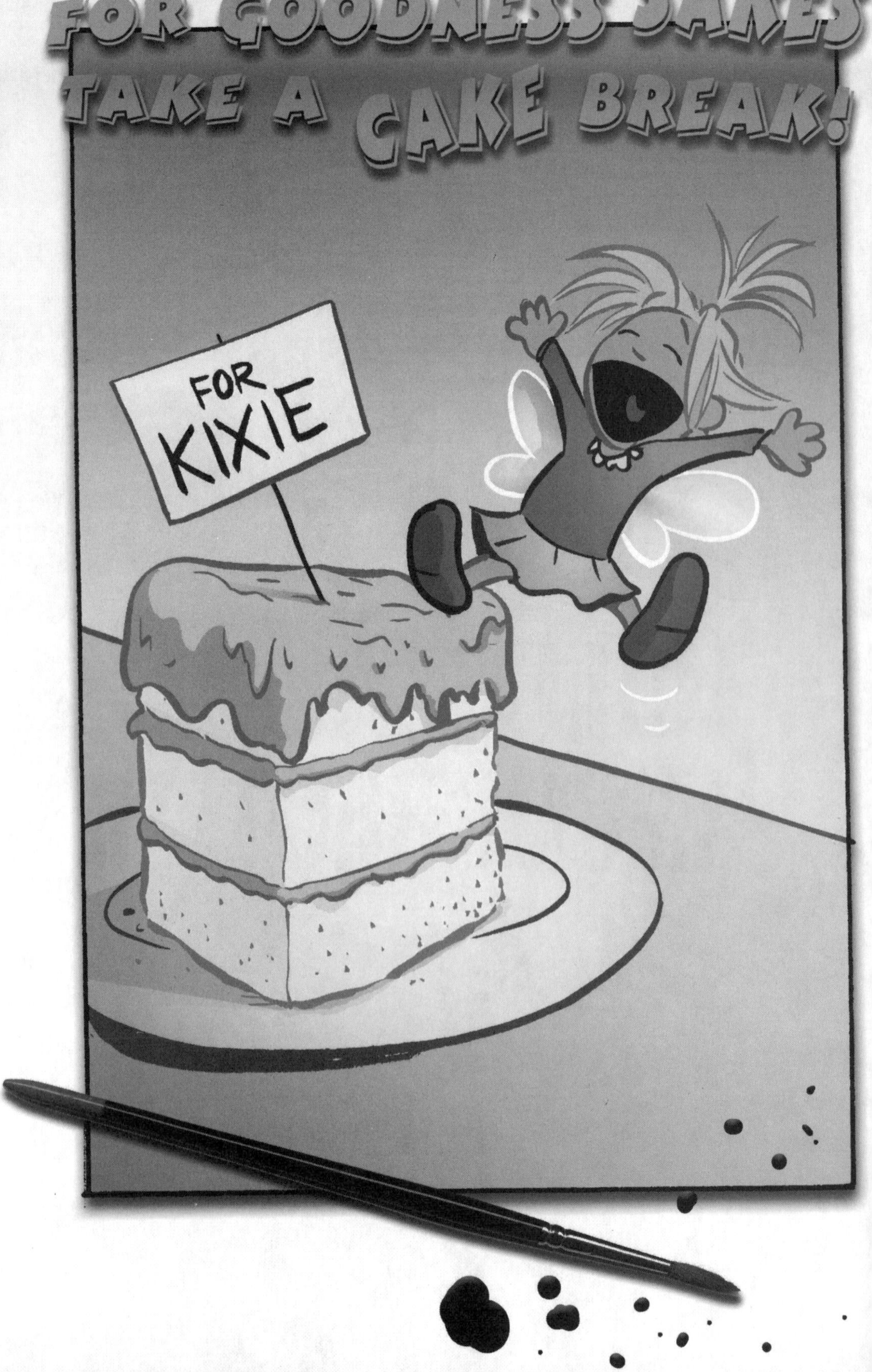
FOR GOODNESS SAKES
TAKE A CAKE BREAK!
FOR KIXIE

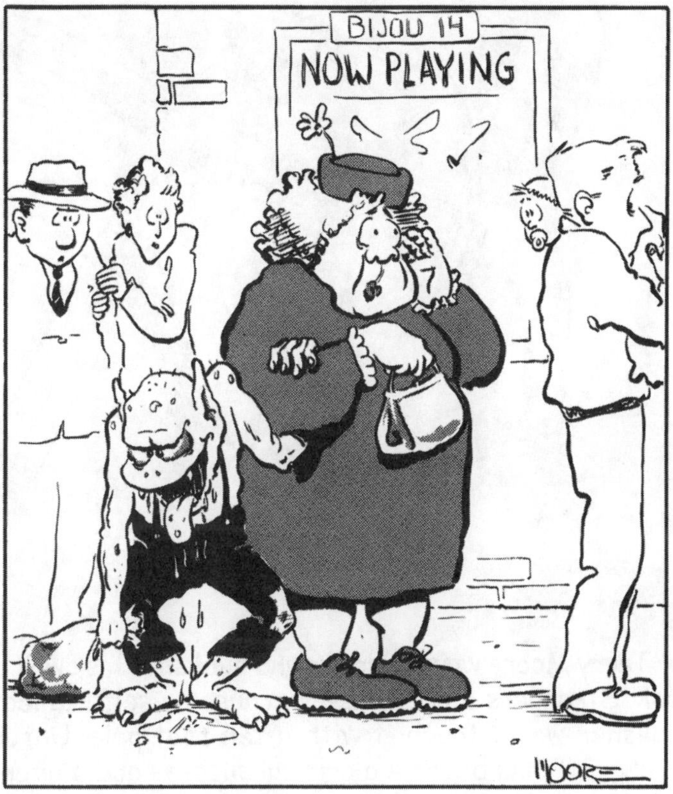
BIJOU 14
NOW PLAYING
MOORE

Martha was ashamed to admit she was dating a sewer snoid.

Terry Moore writes, draws and publishes his own comic book, Strangers In Paradise, because no self respecting publisher would touch it with a ten foot pole. Unfortunately, SIP has become a critical success and a phenomenal cash cow, making Moore the wealthiest young man in America to not own a palmtop computer.

Moore continues to plague the comic book syndicates with bribes and submissions, despite numerous restraining orders, and can often be found muttering to himself at mannequin trade shows. He lives in Houston with a beautiful woman who should know better, a teenage son who does, and a Shih Tzu who remains, to this day, completely clueless.

If you like one of the comic strip ideas in this collection, for heaven's sake, let the poor bastard know. The future of our newspapers depends on it.